Law & American Society

Second Edition

Samuel D. Hodge, Jr.
Temple University

Mc
Graw
Hill
Education

1 2 3 4 5 6 QVS/QVS 20 19 18 17 16

ISBN-13: 978-1-259-97340-6
ISBN-10: 1-259-97340-9

Solutions Program Manager: Nicole Schmitt
Project Manager: Nikki Schmitt
Cover Designer: Paul L. Illian

ACKNOWLEDGMENTS

The author gratefully acknowledges the editorial assistance
of Kamina Richardson and Matthew Hoffer

DEDICATION

This book is dedicated to Samuel Tyler Roseman,
a special little boy who won his battle with adversity while
putting smiles on the faces of those around him.

TABLE OF CONTENTS

CASES LISTED ALPHABETICALLY

PART ONE

THE SUBSTANTATIVE LAW

CHAPTER 1

LAW IN AMERICAN SOCIETY, AN OVERVIEW

SECTION 1.1
INTRODUCTION

Law is a dynamic force that is not capable of a single or simple definition. For instance, the Greek philosopher *Aristotle* believed that "law is a pledge that citizens of a state will do justice to one another." *Black's Law Dictionary* defines the term as "that which must be obeyed and followed by citizens, subject to sanctions or legal consequences." Regardless of how the term is defined, the law affects all aspects of life and establishes the parameters of acceptable conduct within our society. These rules can be created by the legislature, administrative regulation, or be imposed by court decree. While one may not always agree with the law, deviations from these mandates may result in both criminal and civil liabilities.

In the face of expanding government regulations and a litigation-oriented society, individuals and businesses must be cognizant of the legal implications of their actions. Seemingly minor violations of the law may have significant financial and emotional consequences. Million dollar verdicts occur with some frequency in the United States, and the courts continually recognize new or expanded theories of liability.

Law books tend to be theoretical and discuss the economic, sociological, and political framework within which the law operates. This text will examine the forces that shape the law in American Society and will provide the reader with the opportunity to observe the legal system in action. As the semester unfolds, the reader will be introduced to several families in a neighborhood who become involved in a variety of squabbles. Minor disturbances become major confrontations and the neighbors are soon embroiled in various civil and criminal proceedings. Students will learn of these legal controversies through a series of problems that the reader will be requested to help solve.

The text is broken down into two segments. Part One will examine some of the basic laws that govern this country and maintain order among members of society. Part Two of the text will expose the reader to legal procedure. These are the so-called "technicalities" that govern lawsuits. Each chapter will conclude with a discussion of ethics.

SECTION 1.2
THE STUDY OF LAW

Ignorantia juris non excusat is a legal maxim that goes back thousands of years to ancient Rome. It means ignorance of the law is no excuse and the concept is part of the fabric of our legal system. The basis for this phrase is simple. Someone accused of committing a crime or the subject of a civil claim could merely say he or she was unfamiliar with the law to escape responsibility. Therefore, we are presumed to know the legal consequences of our actions. It is the only way to insure fairness in the application of the law and to prevent willful ignorance for our actions.[1] As responsible members of society, it is incumbent upon us to know the various laws and court decisions that regulate our conduct.[2] The problem is that the rules, regulations and judicial edicts that make up the American legal system are numerous; often time's complex and difficult to understand. While our system is not perfect, it does establish a system of order and justice. What would automobile traffic be like if we didn't have a motor vehicle code to establish rules of the road? How could we be secure in our homes if we didn't have the threat of imprisonment for those who enter our residences without permission?

Unlike any other facet of life, the law operates in an adversarial setting. There are two sides to every dispute and one party must lose. Who is to obtain custody of the children in a divorce proceeding? If the court awards custody to the mother, does that mean the father loves the children any less?

Law influences politics, governmental action, police conduct and society in a multitude of ways. It acts as a social mediator of conduct between the people and the government. Examples are contract law which regulates and enforces the voluntary agreements between individuals or entities, tort law allows aggrieved individuals to be compensated because of the wrongful acts of another such as when a person is injured in a car accident or property law that determiners the ownership and possession of real estate or personal property. Laws can also affect society as a whole such a criminal law which provides a mechanism to punish those who commit crimes or constitutional law which safeguards our fundamental rights like the freedom of speech or our protection against an unreasonable search and seizure by the police.[3]

Judges make difficult decisions which are not always popular with all members of society. For instance, the rulings by various courts on same-sex marriages is an example. Despite the Supreme Court's clear pronouncement on the validity of these unions, a minority of citizens remain opposed to same-sex marriages. Nevertheless, the law is clearly superior to the alternative, uncontrolled behavior, military rule, or dictatorship where the people have no rights or say in the operation of the government. Some of the landmark decisions on same-sex marriages will be discussed as part of this education process as we exam the development of the law in a specific area.

The law can be complicated because legal documents are not always easy to understand and seem to be filled with Latin phrases. Instead of simply saying a person has filed an appeal to the United States Supreme Court, this procedure is labeled a *Writ of Certiorari*. Precedent becomes *stare decisis* and legal papers are filled with wherefore's and hereinafter's.

Change is occurring, but reform takes time. More and more contracts are required to be written in easy-to-understand language. For instance, we now have "plain language" leases and authors of contracts are penalized by the court who construe ambiguities in a document against the drafter.

This text will attempt to simplify the law by explaining how the law affects members of American Society in both theory and practice. Legal terms will be translated into common English and a variety of contemporary legal issues will be explored. It is only through this type of learning process that one may gain a better appreciation of the American system of jurisprudence.

SECTION 1.3
THE COURTROOM

Judges are the final arbiters of legal disputes and the courtroom is like a stage filled with drama and suspense. It is through this forum that stories unfold with people's futures hanging in the balance. Did the suspect really kill his wife to collect the proceeds of a million dollar life insurance policy, or was her death caused when his car was forced off the road by an unknown assailant who robbed the couple at gunpoint, killing the woman because she started to scream? The outcome is never certain until the verdict is announced. Therefore, there is no better place to start this educational experience than to introduce the players in the courtroom.

The master of ceremonies is the judge who sits facing the parties on an elevated platform. All are bound by the judge's rulings and the jurist oversees everything that occurs within the courtroom. The starting and concluding times of the hearing and legal determinations are within the province of the judge.

The directors in the drama are the attorneys. They orchestrate the presentation of evidence and determine the sequence of witnesses to maximize the impact of their testimony.

The parties to the suit are the plaintiff and the defendant. The plaintiff initiates the case, and the defendant is the one being sued. The easiest way to remember the difference is to look at the word "defendant." Note that the term contains "defend" in its spelling.

The positions of the parties in the courtroom is predetermined by custom. The party with the burden of proof, sits closest to the jury. In a civil case, the plaintiff has the burden of proof and in a criminal case, the government must prove that the accused is guilty of the crime. The other side of the courtroom is reserved for the defense or the party being sued.

The jury sits to the side of the judge and is segregated from all others in the courtroom. This is done to guard against tampering and undue influence. Jurors are instructed not to discuss the case with anyone and to refrain from contact with those involved in the dispute. Jurors are brought into and leave the courtroom separately from all the other parties. While the judge makes all decisions concerning the applicable law, the jury resolves the factual issues. For instance, the judge will decide whether it is improper for a motorist to enter an intersection after the traffic light has turned yellow, while the jury will make the factual determination as to whether the defendant actually entered the intersection on a yellow light.

As for the actual litigation, cases are tried by the presentation of evidence. Witnesses testify as to the facts and occasionally act as character witnesses. The witness stand is located next to the judge, and is in close proximity to the jury because of the importance of the stories being told.

All dramas need an audience and trials are no different. Courtrooms are generally open to the public and interested parties are seated in the back of the room.

As a theater needs a production crew, a courtroom needs a staff. A stenographer records everything that is said for appellate review. A court clerk keeps track of the exhibits, administers the oath to all who testify, and oversees the jury. Each judge has a court officer who helps run the courtroom and assists the judge in the daily operation of the office.

SECTION 1.4
THE EVOLUTION OF
THE JURY TRIAL

The right to a jury trial has been around for thousands of years and was an integral part of the legal systems in ancient Greece and Rome. The American jury system, however, has its origins in medieval England where groups of 12 "free and lawful" men from the area were convened to assist the king in dispensing justice.[4] These panels based their findings upon what they knew about the matter. As the population of England grew, these individuals no longer were able to base their verdicts upon local rumors and they started to decide the cases upon what people said in court about the matter. As the British model become more engrained in the American legal system, fact finders were told to ignore whatever they knew or heard about the dispute and to decide the outcome based solely upon the evidence presented in court.[5]

This incorporation of the British system into the American colonies was not an easy transition. In fact, the curtailment by the British of the right to a jury trial in the colonies partial lead to the Revolutionary War. That is why the Constitution contains two Amendments guaranteeing the right to be tried by one's peers. Few other countries afford their citizens this right and it is estimated that the United States accounts for more than 80% of the jury trials in the world.

Jury trials are fairly straight forward and they will be covered in more detail in Chapter 7. Needless to say, the linchpin of the modern jury trial is that factual evidence is presented through witnesses and the jury decides which side is more credible in making their ultimate determination. This process, however, was not always so logical.

In ancient England, a trial was conducted not by one's neighbors but according to wager the law, compurgation or trial by ordeal. **Wager the law** was very simple. In ancient times, a person's oath was of critical importance. Therefore, the accused took a pledge swearing to the facts. Those who enjoyed good reputations merely had to swear that they did not commit the crime to be declared innocent.[6] However, if someone challenged the oath of the defendant, a **trial by compurgation** took place. This process mandated that the accused produce 11 other people who would swear on the accused's behalf. These witnesses did not swear about the facts of the case. Rather, they would testify to the person's good reputation or act as what is known today as a "character witness." The court in ancient times had a simple way to insure that the compurgators were sincere and not just paid actors. If the defendant was found guilty following the testimony, the character witnesses would also be punished since they would be implicated in the accused's guilt.[7]

If the accused was a common criminal or could not locate 11 people to take an oath on their behalf a **trial by ordeal** ensued. As its name implies, the accused was subjected to some kind of physical test with guilt or innocence hinging on how the person performed during the ordeal. These tests frequently involved fire or water and were a symbolic appeal to God to provide a signal as to the person's innocence or guilt. Since the tests determined the outcome through an unpleasant experience, the accused frequently suffered bodily injury thereby creating a no-win situation.[8] For instance, a cauldron of boiling hot water would be placed in front of the accused who had to reach into the scaling water and pick up a hot iron ring from the bottom of the pot. If the defendant's arm did not burn, he was deemed innocent. In this way, God was able to render judgment by proving a physical sign thereby instilling the fear of God in the citizens.[9]

PARK, BROWN & SMITH, P.C.
ATTORNEYS AT LAW
MEMORANDUM

To: All Students

FROM: Peter Smith, Esquire

RE: Biographical Sketches

My name is Peter Smith, and I am the managing partner of the law firm of *Park, Brown & Smith, P.C.* We are a multi-faceted firm which provides representation in all types of cases. We have been retained by Joseph Roberts to represent him in several disputes that have arisen with his neighbors. I am providing you with brief biographical sketches of the people whose legal problems you will hear about during the next few months.

Estelle Worthington Roberts

Estelle Worthington met Joe Roberts when they were sixteen, and they married shortly after graduating from high school. Within a year of their marriage, Estelle became pregnant and gave birth to a son, Anthony. Over the ensuing years, the couple had three more children: Kathy, Brad, and Greg.

In addition to being a full-time mother, Estelle is very involved in community service and has developed a reputation as a tenacious consumer advocate. Her causes have included lobbying for warning labels on sexually explicit music, banning the selling of soda and junk food at schools and advocating for the rights of children with learning disabilities.

Joseph Roberts

Because Joseph Roberts became a father shortly after graduating from high school, he was unable to attend college and had to obtain work with a construction firm as a bulldozer operator. As the pressures of married life mounted, Joe developed a drinking problem that caused numerous conflicts. Events climaxed when Joe accidently hit his supervisor's new car with a piece of construction equipment while inebriated. Joe was fired and was unable to pay his mounting bills. His creditors eventually sold Joe's house at Sheriff's sale.

With his last bit of money, Joe jumped on a bus and headed to the casinos. Much to his disbelief, Joe hit the jackpot and won a million dollars while playing a progressive slot machine. With his new found wealth, Joe purchased the construction company that had fired him. He renamed the entity, Joro Construction Company, and assumed the title of President and CEO. Joe quickly doubled his wealth and made two unusual purchases: He purchased a baby bear from a bankrupt circus which he named "Harry," and a yacht that he called *ONLY IN AMERICA;* to reflect his life story.

Anthony Roberts

Anthony Roberts Joe and Estelle's son, Tony, is 23 years old. Throughout high school, Tony excelled in athletics and was the goalie on the soccer team.

During his junior year, Tony took up football. His soccer background enabled him to become an outstanding place kicker, and his high school team went on to win the state championship.

Tony was offered a full-paid scholarship to play college football. During his last year, he set a number of school records for points and field goal accuracy. The various scouting combines rated him as one of the top kickers in collegiate football. He subsequently tried out for the Stallions, the latest professional football expansion team and was signed to a three-year contract.

Kathleen Roberts

Kathy is 16 years old and spends hours talking on the phone, texting or surfing the internet. One might assume that she is a normal teenager, but Kathy has a serious problem.

Ever since she started experimenting with drugs, her grades have gone from A's to F's and she has detached herself from the day-to-day life of her family. Whenever her parents try to communicate with her, Kathy reacts with great hostility. Since her parents increasingly avoid any sort of confrontation with her, Kathy's decline accelerates.

Peter Christopher

Peter Christopher Peter Christopher was born one of a pair of identical twins. Since no one was able to tell them apart, their father gave each boy an identical tattoo of a shark on opposite shoulders. The Christopher brothers enlisted in the military after graduating from high school and specialized in military intelligence and photographic analysis. They spent their army days in Iraq and Afganistan where they conducted undercover surveillance for the government.

After leaving the military, they started a private investigation service specializing in surveillance and industrial espionage. However, Peter relocated to the Philadelphia area after he had a falling out with his brother over the allocation of profits from their business and moved next door to the Roberts family.

Donald Jones, M.D.

Donald Jones always wanted to be a physician, and studied diligently to achieve this lofty goal. Upon graduating from medical school, he became a surgical resident at a hospital in Chicago. Following several years in a clinical rotation, he relocated to Philadelphia and is now a successful surgeon. Dr. Jones is Joe's other neighbor.

Officer John O'Brien   John O'Brien is the oldest of five children. Both his father and grand-father were members of the police force, and it has always been John's ambition to follow in their footsteps. He graduated from college with a degree in criminal justice and secured a job as a police officer with a suburban police department. He is presently assigned to patrol the neighborhood in which Joe Roberts lives.

SECTION 1.6
CASE ANALYSIS

COMMON LAW AND STATUTORY LAW

The creation of statutory law is the primary function of the legislature, whether it is on the federal, state, or municipal levels. These laws are designed to address specific problems in our society and to set forth rules to regulate the areas of concern. This process is so important to the governance of this country that this lawmaking function is found in Article One of the United States Constitution.

The Constitution also empowers the judiciary with the authority to interpret the laws and to establish standards of care. This process is known as common law or judge-made law. The court is empowered to pass judgment on what type of conduct is proper and valued in our society. These pronouncements are based upon the judge's perception of what is in the best interest of the people given the political, sociological, and economic climate of the time. The court even has the power to review a law passed by the legislature to ensure its constitutionality or to ascertain whether certain conduct falls within the contemplation of the statute.

These judicial pronouncements are rendered in the form of written explanations called **opinions** so that the parties to the litigation and the general public may understand the basis for the court's resolution of the dispute.

The study of law requires a review of these court decisions in order to gain an appreciation as to how legal determinations are made, to learn the rules that govern our conduct, and to understand the factors that a judge weighs in rendering a decision.

Reading and understanding court decisions is an acquired skill that takes time to learn. This skill, however, is extremely important to master, as judicial decisions affect every aspect of our lives.

Chapter One will introduce students to the judicial decision making process. Many factors are utilized by the court in arriving at its decisions. Most times judges will be guided by prior case law or precedent. Courts are also influenced by popular opinion, changing values or a sense for what is good for the community. Students will start their educational experience on how to read and understand court opinions by examining two unrelated decisions; one involving a common law determination by the court and the second dealing with the interpretation of a statute.

The second step in this learning process will involve the examination of one legal issue over a time: same sex marriage. The reader will follow the legal developments involving this contemporary issue as it wound its way through the courts and Congress before being decided by the Supreme Court in 2015.

The first case provides an example of judge made law and involves whether the long standing rule that spectators assume the risk of being exposed to those risks inherent in watching a sports contest applies to a patron who is hit in the eye by a hotdog thrown into the stands by the team's mascot. The second matter provides an illustration of statutory law and the interpretation of the Copyright statute.

JOHN COOMER V. KANSAS CITY ROYALS BASEBALL CORPORATION
437 S.W.3D 184 (MO. 2014)

Coomer claims he was injured when hit in the eye with a hotdog thrown by Sluggerrr, the Kansas City Royals mascot. Coomer is a frequent spectator at Royals games. On September 8, 2009, he brought his father along to watch the Royals host the Detroit Tigers. Sluggerrr mounted the visitor's dugout to begin the "Hotdog Launch." The launch occurs between innings, when Sluggerrr uses an air gun to shoot hotdogs from the roof of the visitor's dugout to fans seated beyond hand-tossing range. When his assistants are reloading the air gun, Sluggerrr tosses hotdogs by hand to the fans seated nearby. Coomer admits that he frequently watched Sluggerrr toss hotdogs from the roof of the visitor's dugout and, on September 8, he saw Sluggerrr mount the dugout to begin the Hotdog Launch. Coomer was seated 15 to 20 feet from Sluggerrr, directly in his view. Coomer saw Sluggerrr turn away from the crowd as if to prepare for a behind-the-back throw, but, because Coomer chose that moment to turn and look at the scoreboard,

he admits he never saw Sluggerrr throw the hotdog that he claims injured him. Coomer testified only that a "split second later ... something hit me in the face," and he described the blow as "pretty forceful."

Coomer felt something "wasn't right" with his left eye. Coomer saw a doctor and was diagnosed with a detached retina. Coomer underwent surgeries to repair the retina and to remove a "traumatic cataract" in the same eye.

Coomer filed this lawsuit asserted that the Royals failed to exercise ordinary care in throwing hotdogs into the stands, that the team failed to adequately train Sluggerrr on how to throw hotdogs into the stand safely, and that the team failed to adequately supervise Sluggerrr's hotdog toss. The Royals asserted the defense of assumption of the risk.

Coomer argued that assumption of the risk only applies to risks that are inherent in the nature of the activity and the harm of getting hit with a hotdog has absolutely no relationship to going to a baseball game.

When the risk arises from the circumstances, e.g., from a condition on the defendant's property or the inherent nature of the defendant's activity, "assumption of the risk" bars recovery by a plaintiff who knowingly and voluntarily encounters that risk. ·

A majority of courts recognize that spectators at sporting events are exposed to certain risks that are inherent merely in watching the contest. These courts hold that the home team is not liable to a spectator injured as a result of such risks. There remains a hazard that spectators in unscreened seats may be struck and injured by balls which are fouled or otherwise driven into the stands. This risk is a necessary and inherent part of the game and remains after ordinary care has been exercised to provide the spectators with seats which are reasonably safe. It is a risk which is assumed by the spectators because it remains after due care has been exercised and is not the result of negligence on the part of the baseball club.

But the rationale for this rule extends only to those risks that the team is powerless to alleviate without fundamentally altering the game or spectator's enjoyment of it. Can this be said about the antics of the mascot? We think not.

Accordingly, the proper application of assumption of the risk in this case—is this: if Coomer was injured by a risk that is an inherent part of watching the Royals play baseball, the team had no duty to protect him and cannot be liable for his injuries. But, if Coomer's injury resulted from a risk that is not an inherent part of watching baseball in person—or if the negligence of the Royals altered or increased one of these inherent risks and caused Coomer's injury—the jury is entitled to hold the Royals liable for such negligence.

Some fans may find Sluggerrr's hotdog toss fun to watch between innings, and some fans may even have come to expect it, but this does not make the risk of injury from Sluggerrr's hotdog toss is an "inherent risk" of watching a Royals game. There is nothing about the risk of injury from Sluggerrr's hotdog toss that involves the "constitution or essential character" of watching a Royals game at Kauffman Stadium.

Accordingly, the Court holds as a matter of law that the risk of injury from Sluggerrr's hotdog toss is not one of the risks inherent in watching the Royals play baseball that Coomer assumed merely by attending a game. As a result, Sluggerrr owes the fans a duty to use reasonable care in conducting the Hotdog Launch and can be held liable for damages caused by a breach of that duty. Sluggerrr's tosses may—or may not—be negligent; that is a question of fact for the jury to decide.

Statutory law is a written pronouncement made by the legislature which can be passed on the federal, state or local levels and they are considered the primary source of laws in the United States.[10] Statutes are arranged by subject matter in multiple volume books called codes. For instance, the federal laws are published in the United States Code and become law when enacted unless a contrary date for their implementation is noted.[11] These laws must be distinguished from common law or judge made law which is based upon the customs and traditions of the people. While laws are created by the legislature, they are interpreted and applied by the courts.

Understanding the meaning of a statute begins with an examination of the plain language used in the legislation to ascertain its intent. This is done by utilizing the ordinary and customary meaning of a word or term. If that does not prove useful, judges will examine the intent of the legislature in passing the law. Courts also try not to apply an interpretation that would lead to an illogical meaning.[12]

A "selfie" is a new term coined in the 21st Century to refer to a self-portrait created by a small digital device like a cell or smart phone, webcam or I pad and uploaded to a social media location. They are everywhere. Just type "selfie" into a google or Twitter search bar and thousands of images will be displayed.[13] These images are revolutionizing how we collect autobiographical data about ourselves and our acquaintances.[14]

A host of legal issues arises over selfies. For instance, a copyright arises when the creator posts the image in a tangible medium. In another words, a copyright becomes a creative work when it exists physically. Generally, the image taker is both the author and copyright owner. However, adding other people, places or things to the image can complicate the issue.[15] Taking a selfie that includes the image of another raises invasion of privacy issue. The laws try to safeguard the disclosure of a person from confidential or privileged information including pictures of a private moment without that person's consent. As a result, the laws of privacy can impact the publishing of a selfie of another person.[16]

Few selfies, however, have created more of a furor that the selfie taken by a monkey in a tropical forest after a nature photographer handled the primate his camera. A macaque monkey named Naruto took a series of vivid and unusual candid pictures that were published by the nature photographer. These images set off a firestorm concerning the ownership of the pictures and who was entitled to the royalties on the published images. The case ended up in federal court when the People for the Ethical Treatment of Animals sued the nature photographer on behalf of the monkey claiming that the animal enjoyed the copyright to the picture since Naruto took the images. The case required the court to interpret the Copyright statute in order to see if an animal can own this intangible right.

NARUTO V. DAVID SLATER
2016 WL 362231 (N.D. CAL. 2016)

This case arises out of allegations that Naruto, a six-year-old crested macaque, took multiple photographs of himself ("Monkey Selfies") using Slater's camera. The complaint, filed by the People for the Ethical Treatment of Animals ("PETA") alleges Slater violated Naruto's

copyright by displaying, advertising, and selling copies of the Monkey Selfies.

Naruto is a six-year old crested macaque who lives on the island of Sulawesi in Indonesia. He is "highly intelligent" and possesses grasping hands and opposable thumbs with the ability to move his fingers independently. Because he lives immediately adjacent to a human village, Naruto has encountered tourists and photographers throughout his life. He was accustomed to seeing cameras, observing cameras being handled by humans, hearing camera mechanisms being operated, and experienced cameras being used by humans without danger or harm to him and his community. Naruto authored the Monkey Selfies by independent, autonomous action in examining and manipulating Slater's unattended camera and purposely pushing the shutter release multiple times, understanding the cause-and-effect relationship between pressing the shutter release, the noise of the shutter, and the change to his reflection in the camera lens.

PETA alleges that Slater has repeatedly infringed on Naruto's copyright on the Monkey Selfies by falsely claiming to be the photographs' author and by selling copies of the images for profit. PETA claims that defendant has violated the Copyright Act, by displaying, advertising, reproducing, distributing, offering for sale, and selling copies of the Monkey Selfies. They allege that Naruto is entitled to defendant's profits from the infringement and seek to permanently enjoin defendants from copying, licensing, or otherwise exploiting the Monkey Selfies and to permit PETA to "administer and protect" Naruto's authorship of and copyright in the Monkey Selfies.

The starting point for interpreting a statute is the language of the statute itself. The Copyright Act protects "original works of authorship fixed in any tangible medium of expression from which they can be perceived, reproduced, or otherwise communicated, either directly or with the aid of a machine or device." The "fixing" of the work in the tangible medium of expression must be done "by or under the authority of the author." The Copyright Act defines neither "works of authorship" nor "author."

Defendant argues that the Copyright Act confers no rights upon animals such as Naruto. PETA responds that the Act has "no definitional limitation." They contend that standing under the Copyright Act is available to anyone, including an animal, who creates an "original work of authorship."

I disagree with PETA. The Copyright Act does not "plainly" extend the concept of authorship or statutory standing to animals. To the contrary, there is no mention of animals anywhere in the Act. The Supreme Court has repeatedly referred to "persons" or "human beings" when analyzing authorship under the Act. PETA has not cited, and I have not found, a single case that expands the definition of authors to include animals.

Moreover, the Copyright Office agrees that works created by animals are not entitled to copyright protection. It directly addressed the issue of human authorship in the Compendium of U.S. Copyright Office Practices which concludes that it "will register an original work of authorship, provided that the work was created by a human being." Naruto is not an "author" within the meaning of the Copyright Act.

SECTION 1.7
ELEMENTS OF A
JUDICIAL OPINION

Few issues in the past several decades has been more controversial and debated than same-sex marriages. Traditionally, marriage has been defined as "the state of being united to a person of the opposite sex as husband or wife in a consensual and contractual relationship recognized by law."[17] It is based on the concept that men and women are complementary and reproduction depends upon both sexes. As the result, it has been the foundation of civilization for thousands of years and governments recognize marriage because it is an institution of great benefit to society and it is the "least restrictive means of ensuring the well-being of children."[18]

In 1971, these traditional notions of marriage were challenged when Richard Baker and James McConnell applied for a marriage license in Minnesota. In upholding the refusal to issue the license, the Minnesota Supreme Court said:

> The institution of marriage as a union of man and woman, uniquely involving the procreation and rearing of children within a family, is as old as the book of Genesis. Marriage and procreation are fundamental to the very existence and survival of the race. This historic institution manifestly is more deeply founded than the asserted contemporary concept of marriage and societal interests for which petitioners contend. The Due Process Clause of the Fourteenth Amendment is not a charter for restructuring it by judicial legislation.[19]

The majority of the Americans fully supported **Baker v. Nelson** at the time and it remained the seminal decision on the issue for years. However, critics of the ban on same sex-marriages became more vocal and in 1979, a new classification of a relationship was proposed; domestic partnership. In 1982, the idea was adopted by the San Francisco Board of Supervisors for the first time but rejected by the mayor as the result of intense pressure from the Catholic Church.[20]

Hawaii, however, became the battle ground in 1991 when a women and her partner were denied a marriage license. This dispute ended up before the Supreme Court of Hawaii that ruled its prohibition against same sex-marriages was unconstitutional because it constitutes discrimination based upon one's sex.[21] While the court did not explicitly rule that same sex-marriages were acceptable proponents of same sex-marriages were buoyed by this ruling and the tide of public opinion seemed to be slowly turning in favor of these unions.

In 1996, Congress stepped into the fray by enacting the Defense of Marriage Act or "DOMA." This law, which was passed by President Bill Clinton, declared that marriage may be defined only as:

> "A legal union between one man and one woman as husband and wife, and the word `spouse' refers only to a person of the opposite sex who is a husband or a wife."

The effect of this legislation is that it prohibited the federal government from accepting or acknowledging any marriage between same-sex partners for the purpose of federal laws or programs, despite the fact that the couple was recognized as legally married by the state in which they live.[22] This statute had the effect of barring same-sex partners from receiving such things as insurance benefits for government employees, social security survivors' benefits, and the filing of joint tax returns.[23]

Despite this pronouncement by Congress, the states continued to battle over the definition of same-sex marriage.[24] California became the first state to enact a domestic partnership law in 1999 and civil unions were recognized in Vermont. The firestorm over this controversial issue, however, erupted in 2001, when seven same-sex couples from Massachusetts applied for a marriage license but were turned down. Let us roll the clock back that time to begin our lesson on how to understand the elements of a judicial opinion by examining the decision of the Massachusetts trial court who refused to recognize same-sex marriages on the theory that history, statutory construction and the need to procreate only recognizes marriage as a union between a man and woman. This decision was then appealed to the Massachusetts Supreme Court which ruled that a statute barring same-sex couples from marrying was unconstitutional. This case became the catalyst that eventually lead to the Supreme Court of the United States declaring in 2015 that a ban on same-sex marriage is unconstitutional. The reader will see how a specific legal issue undergoes a metamorphous as the result of changing public opinion.

It is important to be familiar with the elements of a judicial opinion so one may better understand the law that the court has established.

The full name of the important case on same-sex manage is **Goodridge v. Department of Public Health;** this is known as the caption of a case since it identifies the parties to the lawsuit. In other words, Goodridge sued the Department of Public Health so she is known as the plaintiff. The Department of Public Health is the defendant since it has been sued. When a case is appealed to a higher court, the names of the parties change. The person who appeals the lower court's decision is the **"appellant."** The party against whom the appeal is filed is the **"appellee."**

The **citation** tells a person how to locate the case. In this instance, the citation of the trial court decision is 14 Mass. L. Rptr. 591 (Mass. Super. 2002). "Mass. L. Rptr." refers to the book that contains this decision or the Massachusetts Law Reporter. The number "14" refers to the volume of the book that contains the decision, and "59" is the page number on which the case is published. Goodridge was initially decided by the trial court. In Massachusetts, the trial court is known as the Superior Court. By way of comparison, the Superior Court in Pennsylvania refers to an intermediate appellate court. If a federal court decided the case, the initials F. or F. Supp. would appear. Finally, "2002" is the year in which the case was decided.

Goodridge v. Department of Public Health was appealed and assigned a new number to reflect that fact. The appellate decision is located at 798 N. E. 2d 941 (Mass. 2003). The abbreviation "N.E. 2d" refers to the Northeast Reporter, Second Series. The Northeast Reporter contains appellate court decisions in Massachusetts, Illinois, Indiana, New York and Ohio. By comparison, California decisions are published in the Pacific Reporter, and Pennsylvania cases are set forth in the Atlantic Reporter.

The next item after the caption is the name of the judge who authored the opinion. On appeal, one judge writes the opinion or body of the case for the "majority" of the court. Because an appellate court consists of a panel of three or more judges, a decision reached by more than half of the judges constitutes the **"majority opinion."** A decision rendered by the majority is the law. A judge authors a **"dissenting opinion"** when he or she disagrees with the result reached by the majority— however, the dissent has no value as precedent. A judge may also write a **"concurring opinion"** when the jurist agrees with the outcome of the case but wants to note a difference in logic for reaching the decision.

**SECTION 1.8
BRIEFING OF A CASE**

Breaking a case down into its component parts simplifies a person's understanding of the opinion. An opinion has four main parts:

1. The Action;

2. The Facts;

3. The Issue; and

4. The Opinion of the Court.

The Action — What kind of case is it? What remedy is being sought? For instance, does the case involve a criminal prosecution or a civil lawsuit for money damages?

The Facts — What happened? The reader should be concerned with the three *W's*: specifically, *Who* did *What* to *Whom?* The facts of a case are discussed in a narrative form.

The Issue — What question is presented to the court for it to decide?

The Opinion of the Court — First, the reader must ascertain what the court decided. In other words, how did the court answer the question posed in the Issue section? Second, and more importantly, what justification does the court provide for coming up with its answer? For example, what sociological, economic or political policies does the court use to justify its decision? Any dissenting or concurring opinions should also be noted in this section, but the discussion will be less detailed than that of the majority opinion.

An appellate court can affirm, reverse or remand the decision of a lower court. When a decision is **affirmed**, the appellate court determines that the lower court reached the correct decision. The appellate court **reverses** a decision when it finds that the lower court's decision was incorrect. A case may also be **remanded** to the trial court. This occurs when the appellate court finds that the trial judge committed an error in deciding the case, additional evidence must be obtained, or the lower court's decision must be clarified.

The reader should now examine the two opinions in **Goodridge v. Department of Public Health** and break the cases down into their component parts.

Marriage is part of the basic fabric of Western civilization that is created and regulated by state law. More than 100 years ago, the Supreme Court in **Maynard v. Hill** acknowledged the connection between marriage and a free society when it pronounced marriage as "the foundation of the family and society, without which there would be neither civilization nor progress." Other courts have followed this principle by stating that "the structure of society itself largely depends upon the institution of marriage ... The joining of the man and woman in marriage is the most socially productive and individually fulfilling relationship that one can enjoy in the course of a lifetime." **Marvin v. Marvin, 557 P. 2d 106 (Cal. 1976).**

Over the years, however, the institution of marriage has not been without its controversies. For instance, interracial couples were prohibited from marrying until 1967 when the United States Supreme Court found the following Virginia statute unconstitutional:

> All marriages between a white person and a colored person shall be absolutely void without any decree of divorce or other legal process.

In announcing its decisions, the court noted that "marriage is one of the 'basic civil rights of man,' fundamental to our very existence and survival. To deny this fundamental freedom on so unsupportable a basis as racial classifications ... is surely to deprive all the State's of liberty without due process of law."

The last few decades have witnessed a new controversy—same-sex marriages. Countries around the world are being asked to recognize these unions in increased frequency. Massachusetts, however, is the first state in this country to recognize same-sex marriages in **Goodridge v. Department of Public Health.** The case was initially heard by a trial judge who refused to recognize the union on the theory that history, statutory construction and the need to procreate only recognizes marriage as a union between a man and a woman. This decision was reversed by the Massachusetts Supreme Judicial Court which ruled that marriage is a voluntary union between two individuals as spouses and that any prohibition against same-sex marriages would be constitutionally invalid. These decisions are presented so that the reader may gain an appreciation of how the courts arrive at a decision when there is no precedent in the jurisdiction.

HILLARY GOODRIDGE V. DEPARTMENT OF PUBLIC HEALTH
14 MASS. L. RPTR. 591 (MASS. SUPER. 2002)

Thomas Connolly, Justice

This case concerns the most fundamental institution: marriage. The plaintiffs are seven samesex couples who want the state and society to recognize their commitment to each other through marriage. Plaintiffs argue that the Commonwealth's marriage statute should be interpreted gender-neutrally so as not to restrict marriage to a man and a woman.

The Supreme Judicial Court defines marriage as follows:

> Marriage is...a civil contract, founded in the social nature of man, and intended to regulate, chasten, and refine the intercourse between the sexes; and to multiply, preserve, and improve the species. It is an engagement by which a single man and single woman, of sufficient discretion, take each other as husband and wife. From the nature of the contract, it exists during the lives of the two parties, unless dissolved for causes which defeat the object of marriage...

The Supreme Judicial Court has interpreted "marriage," within Massachusetts' statutes, "as the union of one man and one woman." Likewise, other jurisdictions' courts have interpreted their marriage statutes to apply only to one man and one woman.

Second, the statutory construction of the marriage statutes demonstrates the Legislature's intent to limit marriage to a man and a woman. Because marriage is not defined in the statue itself, the term must be construed as it is "commonly understood." Accordingly, Black's Law Dictionary defines "marriage" as "[t]he legal union of a man and woman as husband and wife." Similarly, Webster's Third New International Dictionary defines marriage as "the state of being united to a person of the opposite-sex as husband or wife."

The history of marriage further illuminates the purpose of the modern marriage statutes. Marriage emphasized the unity of husband and wife. Within that unity, the man and woman divided gender-specific responsibilities with the husband responsible first for farming and later for financial support and the wife responsible for domestic work, childbearing, and child rearing.

Based on the legal application of the word "marriage," the construction of the marriage statutes and the history of marriage, Massachusetts' marriage statutes cannot support same-sex marriage.

Plaintiffs assert that the right to marry the person of their choice is a fundamental right. Therefore, to construe the state marriage statutes to exclude same-sex couples is unconstitutional.

Massachusetts has recognized as fundamental those rights that are deeply rooted in the Commonwealth's history and tradition. Restricting marriage to the union of one man and one woman is deeply rooted in the Commonwealth's legal tradition and practice.

No state legislature has enacted laws permitting same-sex marriage; and a large majority of states, as well as the United States Congress, have affirmatively prohibited the recognizing of same-sex marriage. Thus, this court cannot conclude that "a right to same-sex marriage is so rooted in the traditions and collective conscience of our people that failure to recognize it would violate the fundamental principles of liberty and justice that lie at the base of all our civil and political institutions."

This court acknowledges the inherent contradiction that the Commonwealth allows samesex couples to establish legal relationships with their children but not with each other. Furthermore, the Legislature amended the adoption laws to allow adoption of children by same-sex couples. Commonwealth's elected representatives, not the courts, should resolve this paradox. While this court understands the plaintiffs' efforts to be married, they should pursue their quest on Beacon Hill.

For the foregoing reasons, it is ORDERED that plaintiffs' motion for summary judgment be DENIED.

This trial court decision was immediately appealed by the plaintiffs to the Supreme Judicial Court of Massachusetts which reached the opposite result. This state's highest court found that a ban on same-sex marriage would be a violation of its constitution. While the Massachusetts Supreme was not unanimous in its historic decision, the 4-3 opinion was the first appellate court decision in the United States to recognize same-sex marriages.

HILLARY GOODRIDGE v. DEPARTMENT OF PUBLIC HEALTH
798 N.E. 2D 941 (MASS. SUPREME. 2003)

The plaintiffs are fourteen individuals from Massachusetts. In March and April, 2001, each of the plaintiff couples attempted to obtain a marriage license from a city clerk's office. In each case, the clerk either refused to accept the notice of intention to marry or denied a marriage license on the ground that Massachusetts does not recognize same-sex marriage. Because obtaining a marriage license is a necessary prerequisite to civil marriage in Massachusetts, denying marriage licenses to the plaintiffs was tantamount to denying them access to civil marriage itself, with its social and legal protections, benefits, and obligations.

We interpret statutes to carry out the Legislature's intent. The everyday meaning of "marriage" is "[t]he legal union of a man and woman as husband and wife," Black's Law Dictionary. The plaintiffs do not argue that the term "marriage" has ever had a different meaning.

The larger question is whether, government action that bars same-sex couples from civil marriage constitutes a legitimate exercise of the State's authority to regulate conduct, or whether this categorical marriage exclusion violates the Massachusetts Constitution.

We begin by considering the nature of civil marriage itself. Simply put, the government creates civil marriage. In a real sense, there are three partners to every civil marriage: two willing spouses and an approving State. While only the parties can mutually assent to marriage, their terms of the marriage—who may marry and what obligations, benefits, and liabilities attach to civil marriage—are set by the Commonwealth.

The plaintiffs challenge the marriage statute on both equal protection and due process grounds. The department posits three legislative rationales for prohibiting same-sex couples from marrying: (1) providing a "favorable setting for procreation;" (2) ensuring the optimal setting for child rearing, which the department defines as "a two-parent family with one parent of each sex;" and (3) preserving scarce State and private financial resources. We consider each in turn.

Our laws of civil marriage do not privilege procreative heterosexual intercourse between married people above every other form of adult intimacy and every other means of creating a family. Fertility is not a condition of marriage, nor is it grounds for divorce. It is the exclusive and permanent commitment of the marriage partners to one another, not the begetting of children, that is the sine qua non of civil marriage.

The department's first state rationale, equating marriage with unassisted heterosexual procreation, shades imperceptibly into its second: that confining marriage to opposite-sex couples ensures that children are raised in the "optimal" setting. Protecting the welfare of children is a paramount State policy. Restricting marriage to opposite-sex couples, however, cannot plausibly further this policy.

The third rational advanced by the department is that limiting marriage to opposite-sex couples furthers the Legislature's interest in conserving scarce State and private financial resources. An absolute statutory ban on same-sex marriage bears no rational relationship to the goal of economy. The department's generalization, that same-sex couples are less financially dependent on each other than opposite-sex couples, ignores that many same-sex couples, such as many of the plaintiffs in this case, have children and other dependents (here, aged parents) in their care.

We declare that barring an individual from the protections, benefits, and obligations of civil marriage solely because that person would marry a person of the same sex violates the Massachusetts Constitution. Entry of judgement shall be stayed for 180 days to permit the Legislature to take such action as it may deem appropriate in light of this opinion.

As one might imagine, the reaction to the decision was swift and furious with the battle lines clearly being drawn. A professor of political science at Boston College exclaimed that "this comes pretty close to an earthquake politically. I think it's exactly the right kind of material for a backlash."[25] The justice who authored the majority opinion in **Goodbridge v. Department of Public Health** received death threats and President George W. Bush proclaimed: "Activist judges ... have begun redefining marriage by court order, without regard for the will of the people and their elected representatives. On an issue of such great consequence, the people's voice must be heard. If judges insist on forcing their arbitrary will upon the people, the only alternative left to the people would be the constitutional process. Our Nation must defend the sanctity of marriage."[26]

Subsequently, 18 states passed constitutional amendments prohibiting same-sex marriages but in 2008, the courts in California and Connecticut legalized these unions. Same-sex marriage continued to be debated in the state legislatures and the courts continued to weigh in on the issue with varying results. But by 2013, the opinion of the public had clearly changed with 57% of those in this country in favor of same-sex marriage. With a split in the courts on the validly of these unions and a growing attack on the constitutionality of the Defense of Marriage Act, this issue was primed to land on the dockets of the United States Supreme Court.

SECTION 1.9
STATUS AND PROCESS

Status and process is a concept that makes judicial decisions a little easier to understand. The principle is quite simple. If one is able to ascertain who enjoys favored status with the law, it is often possible to predict the outcome of a case without even knowing the law.

Status and process requires an examination of the parties to the litigation. The outcome of the case will depend on whom the courts want to protect and what goals society wants to achieve.

For example, consider the institution of marriage. Does the law favor or frown upon marriage? Historically, the laws supported marriage and the outcome of a case was frequently decided to uphold that institution. From a sociological point of view, marriage serves three functions:

1. It is a way of regulating the struggle between men and women. This is amply reinforced during the marriage vows when one takes a spouse for better or for worse, and through sickness and in health.

2. The law recognizes marriage as the accepted way of producing children, albeit not the only way. A child born out of wedlock is frowned upon and labeled "illegitimate."

3. Marriage is favored since it offers a logical way of transferring assets from generation to generation. Assets are passed down to children and spouses rather than being given to the first person that arrives at the home of the decedent.

To prove that the law historically favored the institution of marriage, one merely has to think of how easy it was to become married and how difficult it was to obtain a divorce. Everyone is aware that a marital union can be created through a religious or civil ceremony. The law, however, went out of its way to establish marital relationships and had created the fiction of a common-law marriage.

In **Hall v. Duster, 727 So. 2d 834 (Ala. Civ. App. 1999),** the court outlined three general requirements for a common law marriage. First, the parties must have the capacity to marry. Next, they must agree to enter into a marital relationship, but no particular words are necessary to show a present agreement to marry. This is demonstrated in **In re Estate of Garges, 378 A. 2d 307 (Pa. 1977),** where the court stated:

> A marriage contract does not require any specific form of words. In particular, words of taking or explicit utterances, such as "I take you to be my wife" or "I hereby marry you" are unnecessary. All that is essential is proof of an agreement to enter into a legal relationship of marriage at the present time. For example, a marriage contract was found where a man gave a woman a ring and said, "Now you have the right and you are my wife," whereupon she replied, "That is fine, I love it."

Finally, the parties must consummate the marriage; that is, they must live in such a way as to gain public recognition that they are living as husband and wife. For instance, the fact that a man "made no comment" when introduced as a woman's husband was taken as an objective manifestation of an intent to be married. Sexual relations between the parties is also not an indispensable element of co-habitation.

The implications of these informal arrangements are dramatic. A common law marriage is just as valid as a religious or civil ceremony and requires a formal divorce decree to dissolve.

What other institutions enjoy favor with the law? These groups would include children, incompetents, the government, and religious organizations. For instance, the government, its agencies, and high ranking officials enjoy immunity from suit in most cases.

Status and process, however, requires that one analyze the institution as it existed at the time of the court decision. As times change, so do the institutions that the law protects. With regard to marriage, women were traditionally viewed as the weaker of the sexes. Therefore, women in the past were automatically awarded one-third to one-half of the husband's net income in a support proceeding. Following the Equal Rights movement, and the shifting of public opinion, the role of women in today's society has vastly changed. They are considered equal to men and have made significant inroads in the market place. It is now common to see a female doctor, lawyer, construction worker, police officer or soldier. This equality of the sexes has resulted in change in the support laws. The courts now examine the earning capacity of each person instead of making an automatic award to the wife. This has resulted in court decisions requiring wives to pay support to husbands and giving husbands custody of the children.

Traditional notions of marriage are also being reexamined in view of the number of people who choose to cohabitate instead of becoming married. The U.S. Census Bureau estimates that unmarried couples make up about 5.5 million households with about 40 percent of those households having children. New terms are being coined to identify this growing group such as domestic partners who seek the same benefits afforded to their married counterparts. For example, a number of employers now offer benefits to this group with increasing frequency similar to those provided to a married couple. In view of this trend, has the concept of a common law marriage outgrown its usefulness?

Common-law marriage was created because of the difficulties in obtaining a marriage license during the early years of this nation. Women were also considered the weaker partner and needed to be protected at all costs. In view of the current ease in obtaining a marriage license and the economic power of women, the continued validity of common law marriage is the issue.

Judicial criticism of the doctrine has increased in recent time. For instance, the Illinois Supreme Court noted:

> "Despite its judicial acceptance in many states, the doctrine of common-law marriage is generally frowned on in this country, even in some of the states that have accepted it." Judicial criticism has been widespread even in States recognizing the relationship [sicne it is] a fruitful source of perjury and fraud ..." It tends to weaken the public estimate of the sanctity of the marriage relation. It puts in doubt the certainty of the rights of inheritance. It opens the door to false pretenses of marriage and the imposition on estates of supposititious heirs."[27]

Pennsylvania, which once recognized common-law marriages, declared in 2002 that it will no longer acknowledge their validity:

> There has been a growing judicial impatience of the invitation to perjury in cases depending for recovery on marriage at common-law and a progressive change in judicial view requiring higher degrees of proof where such marriages are asserted. ... But it is still not difficult for unprincipled claimants to convert illicit relationships into honest marriages, to their advantage, on spurious claims for workmen's compensation or against the estate of a decedent.[28]

Currently, common-law marriages are only recognized in a handful of jurisdictions such as Colorado, Iowa, Kansas, Montana, New

Hampshire, South Carolina, Texas and Utah. Because there is no longer a need to protect the parties of this type of union, several states that previously acknowledged common law marriages will no longer do so after a specific date. These include Pennsylvania, Ohio, Indiana, Georgia and Florida.[29]

SECTION 1.10
CHRISTOPHER V. ROBERTS

PROBLEM ONE—A

PARK, BROWN & SMITH, P.C.
ATTORNEYS AT LAW
MEMORANDUM

To: All Students

From: Peter Smith, Esquire

Re: Kathy Roberts and the Purchase of Her Car

Kathy Roberts, a 16 year-old, related the following story to me:

Immediately after passing her driving test, Kathy decided she must have a car. Unfortunately, she and her father, Joe Roberts, disagreed as to whether she was ready for what her father considered an "unnecessary extravagance." Joe had called his insurance agent and learned that the annual premium for insuring the car was more than what the automobile was worth.

Despite her father's objections, Kathy decided to secretly purchase a vehicle on her own. While walking home from school, she noticed that her next-door neighbor, Peter Christopher, had a *For Sale* sign in the window of a Honda parked in his driveway. The vehicle seemed perfect for Kathy's needs, and was in good mechanical condition. Kathy was certain that her father would be favorably impressed with her choice of transportation. Kathy contacted the neighbor and purchased the vehicle for $5,000.

When Kathy's father learned of the purchase, he exploded. "How dare you buy a car after I told you no." Kathy had never seen her father more outraged. Even her sweetest smile couldn't calm him down. Not only did he suspend her driving privileges, he even attempted to return the car to Christopher but the neighbor refused to take the car back, claiming that a "deal is a deal." Two days later, Kathy figured that her father had calmed down enough for her to start driving the vehicle. Unfortunately, Kathy was unable to negotiate a sharp turn a block from home and demolished the Honda. As she sat on the curb crying, the hubcap of the vehicle rolled by her. Since this was the only thing left of the car, she picked it up and walked home.

Kathy spent the rest of the day calling friends for advice. One girlfriend told Kathy that she could obtain the return of her money from Christopher since she was only sixteen. The girlfriend had her money refunded from a computer software club that she had joined when she was fifteen. Relying on this advice, Kathy approached her neighbor and demanded her money back. She even offered Christopher the return of the hubcap. After all, that was all that was left of the car. Christopher laughed and said that Kathy had entered into a valid contract and she had destroyed the car.

Please read **Swalberg v. Hannegan** and apply the case to Kathy's problem. You must decide the following:

1. Should Kathy be able to rescind the contract and get her money back from Christopher?

2. Does it matter that the only thing she can return to Christopher is the hubcap, or must she pay to have the car repaired before she can disaffirm the contract?

3. Did status and process play any part in the Swalberg decision? Explain your answer.

LARRY SWALBERG v. TODD HANNEGAN
883 P. 2D 931 (CT. APP. UTAH 1994)

In 1990, Hannegan contracted with Swalberg to purchase plaintiff's 1974 Ford truck for $2,500. Defendant's minority was apparently not discussed when the parties entered into the contract, and there is no allegation that defendant made any misrepresentation as to his age. Defendant paid plaintiff $640 and agreed to pay the balance three months later. Rather than paying the balance, however, defendant disaffirmed the contract on the basis of his minority. Plaintiff filed a complaint asking that the contract be enforced, or in the alternative, that the truck be returned and that defendant be held responsible for the reasonable value of his use of the truck or for the amount it depreciated while in defendant's possession.

Plaintiff argued that when defendant disaffirmed the contract, defendant did not properly "restore" the truck since he purchased it for $2,500 and returned it in a condition worth only $700. The court awarded $1,160, which was the remaining balance minus the value placed upon the truck in its returned condition.

The dispositive issue on appeal is whether a minor who disaffirms a contract is required to restore the full value of the property received under the contract. Defendant argues that the law does not require a disaffirming minor to restore the other party to his or her precontractual status. We agree.

Utah Code Ann. § 15-2-2 (1986) provides:

A minor is bound not only for the reasonable value of necessities but also for his contracts, unless he disaffirms them before or within a reasonable time after he obtains his majority and restores to the other party all money or property received by him and remaining within his control at any time after attaining his majority.

This statute requires only that the property remaining within the minor's control be returned to the other party. The trial court held, however, that defendant was required to return the property in its original condition or be liable for the difference in value. This holding is clearly contrary to the provisions of this statute and case law.

In **Blake v. Harding, 54 Utah 158 (1919),** a minor sold a pony, harness, and buggy to an adult at an agreed value of $150, for which the adult delivered 3,000 shares of stock in a mining company. The minor later disaffirmed the contract and returned the stock to the adult. The minor sued to recover $150 since the adult had sold the pony, harness, and buggy. The jury was instructed that "if you believe that the contract was reasonable, and if you further find that the mining stock traded to the minor by the adult is now worthless, the minor is not entitled to recover in this action." A jury returned a verdict in favor of the adult. The Utah Supreme Court reversed the verdict and held that the jury instruction was in "direct conflict with our statute." The Supreme Court stated that this jury instruction would require the minor to place the adult in his precontractual status, which would "disregard and misapply the purpose of the law. The law is intended for the benefit and protection of the minor; and hence an adult, in dealing with a minor, assumes all the risk of loss."

Further, in **Harvey v. Hadfield, 13 Utah 2d 258 (1962),** a minor contracted with an adult to buy a house trailer. The minor paid $1,000 as a down payment without selecting a trailer. The minor later disaffirmed the contract, requesting the return of his money. When the adult refused to return the money, the minor brought an action against the adult. The trial court returned a judgment in favor of the adult. The Utah Supreme Court reversed the trial court, holding that the minor could recover the down payment without compensating the adult for the loss of a sale.

Section 15-2-2 requires that a disaffirming minor must only return the property remaining within his or her control. The court has interpreted this statute to allow a minor to effectively disaffirm the underlying contract without restoring the full value of the property received under the contract.

We find in favor of the defendant.

PROBLEM ONE—A
ANSWER SHEET

Name _____   **Please Print Clearly**

1. Should Kathy be able to rescind the contract and get her money back from Christopher? (Support your answer with case law.)

_____
_____
_____
_____
_____
_____
_____
_____
_____
_____
_____
_____
_____
_____
_____
_____
_____
_____
_____
_____

2. Does it matter that the only thing Kathy can return to Christopher is the hubcap, or must she pay to have the car repaired before she can disaffirm the contract?

_____

_____

_____

_____

_____

_____

_____

_____

_____

3. Do you think that the concept of status and process played any part in the **Swalberg** decision? Explain your answer.

Absolutely, it did. In this case, the court defended a minor even though he broke a contract with the previous owner of the car.

_____

_____

_____

_____

_____

_____

**SECTION 1.11
PRECEDENT:
THE BACKBONE OF
AMERICAN
JURISPRUDENCE**

Precedent is the process whereby judges apply prior rules and decision of similar cases to the matter over which they are currently presiding. The correct legal term for this concept is **stare decisis**. This doctrine forms the backbone of the American legal system and offers litigants certainty and uniformity in the application of the law. As noted in **In re Larry A. Deboer,** 1999 WL 33486710 (Bankr. D. Idaho), stare decisis provides that when the court has once laid down a principle of law as applicable to a given state of facts, it will adhere to that principle and apply it in future cases where the facts are substantially the same. This principle has long been a cornerstone of common law.

Judges will generally follow precedent but are not bound to do so in every situation. A legal principle may be changed by the legislature and the court has the discretion to change the law as the social, political, or economic conditions change. Changes are also observed as members of the court, especially the United States Supreme Court, are replaced by jurists with different judicial or political philosophies.

A change in precedent may occur for a number of reasons including: (1) when the court is convinced that prior decisions are irreconcilable; (2) the application of a rule or principle has created confusion; (3) a rule of law has been inconsistently applied; (4) to correct a misconception in a decision; or (5) where the court believes that the reason for the law no longer exists, justice requires a change, and no vested property interests will be injured by the change. **Niederman v. Brodsky, 261 A. 2d 84 (Pa. 1970).**

In view of the developments of same-sex marriages and their growing acceptance by the American public, what happened to the many years of precedent in ruling that a marriage must be a union between a man and women? Obviously, change was in the wind.

The first shoe to drop occurred in 2013 when the Supreme Court tackled the constitutionality of the Defense of Marriage Act. That occurred in **United States v. Edith Windsor** when the court determined that this federal legislation denying benefits to couples of the same-sex was unconstitutional.

UNITED STATES V. EDITH WINDSOR
133 S. CT. 2675 (2013)

Two women then residents in New York were married in Canada. Edith Windsor and Thea Spyer returned to their home in New York City. When Spyer died in 2009, she left her estate to Windsor. Windsor sought to claim the estate tax exemption for surviving spouses. She was barred from doing so, however, by a federal law, the Defense of Marriage Act, which excludes a same-sex partner from the definition of "spouse" as that term is used in federal statutes.

In 1996, as some States were beginning to consider the concept of same-sex marriage, see, e.g., **Baehr v. Lewin,** 74 Haw. 530 (1993), and before any State had acted to permit it, Congress enacted the Defense of Marriage Act (DOMA). Section 3 provides a federal definition of "marriage" and "spouse." It provides as follows: "In determining the meaning of any Act of Congress, or of any ruling, regulation, or interpretation of the various administrative bureaus and agencies of the United States, the word 'marriage' means only a legal union between one man and one woman as husband and wife, and the word 'spouse' refers only to a person of the opposite sex who is a husband or a wife."

When Windsor and Spyer longed to marry, neither New York nor any other State granted them that right. In 2007, they traveled to Ontario to be married. It seems fair to conclude that, until recent years, many citizens had not even considered the possibility that two persons of the same sex might aspire to occupy the same status and dignity as that of a man and woman in lawful marriage. For marriage between a man and a woman no doubt had been thought of by most people as essential to the very definition of that term and to its role and function throughout the history of civilization. For others, however, came the beginnings of a new perspective, a new insight. Accordingly, some States concluded that same-sex marriage ought to be given recognition and validity. The limitation of lawful marriage to heterosexual couples, which for centuries had been deemed both necessary and fundamental, came to be seen in New York and certain other States as an unjust exclusion.

The laws of New York came to acknowledge same-sex marriage. New York, in common with 11 other States, decided that same-sex couples should have the right to marry and so live with pride and in a status of equality with all other married persons. Against this background of lawful same-sex marriage in some States, the design, purpose, and effect of DOMA should be considered.

DOMA enacts a directive applicable to over 1,000 federal statutes and the whole realm of federal regulations. And its operation is directed to a class of persons that the laws of New York, and of 11 other States, have sought to protect. State laws defining and regulating marriage, of course, must respect the constitutional rights of persons; but regulation of domestic relations is an area that has long been regarded as an exclusive province of the States.

The recognition of civil marriages is central to state domestic relations law applicable to its residents and citizens. The definition of marriage is the foundation of the State's broader authority to regulate the subject of domestic relations with respect to the protection of offspring, property interests, and the enforcement of marital responsibilities. Against this background DOMA rejects the long-established precept that the incidents, benefits, and obligations of marriage are uniform for all married couples within each State. DOMA, because of its reach, departs from this tradition of reliance on state law to define marriage.

In acting to allow same-sex marriages, New York was responding to the initiative of those who sought a voice in shaping the destiny of their own times. These actions were without doubt a proper exercise of its sovereign authority within our federal system, all in the way that the Framers of the Constitution intended. DOMA seeks to injure the very class New York seeks to protect. By doing so it violates basic due process and equal protection principles applicable to the Federal Government. DOMA's unusual deviation from the usual tradition of recognizing and accepting state definitions of marriage here operates to deprive same-sex couples of the benefits and responsibilities that come with the federal recognition of their marriages.

When New York adopted a law to permit same-sex marriage, it sought to eliminate inequality; but DOMA frustrates that objective. DOMA writes inequality into the entire United States Code. DOMA's principal effect is to identify a subset of state-sanctioned marriages and make them unequal. DOMA divests married same-sex couples of the duties and responsibilities that are an essential part of married life and that they in most cases would be honored to accept were DOMA not in force. And though Congress has great authority to design laws to fit its own conception of sound national policy, it cannot deny the liberty protected by the Due Process Clause of the Fifth Amendment.

Did the **Windsor** decision end the controversy and legal issues involving same-sex marriages? No, the decision only declared a part of DOMA unconstitutional. It did not rule that same-sex marriages were lawful so a conflict remained between states that allowed these unions and those that did not. This created a degree of uncertainty. For instance, what would happened if a same-sex couple married in a state that recognized the union but then moved to a state that did not permit it?

The validity of same-sex marriage was decided by the Supreme Court in 2015 in **Obergefell v. Hodges.** The Supreme Court felt mandated to tackle the issue because of a split between the Federal Circuit Courts of Appeal. In overturning a prior Supreme Court decision, the court established new precedent by determining that the right to marry is a fundamental right guaranteed under the Due Process and Equal Protection Clauses of the Fourteenth Amendment. As the court takes us through a history of marriage including the court cases on same-sex marriages, the court is vigilant to point out that the law is not stagnate and must reflect the changing attitudes of society. The traditional notions of marriage; to have a permanent relationship between two people and to rise a family is equally applicable to people of the same-sex so it must be protected by the United States Constitution.

OBERGEFELL V. HODGES
135 S. CT. 2584 (2105)

The petitioners seek to find that liberty by marrying someone of the same-sex and having their marriages deemed lawful on the same terms and conditions as marriages between persons of the opposite sex. These cases come from Michigan, Kentucky, Ohio, and Tennessee, States that define marriage as a union between one man and one woman. The petitioners are 14 same-sex couples.

The annals of history reveal the transcendent importance of marriage. The lifelong union of a man and a woman always has promised nobility and dignity to all persons, without regard to their station in life. The ancient origins of marriage confirm its centrality, but it has not stood in isolation from developments in law and society. The history of marriage is one of both continuity and change. That institution—even as confined to opposite-sex relations—has evolved over time. In the late 20th century, following substantial cultural and political developments, same-sex couples began to lead more open and public lives and to establish families. Against this background, the legal question of same-sex marriage arose. In 1993, the Hawaii Supreme Court held Hawaii's law restricting marriage to opposite-sex couples constituted a classification on the basis of sex and was therefore subject to scrutiny under the Hawaii Constitution. **Baehr v. Lewin,** 74 Haw. 530, 852 P.2d 44. Although this decision did not mandate that same-sex marriage be allowed, some States were concerned by its implications and reaffirmed that marriage is defined as a union between opposite-sex partners. So too in 1996, Congress passed the Defense of Marriage Act (DOMA), defining marriage for all federal-law purposes as "only a legal union between one man and one woman as husband and wife."

The new and widespread discussion of the subject led other States to a different conclusion. In 2003, the Supreme Court of Massachusetts held the State's Constitution guaranteed same-sex couples the right to marry. See **Goodridge v. Department of Public Health,** 440 Mass. 309, 798 N.E.2d 941 (2003). Two Terms ago, this Court invalidated DOMA to the extent it barred the Federal Government from treating same-sex marriages as valid. After years of litigation, legislation, referenda, and the discussions that attended these public acts, the States are now divided on the issue of same-sex marriage.

Under the Due Process Clause of the Fourteenth Amendment, no State shall "deprive any person of life, liberty, or property, without due process of law." In addition these liberties extend to certain personal choices central to individual dignity and autonomy. Applying these established tenets, the Court has long held the right to marry is protected by the Constitution. It cannot

be denied that this Court's cases describing the right to marry presumed a relationship involving opposite-sex partners. The Court, like many institutions, has made assumptions defined by the world and time of which it is a part.

In defining the right to marry, these cases have identified essential attributes of that right based in history, tradition, and other constitutional liberties inherent in this intimate bond. And in assessing whether the force and rationale of its cases apply to same-sex couples, the Court must respect the basic reasons why the right to marry has been long protected. This analysis compels the conclusion that same-sex couples may exercise the right to marry. Marriage is fundamental under the Constitution apply with equal force to same-sex couples. The right to personal choice regarding marriage is inherent in the concept of individual autonomy like choices concerning contraception.

A second principle is that the right to marry is fundamental because it supports a two-person union. Same-sex couples have the same right as opposite-sex couples to enjoy intimate association. A third basis for protecting the right to marry is that it safeguards children and families and thus draws meaning from related rights of childrearing, procreation, and education. As all parties agree, many same-sex couples provide loving and nurturing homes to their children, whether biological or adopted.

The limitation of marriage to opposite-sex couples may long have seemed natural and just, but its inconsistency with the central meaning of the fundamental right to marry is now manifest. With that knowledge must come the recognition that laws excluding same-sex couples from the marriage right impose stigma and injury of the kind prohibited by our basic charter.

These considerations lead to the conclusion that the right to marry is a fundamental right inherent in the liberty of the person, and under the Due Process and Equal Protection Clauses of the Fourteenth Amendment couples of the same-sex may not be deprived of that right and that liberty.

SECTION 1.12
COMMONWEALTH
OF PENNSYLVANIA
v. JOSEPH ROBERTS

PROBLEM ONE—B

PARK, BROWN & SMITH, P.C.
ATTORNEYS AT LAW
MEMORANDUM

To: All Students

From: Peter Smith, Esquire

Re: The Skateboarding Accident

Joe Roberts is an avid skateboarder and is so proficient that he often skateboards many miles to work. During one particularly hot and humid day, Joe suffered heat exhaustion after practicing for several hours. Therefore, he consumed several cans of beer to quench his thirst and skateboarded to a nearby park that had several mountain trails to build up his endurance.

As Joe was skateboarding down the street, he waved to a neighbor. Unfortunately, Joe was going so fast that he lost his balance and crashed into Officer John O'Brien who was crossing the street. As Officer O'Brien helped Joe to his feet, the police officer smelled alcohol on Joe's breath. A breathalyzer revealed a blood-alcohol level of .09, so Joe was arrested for driving under the influence of alcohol. Joe is shocked by the absurdity of the situation and has come to our office for advice. He cannot understand how a person can be arrested for driving under the influence when he is using a skateboard and not an automobile. Joe is particularly distressed since he will lose his driver's license if found guilty of the charge.

Pennsylvania has lowered the legal requirements to convict a person for driving under the influence of alcohol from a blood-alcohol level of .10 to the lower level of .08. This change was made in order to receive federal highway construction funds. That new law is as follows:

§ 3802. Driving under the influence of alcohol or controlled substance

(a) General impairment.—

(1) An individual may not drive, operate or be in actual physical control of the movement of a vehicle after imbibing a sufficient amount of alcohol such that the individual is rendered incapable of safely driving, operating or being in actual physical control of the movement of the vehicle.

(2) An individual may not drive, operate or be in actual physical control of the movement of a vehicle after imbibing a sufficient amount of alcohol such that the alcohol concentration in the individual's blood or breath is at least 0.08% but less than 0.10% within two hours after the individual has driven, operated or been in actual physical control of the movement of the vehicle.

I told Joe that you would do a fine research job. Please read **Commonwealth v. Brown** and apply the holding to Joe's case. You will need to answer the following questions:

1. Does new *Section 3802 of the Motor Vehicle Code* apply to an individual riding a skateboard while under the influence of alcohol?

2. According to the case, what factors should the Court consider in determining the legislature's intention in enacting a statute?

3. Is there enough evidence to convict Joe of driving under the influence? Support your answer with case law.

COMMONWEALTH OF PENNSYLVANIA v. LEE BROWN
620 A. 2D 1213 (PA. SUPER. 1993)

On September 20, 1990, Brown was riding her bicycle in the wrong lane of Miller Avenue, Clairton, Pennsylvania, and traveling in the wrong direction. As the bicycle weaved down the street, Brown struck an automobile whose driver had attempted to avoid her by swerving his vehicle. After the accident, a state police officer observed a strong odor of alcohol on Brown's breath. She consented to a blood alcohol test which revealed a blood alcohol content of 0.29%. She also admitted to the police officer that she had been consuming beer.

Based on this incident, the Commonwealth charged Brown with two counts of driving under the influence of alcohol or controlled substances, and with riding on the wrong side of the roadway, a summary offense. The Commonwealth raises the following issue: Whether the trial court erred in holding that bicycles are not "vehicles" for purposes of *75 Pa.C.S.A. Section 3731*, and therefore, that a person cannot be convicted of driving under the influence for operating a bicycle on a public highway while under the influence of alcohol or controlled substances?

Because this case presents a question of the proper interpretation of a legislative enactment, we will review the relevant rules of statutory construction. The cardinal principle in interpreting legislative enactments is "to ascertain and effectuate the intent of the General Assembly." When the words of a statute are clear and free from all ambiguity, the letter of the law is not to be disregarded under the pretext of pursuing its spirit. A court interpreting a statute must ascertain and effectuate the intention of the legislature and give full effect to each provision of the statute if at all possible. **Fireman's Fund Insurance Company v. Nationwide Mutual Insurance Company, 317 Pa. Super. 497, 464 A.2d 431 (1983).** "When the words of a statute are not explicit, the intention of the General Assembly may be ascertained by considering, among other factors:"

1. The occasion and necessity for the statute.

2. The circumstances under which it was enacted.

3. The mischief to be remedied.

4. The object to be attained.

5. The former law, if any, including other statutes upon the same or similar subjects.

6. The consequences of a particular interpretation.

7. The contemporaneous legislative history.

8. Legislative and administrative interpretations of such statute.

The statute which requires interpretation herein is *Section 3731 of the Motor Vehicle Code*, which provides:

a. Offense defined. A person shall not drive, operate or be in actual physical control of the movement of any vehicle while:

   1. under the influence of alcohol to a degree which renders the person incapable of safe driving;

   2. under the influence of any controlled substance, to a degree which renders the person incapable of safe driving;

   3. under the combined influence of alcohol and any controlled substance to a degree which renders the person incapable of safe driving; or

   4. the amount of alcohol by weight in the blood of the person is 0.10 percent or greater.

The issue presented by this case is whether *Section 3731* applies to an individual operating a bicycle, as opposed to a motor vehicle.

Keeping in mind the principle that a statute must be construed to give effect to all of its parts, we note the definitions of "vehicle" and "motor vehicle" as set forth in the Vehicle Code. A "vehicle" is defined as "[e]very device in, upon or by which any person or property is or may be transported or drawn upon a highway, except devices used exclusively upon rails or tracks." 75 Pa. C.S.A.§102. "Motor vehicle" is defined as "a vehicle which is self-propelled except one which is propelled solely by human

power or by electric power obtained from overhead trolley wires, but not operated upon rails." *Section 3731* prohibits the driving or operating of a "vehicle"—while under the influence of alcohol. A bicycle clearly falls within the confines of that definition. It is a "device" upon which a person or property may be "transported or drawn upon a highway," and it is not a device which is "used exclusively upon rails or tracks." See *Section 102*, supra ("vehicle"). A bicycle is clearly not a motor vehicle as it is a vehicle "which is propelled solely by human power." However, it is the operators of vehicles, not the operators of motor vehicles, who are regulated under *Section 3731*. Since *Section 3731* applies to the operators of vehicles, and since the bicycle which appellee was riding falls within the definition of that term, the lower court erred in holding that appellee could not be prosecuted under *Section 3731* for operating her bicycle while purportedly under the influence of alcohol.

For these reasons, we hold that the lower court abused its discretion in dismissing the charges against appellee under *Section 3731.*

Order reversed; case remanded for further proceedings in accordance with this memorandum.

DEL SOLE, J., concurring.

I join the opinion of my distinguished colleague, Judge Cercone. I only wish to point out that the Vehicle Code evidences the Legislature's understanding that the word "vehicle" does include bicycles. At **Pa. C.S.A. Section 1101,** all vehicles are required to be titled except those exempted in *Section 1102.* There, in subparagraph 7, vehicles "moved solely by human or animal power" are excluded from this requirement. This same limitation also applies to the registration requirements of *Section 1301* at. seq. These sections demonstrate to me that the members of the General Assembly fully understood that bicycles were included in the definition of "vehicle" when used in *Section 3731.*

PROBLEM ONE—B
ANSWER SHEET

Name   **Please Print Clearly**

1. Does the amended **Section 3802 of the Motor Vehicle Code** apply to an individual riding a skateboard while under the influence of alcohol?

_____

_____

_____

_____

_____

_____

_____

_____

2. According to **Commonwealth of Pennsylvania v. Brown,** what factors does the court indicate should be examined in order to ascertain the intention of the legislature when the words of a statute are not specific?

_____

_____

_____

_____

_____

_____

_____

_____

_____

3. Is there enough evidence to convict Joe of driving under the influence? Please explain.

_____

_____

_____

_____

_____

_____

_____

_____

_____

_____

_____

_____

_____

_____

_____

_____

_____

_____

_____

_____

_____

SECTION 1.13
INTERNET RESEARCH
ON MALPRACTICE

PROBLEM ONE—C

PARK, BROWN & SMITH, P.C.
ATTORNEYS AT LAW
MEMORANDUM

To: All Students

FROM: Peter Smith, Esquire

RE: Internet Research on Medical Malpractice

It has become very expensive to maintain a law library, so I am interested in learning how to conduct legal research on the internet. I have been told that many courts have posted their decisions on the web and a number of excellent search engines and websites provide answers to a variety of legal problems.

Park, Brown & Smith, P.C. has been consulted by a client who suffered a tragic loss as the result of the amputation of her foot due to the negligence of Dr. Jones. The client had a cancerous tumor on the right foot that required amputation. However, in the operating room, Dr. Jones became confused and mistakenly amputated the left foot. I believe this is a clear case of medical malpractice, and we should recover millions.

Please research the issue of medical malpractice on the internet. I want to learn if there are any legal resources on this topic. Let me know the results of your internet research and provide me with an explanation on how you uncovered the information. Print out two of these resources and attach the first page of each site to this assignment. Your research should not be confined to cases involving the amputation of a leg or foot.

PROBLEM ONE—C
ANSWER SHEET

Name   **Please Print Clearly**

1. Does the Internet have legal resources on the topic of medical malpractice? If so, please list and describe five of these resources.

_____

_____

_____

_____

_____

_____

_____

2. Please explain how you found these resources. How many resources were there?

_____

_____

_____

_____

_____

_____

_____

_____

_____

3. Please print out two of these references and attach the first printed page of each site to this assignment.

_____

_____

_____

_____

_____

_____

_____

_____

_____

_____

_____

_____

_____

_____

_____

_____

_____

_____

_____

_____

_____

_____

_____

SECTION 1.14
ETHICAL THEORIES

If ethics is about choosing the right behavior, the moral way to live one's life, how does society achieve this goal? There are many different ethical beliefs individuals can hold. Abortion is just one example of an issue that separates people who have very strong but completely opposite ethical beliefs. And in a multicultural society, doesn't it become even more difficult to decide on one single ethically correct position? Who is to say which personal or cultural ethical standard is correct or is there a universal ethic?

For centuries, human beings have struggled to determine the answers to these types of questions. Within Western civilization, two major philosophical theories about ethics have evolved:

1. **Utilitarian Theory:** Focuses on the consequences—both short and long term—of any particular action for all individuals affected. Benefits and harms are balanced against one another, to determine which action produces the most happiness for the greatest number of people.

2. **Rights Theory:** Concerned with the reasons for action, not just the results. People have certain basic rights—the right to life, freedom of expression, privacy, for instance—that are of value in themselves and must be protected. This theory also includes the notion of "Universality:" Whatever we choose to do must be behavior we would be willing to have done to everyone, including to ourselves—a version of the Golden Rule.

Sometimes these two theories serve the same purpose. For example, a student who sees another student cheating on an exam employs her freedom of expression to alert the professor. Not only has she acted for ethical reasons — the Rights Theory — but she has come to the aid of the rest of the class, who benefit by having their grades accurately measured. Thus, she has also acted in accordance with the Utilitarian Theory, the greatest good (better grades) for the greatest number (the rest of the class).

Occasionally, however, the two theories are diametrically opposed to each other. The classic example is slavery, where a minority of the population is enslaved, but the rest of society benefited economically. Before the Civil War, the economy of the Southern states prospered, providing the greatest good to the greatest number and satisfying the Utilitarian Theory. But the Rights Theory suffered, since human beings were enslaved, prevented from enjoying the same rights as the other members of society.

Can you think of other examples where the two philosophies go hand-in-hand? How about situations where they diverge? Consider these examples when you work on the following problem.

PARK, BROWN & SMITH, P.C.
ATTORNEYS AT LAW
MEMORANDUM

TO: All Students

FROM: Peter Smith, Esquire

RE: Kathy Roberts and Eastcoast Airlines

Kathy Roberts decided to obtain a summer job in order to prove that she has finally grown up. To her credit, she landed a clerk's position in the real estate department of Eastcoast Airlines.

Eastcoast has tried to diversify by acquiring a number of properties in Florida. Eastcoast Airlines, like so many of its competitors, has been suffering substantial losses in the years since airline deregulation, and has a negative cash flow. Unless the company could control its high labor costs and increase its popularity with the flying public, bankruptcy is a possibility. Kathy's boss, Robert Stingle sees selling off the Florida properties, as an important way of alleviating the company's financial crisis.

Kathy contacted Silvertooth, Inc., a developer of nursing homes, about the Florida properties and found an interested buyer. The corporation thought that one of the parcels would be perfect for a retirement villa and would feature elaborate walking trails and outdoor recreational facilities.

Eastcoast had conducted a full environmental audit of the property six months earlier, and no problems were revealed. A copy of the report was given to a Silvertooth representative who also examined the property and discovered no problems.

As negotiations progressed with Silvertooth, Kathy was approached by one of her friends at Eastcoast, Steve Flame. He told Kathy that there is highly toxic waste on the property that she is attempting to transfer to Silvertooth, Inc. The person who told Steve about the situation was recently in Florida at the site, and had found several buried metal containers marked "Danger! Biohazard. Radioactive medical waste." The containers were cracked and liquid was seeping out onto the ground. Steve said he wanted Kathy to know about the dangerous condition because he is concerned that innocent people could be harmed if the sale goes through.

Kathy contacted her boss, but before she could mention the containers, Stingle told her it is vital that the sale be closed quickly, and that their jobs depend on it. Kathy consulted with a lawyer who explained that Florida law does not require disclosure of hazardous substances on commercial property so long as there hasn't been a fraudulent misstatement about the condition of the property.

Kathy is very upset. She knows that Silvertooth is considering other similar properties, and if she mentions the toxic spill problem to the potential buyer, they will back out of the sale. Kathy also realizes that she will never deal with Silvertooth again since Eastcoast didn't own any other property that is suitable for a retirement community.

Although there appears to be no legal consequences if Kathy says nothing, and allows the sale to go through, from an ethical perspective the situation might be different. Write an advisory memo to Kathy on the ethics of the choice she must make, "To Disclose or Not To Disclose?"

1. First apply the Utilitarian Theory. Who are the people affected by Kathy's decision? What choice would result in "the greatest good for the greatest number?"

2. Now do the analysis from the Rights Theory perspective. What rights do the various affected individuals and groups have in this situation? How do they weigh against one another? What would be the result if Kathy thinks about the Golden Rule?

3. Finally, summarize your own ethical opinion: If you were in Kathy's shoes, what would you do, and why?

PROBLEM ONE—D
ANSWER SHEET

Name _____   **Please Print Clearly**

1. First apply the Utilitarian Theory. Who are the people affected by Kathy's decision? What choice would probably result in "the greatest good for the greatest number?"

_____

_____

_____

_____

_____

_____

_____

_____

2. Now do the analysis from the Rights Theory perspective. What rights do the various affected individuals and groups have in this situation? How do they weigh against one another? What would be the result if Kathy thinks about the Golden Rule?

_____

_____

_____

_____

_____

_____

_____

_____

_____

3. Finally, summarize your own ethical opinion: If you were in Kathy's shoes, what would you do, and why?

_____

_____

_____

_____

_____

_____

_____

_____

_____

_____

_____

_____

_____

_____

_____

_____

_____

_____

_____

**SECTION 1.16
REVIEW CASES**

1. A 16-year-old went to a local car dealer in order to purchase an automobile. When the salesman learned of the customer's age, he refused to sell the car unless the purchase was made by an adult. A few hours later, the minor returned with an adult that the child had just met. The salesman sold the car to the adult and then assisted the buyer in having the title transferred to the youth. A few days later, the 16-year-old returned with his father and attempted to rescind the contract. Will the car dealer be required to take the automobile back and return the money? **Quality Motors, Inc. v. Johnny Hayes, 225 S. W. 2d 326 (Ark. 1949).**

2. The mother of a mentally challenged female was concerned that her 15-year-old daughter would become pregnant without understanding the consequences. The mother filed a "Petition To Have A Tubaligation Performed On A Minor" with the court. Although there was no legal authority for the court to order the sterilization, the judge felt that the procedure would be in the best interest of the child in order "to prevent unfortunate circumstances..." The child was taken to the hospital under the pretext of having her appendix removed, and the tubaligation was performed. Several years later, the child married and attempted to become pregnant. At this time, she learned that she had been sterilized. As a result of her inability to have children, she sued the judge, claiming that he violated her constitutional rights. Under the concept of status and process, will the judge be immuned from suit for his actions? **Judge Harold Strump v. Linda Sparkman, 435 U.S. 349 (1978).**

3. The parties to a lawsuit attended a settlement conference before the trial judge. During a break, the judge confronted the plaintiff in the hallway, and in a loud, angry voice, yelled at the plaintiff that his settlement demand was "Bull - - - -", and if he thought that there was money in the case, the plaintiff had "s - - - for brains!" The judge then told counsel for the plaintiff that the client "had to deal with him and now he was their enemy." Sometime later, the judge was interviewed by a reporter about the incident and denied that he had acted improperly as the plaintiff was alleging. This made it appear as though the plaintiff was lying. Subsequently, the plaintiff filed suit against Judge Williams for his improper conduct. Will the judge enjoy immunity for his actions, or should he be held responsible for the outbursts? Do you see a difference between the statements that the judge made during the settlement conference as opposed to those he made to the reporter? **Robert Soliz v. Alexander Williams, III, 74 Cal. App. 4th 577 (1999).**

4. Charles Kuralt, the former "On The Road" correspondent with CBS, maintained a longtime and intimate relationship with Elizabeth Shannon. This relationship was kept secret because Kuralt

was married; Kuralt was the primary source of financial support for Shannon at the time. In 1989, the television personality sent Ms. Shannon a letter indicating that in the event of his death, he wanted her to own the property in Montana which was used as their retreat. In 1994, Kuralt executed a will naming his wife and children as the beneficiaries of his Estate. The will said nothing about the Montana property. In 1997, Kuralt decided to transfer the property to Shannon. The transaction was disguised as a sale, but it was Kuralt's intention to give Shannon the money for the transfer. Prior to the completion of the sale, Kuralt become critically ill. While in the hospital, he wrote a letter to Shannon and enclosed a check to complete the transfer with a notation that it was his intent for her to inherit the Montana property. Before the transfer could take place, Kuralt died. Subsequently, conflicting claims were made against the Montana property by both Kuralt's family and Ms. Shannon. Who do you believe is entitled to the property? Does status and process play any part in your decision? **In re: The Estate of Charles Kuralt, 2000 Mont. LEXIS 375 (2000).**

Footnotes:

1. "Ignorantia juris non excusat," Wikipedia, The Free Encyclopedia, https://en.wikipedia.org/wiki/Ignorantia_juris_non_excusat (last visited February 10, 2016).

2. Radley Balko, "Ignorance of the Law Is No Excuse," reason.com, http://reason.com/archives/2010/08/02/ignorance-of-the-law-is-no-exc (last visited February 10, 2016).

3. "What Is The Purpose Of Having Laws In Our Society?," Legal Framework for Multimedia," https://hsienminglaw.wordpress.com/2009/11/12/what-is-the-purpose-of-having-laws-in-our-society/ (last visited February 10, 2016).

4. "Anatomy of a Jury Trial," E Journal USA, US Department of State, Vol. 14, Number 7, July 2009, http://photos.state.gov/libraries/korea/49271/dwoa_122709/ewoa_0709.pdf (last visited March 10, 2016).

5. *Id.*

6. "When Justice is Up to You, American Association for Justice and the National Institute for Citizens Education in the Law, 1992.

7. *Id.*

8. *Id.*

9. "Justice Medieval Style," Boston.com, http://www.boston.com/bostonglobe/ideas/articles/2010/01/31/justice_medieval_style/ (last visited February 10, 2016).

10. "Statute," The Electric Law Library," http://www.lectlaw.com/def2/s071.htm (last visited February 10, 2016).

11. *Id.*

12. Statutory Construction," LII, Cornell University Law School, https://www.law. cornell.edu/wex/statutory_construction (last visited February 12, 2016).

13. "How Selfies Became a Global Phenonium," The Guardian, July 13, 2013, http:// www.theguardian.com/technology/2013/jul/14/how-selfies-became-a-global-phenomenon (last visited February 16, 2016).

14. *Id.*

15. "Selfies-Unexpected Legal Issues," Klemuchk, LLP, http://www.klemchuk. com/774-selfies-unexpected-legal-issues/ http://www.merriam-webster.com/ dictionary/marriage (last visited February 13, 2016).

16. *Id.*

17. Merriam-Webster Dictionary, http://www.merriam-webster.com/dictionary/ marriage (last visited February 13, 2016).

18. Ryan Anderson, "Marriage: What It Is, Why It Matters, and the Consequences of Redefining It," http://www.heritage.org/research/reports/2013/03/marriage-what-it-is-why-it-matters-and-the-consequences-of-redefining-it (last visited February 13, 2016).

19. *Baker v. Nelson,* 291 Minn. 310, 191 N.W.2d 185 (Minn. 1971).

20. "Domestic Partnership," Wikipedia, https://en.wikipedia.org/wiki/Domestic_ partnership (last visited February 13, 2016).

21. *Baehr v. Lewin,* 74 Haw. 530, 852 P.2d 44 (Haw. 1993).

22. "Frequently Asked Questions: Defense of Marriage Act (DOMA)," Glaad, http:// www.glaad.org/marriage/doma (last visited February 12, 2016).

23. Defense of Marriage Act, Wikipedia, https://en.wikipedia.org/wiki/Defense_ of_Marriage_Act (last visited February 12, 2016).

24. Richard Wolf, "Timeline: Same-Sex Marriage Through The Years," USA Today, http://www.usatoday.com/story/news/nation/2015/04/22/gay-marriage-timeline/70497376/# (last visited February 12, 2016).

25. *"Goodridge v. Department of Public Health,"* Wikipedia, https://en.wikipedia.org/ wiki/Goodridge_v._Department_of_Public_Health (last visited February 13, 2016).

26. *Id.*

27. *Hewitt v. Hewitt,* 77 Ill.2d 49, 31 Ill. Dec. 827, 394 N.E.2d 1204 (1979).

28. *PNC Bank Corporation v. Workers' Compensation Appeal Board,* 831 A.2d 1269 (Pa. Cmwealth. 2002).

29. "Common Law Marriage by State," NCSL, August 4, 2014, http://www.ncsl. org/research/human-services/common-law-marriage.aspx / (last visited February 13, 2016).

KEY TERMS

Affirmed	Jury
Appellant	Judicial Decree
Appellee	Judicial Opinion
Article One of the Constitution	Legislative Enactment
Briefing of a Case	Majority Opinion
Burden of Proof	Plaintiff
Caption	Precedent
Citation	Questions of Fact and Law
Common Law	Remanded
Common Law Marriage	Reversed
Compurgation	Same-Sex Marriage
Concurring Opinion	Stare Decisis
Court Clerk	Status and Process
Defendant	Statutory Law
Defense of Marriage Act	Trial by Ordeal
Dissenting Opinion	Trial by Water and Fire
Domestic Partnership	Voyeurism
Internet Research	Wager of Law
Judge	Witness

CHAPTER 2

CLASSIFICATIONS OF LAW

SECTION 2.1
PUBLIC LAW v.
PRIVATE LAW

The major classifications of law are public law and private law. **Public law** involves the rights of society, and those rights are usually represented by a governmental agency. An example of a public law is the crime of murder. This criminal offense affects the rights of all members of society to be safe and secure. The categories of public law are criminal law, constitutional law and administrative law.

Private law, on the other hand, involves matters between individuals, such as the leasing of an apartment, a claim against a doctor for making a mistake during surgery, or the purchasing of a new car. These matters are personal between the parties to the transaction or incident. The major classifications of private law are contract law, tort law, property law, and family law.

Take for example the shooting of a gun as an activity that involves both public and private law. It is crime to discharge a gun in the street and it would violate a public law. Gun enthusiast, however, can join a gun club where they can engage in target practice at a gun range. This would be an example of private law because the activity is being done on private property as the result of a contract between the parties. It involves no government regulation.

SECTION 2.2
CRIMINAL LAW

A **crime** is a violation of those duties that an individual owes to his or her community and the breach of which requires the offender to make satisfaction to the public. As a result, a crime is a violation of the rights of society and not of the individual victim. This distinction is immediately apparent when the victim of a crime does not want to prosecute the offender. While the prosecutor will usually follow the victim's wishes, a district attorney can force a victim to testify against the accused if there is a compelling societal interest, such as in cases of child or spousal abuse or rape. Since the government is responsible for taking action against a criminal defendant on behalf of society, the caption of the case contains the name of the governmental unit, such as the "United States," "The State," or "The People" versus the defendant.

The FBI keeps tract of the crimes committed in the Unites States. These statistics show that in 2012, there were an estimated 1,214,462 violent crimes including murder, manslaughter, forcible rape, and aggravated assault. Nationwide, there were 8,975,438 crimes involving property with victims of these crimes suffering losses pegged at $15.5 billion.

The arrest rate for the commission of a violent crime was 166.3 per 100,000 people, and the rate for property crime was 528.1 per 100,000 inhabitants.

Criminal laws are established by the legislature and are broken down into different categories based upon one thing—the penalty for the offense. While each jurisdiction will differ on what crimes go into a specific category, these classifications are treason, felonies, misdemeanors, and summary offenses. **Treason** is defined in the United States Constitution because it is considered the most serious offense against the country. **Article III, Section 3** states: "Treason against the United States shall consist only in levying war against them or in adhering to their enemies, giving them aid and comfort." A person cannot be convicted of treason unless two witnesses testify to the commission of the same overt act done to betray the United States, or if the accused confesses in open court. Because this burden of proof is so high, the government has prosecuted less than 100 cases involving treason in its history. Examples of people accused of being traitors include Benedict Arnold, Aaron Burr, Julius and Ethel Rosenberg, Anthony Cramer, and John Walker Lindh, the 20-year-old American who was captured while fighting for the Taliban. The penalty for treason can range from death to a minimum of five years in prison along with a fine of $10,000.

Although penalties for most crimes vary from state to state, a felony is a crime generally punishable by more than one year in jail. Examples include such offenses as murder, rape, burglary, and arson. A **misdemeanor** is usually punishable by less than one year in jail and includes such matters as assault, criminal trespass, and harassment. A defendant accused of a **summary offense** will generally be responsible for the payment of a fine, such as that which occurs with a traffic ticket.

The government has the burden of proving a defendant guilty **beyond a reasonable doubt**. This phrase has been interpreted to mean "fully satisfied," "entirely convinced," or "satisfied to a moral certainty." This is a very strict standard requiring the prosecutor to prove that the defendant actually committed the crime or **actus reus,** and that he or she had the necessary state of mind to commit the crime. This requisite state of mind, or criminal intent, is called **mens rea**. The legal system is concerned with what the defendant intended, knew, or should have known when he or she committed the crime.

There are various ways of proving mens rea. Criminal intent may be proved through an intentional, knowing, reckless, or negligent act. For example, in **Commonwealth of Pennsylvania v. Cheatham, 615 A. 2d 802 (Pa. Super. 1992),** the court had to decide whether a seizure-induced-black-out caused by epilepsy was an involuntary act which relieved the driver of a car of criminal responsibility for a fatal motor vehicle accident. The driver was found guilty because he possessed the necessary mens rea to commit the offense. The court concluded that the driver clearly knew that he suffered from unannounced seizures and was ordered not to operate a car. By choosing to drive a motor vehicle, the motorist exhibited recklessness under the circumstances. A different resolution would occur, however, if a person causes an accident by suffering an unexpected heart attack. Mens rea would be lacking since the act would be involuntary and the accident unforeseeable.

Criminal intent may also be inferred by the circumstances and actions of the accused. For instance, the actress Gwyneth Paltrow was the recipient of unwarranted advances by an overzealous fan who appeared at her parents' doorstep and sent the actress letters and packages on a daily basis. The man was charged with stalking under the California Penal Code; this statute requires the defendant's intent to place a person in fear for his or her safety in order to sustain a conviction. The defendant argued that his behavior was motivated by a desire to have a romantic relationship with the actress rather than the intent to cause her fear. The court disagreed and found that mens rea was present because the stalker did not stop his unwelcomed advances after he was informed that Ms. Paltrow and her family were fearful of his actions.

A number of crimes are committed by people while intoxicated. It is a frequent refrain for a defendant to exclaim that she did not have the requisite "mens rea" because she was so intoxicated that she did not appreciate the consequences of her actions. Generally, the law looks disapprovingly upon those who perpetrate crimes while intoxicated; but it can be a defense in certain situations.[1] Intoxication is not considered a defense unless it removes a component of the crime. Take for example burglary. This crime is defined as the unlawful entry into a building or occupied structure with the intent of committing a crime. If a defendant enters a structure in such an intoxicated state that he cannot appreciate his actions, one may argue that the intoxication removes the *specific intent* to commit the crime.[2] This is represented by the following case. A young man was so intoxicated that he entered a neighbor's home about a block away from his residence. The townhomes were identical in design and he merely opened the front door and pushed past the startled neighbor in order to go upstairs to bed. When the police arrived, the defendant was found asleep in the master bedroom. He was arrested for burglary but found not guilty at trial. The man was simply confused as to the location of his because of his intoxicated stupor and thought that he had

house. He had no intent of committing a crime; he merely wanted to sleep off his stupor.

State of New Jersey v. Eugene Baum examines whether an alcoholic, who has no control over is drinking, can assert his addiction to liquor as a defense to aggravated manslaughter to remove the element of intent.

STATE OF NEW JERSEY V. EUGENE BAUM
2016 WL 456773 (N.J. 2016)

[The defendant was convicted of two counts of aggravated manslaughter and has filed this appeal.]

On the night of April 20, 2006, defendant struck and killed two teenage girls walking in the bike lane of Kinnelon Road, in Morris County. Responding officers found two beverage containers in defendant's car, one of which contained liquid that was 7.7 percent ethyl alcohol (15 proof), and they reported that defendant could not maintain his balance and smelled strongly of alcohol. Defendant told the police, "I think I hit a deer, but I don't know."

Defendant was transported to Chilton Memorial Hospital where blood was drawn revealing that his blood alcohol content (BAC) was between .289 and .320. The blood test also revealed traces of Librium, a drug used to control the consequences of alcohol withdrawal, and which exacerbates the effects of alcohol. Defendant stated that he took Paxil the night before the accident and Librium the morning of the accident to control his "shakes." Even though defendant knew Librium would intensify his intoxication, he consumed more ~an two alcoholic beverages before driving ~ximately fifteen miles from his home ~other's home. Defendant stated that ~ecause he was an alcoholic, that

he had struggled with alcoholism for about seven years, and that he was receiving therapy for his addiction.

At trial, defendant presented the expert testimony of Dr. Frederick Rotgers, and he analogized defendant's alcohol consumption to "chain smokers" who unconsciously light cigarette after cigarette. Dr. Rotgers opined that defendant consumed alcohol without ever forming the conscious intent to do so, and it was "very likely" defendant did not realize that he was drinking because his alcohol consumption had become "automatic behavior."

The State called Dr. Daniel Greenfield, an expert in addiction medicine, who explained that alcohol consumption is a "conscious," "goal directed behavior." When a person makes a decision to buy alcohol, to drink it at various periods of time in different states of mind and when a person carries alcohol in his car, these are all purposeful goal-directed behaviors that people engage in. They're making a conscious decision to drink.

Our law considers an act to be voluntary, even if the bodily effort was the result of conscious decision or done as a matter of habit. Whether an act is voluntary is not determined by whether such bodily movements were done as a matter of choice or freewill. An act is involuntary only if it is not the product of the effort or determination of the actor.

The Criminal Code authorizes a defendant to present evidence of a mental disease or defect to negate the presence of an essential mental element of the crime. This defense was designed by the Legislature not as a justification or an excuse, nor as a matter of diminished or partial responsibility, but as a factor bearing on the presence or absence of an essential element of the crime as designated by the Code. Thus, a jury considers evidence of diminished capacity in relation to the State's burden to prove the essential elements of the crime."

A defendant may raise a diminished capacity defense if (1) he or she has presented evidence of a mental disease or defect that interferes with cognitive ability sufficient to prevent or interfere with the formation of the requisite intent or mens rea and (2) the record contains evidence that the claimed deficiency did affect the defendant's cognitive capacity to form the mental state necessary for the commission of the crime."

Evidence of intoxication may be introduced to disprove that a defendant acted purposely or knowingly. However, when recklessness establishes an element of the offense, if the actor, due to self-induced intoxication, is unaware of a risk of which he would have been aware had he been sober, such unawareness is immaterial. Consequently, a defendant claiming to have been voluntarily intoxicated at the time of the commission of a crime for which the requisite mental state is recklessness, such as aggravated manslaughter or death by auto, may nonetheless be found guilty.

Defendant claims that his mental diseases or defects negated the voluntariness of his intoxication. Hence, defendant contends his intoxication should have been considered as evidence of his mental diseases or defects. Self-induced intoxication means intoxication caused by substances which the actor knowingly introduces into his body. Our law considers an act to be voluntary, even if the bodily effort was the result of conscious decision or done as a matter of habit. Whether an act is voluntary is not determined by whether such bodily movements were done as a matter of choice or freewill. An act is involuntary only if it is not the result of bodily movement which is not the product of the effort or determination of the actor.

For the reasons outlined above, the judgment is affirmed.

SECTION 2.3
CONSTITUTIONAL LAW

The idea of a constitution to govern and protect the citizens of a country is not a novel idea. Ancient Rome was formed as a republic that granted certain fundamental freedoms to its citizens. King John of England approved the Magna Carta in 1297. This historic document provided that the people of England had certain fundamental rights that could not be abridged and the threads of this document are found in this country's Bill of Rights.

Following the Revolutionary War, the states decided to create a lasting document to govern the people of America. In the summer of 1787, fifty-five men gathered in secret session in Philadelphia to amend the Articles of Confederation, a document that joined 13 independent colonies into a loose confederation of states with a weak central government. An infirmed Ben Franklin was the oldest delegate at 81 and Jonathan

Douglas was the youngest at 26. George Washington presided over the meetings, but Thomas Jefferson and John Adams were unable to attend. Rhode Island refused to send a delegation.

After much debate, the delegates agreed upon the United States Constitution, which document created a strong centralized government whose primary purpose is to serve its citizens.

The document was then forwarded to the thirteen original states for ratification. One year later, the United States Constitution became the law of the land, and no federal or state law may conflict with that document. Today, the Constitution is the oldest written national constitution in effect. For instance, Italy did not become a democratic republic until 1948 at which time its constitution was enacted. Likewise, Japan did not create its constitution until after World War Two.

The Constitution is the most important legal document in American jurisprudence. It establishes the branches of the government, creates the fundamental rights of the people and protects them from unlawful governmental interference.

The Constitution is purposely written in broad and often vague terms so that it can adapt to changing times. This concept is called **constitutional relativity** and insures that this legal document will maintain its vitality. How does this occur? The courts continually interpret and apply the Constitution to current issues. This power of the judiciary was established by John Marshall, Chief Justice of the United States Supreme Court, in the landmark decision of **Marbury v. Madison, 1 Cranch 137 (1803)**.

The application of constitutional relativity is demonstrated by the evolution of the **Fourth Amendment**. This Amendment provides:

> The right of the people to be secure in their persons, houses, papers, and effects, against unreasonable searches and seizures, shall not be violated, and no warrants shall issue, but upon probable cause.

How could this Amendment, which was adopted more than 225 years ago, have application to a police search of a computer hard drive when this technology was clearly not within the contemplation of the drafters of the Constitution? Quite simply, the Fourth Amendment does not identify what is to be searched but merely specifies that warrants must be issued upon probable cause. This allows the court to decide what is and is not subject to police searches over the course of time.

The Constitution of the United States starts with the following Preamble:

> We the people of the United States, in order to form a more perfect Union, establish justice, insure domestic tranquility, provide for the common defense, promote the general welfare,

and secure the blessings of liberty to ourselves and our posterity, do ordain and establish this Constitution for the United States of America.

This introductory sentence provides the framework for the origins, purpose and beneficiaries of this historical document. The Preamble clearly reflects that the Constitution originates with the citizens and not with the states and its purpose is to form a better government that will insure fairness and protection of the people over time.

The body of the Constitution consists of seven **Articles** and twenty-seven **Amendments**. The framework of the document creates an intentional distribution of power. The framers realized the need for a Federal or National system rather than a loose confederation of states. They also realized the need to prevent a concentration of power in a single branch of the government. With this in mind, the drafters created a framework of limited government power through the concept of the separation of powers. The first three Articles of the Constitution apportion the power to run the country among the legislative, executive, and judicial branches of the government. Article I empowers the legislature to make the laws which the executive branch enforces pursuant to the authority granted to the President in Article II. Article III designates the judiciary as that branch of the government that interprets the Constitution.

Ratification of the Constitution by the original states was not a certainty because of the lingering doubt that a strong central government would infringe upon the individual rights of its citizens. In fact, some states ratified the Constitution only after noting that the document had to be amended to include a list of individual protections that people would enjoy from governmental interference.

This concern was addressed by James Madison two years after the ratification of the Constitution when he drafted the Bill of Rights. Twelve Amendments were proposed but only ten were adopted. These personal safeguards include the right to freedom of speech, protection of religion, and right to assemble. The Amendments also guarantee that people will be secure in their person, the government will not conduct unreasonable search and seizures, and no person shall be forced in a criminal case to testify against himself. Citizens are also guaranteed the right to a speedy and public trial by an impartial jury.

Over the years, these protections have generated a number of lawsuits that have tested the limits of what is meant by these personal freedoms. For instance, does the First Amendment protect the burning of the American Flag or hate speech that has the ability to incite a riot? Does the First Amendment protect religious groups from holding anti-gay protests at military funerals? Does the law against unlawful search and seizures prohibit the government from conducting warrant-less searches of computer hard drives or cell phones and does a prohibition against cruel and unusual punishment prohibit the state from executing a defendant?

While many people think that the last Amendment to the Constitution was the 26th, which granted 18-year-olds the right to vote, the last Amendment was passed in 1992. This 27th Amendment provides:

> No law, varying the compensation for the services of the Senators and Representatives, shall take effect, until an election of Representatives shall have intervened.

In other words, the Constitution prohibits the legislature from granting itself a pay raise that is effective before those representatives run for re-election.

Passing an amendment to the Constitution is a very difficult task. This is amply demonstrated by the fact that over 11,000 amendments have been proposed since the Constitution's inception but only 27 have been adopted. Article V of the Constitution requires that an amendment be passed by two-thirds of each House and by three-fourths of the State Legislatures. The framers did not want the Constitution to be amended every time the population was impassioned by a controversial court decision or legal issue.

The call for an amendment to protect the American flag from desecration is a prime example of such constitutional politics. Whether an amendment to prevent the burning of a flag is necessary or appropriate has become the source of great debate. To put the matter in the proper context, should an amendment be passed to protect the American flag when the country could not agree on the passage of the Equal Rights Amendment which guaranteed equal rights for men and women? It is possible that a constitutional amendment to prevent flag burning may be adopted by appealing to the emotional support of the population. This, however, is the type of issue the framers hoped to avoid by making the amendatory process so difficult to fulfill.

Another proposed amendment that has sparked much discussion is an amendment to limit the terms of those in Congress. This proposal stems from disgruntled voters who believe that career politicians have lost touch with the American people and should not be allowed to stay in office for an indefinite period. The United States Supreme Court in **U.S. Term Limits Inc. v. Thronton** decided that a state cannot limit service in Congress without amending the Constitution. The Court stated that any change in term limits must not come by legislation adopted by Congress or an individual state, but through amendment procedures. The passage of such a constitutional amendment would require a two-thirds vote in the House of Representatives and the Senate, as well as ratification by thirty-eight states.

SECTION 2.4
JOE ROBERTS'
CONSTITUTIONAL
LAW PROBLEMS

PROBLEM TWO—A

PARK, BROWN & SMITH, P.C.
ATTORNEYS AT LAW
M E M O R A N D U M

To: All Students

FROM: Peter Smith, Esquire

RE: Joe Roberts' Constitutional Law Problems

Joe Robert and his family are again in trouble. This particular incident occurred on Election Day.

Joe started brewing beer in the basement of his summer home at the New Jersey shore. He calls it "Jersey Joe's Home Brew," and he transported the liquor into Pennsylvania on Election Day to sell to his neighbors. Joe has a bar in the basement of his house and enough neon signs to light up a street. Unfortunately for Joe, Pennsylvania doesn't allow anyone to bring liquor into the state to sell to customers on Election Day. The state wants to make sure people are sober when they vote.

As Joe was unloading the last of the beer, Officer O'Brien showed up with the FBI. Even though they had no search warrant, these law enforcement officials stormed past Joe, went into his basement and confiscated the beer, taps and the neon signs. They then began loading the contraband into their cars.

"Hey, Tony," Joe yelled, calling to his son, who was asleep on the living room couch. "Help me; I'm being robbed." Tony ran to his father's aid, carrying a 9-mm pistol. An FBI agent grabbed the gun and confiscated the weapon. "Only law enforcement officials are allowed to have these types of guns," O'Brien told them.

Joe protested, claiming that he had the right to keep guns in his house. It was the American way, he said, but O'Brien ignored him. I have since learned that there is a law in Pennsylvania that prohibits citizens from having semi-automatic weapons.

Suddenly, two men walked out of the house. Joe told O'Brien they worked for him. "For how much?" O'Brien asked. "For nothing," Joe said. "They work when I tell them to, and they don't go anywhere else. They live here in the basement." Indeed, the men told Officer O'Brien, they owed Joe several thousand dollars in gambling debts, and Joe was forcing them to pay it back by working for him.

Officer O'Brien took Joe to the police station and tossed him into a holding cell. "Hey, how come you're doing this to me?" Joe asked. "I don't have to tell you anything," O'Brien replied. "You'll stay in there until you tell us where you obtained the ingredients for the beer. Or you can pay a million dollar's bail, and then we'll let you out."

Meanwhile, New Jersey state officials read about Joe's arrest and used the opportunity to seize Joe's summer home. The state has a law that provides for the confiscation of property used in the commission of a crime. Joe doesn't buy it. The state has been after his land for years to use it for a public parking lot for one of the nearby casinos. Joe swears this is a scheme by the state to take his property without paying for it. In addition, the state wants Pennsylvania to return Joe to New Jersey, since Joe made the mistake of starting his brewery in a "liquor-free town." But Pennsylvania refuses to honor New Jersey's wishes.

The Internal Revenue Service has also informed Joe he owes the government back taxes for the money he made on selling his beer. And, to make matters worse, the National Guard has decided that the shore home would make a great barracks, so they moved a couple of soldiers from an Air Force base into Joe's living room.

Estelle got into the act, too. She put on her most patriotic shirt—the one she stitched together from an American flag—and went to the police station. Estelle then started to yell insults at Officer O'Brien. A crowd started to form around her. "She's right," said a woman in the crowd, "O'Brien was mean to me, too. Let's go to the mayor's office and complain." Just as Estelle was building momentum, several police officers grabbed her microphone and threatened to arrest Ms. Roberts for inciting a riot and defacing the American flag.

Joe and Estelle want to sue the states of Pennsylvania and New Jersey, but we're not sure they can do it. Read the Constitution and answer the following questions so that we can advise our clients on how to proceed.

QUESTIONS FOR DISCUSSION:

1. Which provisions in the Constitution support the actions of Joe and Estelle; which provisions prohibit what they did?

2. Is there anything in the Constitution that shows that O'Brien, the township police, the FBI, and the election officials were wrong in their actions?

3. How does someone propose a new amendment to the Constitution?

4. What other amendments do you believe should be included in the Constitution?

ANSWER SHEET
PROBLEM TWO—A

Name   **Please Print Clearly**

1. Which provisions in the Constitution support the actions of Joe and Estelle; which provisions prohibit what they did?

2. Is there anything in the Constitution that shows that O'Brien, the township police, the FBI, and the election officials were wrong in their actions?

3. How does someone propose a new amendment to the Constitution?

_____

_____

_____

_____

_____

_____

_____

_____

_____

4. What new amendments would you propose to the Constitution?

_____

_____

_____

_____

_____

_____

_____

_____

_____

SECTION 2.5
ADMINISTRATIVE LAW

As the United States has grown in complexity, the task of running the country has become extremely difficult, and the needs of the population too great for the legislative branch to handle on its own. In an effort to ease its burden, Congress has created administrative agencies to deal with specialized areas and has staffed the agencies with experts who know how to deal with the particular problems encountered in each area.

An **administrative agency** is a "governmental body charged with administering and implementing particular legislation." Administrative agencies have greatly increased in number over the past several decades in order to effectuate general policy mandates of the legislative and executive branches of the government at the national, state, and local levels. Administrative agencies are created through congressional action called *Enabling Acts.*

Administrative or regulatory law, therefore, is concerned with the legal rules and principles that regulate governmental agencies. These agencies are unique because they enjoy legislative, executive and judicial powers. As public agencies, they protect a public interest or sector instead of a private right or person.

Administrative agencies can exist at any level of the government including the federal, state and local levels. The following are examples of federal administrative agencies:

- *Environmental Protection Agency* **(EPA)**. This agency is designed to protect human health and to safeguard the environment, including the air, water, and land upon which life depends. The **EPA** has been responsible for environmental safeguards such as the banning of DDT, which is used in pesticides and has been found to be a cancer-causing agent. They have also banned the use of lead in gasoline, limited discharges by factories of pollution into waterways, and established fuel economy standards for motor vehicles. The **EPA's** website is: **www.epa.gov**.

- *Securities and Exchange Commission* **(SEC)**. This regulatory body is designed to protect investors and maintain the integrity of the securities market. This agency was created following the economic collapse in the 1930s. The **SEC** oversees the various stock exchanges, mutual fund markets, broker/dealers, and public utility-holding companies. The **SEC** is aggressive in its enforcement function and brings between 400 to 500 enforcement actions each year against individuals and companies that break the security laws. Examples of infractions include insider trading and providing false or misleading information about securities or the companies that issue them. The website for the **Securities and Exchanges Commission** can be found at: **www.sec.gov**.

- *Occupational Safety and Health Administration* **(OSHA).** The bureau is designed to reduce the number of safety and health hazards at work. **OSHA** regulates work environments to ensure that they are free from recognized hazards that are likely to cause death or serious physical harm to workers. This goal is accomplished through work place inspections and by establishing protective standards. Since this agency was created in 1970, the overall workplace death rate has been cut in half. The website for this agency is: **www.osha.gov.**

- *Food and Drug Administration* **(FDA).** This agency protects the health of the public by monitoring products for safety, and helps safe and effective products reach the marketplace in a timely fashion. The *FDA* regulates the sale of food, drugs, medical devices, and radiation-emitting products such as cell phones, lasers, and microwaves. The agency's website is: **www.fda.gov.**

- *Federal Trade Commission* **(FTC).** The **FTC** enforces anti-trust and consumer protection laws. The bureau investigates and prosecutes unfair or deceptive business practices, seeks monetary damages for conduct detrimental to consumers, is responsible for the labeling of cigarettes with health-related warning labels, requires the labeling of ingredients for food, drugs, and cosmetics products, and regulates automatic teller machines. The agency's website is: **www.ftc.gov.**

- *Federal Communications Commission* **(FCC).** This agency was created in 1934 and is responsible for regulating communications by radio, television, satellite, wire, and cable. It also oversees the nation's emergency alert system, which notifies the public about a local or national emergency. The **FCC's** website is: **www.fcc.gov.**

The functions of all of these administrative agencies include the imposition of sanctions; licensing and other regulatory decisions; environmental and safety decisions; awards of benefits, loans, grants and other subsidies; inspections, audits, and approvals; and planning and policy-making.

Administrative agencies are unique because they are created with legislative, executive and judicial powers. An agency acts as a legislative body in the sense that it can issue rules and regulations. Its regulations are promulgated through a daily publication called the **Federal Register**. This power allows the agency to investigate alleged violations of the Act.

Administrative agencies also possess a judicial power called agency adjudication. Administrative hearings are very similar to court proceedings. Witnesses are heard, and evidence is presented so that an administrative law judge can decide the case. Because agencies possess rule-making, adjudicating and investigative powers, they have been considered by some to be a fourth branch of government.

The theory behind the creation of administrative agencies is that the administrator's expertise allows them to resolve problems within a particular area or industry quickly and effectively. The administrator's expertise should lead to proper decisions in the problem areas, as opposed to improper decisions that might be handed down by Congress or the courts due to good intentions but inadequate knowledge.

Because administrative agencies are empowered to regulate and develop the law for a specific area, the scope of review of an agency's adverse determination is very limited. The courts often feel that agencies possess the expertise in their field. Thus, their decisions are rarely overturned unless they are arbitrary, capricious, or an abuse of discretion. Factual findings, however, are conclusive so long as they are supported by **"substantial evidence."** Under this standard, a finding will not be changed on appeal if it is supported by relevant evidence that a reasonable mind might accept as adequate to support a conclusion. This is a very difficult burden for an aggrieved party to overcome.

Super Bowl XXXVIII is not remembered because it was an extraordinary football contest but because of an incident that occurred during the half-time show. What has become dubbed "Nipplegate," Janet Jackson's breast was exposed by Justin Timberlake during a dance routine.[3] The Federal Communications Commission received numerous complaints and levied a $550,000 fine against CBS. This resulted in an appeal of the administrative agency's ruling. The network argued that the FCC for more than 30 years had frequently declined to find broadcast programming indecent. The issue before the court was whether this selective enforcement was arbitrary, capricious or an abuse of discretion because it represented a change in policy that had not been announced in advance.

CBS BROADCASTING, INC. v. FEDERAL COMMUNICATIONS COMMISSION
663 F.3D 122 (3RD CIR. 2008)

CBS presented a live broadcast of the National Football League's Super Bowl XXXVIII, which included a halftime show produced by MTV Networks. Nearly 90 million viewers watched the Show, which lasted about fifteen minutes. The Show featured a variety of musical performances, with Janet Jackson as the headlining act and Justin Timberlake as a "surprise guest" for the final minutes of the show.

Timberlake was unveiled on stage near the conclusion of the Show. He and Jackson performed his popular song "Rock Your Body" as the show's finale. Their performance, which the FCC contends involved sexually suggestive choreography, portrayed Timberlake seeking to dance with Jackson, and Jackson alternating between accepting and rejecting his advances. The performance ended with Timberlake singing, "gonna have you naked by the end of this song," and simultaneously tearing away part of Jackson's bustier. As a result, Jackson's bare right breast was exposed on camera for nine-sixteenths of one second.

Jackson's exposed breast caused a sensation and resulted in a large number of viewer complaints. The Commission concluded the Halftime Show broadcast was indecent because it depicted a sexual organ and violated "contemporary community standards for the broadcast medium." In making this determination, the FCC relied on a contextual analysis to find the broadcast of Jackson's exposed breast was: (1) graphic and explicit, (2) shocking and pandering, and (3) fleeting. The standard applied by the Commission is derived from its policy statement setting forth a two-part test for indecency: (1) the material must describe or depict sexual or excretory organs or activities, and (2) it must be patently offensive as measured by contemporary community standards for the broadcast medium.

CBS filed a petition for review, contending that the FCC's ruling that the fleeting nude image was actionable indecency constituted a change in policy, and its application to CBS was arbitrary and capricious.

During a span of nearly three decades, the Commission frequently declined to find broadcast programming indecent. Throughout this period, the Commission consistently explained that isolated or fleeting material did not fall within the scope of actionable indecency. The FCC contends its restrained policy applied only to fleeting utterances—specifically, fleeting expletives—and did not extend to fleeting images.

The balance of the evidence weighs heavily against the FCC's contention that its restrained enforcement policy for fleeting material extended only to fleeting words and not to fleeting images. The Commission's entire regulatory scheme treated broadcasted images and words interchangeably for purposes of determining indecency. Accordingly, we find the FCC's conclusion so implausible that it could not be ascribed to a difference in view or the product of agency expertise. The Commission's determination that CBS's broadcast of a nine-sixteenths of one second glimpse of a bare female breast was actionably indecent evidenced the agency's departure from its prior policy. [A]n agency cannot ignore a substantial diversion from its prior policies.

Our standard of review of agency decisions is governed by the Administrative Procedure Act. Under the Act, we "hold unlawful and set aside agency action, findings, and conclusions" that are found to be "arbitrary, capricious, an abuse of discretion, or otherwise not in accordance with the law." The scope of review under the "arbitrary and capricious" standard is "narrow, and a court is not to substitute its judgment for that of the agency."

The Commission's determination that CBS's broadcast of a nine-sixteenths of one second glimpse of a bare female breast was actionably indecent evidenced the agency's departure from its prior policy. Its orders constituted the announcement of a policy change—that fleeting images would no longer be excluded from the scope of actionable indecency. Accordingly, an agency changing its course by rescinding a rule is obligated to supply a reasoned analysis for the change beyond that which may be required when an agency does not act in the first instance.

Consequently, the FCC's new policy of including fleeting images within the scope of actionable indecency is arbitrary and capricious under the Administrative Procedure Act, and therefore invalid as applied to CBS.

SECTION 2.6
CONTRACT LAW

We enter into a variety of contracts every day. However, because of their informal nature we rarely think of these agreements as contracts. Buying gas, getting lunch, taking public transportation, or buying a newspaper are all examples of agreements entered into by the parties that represent valid contracts. Merely walk out of a restaurant without paying for lunch, and the legal significance of your actions will be quickly realized.

The courts face a dilemma, however, when asked to enforce a promise that seems social in nature. For instance, how should a court decide a case where a high school student sues her prom date who never showed up for the prom? Suppose the student bought a prom dress and had her hair done. Should a court allow her to collect damages from her date in the form of payment for her dress and beauty treatment? Is this the type of agreement that will give rise to an enforceable contract, or is it merely a social agreement?

A **contract** is the exchange of promises voluntarily made by the parties, which agreement is enforceable in court. While the terms may vary from bargain to bargain, five essential elements must be present. They are:

1. an offer
2. acceptance
3. consideration
4. capacity
5. legality

An offer is a proposal by one party (offeror) to the other (offeree) manifesting a willingness to enter into a valid contract. An offer has three requirements. It must be: (1) definite, (2) made with the intent to contract, and (3) be communicated to the party for whom the offer is intended.

An acceptance is the unconditional promise by a party to be bound by the terms of the offer. For example, the words "I accept your offer to purchase my car for $25,000" shows intent to be bound by the offer. Until this occurs, there has been no meeting of the minds. Also, a change in the proposal by the offeree constitutes a rejection of the offer and becomes a counter-offer. If the buyer responds to an offer to sell a car for $25,000 by saying, "I really like your car but I can only pay $23,500." This statement constitutes a counter-offer. The acceptance must also follow the same format as the offer, and: (1) be made with the intent to contract, (2) be communicated to the offeror, and (3) be unconditional.

Consideration is the third element of a contract and refers to what each party gives up in return for the act or promise of the other. This is called the quid pro quo, or "bargained for exchange." Two elements must be present to satisfy the requirements of consideration. It must appear that the parties intended to incur legal rights and liabilities, and the bargain for exchange must have legal value. For example, if a person purchases a slice of pizza from a vendor for two dollars, what is the consideration? The vendor is giving up a slice of pizza in exchange for two dollars. The consumer is giving up two dollars but is receiving a slice of pizza in return. This bargain for exchange is supported by consideration from both parties. If the merchant only has one slice of pizza left, and the customer offers the vendor $20.00 in order to outbid three other customers, is the contract valid since the consideration offered by the buyer is so much more than what the slice of pizza is worth? The value of a bargain does not have to be equal as long as fraud or undue influence is not present.

The courts will not usually disturb a contract freely entered into by the parties of similar bargaining power. Nevertheless, when one of the individuals does not have the capacity to fully understand the ramifications of the contractual obligation, mutual consent to bargain is lacking. The law provides protection to certain groups deemed to lack the capacity to contract. These include children, insane people, and intoxicated individuals.

The contracts of a minor are voidable at the child's election. This means that the child may disaffirm the contract but the adult is still bound by the agreement. In order to disaffirm, the child does not have to return the adult to the status quo or return the adult to the same position as the adult was in before the contract was formed. The minor merely has to return what is left of that purchased or received. In addition, a minor may ratify a contract upon reaching majority. Ratification occurs when a child reaches maturity and expresses an intention to be bound by the agreement or fails to disaffirm the contract. For instance, a child who purchases a car while a minor but continues to drive a car that he purchased as a minor after reaching majority will be found to have ratified the contract.

The last element of a contract requires the purpose and subject matter of the agreement be legal. A contract is illegal if its performance is criminal, tortuous or against public policy. For instance, a contract to purchase drugs or the agreement to reward a person for assaulting another are illegal contracts and void as a matter of law. In other words, neither party may seek court intervention to enforce the obligations even when one party has performed the act or promise specified in the agreement. Courts will simply leave the parties where it finds them. For example, the court will not enforce a gambling debt between two friends over a college football game. The court takes the position that the enforcement of an illegal transaction makes the judiciary an indirect participant in the wrongful conduct.

On the rare occasion that a party does enter into a formal written contract, each term must be carefully analyzed and understood. An Agreement of Sale to purchase a home, an employment contract, an apartment lease, or the loan documentation from a bank are complex written documents containing many provisions, each paragraph of which has legal significance.

Nothing is more frustrating than when a client seeks legal advice about a contract that has already been signed without review by the attorney. This is reinforced over and over again when a distraught client calls about the purchase of a home. A buyer will eagerly sign an Agreement of Sale without the advice of counsel. Disputes over the perfect house soon arise when the buyer fails to qualify for the mortgage or learns that the refrigerator is not included in the purchase. There is little an attorney can do at this time to overcome the deficiencies in the legal document.

When a party breaches a contract, the consequences are almost always a question of damages. The penalty can vary from nothing to forfeiting the down payment or losing a substantial amount of money. A written

---

MOTION PICTURE CONTRACT

THIS AGREEMENT made by and between **Five Star Motion Pictures**, hereinafter referred to as "Employer" and **Jason Versace** (hereinafter **"Actor"**) .

1. **Employer** agrees to employ the **Actor**, and **Actor** agrees to render services exclusively to the **Employer** during the duration of the filming of the motion picture *"Hot Ice,"* in the parts of such characters or roles and in such plays or subjects as the **Employer** may select.

2. The **Actor** agrees that he will, during the term of this contract, devote his services exclusively to the **Employer** and will not engage in any other occupation.

3. The **Actor** grants the right to the **Employer** to use his name and photograph in any way **Employer** deems fit in connection with the advertising of said motion picture film.

4. The **Employer** agrees to pay the **Actor** for his services, the sum of $100,000.00 payable at the end of the filming of the Motion picture.

5. It is agreed that the services of said **Actor** are extraordinary and unique, and there is no adequate remedy at law for breach of contract by the **Actor**, and that in the case of such a breach, the **Employer** shall be entitled to equitable relief by way of injunction or otherwise.

6. The **Employer** is to supply the **Actor** with all of the costumes required for the assignment under the terms of this contract.

IN WITNESS WHEREOF, we hereto set our hands and seals.

Jason Versace   *Ira Jones*

JASON VERSACE   FIVE STAR MOTION PICTURES

contract will frequently dictate the penalty for the breach of the agreement. In fact, the contract can even specify how the dispute is to be resolved. Do the parties resort to the traditional remedies of court, or does the contract provide for an alternative dispute resolution process such as binding arbitration? Only a review of the document will provide an answer to a party's legal rights and obligations.

The following is a sample motion picture contract so that one may appreciate the individual elements of a contract.

Not all transactions and relationships give rise to a contract. This is demonstrated in **Yarde Metals, Inc. v. New England Patriots** where a season ticket holder's privileges were revoked because of the actions of a business associate who had been given one of the tickets to a Patriots game and misbehaved during the event.

YARDE METALS, INC. v. NEW ENGLAND PATRIOTS
834 N.E.2D 1233 (MASS. APP. CT. 2005)

After twenty years as a season ticket holder of the New England Patriots (Patriots), Yarde Metals, Inc. (Yarde), received a letter from the Patriots' front office advising that Yarde's season ticket privileges had been terminated, "effective immediately." As the reason, the Patriots stated that on October 13, 2002, an individual named Mikel LaCroix, using a ticket from Yarde's account, was "ejected from Gillette Stadium for throwing bottles in the seating section." The letter requested return of Yarde's remaining season tickets and offered a refund of their value. Yarde admitted that LaCroix, a business associate, had been given a ticket for the October 13, 2002, game. Yarde denied that LaCroix had thrown any bottles and offered the following account. Gillette Stadium had an insufficient number of men's restrooms in use for football games. On the date in question, LaCroix, along with others, used available women's restrooms to answer the call of nature. These patrons were unimpeded by security guards, but for some unexplained reason, as he left the women's restroom, LaCroix was arrested, removed from the stadium, and charged with the crime of disorderly conduct.

Yarde argues that its twenty-year relationship with the Patriots created a contractual right to renew its season tickets annually. That such a right was part of the bargain between it and the Patriots, Yarde maintains, is evidenced by the Patriots' annual offer of the opportunity to purchase season tickets for the upcoming football season to Yarde because of Yarde's status as a season ticket holder. Yarde claims that by revoking its tickets for the actions of its guest, a course the Patriots originally took believing he had been ejected for throwing bottles rather than for using the women's room, the Patriots breached that contractual obligation. Specifically, Yarde argues that the process the Patriots followed in terminating Yarde's season tickets constituted a violation of the covenant of good faith and fair dealing that would be implied in any contractual right to renew annually.

The purchase of a ticket to a sports or entertainment event typically creates nothing more than a revocable license. No Massachusetts cases, however, address the nature of the relationship between season ticket holders and ticket issuers, and the cases do not preclude parties from contracting for such things as renewal or transfer rights. Picking up on that fact, Yarde suggests we should follow cases from other jurisdictions where it has been concluded that season ticket holders have some protected expectations regarding their season ticket accounts.

In particular, Yarde urges us to extrapolate from two bankruptcy court decisions that ruled that the opportunity to transfer renewal rights to season tickets was an asset of the bankrupt season ticket holder's estate. The contractual right Yarde asks this court to imply here would substantially expand the reasoning of the decisions that it cites for support. The bankruptcy decisions focus on the nature of the season ticket as an asset of the bankrupt ticket holder's estate. In those cases, the teams did not attempt to revoke season tickets, but rather intervened only when the estate tried to transfer season ticket accounts, a practice both teams typically allowed. Therefore, they provide little support for the proposition that a court can enforce a contractual right to renew that trumps a ticket issuer's decision to cancel a specific season ticket on account of the behavior of the ticket holder.

Despite the fact that the parties themselves are not precluded from contracting for renewal rights, Yarde's allegations would not justify implying a contractual right that would contradict the explicit language on the ticket. The annual "automatic and unsolicited" offer from the Patriots to purchase season tickets may not thwart the Patriots' right to revoke ticket privileges for cause that the ticket holder agreed to as part of the season ticket package. Where there is a seemingly clear transaction-Yarde purchased six tickets to ten games at $100 each-we cannot infer an annual renewal right, the value of which would dwarf the value of the otherwise clear commercial exchange. More importantly, such a theory would disregard the Patriots' express disclaimers of any right of the purchaser to renew in subsequent years printed on game tickets and informational material provided to season ticket holders. The ticket specifically stated that "[p]urchase of season tickets does not entitle purchaser to renewal in a subsequent year." Yarde has articulated no basis on which we can ignore the language on the ticket.

In sum, Yarde's complaint did not plead a justifiable cause of action. The judge did not err in dismissing the complaint.

SECTION 2.7 TORT LAW

A **tort** is a private or civil wrong against an individual for which the court will award money damages. The word "tort" is derived from the Latin term "torquer," meaning "to twist." Torts are classified into the categories of negligence or intentional torts. **Negligence** arises when one fails to act as a reasonable person under the circumstances. Four elements must be established to make out a case of negligence: (1) the defendant must owe a duty, (2) there must be a breach of that duty, (3) that negligence must be the proximate cause of the harm, and (4) damages must flow from the wrongful conduct. For example, a motorist is negligent when the driver loses concentration and unintentionally runs into another car. The motorist did not intentionally try to injure the driver of the second car, however, he will be responsible for money damages in causing the accident.

The plaintiff has the burden of proving all of these elements by the preponderance of the evidence. Suppose Joe Roberts is stopped at a traffic light when Peter Christopher loses control of his vehicle and rams the rear of Joe's car. The force of the impact propels Joe forward and he sustains a whiplash type injury. Is Christopher negligent? Christopher owed a duty to drive his car carefully and avoid hitting another vehicle. Christopher breached that duty by striking the rear of the Roberts' vehicle. Finally, the negligence of Christopher in the operation of the car was the proximate cause of Joe's neck injury causing him to incur medical expenses and conscious pain and suffering. Not all cases are as easy to prove and a more detailed examination of each element of negligence is required.

Duty of care establishes the type of behavior a person must exhibit in a given situation. The basic rule is that a person must conform to the standard of care of a reasonable person under the circumstances. This duty can vary from case to case depending upon the age of the person, and his or her expertise in the specific situation. Generally, the law does not make a distinction concerning the standard of care between adults of different ages. A 65 year-old-man will be held to the same standard of care as a person 18 years of age in driving a car. That standard of care is simply the "average driver." A professional, however, is held to a higher standard of care when he or she is engaged in that professional capacity. This type of claim is called malpractice and the defendant is held to the standard of care of the average professional in that discipline. For example, a neurosurgeon who makes a mistake during surgery is held to the standard of care of the average neurosurgeon and not to the standard of care of the average person performing surgery – or even the average physician. The neurosurgeon has been selected because of this individual's specialized skill so the doctor must possess the skill and expertise of the average neurosurgeon.

Children develop differently each year of their lives. There is a vast difference in the motor and intellectual skills of a child of six years of age and a child of twelve. Therefore, minors are held to a different standard of care than the average adult. A minor is held to the standard of care of a child of similar age, intelligence, and experience. The exception to this rule is when the child engages in adult activity, such as the driving of a car or the flying of an airplane. In those cases, children are held to the standard of care of the average person engaged in those activities.

The second element of a negligence action is quite simple. If a duty is owed, and a person fails to fulfill that obligation, a breach of duty has occurred. For example, a property owner owes a duty to a business visitor to make the property safe. This includes the obligation to inspect the premises on a reasonable basis. If a department store does not inspect its facility, and a business visitor is injured because a broken bottle is not picked up from the floor, the merchant has breached the duty of care.

Proximate cause is the third element and requires there be a reasonable connection between the negligence of a defendant and the harm suffered by the plaintiff. The fact that a party is careless and another suffers an injury is not by itself enough to impose liability. Rather, the negligent conduct must be a substantial factor in causing the harm. For instance, a surgeon who leaves an instrument in a patient's abdomen following surgery has obviously breached the duty of exercising reasonable medical care. The patient's need for additional surgery to remove the medical instrument would be directly related to the doctor's malpractice.

The last element of a negligence claim is damages. This is the amount of money awarded to an injured person as the result of the wrongful or improper conduct of the defendant. This recovery may take the form of compensatory and punitive damages.

The purpose of compensatory damages is to make an injured party whole by providing a sum of money that would return the aggrieved party to the same position as though nothing had happened. These damages must always have a reasonable relationship to the negligent act of the defendant and cannot be speculative. In a tort action, the damages should place an injured party in substantially as good of a position as that occupied before the injury. Those damages, however, are not always easy to quantify. While one may quantify the amount of lost wages, how much is a broken arm worth? Would it matter if the injured party is a painter and could no longer use his arm?

Reasonable people differ on the value of the case but the following elements must be considered when arriving at a dollar figure: medical expenses, lost wages, property damage, and pain and suffering.

Pain and suffering is the most controversial element of recoverable damages because it is subjective and cannot be calculated with mathematical certainty. The value of each case will also change depending upon the circumstances. For instance, if the victim of a broken arm makes a good recovery after six weeks, the case will have one value. If the injury, however, results in permanent impairment of a person's range of motion of the arm, it is worth a much greater sum of money.

Even though a defendant is negligent, the injured party's own conduct may preclude recovery. There are two basic defenses to a negligence action—contributory negligence and assumption of the risk.

Contributory negligence is the failure of the plaintiff to act as a reasonable person under the circumstances. For instance, a driver who fails to stop for a red light is negligent. While the operator of the other vehicle with the green light has the right of way, that driver may not blindly proceed through the intersection without first looking to the left and right. If the two vehicles collide, and neither driver looked for the other, they are both negligent. Since the individual who went through the red light bears the bulk of the liability, can the motorist with the green light collect damages? The answer is no. A plaintiff may not recover if he or she has any degree of contributory negligence even if that fault is 1% of the responsibility for the accident.

Most jurisdictions find this principle too harsh and have adopted a modified concept called, **comparative negligence.** Basically, as along as the plaintiff's negligence is not greater than the defendant's misdeeds, the plaintiff may recover damages, but the verdict will be reduced by the percentage of the plaintiff's negligence. In other words, if the plaintiff is found to be 30% of fault and the verdict is $10,000, the award will be reduced to $7,000. Pennsylvania and New Jersey follow this approach while Maryland and the District of Columbia use the more rigid contributory negligence standard.

The second defense to a negligence action is **assumption of the risk.** If the plaintiff knows of the danger, but voluntarily exposes himself to the harm, the plaintiff will be barred from recovery. For example, if a person jumps over an open manhole instead of walking around it, he will have assumed the risk of injury if he falls into the hole.

When the wrongdoer purposely sets out to harm another, that conduct gives rise to an **intentional tort** and may result in the imposition of money damages. Theories of liability include actions for a battery, assault, defamation, false imprisonment, and infliction of emotional distress.

Intentional torts are treated more seriously by the courts and verdicts frequently include an award of **punitive damages**, which sum is to punish the wrongdoer for his actions. These types of claims are generally not covered by insurance.

One must always be mindful, however, that the mere fact someone suffers a loss does not mean that he or she is entitled to recover money. The claimant must prove that another person was at fault in causing the harm and that the law recognizes a theory of liability.

For instance, in **Ali v. Gates, 1998 WL 317584 (W.D. N.Y.),** an individual instituted suit against Bill Gates and a number of others alleging that his constitutional rights were being violated by the defendants, who were trying to murder him through a Windows program hooked to his mind. This case was dismissed by the court because Mr. Ali failed to establish a recognized cause of action under the various theories he asserted in his lawsuit.

Who remembers the elderly woman who purchased a cup a hot coffee from McDonald's and received a verdict of more than two millions dollars when the coffee spilled? The case became the poster child for frivolous lawsuits. The facts showed that Stella Liebeck was trying to hold the cup of coffee between her legs while removing the lid. However, the cup spilled, pouring hot coffee onto her lap. This resulted in severe burns over 16 percent of her body, necessitating a hospital stay of eight days, debridement of her wounds, skin grafting and disability for more than two years.[4]

What is not known by the general public is that McDonald's Operations Manual required the franchisee to brew its coffee at 180 to 190 degrees Fahrenheit and coffee at that temperature results in third-degree burns which do not heal without extensive and painful care. The fast-food business acknowledged that it knew of the risk of serious burns for more than a decade as the result of other lawsuits and McDonald's coffee had injured more than 700 customers, many receiving severe burns.[5]

Triche v. McDonald's Corporation represents another lawsuit against McDonald's for hot coffee that spilled on the customer causing injury. However, the results of that lawsuit were much different.

BARRY TRICHE V. MCDONALD'S CORPORATION
164 SO.3D 253 (CT. APP. LA. 2015)

Plaintiff filed suit alleging he sustained personal injuries when three large cups of coffee that he ordered from a McDonald's drive-thru fell out of a cup holder, spilling hot coffee onto his foot, ankle and groin. Plaintiff claimed that the coffee cups were not properly secured in the cup holder by the McDonald's employee in accordance with McDonald's policies and procedures. He further alleged that the temperature of the coffee exceeded the temperature limits set forth in McDonald's policies and procedures. Plaintiff asserted that he suffered first, second, and third degree burns to his body as a result of the incident.

McDonald's filed a motion for summary judgment asserting there were no genuine issues of material fact. McDonald's alleged Plaintiff could not prove the coffee was unreasonably dangerous and pointed to the lack of evidence to support Plaintiff's allegation that the coffee was too hot.

In opposition to McDonald's motion, Plaintiff relied on photographs of his injuries. Plaintiff explained that he returned to the restaurant after seeking treatment for his burns and confronted the employee who served him the coffee. Plaintiff told the employee that she did not push the coffee cups into the holder, at which time the employee allegedly responded that she did not check the cups or push them down before handing the tray to Plaintiff. Plaintiff maintained this created a question of fact as to whether McDonald's firmly and securely placed the coffee cups in the tray.

Plaintiff also alleges that the coffee was too hot and did not contain adequate warnings. He further alleges the McDonald's employee did not properly seat the coffee cups in the tray holder before handing it to Plaintiff. Thus, Plaintiff stated a cause of action under the theory of products liability.

The manufacturer of a product is liable for damages caused by a product that is unreasonably dangerous when it is in normal use. A product may be deemed unreasonably dangerous due to its composition or construction, its design, the manufacturer's failure to provide adequate warning, or the product's failure to conform to an express manufacturer's warning. It is the plaintiff's burden to prove that a product is unreasonably dangerous.

McDonald's stated that Plaintiff had no evidence to support his allegation that the coffee served that day was hotter than it should have been or exceeded industry standards. Plaintiff failed to submit any evidence indicating what the manufacturer's standards were regarding the temperature of the coffee or whether the temperature of coffee on the day of the incident deviated from those standards. The only evidence regarding the temperature of the coffee was Plaintiff's testimony in which he stated, "I've had hot coffee at home spilled on me and it was nowhere near as hot as that." This is insufficient to demonstrate the existence of a genuine issue of material fact as to whether the coffee was unreasonably dangerous in construction or composition.

Although Plaintiff submitted photographs of the burn injury, there was no testimony indicating the temperature of the coffee based on the type of burns Plaintiff suffered. We cannot presume a characteristic of a product, i.e., the temperature of the coffee, is unreasonably dangerous solely from the fact that an accident producing injury occurred.

Plaintiff also failed to show a genuine issue of material fact existed as to whether the coffee was unreasonably dangerous because of an inadequate warning. A manufacturer has a duty to provide an adequate warning of any danger inherent in the normal use of its produce which is not within the knowledge of or obvious to the ordinary user. This duty to warn does not apply when the danger is or should be obvious to the ordinary user. This is particularly so when the user is familiar with the product, making him a 'sophisticated user.

Here, the evidence showed that Plaintiff frequently bought and consumed coffee from this particular McDonald's restaurant. Thus, Plaintiff is a "sophisticated user" who is presumed to know about the inherent danger of hot coffee because of his familiarity with it. Plaintiff presented no evidence that the temperature of the coffee exceeded industry standards. Accordingly, McDonald's had no duty to provide additional warnings to Plaintiff, a regular coffee drinker.

Accordingly, we affirm the trial court's grant of summary judgment in favor of McDonald's Restaurants.

SECTION 2.8
SHOOTING OF
PETER CHRISTOPHER

PROBLEM TWO—B

PARK, BROWN & SMITH, P.C.
ATTORNEYS AT LAW
MEMORANDUM

To: All Students

FROM: Peter Smith, Esquire

RE: Shooting of Peter Christopher

___

Tony Roberts' has been arrested for aggravated assault. My investigation reveals that the football player shot his neighbor, Peter Christopher, to prevent Christopher from stealing his car. Tony claims he was merely defending his property and questions the fairness of prosecuting him for shooting a thief. The following story emerged after I spoke to Tony at the police station.

Tony came home from football practice around 4 p.m. Just as Tony was about to watch TV, he heard rattling noises coming from outside. Tony peered out his bedroom window and saw Peter Christopher standing by his Corvette in the driveway.

When Tony's requests that Christopher get away from the car went unheeded, he ran into his father's study. From there he had access to the deck overlooking the driveway. Tony thought that from this vantage point, he would be able to scare his neighbor away.

Tony again warned Christopher to get away from the car. When it became apparent that the neighbor was determined to steal the vehicle, Tony decided to make his request a little more threatening. He ran back into the study and grabbed a gun from his father's collection. He warned Christopher that he would shoot if the neighbor didn't leave immediately. Christopher responded with obscene words and gestures while continuing to break into the car.

Tony really hadn't expected any trouble. He didn't want to shoot Christopher, but he refused to stand there helplessly while Peter drove away with his most prized possession. So Tony fired a single shot, which pierced the neighbor's left arm.

Having apprehended the neighbor, Tony called the police to report the attempted theft. He also called Dr. Jones to provide medical attention to Christopher. Officer O'Brien arrived almost immediately. Tony greeted the policeman with a big smile, but was shocked when O'Brien handcuffed him. Tony thought O'Brien was joking. In fact, he expected O'Brien to pat him on the back. After all, Tony had just caught a thief. But there was no mistake. O'Brien took the football player to headquarters, where Tony was fingerprinted, booked, and thrown in jail for aggravated assault.

An important decision on the topic is **Katko v. Briney, 183 N.W.2d 657 (Iowa 1971).** According to the rules set forth in that case, decide whether Tony can escape liability. You must answer the following:

1. Is Tony allowed to use force to protect his property? As Tony said, "I warned him to get away from the car. He made an obscene gesture, so I shot him in the arm in self-defense."

2. Was this a reasonable degree of force under the circumstances?

3. Does it matter that Tony warned his neighbor before he shot him?

4. Can Tony be criminally prosecuted and sued civilly for the shooting?

5. Do you agree with the law?

Your decision should include an analysis of these questions along with any other facts or arguments you believe are relevant in deciding Tony's culpability.

Marvin Katko v. Edward Briney
183 N.W.2d 657 (Iowa 1971)

The primary issue presented here is whether an owner may protect personal property in an unoccupied boarded-up farm house against trespassers and thieves by a spring gun capable of inflicting death or serious injury.

At defendants' request plaintiff's action was tried to a jury consisting of residents of the community where defendants' property was located. The jury returned a verdict for plaintiff and against defendants for $20,000 actual and $10,000 punitive damages.

Most of the facts are not disputed. In 1957 defendant, Bertha L. Briney inherited her parents' farmland. Included was an 80-acre tract in southwest Mahaska County where her grandparents and parents had lived. No one occupied the house thereafter.

There occurred a series of trespassing and housebreaking events with loss of some household items, the breaking of windows and "messing up of the property in general."

Defendants boarded up the windows and doors in an attempt to stop the intrusions. They had posted "no trespass" signs on the land. The nearest one was 35 feet from the house. Defendants set a "shot-gun trap" in the north bedroom where they secured it to an iron bed with the barrel pointed at the bedroom door. It was rigged with wire from the doorknob to the gun's trigger so it would fire when the door was opened. Briney first pointed the gun's trigger so an intruder would be hit in the stomach but at Mrs. Briney's suggestion it was lowered to hit the legs. Tin was nailed over the bedroom window. The spring gun could not be seen from the outside. No warning of its presence was posted.

Plaintiff worked regularly as a gasoline station attendant seven miles from the old house and considered it as being abandoned. He knew it had long been uninhabited. Plaintiff and McDonough had been to the premises and found several old bottles and fruit jars which they took and added to their collection of antiques. About 9:30 p.m. they made a second trip to the Briney property. They entered the old house by removing a board from a porch window which was without glass. While McDonough was looking around the kitchen area plaintiff went to another part of the house. As he started to open the north bedroom door the shotgun went off striking him in the right leg above the ankle bone. Much of his leg, including part of the tibia, was blown away.

Plaintiff testified he knew he had no right to break and enter the house with intent to steal bottles and fruit jars therefrom. He further testified he had entered a plea of guilty to larceny in the nighttime of property of less than $20 value from a private building. He stated he had been fined $50 and costs and paroled during good behavior from a 60-day jail sentence.

The main thrust of defendant's defense in the trial court and on this appeal is that "the law permits use of a spring gun in a dwelling or warehouse for the purpose of preventing the unlawful entry of a burglar or thief."

The overwhelming weight of authority, both textbook and case law, supports the trial court's statement of the applicable principles of law.

Prosser on Torts, Third Edition, pages 116–118, states:

> The law has always placed a higher value upon human safety than upon mere rights in property, it is the accepted rule that there is no privilege to use any force calculated to cause death or serious bodily injury to repel the threat to land or chattels unless there is also such a threat to the defendant's personal safety as to justify a self-defense... Spring guns and other

man-killing devices are not justifiable against a mere trespasser, or even a petty thief. They are privileged only against those upon whom the land-owner, if he were present in person would be free to inflict injury of the same kind.

Restatement of Torts, section 85, page 180 states: "The value of human life and limb, not only to the individual concerned but also to society, so outweighs the interest of a possessor of land in excluding from it those whom he is not willing to admit thereto that a possessor of land has no privilege to use force intended or likely to cause death or serious harm against another whom the possessor see about to enter his premises or meddle with his chattel, unless the intrusion threatens death or serious bodily harm to the occupiers or users of the premises.

The facts in **Allison v. Fiscus, 156 Ohio 120, 100 N.E.2d 237, 44 A.L.R.2d 369,** decided in 1951, are very similar to the case at the bar. There plaintiff's right to damages was recognized for injuries received when he feloniously broke a door latch and started to enter defendant's warehouse with intent to steal. As he entered a trap of two sticks of dynamite buried under the doorway by defendant owner was set off and plaintiff seriously injured. The court held the question whether a particular trap was justified as a use of reasonable and necessary force against the trespasser engaged in the commission of a felony should have been submitted to the jury. The Ohio Supreme Court recognized plaintiff's right to punitive or exemplary damages in addition to compensation damages. The jury's findings of fact including a finding defendants acted with malice and with wanton and reckless disregard, as required for an allowance of punitive or exemplary damages, are supported by substantial evidence. We are bound thereby.

Affirmed.

ANSWER SHEET
PROBLEM TWO—B

Name   **Please Print Clearly**

1. Is Tony allowed to use force to protect his property?

_____

_____

_____

_____

_____

_____

_____

_____

_____

_____

2. Was this a reasonable degree of force under the circumstances?

_____

_____

_____

_____

_____

_____

_____

_____

_____

_____

3. Does it matter that Tony warned his neighbor before he shot him in the arm?

_____

_____

_____

_____

_____

_____

_____

_____

_____

4. Can Tony be criminally prosecuted and sued civilly for the shooting? Do you agree with the law?

_____

_____

_____

_____

_____

_____

_____

_____

_____

Katko v. Briney clearly demonstrates that a person cannot use force that will inflict death or serious bodily injury in the protection of property. Human life is simply more important than property. What is the law, however, when a person's life is in danger? A different standard will apply and is known as the **Castle Doctrine** or "stand-your-ground" law. This concept is a common law principle that allows an individual to stand his or her ground while at home and use reasonable force, including deadly force, to defend himself. In this situation, there is no duty to retreat. Outside of the "castle," the person has a duty to retreat, if it is safe to do so, before using deadly force.[6] Forty-six states have adopted this law or a variation of the doctrine as long as the person using the force is not engaging in an illegal activity.[7]

Over the years, the states have strictly construed the application of the Castle Doctrine and the burden of proof for a "stand-your-ground" defense is on the person using the force. The first element of a proper defense is that the individual must be inside her residence or place of business. In other words, the edifice must be the location where the person usually resides or works, such as a house, apartment, or mobile home. The user of the deadly force must also be inside the structure. For instance, the courts have rejected the application of the doctrine if it is used while the person is in their front yard. In that situation, there is a duty to retreat if safely possible.[8]

The Castle Doctrine requires a second component before deadly force may be used. The victim must be committing or attempting to perpetrate an unlawful entry into the defendant's property. Merely standing in the backyard or driveway or walking across the lawn will not trigger the defense. Some type of proof must be shown that the person was at least attempting an unlawful entry.[9]

Would the Castle Doctrine be available to a person visiting someone else's home? That is the issue in the next case.

STATE OF FLORIDA V. ALEXANDER JAMES
867 SO.2D 414 (FLA. APP. DIST. 2006)

James had been acquainted with Samantha Beal for approximately one week before he came to her apartment on April 17, 1997. James had been to Beal's apartment once before to assist her in putting together a bed frame. James and Beal had agreed that on April 17 they would travel together from Beal's apartment to the residence of Beal's mother so that James could perform some electrical work there. When James arrived at Beal's apartment, Beal answered the door wearing a black negligee and invited him inside. They engaged in consensual sex and later showered together.

Shortly thereafter, the victim, Larry Ferguson, Beal's allegedly abusive ex-boyfriend, showed up at Beal's apartment. Beal went to the front door and told the victim to leave because she had a boyfriend in her apartment. Beal and the defendant, thereafter, got dressed to leave.

As Beal and James were exiting the apartment, they spotted the victim who was still waiting outside. The victim grabbed Beal and began to choke her. James intervened to prevent the victim from hurting her. The three ended up back in the apartment. Once there, the defendant and the victim continued to struggle and Beal was able to flee her apartment to telephone for help.

During the struggle between the defendant and the victim, a gun fell to the floor. The defendant picked up the gun and the victim fled into the bedroom. Beal testified that as she was running back to her apartment, she saw the defendant standing in the entrance door to the apartment with his back facing her. The defendant fired a shot through the partially closed bedroom door. The bullet hit the victim in the chest. The victim died a few days later.

Florida permits the use of deadly force in self-defense if a person reasonably believes that such force is necessary to prevent imminent death or great bodily harm. Specifically, "a person ... is justified in the use of deadly force only if he reasonably believes that such force is necessary to prevent imminent death or great bodily harm to himself or another or to prevent the imminent commission of a forcible felony." Even under these circumstances, there is still a common law duty to use every reasonable means to avoid the danger, including retreat, prior to using deadly force.

The "duty to retreat" rule has an exception, known as the "castle doctrine," which espouses that one is not required to retreat from one's residence, or "castle," before using deadly

force in self-defense, so long as the deadly force is necessary to prevent death or great bodily harm.. Florida courts have defined the castle doctrine as a privilege one enjoys in one's own dwelling place. The Florida Supreme Court has said:

> When one is violently assaulted in his own house or immediately surrounding premises, he is not obliged to retreat but may stand his ground and use such force as prudence and caution would dictate as necessary to avoid death or great bodily harm. When in his home, he has "retreated to the wall." A man is under no duty to retreat when attacked in his own home. His home is his ultimate sanctuary. The castle doctrine privilege of non-retreat is "equally available to all those lawfully residing in the premises, provided, of course, that the use of deadly force was necessary to prevent death or great bodily harm."

We have further extended the "castle doctrine" privilege to employees in their place of employment, while lawfully engaged in their occupations. To date, this has been the only extension of the "castle doctrine" protection to a person not attacked in his or her *own dwelling* or residence.

The issue before us comes down to whether the castle doctrine privilege should be further extended to a temporary visitor or guest, since the defendant was not a resident of the apartment at the time of the incident. We believe that an overly broad extension of the castle doctrine would vitiate the retreat rule. The more places there are where one has castle doctrine protection, the fewer places there would be from which one has a duty to retreat. Granting castle doctrine protection to a social guest or visitor would necessarily grant the guest or visitor innumerable castles wherever he or she is authorized to visit. That, in turn, would expand the privilege of non-retreat and encourage the use of deadly force. We decline to extend the "castle doctrine" privilege to a temporary social guest or visitor in the home of another. Thus, given the defendant's status as a temporary social guest or visitor at the time of the alleged incident, he is not entitled to the use of a "castle doctrine" defense.

QUESTIONS FOR DISCUSSION

1. Do you agree with the court's decision?

2. Suppose an intoxicated neighbor entered the wrong house by mistake. Should the homeowner be allowed to use deadly force?

3. Do you agree with Texas and some other states that have expanding the Castle Doctrine by providing a person has no duty to retreat outside of the home before using deadly force if you feel that your life is in danger? These laws are known as the "Make My Day" law.

While the use of a shotgun in the protection of property is clearly excessive force, is the owner of a store liable for an attack by a vicious dog that is allowed to roam the store at night in order to stop trespassers? Based upon the reasoning in **Katko v. Briney,** the store owner will be liable for the attack. The dog has been kept on the premises for the sole purpose of protecting property by inflicting serious harm to the intruder. Will liability, however, be imposed on a homeowner whose pet dog attacks a burglar that enters a home when no one is present? The answer is no. The dog is not kept at the family dwelling for the sole purpose of attacking people. Dogs are territorial and they will protect their master's home against an intruder.

Will the owner of a dog be liable if the animal bites a guest or if a large playful dog, that has a habit of jumping on people, knocks someone down? The law is well settled that a dog's owner will be liable for the actions of the pet if the owner knows or has good reason to know of the dog's dangerous or vicious propensities and fails to take reasonable measures to protect the guest from the pet's actions. The saying that "every dog is entitled to one bite" is not true. If a dog has displayed a vicious propensity in the past, the owner will be liable to another for a dog bite even if the animal has not bitten anyone previously. Likewise, the law imposes a duty of restraint on the owner of a dog when the owner knows of the animal's playful but dangerous propensity of jumping on people and knocking them down.

James Moore v. Michael Gaut
2015 WL 9584389 (Tenn. 2015)

James Moore was at Michael Gaut's residence to do maintenance on his satellite dish when he was bitten by Defendant's dog, a Great Dane. The dog was in Defendant's fenced-in backyard, Plaintiff was on the *other* side of the fence, and the dog bit Plaintiff on his face. Plaintiff argues that the large size of the Great Dane, a breed Plaintiff characterizes as being in a "suspect class," should be enough, standing alone, to establish a genuine issue of material fact as to whether Plaintiff should have known the dog had dangerous propensities.

According to the complaint, Plaintiff was greeted by Defendant's father, who "spoke at great length about the gentle nature and jovial habits of the dog," which was in a fenced area in the backyard of the Defendant's residence. The complaint further alleges that "on the insistence of the Defendant's father, the Plaintiff was requested to introduce himself to the dog" and that "upon approaching the dog, the dog jumped up and bit the Plaintiff." Defendant answered, denying liability on the ground that he neither knew nor should have known of the dog's dangerous propensities because it had never bitten anyone before.

In the present case, not only has there been no showing of any vicious or mischievous tendencies of behavior on the part of the dog, the evidence establishes just the opposite. The defendant's affidavit establishes that the dog had never bitten or attacked anyone. Furthermore, the plaintiff's own complaint alleges that the defendant's father told the plaintiff that the dog was gentle and jovial. ... [T]here is no evidence to show that the dog engaged in any playful behavior that could be considered dangerous by virtue of its size. There is simply no evidence of any behavior on the part of the dog that would have put the defendant on notice that the dog was dangerous. The plaintiff suggests that the dog's size alone is enough to create a genuine issue of material fact, but to so hold would essentially create a "big dog exception" to the notice requirement. This the Court will not do.

The common law principles governing dog bite cases were set forth by the Supreme Court just over a century ago in **Missio v. Williams, 167 S.W. 473, 474 (Tenn. 1914)**: [T]he general rule respecting the liability of owners or keepers of domestic animals for injuries to third persons is that the owner or keeper of domestic animals is not liable for such injuries, unless the animal was accustomed to injure persons, or had an inclination to do so, and the vicious disposition of the animal was known to the owner or keeper. Courts generally hold that acts done by the dog that are dangerous from playfulness or mischievousness are to be considered, as well as acts of viciousness itself. The reason for the rule is that an animal may be of a dangerous propensity from playfulness as well as viciousness.

Under these rules, the owner or keeper of the dog is not answerable for injuries done by it, unless the dog was in fact vicious or otherwise dangerous, the owner or keeper knew, or under the circumstances should have known, of the dangerous disposition of the animal, and the injuries resulted from the known vicious or dangerous propensity of the animal. The basic key to recovery of damages for injuries caused by a dog is the knowledge of the owner or keeper that the animal is vicious or has mischievous propensities.

Plaintiff has presented no evidence that creates a genuine issue of material fact, and has not shown any "specific facts which could lead a rational trier of fact to find in favor of him. All the evidence presented by Plaintiff tends to show that Defendant believed his dog was friendly, gentle, and jovial before the bite occurred. Nor is there any evidence that Defendant was aware of any prior playful or mischievous behavior that could be dangerous. Moreover, it is undisputed that the dog did not get outside the fence, and that Plaintiff is the one who approached the dog.

The trial court's grant of summary judgment to Defendant is affirmed.

**SECTION 2.9
PROPERTY LAW**

Property law deals with the rights and duties that arise out of the ownership or possession of real property and personal property. **Real property** includes land and everything attached to the land. For instance, a building, a tree, or ground are all considered part of the realty. **Personal property** consists of all other property and would include a book, car, money, or even a folding chair. In other words, personal property includes everything not attached to the land.

Personal property is further sub-divided into tangible and intangible property. **Tangible property** is a physical object, such as this textbook. **Intangible property**, on the other hand, is personal property that is not a physical object. The ownership of intangible property is usually evidenced by a legal document. Examples of such property include a patent or invention, a copyright for published material, or a trademark to identify a manufacturer or merchant's product.

The purchase of a home has certain inherent problems. Disputes frequently arise as to what is included in the sale. When the buyer inspected the home, a crystal chandelier hung in the foyer. At the time of settlement, a plastic fixture has replaced the chandelier. The seller refuses to give the buyer the chandelier, claiming that it is a family heirloom worth several thousand dollars. The buyer maintains that the fixture was part of the realty since it was on display at the time the home was inspected. Who is correct? The answer will depend upon whether the item is real or personal property.

In **O'Donnell v. Schneeweis, 73 D. & C. 2d 400 (Chester County Ct. of Common Pleas, Pa. 1975),** the court offered guidelines as to what constitutes a fixture that would be included in the sale of real estate. A **fixture** is an item of personal property which, by reason of its being attached to a building, becomes part of the real estate. In reaching this conclusion, the court noted that personal property used in connection with real estate falls into one of three classes.

First, furniture, such as a couch or table, always remains personal property; second, fixtures, or those things so affixed to the property that they cannot be removed without material injury to the real estate are considered real property; and third, those things which, although physically connected to the real estate, are affixed in such a manner that they may be removed without destroying or materially injuring the item to be removed. This third category of property becomes part of the realty or remains personal property, depending upon the intention of the parties at the time of annexation.

For example, wall-to-wall carpeting remains as a fixture, but a mirror or picture attached to a wall by a wire is considered personal property. If the mirror was affixed in such a way that it provided the impression that it was meant to be permanent, it would be considered a fixture that remained with the house. Such an example would include a mirror that was glued to the wall and could not be removed without causing damage to the wall.

There are many causes of infertility but advances in medicine though drugs, surgery, artificial insemination, or assisted reproductive technology (ART) have greatly enhanced the ability of a couple to conceive. Assisted reproductive technology works by removing eggs from the female and mixing them with sperm to make an embryo. The embryos are then placed back into the woman's body.[10] It is also common for a man's sperm to be frozen for use at a later time for either in artificial insemination or other fertility treatments.[11]

A host of legal and ethics issues arises over infertility issues and a number involve property rights. Because sperm can be frozen for months or years, they are consider property. The following case provides an example of a legal dispute that has arisen over their ownership. The novel question is whether a widow has the right to use her late husband's frozen sperm in an attempt to conceive a child when her deceased husband had signed an agreement with the sperm storage company that the frozen sperm was to be discarded upon his death.

ESTATE OF JOSEPH KIEVERNAGEL v. IRIS KIEVERNAGEL
166 CAL.APP.4TH 1024 (CT. APP. CAL. 2008)

Joseph and Iris Kievernagel were married for 10 years prior to Joseph's death. They contracted with the Northern California Fertility Medical Center, Inc., to perform in vitro fertilization (IVF) to allow Iris to conceive. The fertility center operated a sperm cryopreservation storage program under which sperm was collected and stored. The frozen sperm could then be thawed and used for insemination. As part of the sperm cryopreservation storage program, the center required an IVF Back–Up Sperm Storage and Consent Agreement (the Agreement). Iris completed the Agreement and Joseph signed it. The Agreement provided that the sperm sample was Joseph's sole property and he retained all authority to control its disposition. The Agreement provided for two options for the disposition of the sperm sample upon death or incapacitation: donate the sperm to his wife or discard the sperm sample. The box indicating the sperm sample was to be discarded was checked and Joseph initialed it. The Agreement also provided the sperm sample was to be discarded upon divorce. Iris signed, acknowledging the sperm sample was Joseph's sole and separate property. Joseph died in a helicopter crash in July 2005.

Iris petitioned for a distribution of an "asset of no financial value" but "of immense sentimental value to the widow." The item was a vial of Joseph's frozen sperm. Joseph's parents, objected contended it was contrary to Joseph's express wishes, as set forth in the Agreement, that upon his death, his sperm sample was to be discarded.

After an evidentiary hearing, the court found the following. Joseph and Iris "loved each other deeply and completely." Joseph was opposed to having children, but agreed to the fertility procedures due to Iris's strong desire for children. The couple's dispute over having children led them to marriage counseling. According to the marriage counselor, Joseph believed Iris would divorce him if he did not agree to have children and a divorce would devastate him. The Agreement provided the sperm sample was to be discarded upon Joseph's death. This option was selected instead of the option to donate the sperm sample to Iris. Iris completed the Agreement, making the selections. Joseph signed it. The court found the key issue was the intent of the decedent regarding use of his sperm. The court found the Agreement evidenced the intent of both Iris and Joseph that the sperm be discarded upon his death. The court found Iris failed to prove the Agreement did not express Joseph's intent.

In making its decision, the court below found "little to no guiding precedent." Frozen sperm falls within the broad definition of property.

It looked to ethical standards in the IVF field. The American Fertility Society took the position that gametes and concepti are the property of the donor and the donor has the right to decide their disposition. The decedent's interest in the frozen sperm vials "entitles them to special respect because of their potential for human life." At the time of his death, Joseph "had an interest, in the nature of ownership, to the extent that he had decision making authority as to the use of his sperm for reproduction."

Gametic material, with its potential to produce life, is a unique type of property and thus not governed by the general laws relating to gifts or personal property or transfer of personal property upon death. Joseph, as the person who provided the gametic material, had at his death an interest, in the nature of ownership, to the extent he had decision making authority as to the use of the gametic material for reproduction. Accordingly, in determining the disposition of Joseph's frozen sperm, the trial court properly relied on Joseph's intent as to its use after his death.

Probate Code Section 249.5 addresses the property rights of a child of a decedent conceived and born after the death of the decedent. Such a child is deemed to have been born within the decedent's lifetime if it is proved by clear and convincing evidence that the decedent specified in writing "that his or her genetic material shall be used for the posthumous conception of a child." This law suggests that when the issue is postmortem reproduction using gametic material from a deceased donor, the decedent's intent as to such use should control.

Iris [further] contends the probate court's decision ignores the fundamental right of the donee spouse to procreate. Iris further contends that since procreative rights are based on the right to privacy, and that right ends at death, in balancing the relative interests, hers prevails. We disagree. The right of procreative autonomy "dictates that decisional authority rests in the gamete-providers alone, at least to the extent that their decisions have an impact upon their individual reproductive status." In this case, there is only one gamete-provider. The material at issue is Joseph's sperm. Only Joseph had

"an interest, in the nature of ownership, to the extent that he had decision making authority as to the use of his sperm for reproduction."

Judgment affirmed.

QUESTIONS FOR DISCUSSION

1. Do you agree with the court's decision?

2. Did status and process play any role in the outcome?

3. If the sperm was used to conceive after the donor's death, would that child have any legal rights against his deceased father?

4. Suppose the sperm and egg had been fertilized and frozen. Subsequently, the parties divorced. What should happen to the fertilized eggs? Do they become a piece of property that is disturbed like any other asset in a divorce?

5. Should a fertilized egg or frozen sperm be consider property?

Ownership of property is viewed as consisting of a bundle of rights. Owners have specific rights with their respect to their property; they may use it, prevent others from using it, lend it to someone else, sell it, give it away or destroy it.

It is also common for people to join their own assets with others. The law calls it **concurrent or joint ownership** and it occurs when the title to property is shared by two or more people who hold title to the asset. The most common form of concurrent ownership is **tenancy in common, and joint tenants with the right of survivorship**. Both forms of joint ownership give the owners essentially equal rights to the property. Each owner, however, has given up the right to exclusivity; meaning one owner cannot prevent his co-owner from using the property.

The difference between tenancy in common and joint tenancy with the right of survivorship occurs when one co-owner dies. In tenancy in common, if one co-owner dies, his or her share will pass to that person's heirs. In a joint tenancy with the right of survivorship, when one co-owner dies, the decedent's share will pass to the surviving co-owner. Thus, if Joe Roberts and Peter Christopher have a joint bank account as tenants in common, either one of them may make deposits or withdraw funds. If Joe dies, however, his share will pass to his heirs, usually the family, and Peter will retain his one-half share. If, on the other hand, Joe and Peter are joint tenants with the right of survivorship, and Joe dies, his share will automatically pass to Christopher who becomes the sole owner of the bank account. When property is owned as joint tenants with the right of survivorship, the co-owners forfeit their individual rights to dispose of the property as they wish at the time of death. The property is automatically transferred to the survivor.

Married people enjoy a special form of co-ownership designed to protect the marital assets from creditors and to ensure an easy transition of the property to the surviving spouse upon a tenant's death. Most states recognize **tenancy by the entirety,** which is similar to a joint tenancy with the right of survivorship. It differs from a joint tenancy, however, in that neither spouse can convey his or her interest in the property without the other. In other words, each spouse owns 100% interest in the property and cannot dispose of the asset without the consent of the other. Because each spouse owns 100% of the property, the creditor of one spouse is unable to seize the joint asset. Sophisticated creditors, such as banks and mortgage companies, are aware of this rule and require both spouses to sign the loan documentation even though only one spouse may receive the money.

Several states including California, Arizona, Texas and Nevada have adopted **community property rights.** As with a tenancy by the entirety, neither spouse can convey separately his or her interest during life. In these states, community property will pass to the surviving spouse if one dies unless it is given by will to another. Both the tenancy by entireties and community property rights will be severed by a divorce. The property is then automatically converted to a tenancy in common with each owning a one-half interest. These forms of co-ownership apply to both real and personal property.

SECTION 2.10
FAMILY LAW

The institution of marriage no longer enjoys the same favor that it did historically, and more and more couples are establishing family units without much formality or binding commitment. Regardless of how the family unit is created, issues regarding children, assets and benefits arise. **Family law** encompasses the rights, duties, and obligations involving marriages, domestic partnerships, divorce, custody, child support, paternity, and other family related issues.

This category of private law is exclusively regulated by state law whose rules and regulations vary from jurisdiction to jurisdiction. There are, however, a number of basic concepts that remain constant.

A **marriage** is a contract between two people whereby they take each other to be spouses for life. A handful of jurisdictions recognize

domestic partnerships in which an unwed couple can acquire legal rights and protections. Usually this arrangement can only have legal standing if the parties register with the state by filing a Declaration of Domestic Partnership or similar document. While registration does not create a marriage, it does secure a number of rights such as the ability to collect insurance benefits from a partner's employer.

Marriages have a 50% failure rate and the legal dissolution of a marriage is called a **divorce.** Historically, this dissolution could only be accomplished by an innocent spouse who had to prove that his or her partner was at fault in causing the termination of the marriage by engaging in cruel and barbarous treatment, desertion, indignities, adultery or some other type of conduct that caused the marriage to fail. This rigid requirement has changed and partners are now allowed to obtain no-fault divorces. For instance, Pennsylvania allows a couple to file for divorce if the marriage is irretrievably broken.

An **annulment** occurs when there is a legal impediment to a marriage so that the union is declared null and void from its inception. For example, this occurs when one of the parties is still married to another at the time of the subsequent marriage, impotence, insanity or fraud.

**SECTION 2.11
VIOLATIONS OF PUBLIC
AND PRIVATE LAW**

Can one incident give rise to a violation of both public and private law? The answer is yes. This is a frequent occurrence in situations involving criminal misconduct. For instance, an intoxicated person who is involved in an accident may be criminally prosecuted for drunken driving and sued civilly by the aggrieved party for personal injury. An election of remedies between public and private law need not be made, since both forms of action may be pursued. The government prosecutes the criminal case in the name of the State, and the aggrieved party is merely a witness. A civil lawsuit may be instituted for the same misconduct by the individual harmed to seek monetary compensation. Each suit is independent of the other.

**SECTION 2.12
ETHICS**

Legal and ethical responsibilities do not necessarily overlap. The **"No Duty To Rescue Rule"** or "American Bystander Rule" demonstrates this point. Often the ethically right decision goes beyond the expectations of the law, sometimes far beyond. The gap between law and ethics is demonstrated in the following case involving the duty owed by a victim to her assailant when she injuries or kills him in self-defense. The case also provides an overview of the law involving the duty to rescue.

STATE OF MONTANA V. MONTANA THIRTEENTH JUDICIAL DISTRICT COURT
298 MONT. 146 (MONT. 2000)

Yellowstone County Sheriff's deputies were dispatched on April 19, 1998, to the home of Bonnie Kuntz and Warren Becker to investigate a reported stabbing. When the deputies arrived at the trailer house, Becker was dead from a single stab wound to the chest.

Kuntz told the deputies that she and Becker had argued the morning of April 18, 1998. At some point during the day, both parties left the trailer home. After Kuntz returned that evening, a physical altercation ensued. The alleged facts indicate that Kuntz and Becker, who had never married but had lived together for approximately six years, were in the process of ending a stormy relationship. When Kuntz arrived at the mobile home that night, she discovered that many of her personal belongings had been destroyed and the phone ripped from the wall. Kuntz told the deputies that she then went into the kitchen and Becker physically attacked her, and at one point grabbed her by the hair, shook her, and slammed her into the stove.

Kuntz told the deputies that she could not clearly remember what happened; only that she had pushed Becker away and had then gone outside by the kitchen door to "cool off." When she thought it was safe to go back inside, she returned to the kitchen. She discovered a trail of blood leading from the kitchen through the living room and out onto the front porch where she found Becker collapsed face-down on the porch. Kuntz does not allege that she personally contacted medical or law enforcement personnel; rather, authorities were summoned by Kuntz's sister-in-law.

Kuntz was charged with negligent homicide for causing the death of Becker by stabbing him in the chest. Kuntz entered a plea of not guilty based on the defense of justifiable use of force. Shortly before trial, the State filed amended information alleging that Kuntz caused the death of Becker by stabbing him once in the chest with a knife *and* by failing to call for medical assistance.

For criminal liability to be based upon a failure to act, there must be a duty imposed by the law to act, and the person must be physically capable of performing the act. As a starting point in our analysis, the parties have identified what is referred to as *"the American bystander rule."* This rule imposes no legal duty on a person to rescue or summon aid for another person who is at risk or in danger, even though society recognizes that a moral obligation might exist. This is true even "when that aid can be rendered without danger or inconvenience to" the potential rescuer, **Pope v. State, 284 Md. 309.** Thus, an Olympic swimmer may be deemed by the community as a shameful coward, or worse, for not rescuing a drowning child in the neighbor's pool, but she is not a criminal.

But this rule is far from absolute. Professors La Fave and Scott have identified several common law exceptions to the American bystander rule: 1) a duty based on a personal relationship, such as parent-child or husband-wife; 2) a duty based on statute; 3) a duty based upon voluntary assumption of care; and 4) a duty based on creation of the peril. Our review of the issues presented here can accordingly be narrowed to a duty based upon a personal relationship and a duty based on creation of the peril.

One of the lead authorities on the personal relationship duty arose in **State v. Mally, 139 Mont. 599 (1961).** This Court held that a husband has a duty to summon medical aid for his wife and a breach of that duty could render him criminally liable. The facts of the case described how Kay Mally, who was suffering from terminal kidney disease, fell and fractured her arms on a Tuesday evening. Her husband, Michael Mally, put her to bed and did not summon a doctor until Thursday morning. "During this period of time, she received but one glass of water." Although his wife ultimately died of kidney failure, Mally was found guilty of involuntary manslaughter.

As for a personal relationship other than husband and wife, a duty cannot be extended to a temporary, non-family relationship. For instance, a married defendant has no duty to summon medical help for his mistress, who was staying in his house for the weekend, after she took morphine following a bout of heavy drinking and fell into a "stupor."

When a person places another in a position of danger, and then fails to safeguard or rescue that person, and the person subsequently dies as a result of this omission, such an omission may be sufficient to support criminal liability. The legal duty based on creation of the peril has been extended in other jurisdictions to cases involving self-defense.

The legal duty imposed on personal relationships and those who create peril are not absolute; i.e., there are exceptions to these exceptions. The personal relationship legal duty, for example, does not require a person to jeopardize his own life. See **State v. Walden 306 N.C. 466** (stating that although a parent has a legal duty to prevent harm to his or her child, this is not to say that parents have the legal duty to place themselves in danger of death or great bodily harm in coming to the aid of their children).

Similarly, the law does not require that a person, who places another person in a position of peril, risk bodily injury or death in the performance of the legally imposed duty to render assistance. Therefore, where self-preservation is at stake, the law does not require a person to save the other's life by sacrificing his own.

Does one who justifiably uses deadly force in defense of her person nevertheless have a legal duty to summon aid for the mortally wounded attacker? We hold that when a person justifiably uses force to fend off an aggressor, that person has no duty to assist her aggressor in any manner that may conceivably create a risk of bodily injury or death to herself, or other persons. This absence of a duty necessarily includes any conduct that would require the person to remain in, or return to, the zone of risk created by the original aggressor. We find no authority that suggests that the law should require a person, who is justified in her use of force, to subsequently check the pulse of her attacker, or immediately dial 911, before retreating to safety.

We conclude that the victim has but one duty after fending off an attack, and that is the duty owed to one's self-as a matter of self-preservation-to seek and secure safety away from the place the attack occurred. Thus, the person who justifiably acts in self-defense is temporarily afforded the same status as the innocent bystander.

QUESTIONS FOR DISCUSSION:

1. Could there have been any circumstance in this case that would have resulted in liability against Bonnie Kuntz?

2. Should the duty of rescue when a special relationship exists between the parties be limited to those of spouses and parents and children?

3. Can you think of an example of a duty created by statute to help another?

4. France requires people to go to the aid of another. What country's law do you think is better?

SECTION 2.13
REVIEW CASES

1. Lawmakers from Virginia have approved specialty license plates for a number of organizations for many years. However, the state legislature refused to allow the Sons of Confederate Veterans to obtain license plates that contained a rebel flag logo because it might offend African-Americans. Does this action by the lawmakers violate the Sons of the Confederate Veterans' First Amendment freedom of speech rights?

2. Morris released a computer program known as a "worm" on the internet which spread and multiplied, eventually causing computers at various educational institutions to crash or cease functioning. Morris was charged with violating the *Computer Fraud and Abuse Act* which punishes anyone who intentionally accesses, without authorization, a category of computers known as "federal interest computers," or prevents authorized use of information in such computers. Morris argues that the government did not prove that he had the necessary mens rea to have committed the computer crime since it was necessary for the government to show not only that (1) he intended the unauthorized access of a federal interest computer, but also (2) that he intended to prevent others from using it. The government argued that the criminal intent requirement required then to prove only one part of the crime. Which side do you believe is correct? **United States v. Robert Morris, 928 F.2d 504 (1991).**

3. Following the entry of a civil judgment against O. J. Simpson, Fred Goldman attempted to seize a grand piano at Simpson's home in order to help satisfy the multi-million dollar judgment. O. J. Simpson's mother testified that the piano was given to her as a gift in 1984. Although the grand piano was still in the football player's house, Simpson claimed that it belonged to his mother, and

that she was the only one who could play the musical instrument. Who do you think should obtain possession of this item of personal property? **Ronald Goldman v. O. J. Simpson, Los Angles Superior Court (Sept. 1997).**

4. Bernard Getz boarded a New York subway and sat down on a bench. Four individuals surrounded Getz and asked him for five dollars. Getz stood up and fired four shots striking the individuals that surrounded him. Getz told the police that two youths stood to his left and two stood to his right. After he was asked for the money, Getz said the four had smiles on their faces and they wanted to "play with me." While he did not think that any of the people had a gun, Getz had a fear of harm based upon prior experiences of being "maimed." Will Getz have any liability for using deadly force in either a criminal or civil context? **People of New York v. Bernard Getz, 68 N.Y. 2d 96 (Ct. App. N.Y. 1986).**

5. Clark owned a fifty pound puppy named Rocky that had a habit of jumping on people. In fact, Rocky had a talent for playing football, and striking people with his body just as a tackler would do. Clark asked a friend to watch the dog while he was out of town. He did not, however, inform her of the dog's playful habits. When the Good Samaritan let the puppy out in the back yard, Rocky ran up behind the woman and struck her forcibly at the back of the knees. The friend fell and fractured her left hip. Is Clark liable for the actions of the playful puppy? **Alice Clark v. Kenneth Clark, 215 A.2d 293 (Pa. Super. 1965).**

Footnotes:

1. "Criminal Law Defenses – Intoxication," Lawyers.com, http://criminal.lawyers.com/criminal-law-basics/criminal-defenses-intoxication.html (last visited February 13, 2016).

2. *Id.*

3. "Super Bowl XXXVIII Halftime Show Controversy," Wikipedia, https://en.wikipedia.org/wiki/Super_Bowl_XXXVIII_halftime_show_controversy (last visited February 13, 2016).

4. "FAQ About The Mcdonald's Coffee Case," Hot Coffee, http://www.hotcoffeethemovie.com/default.asp?pg=mcdonalds_case (last visited February 13, 2016).

5. *Id.*

6. Mark Randall and Hendrik DeBoer, "The Castle Doctrine and Stand-Your-Ground Law," OLR Research Report, April 24, 2012, https://www.cga.ct.gov/2012/rpt/2012-R-0172.htm (last visited February 14, 2016).

7. *Id.*

8. "What is the Castle Doctrine?," FreeAdvice, http://criminal-law.freeadvice.com/criminal-law/violent_crimes/castle-doctrine.htm (last visited February 14, 2016).

9. *Id.*

10. "Infertility Fact Sheet," Womenshealth.gov, http://www.womenshealth.gov/publications/our-publications/fact-sheet/infertility.html (last visited February 14, 2016).

11. "Freezing and Storing Sperm," Human Fertilization and Embryology Authority, http://www.hfea.gov.uk/74.html (last visited February 14, 2016).

KEY TERMS

Acceptance
Administrative Agencies
Administrative Law
Annulment
Article
Articles of Confederation
Assumption of the Risk
Beyond a Reasonable Doubt
Bill of Rights
Burden of Proof
Capacity
Comparative Negligence
Compensatory Damages
Community Property
Concurrent Ownership
Consideration
Constitutional Amendment
Constitutional Law
Constitutional Relativity
Contract
Contributory Negligence
Crime
Criminal Intent
Criminal Law
Damages
Divorce
Domestic Partnership
Duty of Case
Family Law

Federal Register
Felony
Fixture
Intangible Property
Intentional Tort
Legality
Marriage
Mens Rea
Misdemeanor
Negligence
Offer
Ownership of Property
Pain and Suffering
Personal Property
Private Law
Proximate Cause
Public Law
Real Property
Self-Defense
Substantial Evidence
Summary Offense
Tangible Property
Tenancy in Common
Tenancy by the Entirety
Tenancy with Right of Ownership
Tort
Treason

CHAPTER 3

DUE PROCESS

SECTION 3.1
INTRODUCTION TO
DUE PROCESS

"No law perfectly suits the convenience of every member of the community; the only consideration is, whether upon the whole it be profitable to the greater part."

Levi
"History of Rome," c.10 B.C.
"The Quotable Lawyer" Facts on File, 1986

Due Process is synonymous with fundamental fairness and the concept is deeply rooted in history. For instance, ancient Egyptians required judges to hear both sides of a dispute before issuing a ruling. The Romans and Greeks provided for juries. Even Jesus Christ was allowed to confront his accusers and to present evidence during his trial.[1]

Citizens of the world have always expected their governments to establish a system of rules to maintain law and order. However, the actual balance between individual freedoms and government regulation differs from society to society.

In 1215, the **Magna Carta** provided the people of England with a degree of protection against the unchecked power of the King. The "due process" clause in this historic document provided that "no freeman shall be taken or imprisoned or exiled...except by the lawful judgment of his peers or by the law of the land." This Great Charter was not the result of a magnanimous act on the part of King John but stemmed from a bitter conflict between the King and the Barons over finances and royal governance. Events came to a head on the hills of Runnymede when the Barons confronted the unpopular ruler and forced him to sign this historic document guaranteeing that no one is above the law including the King.

The founders of this country did not include a due process clause in the original Constitution. Instead, James Madison drafted this protection as part of the **Bill of Rights** a few years later. More specifically, part of the **Fifth Amendment** provides that no person shall be deprived of life, liberty, or property without **due process** of law. This guarantee is designed to insure that the government acts fairly with members of society. The meaning of this clause, however, is not defined in the Constitution. The drafters wanted the protections to be determined in light of the times so that the Constitution would remain a living and contemporary document. As Justice Cardoza noted, "Due Process guarantees those personal immunities which are so rooted in the traditions and conscience of our people as to be ranked as fundamental... or are implicit in the concept of ordered liberty."[2]

Surprisingly, the Fifth Amendment only extended the protection of the due process clause to the actions of the federal government. This flaw was rectified in 1868 when a second due process clause was written into the United States Constitution through the **Fourteenth Amendment.** This latter clause made due process applicable to the states by providing that "nor shall any State deprive any person of life, liberty, or property without due process of law." Known as the **Reconstruction Amendment,** this clause was originally drafted to protect the recently freed slaves. Not surprisingly, its ratification was rejected by many of the Southern states but the rest of the country voted in favor of the proposal. Over the years, the Fourteenth Amendment has become a cornerstone for the civil rights movement. For instance, it is the basis for overturning laws preventing African Americans from serving on juries.

The original purpose of the Fourteenth Amendment, however, has dramatically changed over the years because of the **Doctrine of Incorporation.** Basically, the courts have used the Fourteenth Amendment to incorporate many of the other protections afforded by the Bill of Rights so that they may have applicability to the state governments.

Due process consists of two parts:

1. **Substantive due process;** and
2. **Procedural due process.**

In order to understand these two concepts, one must first ascertain the meaning of substantive law and procedural law.

Substantive law is the "actual law." It defines the duties and rights of members of society. The Motor Vehicle Code is an example of substantive law. It provides for the proper operation of motor vehicles and prohibits such conduct as speeding, reckless driving, or proceeding through a red light. It is only by the enforcement of the Motor Vehicle Code that the roads are made safer for the public to transverse.

Procedural law is the way that the substantive law is made, enforced, and administered. For example, the Motor Vehicle Code is enforced by issuing an errant driver a traffic ticket and requiring the offender to appear in court to answer the charges.

This Chapter will present an overview of the due process guarantee with an emphasis on legislation and the elements of a fair hearing.

SECTION 3.2
LEGISLATION

The power to make laws on the federal level is vested in **Congress** and is contained in the first Article of the Constitution. Article I, Section 1 of the United States Constitution provides that "All legislative powers herein granted shall be vested in a Congress of the United States, which shall consist of a Senate and House of Representatives."

The **United States Senate** is composed of 100 members. Two senators are elected from each state for six-year terms. On the other hand, **the House of Representatives** consists of 435 members, elected every two years from the 50 states according to population. Together, these chambers make up the U.S. Congress.

The chief function of Congress is to make the laws that govern the people of the United States. In addition, the Senate has the function of consenting to treaties and to certain nominations by the President such as the individuals who serve as judges in the federal court. The House has the power to pass laws raising revenue.

The work of Congress is initiated by the introduction of a proposal in one of four principle forms. These are: the bill; the joint resolution; the concurrent resolution; and the simple resolution. A **bill** is the form used for most legislation. Bills may originate in either the House of Representatives or the Senate. A bill originating in the House of Representatives is designated by the letters "H.R." followed by a number. A Senate bill is designated by the letter "S." followed by its number.

Any member of the legislature may introduce a bill while Congress is in session by simply placing it in the **hopper**, or basket located at the side of the clerk's desk in the House Chamber. The individual who introduces a bill is referred to as the **sponsor** and more than one legislator can co-sponsor a bill. The bill is then assigned to the committee that has jurisdiction over the subject matter of the proposed law. For instance, the House Committee on Armed Services deals with matters involving military installations, service personnel, and military readiness. The Select Committee on Intelligence analyzes issues involving terrorism, homeland security, counterintelligence, and espionage.

One of the most important phases of the congressional process is the action taken by the Committee. It is at the Committee level that the most intense consideration is given to the proposed measures and where citizens are given an opportunity to be heard.

If a bill is of sufficient importance, and particularly if it is controversial, the committee will usually set a date for public hearings. Each committee is required to publically announce the date, place, and subject matter of any hearing to be conducted by the committee. Witnesses may testify either voluntarily or at the request of the committee. A vote of the committee is taken to determine whether it will issue a favorable report or "table" the bill. Committee reports are a valuable element of the legislative history of a law. They are used by courts, executive departments, agencies, and the public, as a source of information regarding the purpose and meaning of the legislation.

When a committee gives a bill a favorable report, the chamber in which the proposed legislation originated votes on the bill. If that chamber passes the bill, the other house then considers it. A bill that is agreed to by both bodies becomes the law if the President signs it. A bill also becomes law when the President fails to return it within ten days with objections to the chamber in which it originated. However, a **pocket veto** may occur if the President receives the legislation within ten days of adjournment by Congress and the Chief Executive fails to sign the bill into law. The President may **veto** a bill that he or she does not want to enact into law. However, two-thirds of the members in each house can vote to override the veto. In that event, the bill becomes law.

There is not a large difference between a joint resolution and a bill. The **joint resolution** is not proposed simultaneously in Congress but originates in either House and generally goes through the same review process as a bill. Their use is usually restricted to advancing a proposed amendment to the Constitution or for emergency appropriations.

The reader may remember Congress providing authorization to President Bush to invade Iraq in 2002 because of the fear that Saddam Hussein was accumulating weapons of mass destruction. This declaration was done through a joint resolution.

Another joint resolution was passed by Congress following 9/11 to allow the President to use the Armed Forces to protect this country:

> Whereas, on September 11, 2001, acts of treacherous violence were committed against the United States and its citizens; and
>
> Whereas, such acts render it both necessary and appropriate that the United States exercise its rights to self-defense and to protect United States citizens both at home and abroad; and
>
> Whereas, in light of the threat to the national security and foreign policy of the United States posed by these grave acts of violence; and
>
> Whereas, such acts continue to pose an unusual and extraordinary threat to the national security and foreign policy of the United States; and
>
> Whereas, the President has authority under the Constitution to take action to deter and prevent acts of international terrorism against the United States: Now, therefore, be it

Resolved by the Senate and House of Representatives of the United States of America in Congress assembled,

To authorize the use of United States Armed Forces against those responsible for the recent attacks launched against the United States.

A **concurrent resolution** is an informal pronouncement by Congress that does not have the effect of a law and does not require the signature of the President. For instance, it can be used to extend congratulations to someone over a special event.

A **simple resolution** is only passed by one chamber of Congress and represents a non-binding resolution that is not presented to the President for signature. They generally deal with the internal affairs of the House or Senate such as the establishment of a new committee.

State and Federal laws are called **statutes**. Local laws are called **ordinances**. To learn more about the activities of Congress, visit the official web sites of the House of Representatives and the Senate. Those addresses are: **www.house.gov and www.senate.gov.**

**SECTION 3.3
SUBSTANTIVE
DUE PROCESS**

If **substance law** is the actual law and **due process** means fundamental fairness, substantive due process can only mean that the law itself must be fundamentally fair. This mandate is directed to the legislative branch of government and requires that (1) the legislation be capable of serving a legitimate public interest; (2) the law may not be broader than is necessary to meet the public program; and (3) the statute cannot be vague. One who does not believe a law satisfies these three conditions may challenge the constitutionality of the legislation in court.

Examine the following example to ascertain whether the law is valid from a substantive due process point of view and satisfies the requirements for constitutionality.

A state legislator is unhappy with the damage to property that is taking place on college campuses, especially in the dorms. He believes that the majority of trouble-makers are students with long hair who drink alcohol and deface school property. To curb the transgressions of these disruptive youths, the legislator introduces a bill requiring "any student with long hair who attends a state related institution to pay an additional $250 in tuition." The state representative believes that this assessment will help defray the cost of damage done to college property by the responsible parties. A student with long hair refuses to pay the extra tuition and claims that his substantive due process rights are being violated. The issue presented is whether the law is capable of serving a legitimate public interest. Just because an individual has long hair does not mean that he or she will be disruptive. The legislation is vague since the statute is silent as to what constitutes "long hair." Also, does the law apply unequally to women? The standard to be applied in ascertaining the constitutionality of the legislation is not what the individual who introduced the bill thinks but whether the average person would believe that the law is sensible and capable of serving a legitimate public interest. This statute is clearly unconstitutional.

Distracted driving is defined as operating a vehicle while engaging in any activity which may distract a motorist from properly and safely operating a vehicle. The following is a sample law on the topic:

> "Distracted driving" means inattentive driving while operating a motor vehicle that results in the unsafe operation of the vehicle where such inattention is caused by reading, writing, performing personal grooming, interacting with pets or unsecured cargo, using personal communications technologies, or engaging in any other activity which causes distractions.

Cell phone and texting legislation clearly fall within the ambit of this term. Distracted driving will also include anything that would divert an operator's eyes from the road, or mental concentration away from driving.[3] This includes shaving, putting on makeup, reading and playing with a pet. Would distracting driving, however, include eating a hamburger that one just purchased from McDonald's? There is no current law that specifically prohibits this conduct but it could be argued that it is a form of activity that would cause a distraction. How about GPS devices in cars? Would entering the address of a location on a built-in GPS device be a violation of the law about texting or would it be an example of distracted driving?

Illegal immigration is controversial throughout the world. This term is applied to someone residing in a country illegally. Other phrases that are used include: undocumented immigrant, illegal immigrant, undocumented alien, illegal alien, migrant, or undocumented worker. Some enter the United States illegally and others overstay their visas. Regardless of how they achieved their status, an illegal alien has decided to take a risk and move to this land in search of a better life.[4]

Over 11 million illegal aliens reside or work in the United States. Proponents say that these individuals benefit the US economy through the expansion of a low-cost labor pool and seek employment in positions that Americans won't take. Others retort that undocumented aliens violate the law by entering in this country without proper documentation or by overstaying their visas. They view these aliens as criminals and an economic burden to tax-paying Americans.[5]

Arizona has taken a very tough stand on illegal immigration. State residents believe that high numbers of illegal immigration and crimes committed by them are among the key factors in the enactment of very harsh laws to prohibit illegal immigration.[6] These laws include penalties for those who harbor or transport illegal aliens, employer sanctions, and provisions dealing with human smuggling.[7]

A question arises as to whether these laws which target those who enter the country illegally, violates substantive due process guarantees. That is the issue in **Angel Lopez–Valenzuela v. Joseph Arpaio.**

ANGEL LOPEZ–VALENZUELA V. JOSEPH ARPAIO
770 F.3D 772 (9TH CIR. CT. APP. 2014)

In 2006, Arizona voters approved an amendment to their state constitution known as Proposition 100 which mandates that Arizona state courts may not set bail "[f]or serious felony offenses if the person charged has entered or remained in the United States illegally." The court must deny bail, irrespective of whether the arrestee poses a flight risk or a danger to the community. In 2008, plaintiffs filed a complaint against Maricopa County challenging the constitutionality of Proposition 100. At the time the complaint was filed, both plaintiffs were charged with state crimes and held in Maricopa County jails as a result of orders finding that they had entered or remained in the United States illegally.

The plaintiffs alleged that the Proposition 100 laws violate the substantive due process guarantees of the Fourteenth Amendment on two theories: (1) arrestees have a liberty interest in being eligible for release on bond pending resolution of criminal charges and the Proposition 100 laws are not narrowly tailored to serve a compelling governmental interest; and (2) the laws impermissibly impose punishment before trial.

The Supreme Court has long recognized constitutional limits on pretrial detention. The Court has prohibited excessive bail and barred punitive conditions of pretrial confinement. The "traditional right to freedom before conviction permits the unhampered preparation of a defense, and serves to prevent the infliction of punishment prior to conviction."

The governing substantive due process standard is a familiar one. "The Due Process Clause ... provides heightened protection against government interference with certain fundamental rights and liberty interests," The defendants suggest what is at stake is "the individual's strong interest in liberty." Freedom from bodily restraint has always been at the core of the liberty protected by the Due Process Clause from arbitrary governmental action. That the Proposition 100 laws regulate persons when there is probable cause to believe they have "entered or remained in the United States illegally," does not alter the analysis. The Due Process Clauses protect every person within the nation's borders from deprivation of life, liberty or property without due process of law. "Even one whose presence in this country is unlawful, involuntary, or transitory is entitled to that constitutional protection."

We also bear in mind that, regardless of whether an arrestee is a citizen, a lawful resident or an undocumented immigrant, the costs to the arrestee of pretrial detention are profound. "Pretrial confinement may imperil the suspect's job, interrupt his source of income, and impair his family relationships. And it may affect "the defendant's ability to assist in preparation of his defense."

The general rule of substantive due process is that the government may not detain a person prior to a judgment of guilt in a criminal trial.

Even if some undocumented immigrants pose an unmanageable flight risk or undocumented immigrants on average pose a greater flight risk than other arrestees, Proposition 100 plainly is not carefully limited because it employs an overbroad presumption rather than an individualized hearing to determine whether a particular arrestee poses an unmanageable flight risk. Demonstrably, many undocumented immigrants are not unmanageable flight risks. The record includes examples of undocumented immigrants who were arrested before Proposition 100, granted bail or released on their own recognizance, and appeared at their court dates and trials.

We next consider whether the Proposition 100 laws violate substantive due process by imposing punishment before trial. There is strong evidence that Proposition 100 was motivated in significant part by a desire to punish undocumented immigrants for (1) entering and remaining in the country.

To conclude, Proposition 100 categorically denies bail or other pretrial release and thus requires pretrial detention for every undocumented immigrant charged with any of a broad range of felonies, regardless of the seriousness of the offense or the individual circumstances of the arrestee, including the arrestee's strong ties to and deep roots in the community. The Supreme Court has made clear that "[i]n our society liberty is the norm, and detention prior to trial or without trial is the carefully limited exception." In contrast, the Proposition 100 laws do not address an established "particularly acute problem," are not limited to "a specific category of extremely serious offenses," and do not afford the individualized determination of flight risk or dangerousness. These laws represent a "scattershot attempt" at addressing flight risk and are not narrowly tailored to serve a compelling interest.

For these reasons, we hold that the Proposition 100 laws violate the substantive component of the Due Process Clause of the Fourteenth Amendment.

Obesity in children and adolescents is a major health concern in the United States affecting 1 in 6 youngsters.[8] These individuals spend less time engaged in physical activities, eat more calories, watch television, use the compute or playing video games on an increased basis. Busy parents have less time to prepare balanced meals and rely on fast food ordering in many instances. Being overweight is a precursor to future health issues such as diabetes, high blood pressure, asthma, sleep disorders and increased lipid levels. Overweight children are also subject to ridicule, depression bulling and low self-esteem.[9]

The federal government has made obesity in children a major component of its efforts to improve the health of Americans by introducing a number of programs that hopefully will have an impact on slowing the rate of obesity in this country.[10] Michelle Obama, when she was the First lady, introduced the Let's Move campaign to stem childhood obesity. The campaign set forth a variety of initiatives such as support for parents, providing healthier food choices in schools, increased physical activity for children and cheaper and healthier foods availability in communities.[11]

Unorthodox initiatives to curb childhood obesity include a proposal in Puerto Rico that would fine parents of obese children.[12] New York is known for the Sugary Drinks Portion Cap Rule which prohibits New York City restaurants, movie theaters and other food service establishments (FSE) from serving sugary drinks in sizes larger than 16 ounces. At what point, however, does the government overstep its bounds and passes a law that does not pass constitutional muster? That is the issue in the next case.

New York Statewide Coalition of Hispanic Chambers of Commerce v. The New York City Department of Health and Mental Hygiene
970 N.Y.S.2d 200 (N.Y. 2013)

On May 30, 2012, Mayor Michael Bloomberg announced the Portion Cap Rule that would require food service establishments to cap at 16 ounces the size of cups and containers used to offer, provide and sell sugary beverages. The Mayor's stated purpose of the rule was to address rising obesity rates in the City.

The Portion Cap Rule limited the maximum self-service cup or container size for sugary drinks to 16 fluid ounces for all food service establishments within New York City, and defined a "sugary drink" as a non-alcoholic carbonated or non-carbonated beverage that is sweetened by the manufacturer or establishment with sugar or another caloric sweetener, has greater than 25 calories per 8 fluid ounces, and does not contain more than 50 percent of milk or milk substitute by volume as an ingredient. The rule thus targeted non-diet soft drinks, sweetened teas, sweetened black coffee, hot chocolate, energy drinks, sports drinks, and sweetened juices, but contained carve-outs for alcoholic beverages, milkshakes, fruit smoothies, mixed coffee drinks, mochas, lattes, and 100% fruit juices. The ban applies to restaurants, delis, fast-food franchises, movie theaters, stadiums and street carts, but not to grocery stores, convenience stores, corner markets, gas stations and other similar businesses.

We must examine whether the Board of Health exceeded the bounds of its authority as an administrative agency when it promulgated the Sugary Drinks Portion Cap Rule. With regard to the exemption for sugary milk or juice drinks, the agency explained that it is based on the Board's conclusion that they, unlike the covered drinks, have some nutritional benefits. The agency, however, ignores the fact that the "soda ban" does more than just target a specific food category. It ignores that the Board has never categorized soda and the other targeted sugary drinks as inherently unhealthy. In essence, it prescribes a mechanism to discourage New Yorkers from consuming those targeted sugary drinks by dictating a maximum single portion size that can be made available in certain food service establishments. Such mechanism necessarily looks beyond health concerns, in that it manipulates choices to try to change consumer norms.

Accordingly, the selective restrictions enacted by the Board of Health reveal that the health of the residents of New York City was not its sole concern. If it were, the "Soda Ban" would apply to all public and private enterprises in New York City. By enacting a measure—one that tempered its strong health concerns with its unstated but real worries about commercial well-being, as well as political considerations—the Board necessarily took into account its own non-health policy considerations. Judged by its deeds rather than by its explanations, the Board of Health's jurisdictional rationale evaporates."

If soda consumption represented such a health hazard, then the Sugary Drink Portion Cap Rule would be exactly the kind of rulemaking intended by the legislature and engaged in by the Board of Health in the past. The Board of Health, however, does not claim that soda consumption can be classified as such a health hazard. Rather, the hazard arises from the consumption of sugary soda in "excess quantity." The risks of obesity and developing diabetes and other illnesses are greater in those who drink soda to excess than in those who drink it in moderation or not at all. Thus, since soda consumption cannot be classified as a health hazard per se, the Board of Health's action in curtailing its consumption was not the kind of rulemaking intended by the legislature.

In sum, we find that the Board of Health overstepped the boundaries of its lawfully delegated authority when it promulgated the Portion Cap Rule to curtail the consumption of soda drinks.

QUESTIONS FOR DISCUSSION

1. The District of Columbia wishes to regulate tattoos, and body piercings because of their long term effects. To illuminate impulsive body art, they wish to enact heath regulations that provide a mandatory 24-hour waiting period before the artist may ply his or her trade by proceeding with the tattoo. Is this a proper exercise of governmental authority? Does the proposed regulation serve a legitimate public interest?

2. Los Angeles enacted legislation called County of Los Angeles Safer Sex in the Adult Film Industry mandating adult film actors to wear condoms when filming sex scenes. Would this law survive a constructional challenge?

3. A number of states have made it illegal to engage in cyberbulling in order to stop the harassment of others by digital means such through emails or cell phone messages. One lawmaker even wants to take the legislation one step further by holding parents liable for cyberbulling by their children. What issues do you see with such a proposed law?

4. Legislators in California have introduced a bill called the Sugar-Sweetened Beverages Safety Warning Act to force soda and other surgery drink manufactures to place labels on cans and bottles warning consumers about the dangers of what they drink. What are the constitutional implications to this bill and would such a label be effective in cutting down on soda consumption?

5. A law that is gaining in popularity is that all welfare recipients must be drug tested. The idea is to make sure that people receiving subsidies from the government are using the funds to buy food and other necessaries. Statically, however, the number of people testing positive for drugs has been exceedingly minuscule. Should the government, threrfore, test welfare recipients for drugs? Does that diminish their need for assistance?

Employers are rightfully concerned about workplace safety and the negative effects of substance abuse. As a result, employers have implemented procedures to reduce these risks, the most controversial of which is drug testing at work. Forty percent of the working population is subjected to **drug-testing,** and marijuana is the illegal substance that surfaces in the majority of positive test results. Employers are in favor of drug-testing because of the financial implications of absenteeism, low productivity, injuries, and theft. Workers are concerned about the accuracy of the test results. For instance, a false positive test result can occur with something as simple as a person eating a poppy seed bagel, which can suggest opium use.

When drug-testing is part of the collective bargaining agreement, employee concerns can be minimized though the negotiation process. Ardent criticism of drug-testing is more apt to occur when the test is unilaterally imposed on members of the workforce. This can happen when the legislature mandates drug-testing of a particular work group. Such legislation usually triggers a constitutional challenge to the drug-testing program on a variety of grounds such as invasion of privacy, due process, and unlawful search and seizure.

The earliest legislative-mandated, drug-testing program focused on railroad employees, who were involved in train accidents. The courts have upheld that legislation because of the need to protect the public against alcohol and drug abuse among transit workers. Random drug-testing of student athletes has also been upheld in order to protect the welfare of children who might be susceptible to the physical, emotional, and social damage of drug abuse.

Drug testing of professional athletes has taken place for years. These programs are implemented through collective bargaining agreements between the players' union and management and may result in the team member's suspension from the sport. Olympic and college athletics have also established rigorous drug testing programs with Olympic medals being forfeited by those who test positive. The justification for this testing is to promote the long-term health of athletes and to level the playing field among the participants in the sport. While drug testing of high school athletes occurs with some frequency, secondary schools are expanding their interest in testing other members of the student population. This ambitious goal to deter the use of illicit drugs among children has generated much debate and controversy over the merits of this approach. Critics maintain that it destroys the element of trust between student and teacher and constitutes an invasion of privacy. The Supreme Court, however, has given its tacit approval for high schools to conduct random drug testing of all those who wish to participate in extracurricular activities.

A small percentage of high schools engage in random drug testing of their students. Nevertheless, the federal government has stepped up its efforts to urge schools to enact drug testing programs and they even offer money to defray the cost of the programs. Drug testing companies are also increasingly their marketing to entice schools to adopt such a policy and to use their products.[13] This has resulted in some educational facilities requiring any students engaged in extra-curricular activities to be randomly drug tested. This policy was challenged in the Supreme Court in **Board of Education v. Earls** and found to be constitutional.The court found that random drug testing is minimally invasive and does not significantly invade the student's rights to privacy. It was also found to be a reasonable and effective means of addressing legitimate concerns in deterring drug use.

Would a college be able to drug test its entire student population? That is the question in **Kittle–Aikeley v. Claycomb.**

BRANDON KITTLE–AIKELEY V. DONALD CLAYCOMB
807 F.3D 913 (W. D. MISS. 2014)

Linn State is a technical college that offers thirty programs for a student body of 1,200 students. Linn State is unique in that its purpose is to make available to students exceptional educational opportunities through highly specialized and advanced technical education and training. The goal is to provide 75% of the class work in the field chosen by the student. For example, students in the Aviation Maintenance program spend roughly 62% of their time doing hands-on training, and work in close proximity to active propeller blades.

On June 17, 2011, Linn State's Board of Regents adopted a mandatory drug-screening policy. The policy states:

Linn State Technical College will begin a drug screening program for student's degree or certificate seeking students returning after one or more semesters of non-enrollment at the Linn State Technical College campus. The purpose of the program is to provide a safe, healthy and productive environment for everyone who learns and works at Linn State Technical College by detecting, preventing and deterring drug use and abuse among students. The testing procedures provide that the test results do not serve law enforcement purposes and will not be revealed to law enforcement personnel.

The public has a valid interest in deterring drug use among students engaged in programs posing significant safety risks to others; some college students that attend Linn State have a diminished expectation of privacy because they are seeking accreditation in heavily regulated industries and industries where drug testing is the norm; Linn State's testing procedures significantly minimize the intrusiveness of Linn State's drug-screening program and are relatively noninvasive, thus the invasion of students' privacy is not significant, and the need to prevent and deter the substantial harm that can arise from a student under the influence of drugs while engaging in a safety-sensitive program provides the necessary immediacy for Linn State's testing policy.

Using drugs while attending classes at a technical school uniquely limited to instruction and training in technical and vocational programs, where a large percentage of the students on campus are performing hands-on work in their respective, industrial programs on a daily basis, poses a unique safety risk that does not necessarily exist on other college campuses, or even at other, more similar, community colleges. The very nature of these programs and the unique vocational focus of the college itself involves dangerous aspects and creates safety risks for students under the influence of drugs or alcohol, as well as others.

By its very nature, this technical school offers a hands-on, in-the-field approach for a vast majority of its students seeking degrees in various traditional vocations. Linn State demonstrated that its students are primarily involved in vocational programs fraught with risks such that anyone participating in these programs who is under the influence, with impaired perception and judgment, creates an unnecessary and dangerous risk to themselves and others.

On balance, testing the entire student population entering Linn State is reasonable and hence constitutional and an effective means of addressing Linn State's interest in providing a safe, healthy, and productive environment.

QUESTION FOR DISCUSSION

1. Based upon this case, would your college or university be allowed to drug test the student population?

Citizens of the United States cherish their individual freedoms. This tenet is reinforced throughout the first Ten Amendments of the Constitution, commonly known as the **Bill of Rights**. For instance, the government may not conduct improper searches of homes or personal property, people have the right to peacefully assemble and to practice their religion without interference from the state. Also, individuals may not be forced to provide incriminating testimony and they have the right to express their opinions without unwarranted governmental interference. Because of these types of constitutional guarantees, legislation must be narrowly tailored to further a legitimate and compelling government interest.

The death of Dale Earnhardt in a racing accident at the Daytona 500 triggered off a court challenge as to whether a law that prohibited the production of his autopsy photographs was overly broad and unconstitutional.

CAMPUS COMMUNICATIONS INC. v. ESTATE OF DALE EARNHARDT
821 So. 2D 388 (CT. APP. FLA. 2002)

Mr. Earnhardt was a car driver who became involved in a fatal crash during the Daytona 500 race on February 18, 2001. An autopsy was performed in accordance with Florida law governing accidental deaths. In performing the autopsy, photographs were taken solely as a back-up to the dictation system utilized by the medical examiner to record his findings.

The written autopsy report, post-crash photographs of Mr. Earnhardt's car, a toxicology report and a sketch showing the markings on Mr. Earnhardt's body were promptly made available to the public. The autopsy photographs, however, were not released because Mrs. Earnhardt sought and obtained an ex parte injunction precluding the medical examiner from releasing them.

On March 29, 2001, the Florida Legislature enacted **Section 406.135 of the Public Records Act**. Campus seeks an order requiring the medical examiner to allow inspection and copying of the photographs.

The issue we are confronted with whether **Section 406.135** is overly broad and therefore unconstitutional.

Both the Florida Constitution and the Public Records Act allow for the creation of exemptions to the Act by the Legislature, provided the exemption 1) serves an identifiable public purpose and 2) is no broader than necessary to meet that public purpose. In order to fulfill these requirements, the Legislature made the following findings:

> The Legislature finds that photographs, video and audio recordings of an autopsy be made confidential. Photographs or video or audio recordings of an autopsy depict or describe the deceased in graphic and often disturbing fashion. As such, photographs, video or audio recordings of an autopsy are highly sensitive depictions or descriptions of the deceased which, if heard, viewed, copied or publicized, could result in trauma, sorrow, humiliation, or emotional injury to the immediate family of the deceased.

As to the requirement that the exemption serve an identifiable public purpose, the Legislature must state with specificity the public necessity justifying the exemption. We find that (the legislature's explanation) clearly satisfies this requirement. The legislative findings detail the graphic and often gruesome nature of such autopsy photographs and the trauma and emotional injury the immediate family of the deceased would likely suffer if these records were disclosed and disseminated to the public.

Campus contends that **Section 406.135** is unconstitutional because it is broader than necessary to meet the statute's public purpose. Specifically, Campus argues that the finding made by the Legislature that some photographs "may" show gruesome scenes and that trauma "could" result from publication of the autopsy photographs is explicit recognition that photographs are not always gruesome and that trauma does not always result from their viewing.

We find the statute to be specific and narrow: it applies only to autopsy photographs and audio and video recordings of the autopsy. It does not apply to other records of the autopsy such as the written autopsy report and, therefore, those materials remain unrestricted public records.

We find that **Section 406.135** serves an identifiable public purpose, is no broader than necessary to meet that public purpose and was enacted in accordance with the constitutional and legislative requirements we have previously discussed. We affirm the judgment under review.

QUESTIONS FOR DISCUSSION:

Are the following laws constitutional?

1. In order to prevent the sexual harassment of women walking past construction sites, a city passes an "antiogling" law for its employees. Looking at someone in a leering manner is considered "ogling" and illegal. First time violators face verbal warnings and repeat offenders can be fired.

2. A beach town enacts an ordinance that prohibits a person who is not physically fit from wearing a bikini on a public beach. The penalty is removal from the beach and a $200.00 fine.

3. A city passes a parental responsibility ordinance that makes parents liable for offenses committed by their children under 18. The law makes the failure to supervise a minor a civil offense. First-time offenders receive a warning. Repeat offenders may be fined as much as $1,000 and be compelled to attend eight-week "parenting courses" approved by the court. In addition, parents must pay for property damage caused by their children.

4. In order to slow down Chicago's increasing murder rate among gang members, the city enacts a law that allows police officers to order the dispersal of individuals whom the officers reasonably believe are street gang members remaining in a public place with no apparent purpose. Those who do not promptly obey the order to move can be arrested.

The drafting of a statute is not an easy task. The problems of society are complex, and the legislature must deal with issues ranging from trash collection to nuclear energy. It is unrealistic to expect that each member of the legislature is an expert in every field of proposed legislation. They must rely upon others for guidance and are subjected to pressures from their peers, constituents, and special interest groups. This requires a constant balancing of personal beliefs against the wishes of others when considering proposed legislation.

In drafting a law, it is a primary goal to avoid using ambiguous words and to make the statute as clear as possible. Unfortunately, this cannot always be done. It is impossible to envision every problem or predict how future events will affect the legislation. For instance, definitions that once seemed obvious become subject to attack as technology changes.

One example is the word "motor vehicle." As automobiles became the favored mode of transportation, statutes were adopted requiring "motor vehicles" used for the transportation of people to be registered with the state. Cars, buses, and trucks are obviously within the contemplation of the legislation, but would airplanes, jet skis, or mopeds be covered?

The following problem will allow the reader to experience the unique issues that arise in trying to properly draft remedial legislation that regulates the conduct in question but is narrowly tailored to prevent an unjustified intrusion into the rights of the citizens.

SECTION 3.4

PROBLEM THREE—A

PARK, BROWN & SMITH, P.C.
ATTORNEYS AT LAW
MEMORANDUM

To: All Students

FROM: Peter Smith, Esquire

RE: Legislation to Prohibit Stalking by Photographers

Congress is considering the adoption of a bill to prohibit paparazzi from stalking famous people in order to sell the pictures to the tabloid magazines. Many support the legislation in light of the general annoyance of movie stars, athletes, and national celebrities by these photographers.

Estelle Roberts is assisting in the lobbying efforts to pass this type of remedial legislation. While Mrs. Roberts understands the desire of fans to learn more about their favorite stars, she believes that celebrities should be able to have some private moments, especially when they take reasonable steps to protect their privacy. After all, famous people should not be prisoners in their own homes. They should have access to public facilities in much the same way that the general public does.

Our firm has been asked to draft the proposed legislation so I have looked into the issue and have spoken to various legislators about the matter. One Senator told me that she was troubled by the constitutionality of this proposed laws. For instance, the Senator thought the bill could criminalize routine news gathering. The Senator also wanted to know who would be covered under the law and how the phrase "reasonable expectation of privacy" would be defined, since that is the term that concerned citizens keep mentioning during their lobbying efforts.

A number of celebrities wrote letters in support of the legislation. Former Governor Schwarzenegger, George Clooney, Sean Penn, and Madonna have had problems with the press. One female celebrity complained about an incident in which a photographer tried to bungy-jump into her backyard in order to take a picture of her infant son. Another celebrity complained about a group of photographers who followed him into the restroom in order to take his picture while in a compromising position.

The tabloids are concerned about this proposed legislation. The media explained that they have the right to take pictures of celebrities because the stars are public figures. They further explained that the general public wants to know anything and everything about their favorite celebrities. Fans' interest ranges from learning about a star's favorite color to learning what flavor ice cream he or she likes. In light of the public's curiosity, the paparazzi believe they are doing a public service whenever they take "candid" pictures of famous people—when they least expect a photographer. Besides, the photographers assert that celebrities know that being famous entails an encroachment into their private lives.

The paparazzi also claim that the proposed bill is unconstitutional because it is overly vague. For instance, the lobbyist want to target photographers who take pictures for profit and would exempt from prosecution a lunatic fan who follows a celebrity. They claim that this distinction makes no sense. After all, the paparazzi do not want to hurt the celebrities, while lunatic fans have actually stalked their favorite stars and can represent an actual and real danger to the celebrities.

The task of drafting the bill has been assigned to you, but you should keep several goals in mind. The proponents of the bill maintain that people have a constitutional guarantee to be left alone, especially when one takes extra steps in order to protect his or her privacy. A professional lobbyist hired by the movie industry also mentioned that the law should target photographers who sell pictures to tabloid magazines.

Please write a draft of the proposed law and focus on the following three aspects:

1. Definitions. Who should be covered under the legislation and how should the phrase "reasonable expectation of privacy" be defined? This section needs careful attention to detail in order to prevent a constitutional challenge on the basis of vagueness.

2. Define what conduct is prohibited. As I mentioned before, the proponents of the legislation believe that photographers should be prevented from taking pictures of an individual when he or she has a reasonable expectation of privacy.

3. What penalties should be imposed for violating the statute? Should the penalty be criminal in nature, or should the remedy be civil in which case the aggrieved person can collect money damages?

I have prepared the following outline for your use in drafting the legislation:

1. Definitions

2. Prohibited Conduct

3. Penalty

Name   **Please Print Clearly**

Section 5005. Regulation of Stalking

1. Definitions

_____

_____

_____

_____

_____

_____

_____

_____

_____

_____

_____

_____

_____

2. Prohibited Conduct

_____

_____

_____

_____

_____

_____

_____

3. Penalty

SECTION 3.5
PROCEDURAL
DUE PROCESS

Procedural due process guarantees that before a person's rights can be determined, he or she must be given a fair hearing. A fair hearing consists of three elements:

1. Notice of the proceeding;

2. Opportunity to be heard; and

3. An impartial tribunal.

The first element necessary to insure a fair hearing is proper notice. Just imagine if you went home and found a certified letter from the court informing you for the first time that you were tried and convicted of burglary the week before. To insure that this does not occur, a party must receive some type of notification of the pending litigation.

In a civil action, the defendant is given a copy of the lawsuit. In a criminal case, the defendant is arrested and informed of the charges against him.

Each party must also be given the opportunity to be heard. This is accomplished by allowing the litigants to be present at trial and to participate in the proceeding. They may sit with counsel during all phases of the trial and assist in presenting or attacking the evidence. It is not uncommon to see a litigant pass a note to counsel during the trial or to speak to the attorney in whispered tones about the case.

Can a party be denied the right to be present during the trial without violating the tenets of due process? The answer is yes. The court has the superior right to make sure that the trial progresses in an orderly fashion. Unruly parties can be excluded from the courtroom.

Finally, a fair hearing requires the right to be tried by an impartial tribunal. Because of the extensive media coverage focused on unusual or notorious cases, the defendant's right to a fair trial is frequently an issue. How can a defendant receive a fair trial when most of the prospective jurors have already heard about the case and have formed an opinion as to the defendant's innocence or guilt?

The Court must exercise great care to minimize outside influences that may improperly affect the verdict. Measures to insure a fair trial range from issuing a gag order to control the dissemination of information to moving the trial to another location where the case is not so well known.

The "Fugitive," was a movie loosely based upon the murder trial of Dr. Sam Shepard, who was convicted of the bludgeoned death of his pregnant wife in the upstairs bedroom of their home. The case went before the United States Supreme Court on the issue of whether Dr. Shepard received a fair trial because of the massive, pervasive and prejudicial publicity that attended his prosecution.

During the murder investigation, the news media published a number of stories that emphasized the evidence that appeared to incriminate Shepard and they pointed out discrepancies in the doctor's statements to the authorities. One editorial asked: "Why don't police quiz top suspect," with a demand that Dr. Shepard be taken to police head-quarters. Another editorial stated: "Why isn't Sam Shepard in jail?" During the trial, which took place two weeks before the general election, the chief prosecutor was a candidate for Common Pleas Court judge, and the trial judge was a candidate to succeed himself. The newspapers published the names and addresses of all potential jurors, and a radio station was permitted to set up broadcasting facilities next to the jury room. When Dr. Shepard was brought into the courtroom before each session, he was surrounded by reporters and extensively photographed for the newspapers and television. During delibera-tions, the sequestered jury was allowed to make telephone calls with-out any type of supervision.

In considering whether Dr. Shepard's procedural due process rights were violated, the Supreme Court noted that the extensive newspaper, radio, and television coverage of the criminal trial, together with the physical arrangements in the courtroom for the news media, deprived Shepard of the judicial serenity and calm to which he was entitled. The Justices noted that our legal system requires that the verdict be reached only according to the evidence and arguments in open court, and not by any outside influences, whether by private talk or pub-lic print. The carnival atmosphere could have been avoided because the courtroom and courthouse were subject to the control of the trial judge. The court should have adopted stricter rules governing the use of the courtroom by reporters, and efforts should have been initiated to control the release of leads, information and gossip to the press. The Supreme Court concluded that the trial court did not protect Dr. Shepard from the inherently prejudicial publicity which saturated the community, and the jurist failed to control the disruptive influ-ences in the courtroom. Due process requires that the accused receive a trial by an impartial jury free from outside influences. This did not occur in the Sam Shepard criminal trial.

In Philadelphia, the trial of Gary Heidnik for the brutal murders and torture of several mentally handicapped women could not proceed until an impartial jury was empaneled. The case was so gruesome and shocking in detail that it received daily press coverage. Very few citi-zens in Philadelphia were unaware of the killings.

Of the 180 potential jurors called, all had heard about Mr. Heidnik, and 124 had already predetermined his guilt or innocence based upon the press coverage. The presiding judge agreed with the defense about the prejudicial affect of the pretrial publicity and noted: "It was impos-sible to get a fair and impartial jury in Philadelphia because this case was turned into nothing short of a freak show." The judge considered moving the trial to Pittsburgh. Instead, a panel of jurors from Pittsburgh were selected and brought to Philadelphia for the trial. In this way, the court balanced the right of the public to know what was going on in the Gary Heidnik case with the defendant's right to have a fair and impartial tribunal.

In Jeffrey Dahmer's murder trial, defense lawyers questioned whether their client could obtain a fair trial given the widespread publicity surrounding the gruesome nature of the murders. Dahmer was accused of killing 17 people and storing their remains in his apartment. His lawyers asked that jurors be selected from outside Milwaukee, where the media focus would be less intense. The court denied this request, citing the worldwide publicity given to the case.

Most people are familiar with the Boston Marathon bombing. Two pressure bombs exploded near the finish line killing several people and injuring hundreds. A video revealed two young men as the suspects and after an intense manhunt, the police apprehended 19-year-old Dzhokhar Tsarnaev. His brother, the other suspect, was killed in a police shootout. The brothers were originally from Kyrgyzstan but lived in this country for approximately ten years prior to the bombings. The heinous crime received a great deal of press coverage and the prosecutor decided to seek the death penalty.[14]

The defendant objected to his trial taking place in the Boston area and requested a **change of venue** because he did not believe he could obtain a fair trial. In other words, he claimed that proceeding with the trial in the Boston area would violate his procedural due process rights to a fair hearing. Should the case have been moved from the location in which it happened or was the case so notorious that everyone in the country knew about and it would not make a difference where the case was held?

UNITED STATES OF AMERICA V. DZHOKHAR A. TSARNAEV
2016 WL 184389 (D. MASS. 2016)

Dzhokhar Tsarnaev was tried arising out of the bombings at the Boston Marathon. The jury returned a verdict in his capital trial finding him guilty under all counts.

The defendant contends that local media coverage, local events, and information or postings on social networks during the trial should raise a presumption of prejudice and require a conclusion that Massachusetts was an improper venue for his trial.

The Supreme Court has identified four factors generally relevant to a determination whether a presumption of prejudice should be indulged: (1) the size and characteristics of the community in which the crime occurred; (2) the nature of the publicity surrounding the case; (3) the time between the crime and the trial; and (4) whether the jury's decision indicated bias. The defendant does not expressly articulate a legal framework for analyzing his claim, but it appears he seeks to advance an argument related primarily to the second and third factors.

The geographic region from which the jury was drawn includes about five million people living not just in Boston, but also in smaller cities and towns, encompassing urban, suburban, rural, and coastal communities.

The main basis for the defendant's motion appears to be the extent and nature of the publicity concerning the case and the events at issue in it. The defendant relies heavily on local marathon-related media coverage. It is certainly true that the local media gave substantial coverage to the anniversary of the bombings, its victims, and the marathon. What the defendant disregards, however, is the national—and international—interest in those same events and people. This was not a crime that was unknown outside of Boston. To the contrary, media coverage of the bombings when they occurred was broadcast live around the world over the Internet and on television.

Although the Boston Marathon is an important event in the city and region, it is also an iconic event known worldwide. The approximately 27,000 registered runners come from all 50 states and many countries. At least 40% of them are from "outside Massachusetts and New England." Similarly, spectators include not only people from the Boston area but also many visitors from elsewhere, coming to watch friends and family members participating in the race. Like the Olympic Games, the event receives worldwide media coverage. Approximately 1,000 media credentials had been issued to representatives of about 80 registered news organizations. The marathon is broadcast live locally, nationally, and internationally to about 20 countries, and it is also live-streamed over the Internet.

Not surprisingly, the trial proceedings were covered not only locally but also nationally and internationally. Many others followed the proceedings from overflow rooms in the courthouse. Newspapers around the world closely followed the trial as it unfolded, both in their print editions and on the Internet, focusing not just on the more significant trial events like opening statements and closing arguments, but even on the more particular aspects of the legal process. There is no reason to think that this extensive coverage would have been any different in kind or degree if the trial had been conducted elsewhere.

I also disagree with the defendant's assertion that the local coverage of the trial was prejudicial to him simply because there was coverage. Not only was the coverage generally factual in nature, rather than inflammatory, but with regard to the appropriate punishment for his crimes much of it was skewed in the defendant's favor. For example, as trial proceeded, media coverage regarding the appropriate punishment suggested a growing disapproval of the imposition of the death penalty by residents in the Boston area.

Consequently, moving the trial to another venue would not likely have eliminated or even substantially reduced the coverage. Furthermore, the media coverage of the trial as it unfolded was not demonstrably prejudicial to the defendant. And finally, the jurors gave repeated assurances that they were avoiding media reports about the case.

Image that you are a University student entering your last semester of school. You have financed your education through student loans and have secured a job with a prestigious accounting firm. Everything seems bright and promising until the fateful day you receive a letter from the Dean of Students charging you with stealing an exam in your business law course with a penalty of explosion from school. You mind is racing with the implications of this news and what to expect at the hearing. What evidence will be used against you? Who is the person that claims you stole the exam? What is the burden of proof and do you have the right to an attorney?[15]

The Fourteenth Amendment provides that no state shall deprive any person of life, liberty, or property without due process of law and a student's desire to pursue a college degree is included within the ambit of protection of liberty and property. Therefore, a student subject to a disciplinary proceeding at a public educational institution is guaranteed due process.[16] The question, however, is what process is due? Due process in the context of a fair procedure, is a flexible criteria which changes based upon the type of the interest affected, and the circumstances of the deprivation.[17] In the context of a student hearing, this includes notice of the hearing, an explanation of the case against the person, and an opportunity to present evidence.[18] This does not mean that a student is entitled to the same protections provided in an adversarial proceeding in a court of law with the right of subpoena, cross-examination by an attorney and strict adherence to the rules of evidence. Rather, the question is whether the student was given the opportunity to answer the charges, explain, and defend.[19] **Osei v. Temple University** provides an example of the type of hearing and safeguards that are necessary in a University disciplinary proceeding.

MICHAEL OSEI v. TEMPLE UNIVERSITY
2011 WL 4549609 CIV. A. 10-2042 (E.D. PA. 2011)

Michael Osei was enrolled in a bachelor's degree program in healthcare management at Temple University. After receiving an allegedly unfair grade in Dr. Krow's chemistry class, Osei sent Dr. Krow a series of e-mails. His second email explained that an unfair grade would result in "a curse against Dr. Krow's life and family forever. In the third e-mail, Osei explained: I just want justice on you physically and spiritually. Your game is

over! Mine begins. You played with the wrong person this time. Cooperate to prevent things from escalating." A follow up email warned: "Mark my words: The year 2010 will not start well for you."

The University Disciplinary Committee informed Osei that he had been charged with violating Temple's Student Code of Conduct for sending "threatening e-mails to Dr. Krow in reference to receiving a poor grade." It quoted a portion of Osei's second email to Dr. Krow and referred to a provision of the Code that prohibits "[a]ny act or threat of intimidation or physical violence toward another person including ... threatened assault or battery."

Osei attended the hearing with an attorney who was not allowed to participate. Dr. Krow did not attend, but others testified that Dr. Krow had "felt threatened," "was worried about what to do," and was "a little spooked" by Osei's emails. The witnesses also referred to issues Osei had with another faculty member. Osei had a chance to speak at the hearing. He apologized, offered letters of good character, and explained that his English was imperfect.

Osei was determined to have violated the Code of Conduct. At the sanctions phase of the hearing, Dr. Luehrmann testified to "a pattern of intimidation" by Osei that included several other faculty members. Osei was suspended until August 15, 2010, required to attend anger management classes, and put on probation until graduation. Osei filed suit alleging, among other claims, a denial of procedural due process.

Procedural due process requires school authorities to provide students facing temporary suspensions with "rudimentary precautions against unfair or mistaken findings of misconduct and arbitrary exclusion from school." This includes "notice of the charges," "an explanation of the evidence" against the student, and "an opportunity to present his side of the story." Nonetheless, what is required of due process is generally a function of: (1) "the private interest that will be affected by the official action"; (2) "the risk of an erroneous deprivation of such interest through the procedures used" and "the probable value, if any, of additional or substitute procedural safeguards"; and (3) "the Government's interest, including the function involved and the fiscal and administrative burdens that the additional or substitute procedural requirement would entail."

Pursuant to these factors, Osei was afforded procedural due process. Although he was only given one day's notice that Dr. Luehrmann was scheduled to testify at his hearing, this was sufficient notice given the context, and there is no allegation that Osei objected at the time of the hearing or sought a continuance. Similarly, because the Notice of Disciplinary Action specifically referenced Osei's threatening e-mails, there was no lack of notice that all his e-mail correspondence with Dr. Krow might be considered. Finally, in light of these e-mails, we are not persuaded by Osei's argument that he was deprived of the opportunity to confront Dr. Krow. To the extent Osei was charged with threats and intimidation, the emails spoke for themselves and he was given ample opportunity to clarify what he meant to communicate.

We are also not persuaded that references by witnesses to prior incidents of alleged intimidation support a claim for a procedural due process violation. [The law] requires that a student receive notice of the charges and an opportunity to explain his side of the story. There is no allegation that Osei was denied the opportunity to challenge the witnesses' testimony or was unable to explain his side of any allegations against him. Finally, to any extent hearsay was permitted at Osei's hearing, the school did not have to abide by the same evidentiary standards as one would in a courtroom.

Thus, Osei has not pled sufficient facts to show a [violation of his procedural due process rights].

Courts must accept, as consistent with due process, "an academic decision that is not beyond the pale of reasoned academic decision making when viewed against the background of [the student's] entire career at the University...."

Under this standard, Wheeler does not come close to showing that TWU did not exercise professional judgment. On this record a rational trier of fact could not find that TWU's treatment of Wheeler and ultimate decision not to award him a doctorate fell beyond the pale of reasoned academic decision-making in light of Wheeler's entire academic career.

Questions for Discussion:

1. How important is the racial makeup of a jury? If it is important, what should the justice system do to make sure a defendant receives a fair trial by an "impartial" jury?

2. It is often said that a defendant must be tried by a jury of peers, but there is nothing in the Constitution that requires it. Should there be? What is a "peer?"

3. Should individuals not be allowed to be excused from jury duty regardless of the reason, so that the litigants obtain a cross section of the population?

4. What is the best way to handle a disruptive party in the courtroom so that due process is not violated?

5. Should the government be required to buy the defendant clothes for a trial so that the jury does not see the defendant in prison garb?

SECTION 3.6
KATHY ROBERTS
AND HER UNFAIR
CRIMINAL TRIAL

PROBLEM THREE—B

PARK, BROWN & SMITH, P.C.
ATTORNEYS AT LAW
MEMORANDUM

To: All Students

FROM: Peter Smith, Esquire

RE: Kathy Roberts and her Criminal trial

Kathy Roberts has been convicted of drug possession. This sixteen year old believes her conviction should be reversed on the basis of a violation of her procedural due process rights. My investigation has uncovered the following information.

Kathy was arrested for possession of drugs after running a stop sign. Officer O'Brien had been keeping his eye on Kathy, so he was right on the scene when she failed to stop. Needless to say, Kathy was quite annoyed. She had a baggy filled with marijuana on the seat beside her and cocaine hidden in the gym bag in her trunk. Somehow O'Brien caught a glimpse of the baggy when he peered through her window while examining her license. His subsequent search of the car uncovered an ounce of marijuana and a kilo of cocaine.

Kathy was arrested for possession of marijuana and cocaine. Following Ms. Roberts' trial, she was convicted of all charges and was awaiting sentencing. Not surprisingly, the trial was a nightmare. From the moment of her arrest, Kathy was belligerent, disruptive, and uncontrollable. On the way into the courtroom, she attempted to run away from the police escorts. When they recaptured her, a struggle ensued with Kathy biting and kicking the officers. It took four officers to eventually contain her. They then had to drag her into the courtroom with her arms handcuffed behind her back and her feet manacled together.

What follows is an excerpt from the courtroom transcript:

THE COURT:	*Ladies and Gentlemen of the jury, you should know that the defendant has been escorted into this courtroom in handcuffs and manacles because she refuses to enter peacefully and of her own volition. You must not look upon these restraints as indicating that she is guilty of the crime charged. I remind you that you must presume the defendant is innocent until the government proves otherwise. Ms. Roberts, the restraints will be removed if you agree to remain peaceably within the courtroom.*
ROBERTS:	I will cooperate, Your Honor.
THE COURT:	*Remove the restraints.*

Kathy was cooperative for the initial stages of the trial and made no further trouble until she took the stand. The defendant became uncontrollable when the judge granted an objection raised by the prosecution. Kathy grabbed a book from the witness box and hurled it at the judge. The court had Kathy removed from the witness stand and handcuffed to her chair.

THE COURT:	*Ms. Roberts, you will remain handcuffed to your seat until I have adequate assurances that you will control yourself.*
ROBERTS:	You're not giving me a fair trial.
THE COURT:	*Ladies and Gentlemen of the jury, please pay no attention to the defendant.*
ROBERTS:	Pay attention to everything. I can't get a fair trial. You're not giving my attorney a chance.
THE COURT:	*You will be bound and gagged if you continue. Now be quiet!*
ROBERTS:	I will not sit here quietly while you railroad me into jail!

THE COURT: *You will be bound and gagged with one more outburst. Be quiet or you will be very sorry you ever set foot in this courtroom!*

At that point, Kathy proclaimed her constitutional right to freedom of speech and started to recite the Pledge of Allegiance. She was finally quieted when the court officer taped her mouth shut. The gag was removed after Kathy promised to contain herself. It was only used for a few minutes.

Ms. Roberts claims that gagging, handcuffing, and manacling her in court in the presence of the jury offended her procedural due process right to a fair and impartial tribunal. The client believes that having a jury see her in restraints was so prejudicial that she was not able to receive a fair trial. Please review the cases of **Commonwealth v. Cruise and State v. Lee** and answer the following questions:

1. According to rules set forth in **State v. Lee,** is it permissible for the judge to merely gag Kathy rather than have her removed from the courtroom as the judge did in **State v. Lee?**

2. What are the pros and cons of the alternative disciplinary measures enumerated in **State v. Lee?** What considerations do you think should be made in determining which approach is the best to use against a disruptive defendant?

3. How does the approach taken to control Kathy compare with the approaches taken in **Lee** and **Cruz?**

4. Even if you do not agree with the approach used by the court, did Kathy's trial comply with the requirements of due process?

COMMONWEALTH OF PENNSYLVANIA V. CRUZ
311 A.2D 692 (PA. 1973)

Cruz contends he is entitled to a new trial because of the prejudicial effect of being seen handcuffed in the courtroom by members of the jury.

Appellant was tried with a co-defendant on the charge of possession of marijuana. The jury found the appellant guilty and the co-defendant not guilty.

The record reveals that appellant was handcuffed when the court recessed for the day while a portion of the jury was still in the jury box and on the following morning he was brought into the courtroom while handcuffed.

The early Common Law recognized that a defendant in a criminal trial had the right to appear in a court free of restraint. "The prisoner must be brought to the bar without irons and all matter of shackles or bonds unless there be danger of escape..." 2 **Hale's Pleas of the Crown**, 219 (1678). Such has been the rule in this country from the time that issue was first discussed.

Under ordinary circumstances a defendant's freedom from handcuffs, shackles or manacles is an important component of a fair and impartial trial, and restraints should not be employed except to prevent him from escaping or injuring others, and to maintain a quiet and peaceable trial.

In **State v. Roberts, 86 N.J. Super. 159, 206 A.2d 200, 205 (1965)**, defendant was compelled to appear before the jury with his feet and hands shackled, the court stated: "In any case where the trial judge, in the exercise of sound discretion, determines that the defendant must be handcuffed or shackled, it is of the essence that he instruct the jury in the clearest and most emphatic terms [which the Judge did not do in the instant case] that it give such restraint no consideration whatever in assessing the proofs and determining guilt. This is the least that can be done toward insuring a fair trial. It may be doubted whether any jury, even with the best of cautionary instructions, can ever dismiss from its mind that the accused has appeared before it in handcuffs or chains. His being restrained must carry obvious implications even to the most fair-minded of juries. Unless the situation is so exceptional as to call for shackles, the trial court should instead arrange for additional guard in the courtroom for the protection of all present and the prevention of any disorder or escape."

Furthermore, the ABA Project on Standards for Criminal Justice, trial by Jury, Approved Draft (1968) suggests:

"[A]s confusion or embarrassment of the person and jury prejudice can

result from wearing the clothing of a convict or prisoner just as it can from the wearing of shackles." (In Eaddy, the defendant was brought into court wearing coveralls with the words "County Jail" in large letters across the back).

In **Commonwealth v. Keeler, 216 Pa.Super. 193 at 195-196, 264 A.2d 407 at 409 (1970)** we held: "A defendant in prison garb gives the appearance of one whom the state regards as deserving to be so attired. It brands him as convicted in the state's eyes It insinuates that the defendant has been arrested not only on the charge being tried but also on other charges for which he is being incarcerated." A clear analogy can be drawn to the appellant being handcuffed in front of the jury and the "prison garb" cases.

The Commonwealth cites **Commonwealth v. Carter, 219 Pa.Super. 280, 281 A.2d 75 (1971)** in support of its position that a mistrial need not be granted in such a case. That case is inapposite to the appeal. In *Carter,* supra, our court upheld the action of the trial judge in dismissing two jurors who had witnessed the appellant being placed in handcuffs, during a trial recess. The trial judge determined that the dismissed jurors had not discussed the observed event with the other jurors.

Prejudice could have easily been created in the minds of the jurors due to the disparity between the co-defendant and the appellant in that co-defendant appeared in court free of restraints. Furthermore, the record does not indicate the appellant was violent while in court, that he conducted himself in an unruly manner, or that he threatened to escape.

For the aforementioned reasons, the judgment of sentence is reversed and the case remanded for a new trial.

STATE OF LOUISIANA V. JAMES LEE
395 SO.2D 700 (LA. 1980)

On July 15, 1977, James Allen Lee was indicted for First Degree Murder. A twelve person jury found the defendant guilty as charged on June 29, 1979. The trial court sentenced the defendant to life imprisonment and the defendant appealed.

The facts incident to the murder are not at issue. The defendant was convicted of shooting Jerry Dennis, the owner of the Shady Oaks Cafe, following an altercation over missing car keys. The defendant turned himself in to police several hours later.

During trial, the defendant persistently interrupted the proceedings by pseudo-Biblical rhetoric and singing the Star Spangled Banner. After numerous warnings by the trial judge, Lee was removed to an adjoining room where he could hear the trial proceedings. After continued outbursts and interruptions from the next room, the defendant was bound and gagged. The jury found him guilty of First Degree Murder.

The defendant urges that the trial court erred in removing the defendant from the courtroom during trial, in overruling defense counsel's objection regarding an alleged inability to communicate effectively with his client, and in having the defendant handcuffed, shackled and gagged. The defendant argues that these measures effectively deprived him of the right to be present during trial, and to confront the witnesses against him.

The selection of prospective juror as well as the trial proceedings were repeatedly interrupted by defendant's disruptive behavior. He began singing the Star Spangled Banner in front of the prospective jurors. Despite a reprimand and warning from the judge the defendant continued by reciting scripture. The judge initially ordered the defendant removed from the courtroom, but reconsidered and warned both defendant and counsel that he would give Lee another chance but remove him if the behavior continued. After additional outbursts and warnings the defendant was ordered removed to an adjoining room, with the understanding that he would be allowed to return once he agreed to act in an acceptable manner. Arrangements were made for the proceedings to be piped into the adjoining room and an attorney was appointed to sit with the defendant. Jury selection continued and the defendant again began sinvging the National Anthem, and speaking in a ministerial fashion. Though these outbursts were in the adjoining room, they were loud enough to disrupt proceedings in the courtroom. The defendant at this point had been handcuffed and shackled following an altercation with deputies. The trial judge stated that he had no alternative but to consider gagging the defendant. After some discussion, however, the judge proceeded without having defendant Lee gagged. At some point the defendant was returned to the courtroom only to interrupt the proceedings again by singing the National Anthem. Again the judge warned him that he would be removed and gagged unless he controlled himself. The defendant's disruptive behavior continued throughout the proceedings and included a prolonged interruption of the state's closing argument. In light of the innumerable interruptions at all stages of the court proceedings it appears that the defendant's arguments objecting to the measures taken by the court are without merit.

In **Illinois v. Allen, 397 U.S. 337, 90 S.Ct. 1057, 25 L.Ed.2d 353 (1970)** the United States Supreme Court held that "a defendant can lose his right to be present at trial if, after he has been warned by the judge that he will be removed if he continues his disruptive behavior, he nevertheless insists on conducting himself in a manner so disorderly, disruptive, and disrespectful of the court that his trial cannot be carried on with him in the courtroom.

The Court concluded that "trial judges confronted with disruptive, contumacious, and stubbornly defiant defendants must be given sufficient discretion to meet the circumstances of each case." Noting also the absence of a panacea for dealing with disruptive defendant, the court further observed that at least three constitutionally acceptable avenues exist for dealing with a defiant defendant:

(1) bind and gag him, thereby keeping him present;

(2) cite him for contempt;

(3) take him out of the courtroom until he promises to conduct himself properly.

The defendant was given every opportunity to remain in the courtroom without restraint if he conducted himself properly. The handcuffs and shackles were utilized only after the defendant struggled with deputies. The judge saw further outbursts as a security risk and only then allowed the restraints. Considering the incessant outbursts it appears the judge acted with considerable restraint. When the defendant was held in an adjoining room he was able to hear the trial proceedings and was accompanied by a second attorney to relay any messages to lead counsel in the courtroom. This Court has stated that: "We recognize that the use of restraining devices, including manacles, is within the sound discretion of the trial judge. In the absence of a clear showing of abuse of discretion on the part of the trial judge, a conviction will not be disturbed on appeal because of restraint imposed upon defendant." **State v. Burnett, 337 So.2d 1096 at 1099 (La. 176).** There was no such abuse of discretion here.

We find these assignments to be without merit.

ANSWER SHEET
PROBLEM THREE—B

Name   **Please Print Clearly**

1. Is it permissible for the judge to merely gag Kathy rather than have her removed from the courtroom?

_____

_____

_____

_____

_____

_____

_____

_____

_____

2. What are the pros and cons of the alternative disciplinary measures discussed in **State v. Lee?** What considerations do you think should be used in determining which approach is the best to use against a disruptive defendant?

_____

_____

_____

_____

_____

_____

_____

3. How does the approach taken to control Kathy compare with the approaches taken in **Lee** and **Cruz?**

_____

_____

_____

_____

_____

_____

_____

_____

_____

4. Even if you do not agree with the approach used by the court, did Kathy's trial comply with he demands of Due Process?

_____

_____

_____

_____

_____

_____

_____

_____

_____

SECTION 3.7
ETHICS

In most jurisdictions in the Western world, it is a crime to assist a person in committing suicide. This ban is not new but reflects a longstanding tradition of the states' commitment to preserve life. In fact, the states have laws imposing criminal penalties on those who assist others in this endeavor.

In 1997, four physicians from Washington State along with several terminally ill patients decided to challenge that state's law prohibition against assisted suicides claiming that the ban was unconstitutional. They asserted a liberty interest protected by the Due Process Clause asserting that the Constitution extends a personal choice to mentally competent, terminally ill adults to commit physician-assisted suicide.

In **Washington v. Glucksberg,** 521 U.S. 702 (1997), the Supreme Court ruled that the Fourteenth Amendment "forbids the government to infringe ... 'fundamental' liberty interests *at all,* no matter what process is provided, unless the infringement is narrowly tailored to serve a compelling state interest." This country's treatment of assisted suicide has been one of rejection of nearly all efforts to permit it. That being the case, our decisions lead us to conclude that the asserted "right" to assistance in committing suicide is not a fundamental liberty interest protected by the Due Process Clause. Washington has an "unqualified interest in the preservation of life." Washington's prohibition on assisted suicide, like all homicide laws, both reflects and advances its commitment to this interest.

1.   Do you agree with the court's decision that a state can ban assisted suicide?

2.   Since this decision, at least four states have enacted laws permitting assisted suicide. What do you think was their rational for such a dramatic change in the law?

3.   What ethical issue do you see arising in an assisted suicide?

SECTION 3.8
PROBLEM CASES

1.   A city passed an ordinance limiting the number of dogs that can be kept at a residential premise to two dogs over the age of six months. A person who wishes to keep three or four adult dogs at home must obtain a permit. Holt runs a "stud service" from her house and rescues Newfoundland dogs until homes can be found for them. When the law went into effect, she had twelve adult dogs at her residence. Is this ordinance constitutional? **Mary Holt v. City of Sauk Rapids, 559 N.W. 2d 444 (Minn. Ct. App. 1997).**

2.   A city passed an ordinance prohibiting the maintenance of a "nuisance." The storage of abandoned or junked motor vehicles is automatically considered a nuisance. A city inspector found a stove, water heater, and car parts on the property owned by Kadash. This

individual was then convicted of violating the ordinance. Do the actions of Kadash constitute a nuisance? Is the ordinance constitutional? **George Kadash v. City of Williamsport, 340 A.2d 617 (a. Cmwlth. 1975).**

3.   During Tribblett's criminal trial for robbery, a spectator stood up and began screaming: "He threatened my life. He's going to jail." The individual continued her ravings while she was physically removed from the courtroom. The court admonished the jurors to eliminate the outburst from their minds and to base their verdict solely on the evidence. The attorney for Tribblett moved for mistrial and claimed that his client's procedural due process rights to a fair trial were violated. Do you agree? **Commonwealth of Pennsylvania v. Tribblett, 363 A.2d 12123 (Pa. Super. 1976).**

4.   Davis was charged with the brutal beating and shooting death of a woman and her two children. The case was the subject of enormous pretrial publicity, including the fact that Davis had failed a lie detector test and had a history of violent crime. During the jury selection process, ten out of forty jurors admitted to having prior knowledge about the case. The trial judge, however, refused to allow these jurors to be questioned individually by defense counsel. As a result, the defense was precluded from learning the specific information that the potential jurors had heard or read . Was the right of Davis to a fair and impartial jury violated by the trial court's action? **Allen Davis v. State of Florida, 473 U.S. 913 (1985).**

5.   Dixon was convicted of attempted robbery. During the course of the crime, he brandished a gun, so he was sentenced to an automatic five-year imprisonment for the weapon's offense. The state legislature had decided to impose a mandatory sentencing scheme for the use of a firearm when committing a crime in order to protect human life. Dixon challenged the statute as being a violation of his due process rights. Specifically, he argues that the law infringes on his constitutional rights because the legislation ignores the right of the judge to sentence a defendant to a shorter term in jail. In other words, the law prohibits a court from imposing a shorter sentence because of mitigating factors such as the defendant's being a first-time offender. Does the statute violate Dixon's substantive due process rights? **Commonwealth of Pennsylvania v. Carl Cooke, 492 A.2d 63 (Pa. Super. 1985).**

Footnotes:

1. *Due Process of Law: Procedural and Substantive Issues,* http://faculty.ncwc.edu/mstevennns/ 410/4101ect06.htm (6/25/03).

2. *Rochin v. California* 342 U.S. 1165 (1952).

3. "Distracted Driving," FindLaw, http://traffic.findlaw.com/traffic-tickets/distracted-driving.html (last visited February 14, 2016).

4. "Illegal Immigration," US Immigration Support, https://www.usimmigrationsupport.org/illegal-immigration.html (last visited February 14, 2016).

5. "What Are the Solutions to Illegal Immigration in America?," ProCon.org, http://immigration.procon.org/ (last visited February 14, 2016).

6. Mariano Castillo, "Crime Stats Test Rationale Behind Arizona Immigration Law," CNN, April 29, 2010, http://www.cnn.com/2010/CRIME/04/29/arizona.immigration.crime/index.html (last visited February 14, 2016).

7. "5 Things to Know About Arizona Immigration Law," Laws, http://immigration.laws.com/arizona-immigration-law (last visited February 14, 2016).

8. "Childhood Overweight and Obesity," CDC, http://www.cdc.gov/obesity/childhood/ (last visited February 14, 2016).

9. *Id.*

10. James Arvantes, "Federal Government Takes Bigger Role in Combating Obesity," AAFP, May 17, 2010, http://www.aafp.org/news/obesity/20100517fed-initiatives.html (last visited February 14, 2016).

11. *Id.*

12. Kimberly Leonard, "Local Governments Seek to Curb Obesity in Kids," US News and World Reports, February 13, 2015, http://www.usnews.com/news/articles/2015/02/13/local-governments-seek-to-curb-obesity-in-kids (last visited February 14, 2016).

13. "Student Drug Testing," Students for Sensible Drug Policy, http://ssdp.org/campaigns/student-drug-testing/ (last visited February 14, 2016).

14. "Boston Marathon Bombings," History Channel, http://www.history.com/topics/boston-marathon-bombings (last visited February 14, 2016).

15. Elizabeth Ledgerwood Pendlay, "Procedure For Pupils: What Constitutes Due Process In A University Disciplinary Hearing?," 82 N.D. L. Rev. 967, 2006.

16. *Raymond Gorman v. University of Rhode Island,* 837 F.2d 7 (1st Cir. Ct. of Appeals 1999).

17. *Id.*

18. *Id.*

19. *Id.*

KEY TERMS

Article One
Bill
Bill of Rights
Congress
Concurrent Resolution
Doctrine of Incorporation
Drug Testing
Due Process
Fifth Amendment
Fourteenth Amendment
Hopper
House of Representatives

Impartial Tribunal
Joint Resolution
Magna Carta
Ordinance
Procedural Due Process
Procedural Law
Reconstruction Amendment
Statute
Substantive Due Process
Substantive Law
United States Senate
Veto

CHAPTER 4

CRIMINAL LAW AND PROCEDURE

<table>
<tr><td>

SECTION 4.1
CRIMES

</td><td>

"The real significance of crime is in its being a breach of faith with the community of mankind."

Joseph Conrad
Lord Jim, 1900

</td></tr>
</table>

As a general rule, an individual can engage in any type of conduct that he or she wishes unless the law specifically prohibits those actions. The legislature, however, will intercede whenever necessary to regulate and prohibit conduct that society deems inappropriate.

A **crime** is an offense against society as determined by the legislature or it is considered a public wrong that carries the punishment of imprisonment or some other public sanction. Crimes number in the thousands, and specific definitions will vary from jurisdiction to jurisdiction. The offense is investigated by law enforcement officials who usually file the criminal charges against the accused, and a governmental agency, such as the District Attorney or United States Attorney, prosecutes the defendant. These crimes range from felonies to summary offenses.

The United States Department of Justice maintains statistics on the categories of crimes committed each year in this country. The most frequently charged offenses deal with non-violent crimes and make up about three-fourths of all arrests. Drug trafficking and other drug related crimes constitute the single largest category of all arrests and make up 36% of the total arrests made in the United States. Violent crimes account for one-fourth of all arrests and assault and robbery lead this category. The Southern states have the highest rate of violent crimes and account for 42% of all violent crimes committed in this country.

Statistically, men are the victims of killings about three-fourths of the time and commit this violent act in almost 90% of the cases. About one-third of murder victims are under 25 and about one-half of the perpetrators are in this age category. Louisiana and Maryland have the highest murder rate by 100,000 people.[1] At what age, however, is a person most likely to die by homicide? According to the Centers for Disease Control, an individual is ten times more likely to be murdered at birth than any other time during one's life. Most of these deaths occurred to children not born in a hospital and the perpetrators were the children's adolescent mothers.[2] Police investigations have

141

determined that arguments are the leading reason for murder in the United States and handguns are by far the weapon of choice.[3]

Not all homicides are illegal nor are all killings punished equally. The law has created a number of categories to reflect these facts with crimes ranging from first degree murder to involuntary manslaughter.

The first part of this chapter will provide definitions for some of the more well-known crimes, such as murder, rape, burglary, and theft. The second part of the chapter will discuss criminal procedure with a focus on the law of search and seizure, police questioning of suspects and will provide a step by step analysis of the arrest procedure through trial.

HOMICIDE

A **homicide** is the killing of another human being but a homicide does not automatically mean that the killing is illegal. In fact, three categories of homicide have been created to designate if the killing is legal or illegal:

1. justifiable homicide;

2. excusable homicide; and

3. criminal homicide.

Justifiable homicide is the killing of another person in self-defense or the execution of an individual carried out by the state or federal governments. California, Michigan, Oklahoma and Louisiana lead the country in justifiable homicides and account for nearly half of these types of killings even though they have only 18% of the population.[4] It is anticipated that the number of justifiable homicides will increase with the growing number of states that have enacted "Make My Day" laws. At least 15 states, including Florida, Colorado, Arizona, and Kentucky, now allow a person to use deadly force against an intruder or attacker in a dwelling, residence, or vehicle and the law provides immunity from for using deadly force. In fact, these laws allow the use of deadly force whenever a person feels threatened in a public area without first having to retreat. An **excusable homicide** is a killing by accident or mistake where the wrongdoer does not have any criminal culpability. A child who is accidentally killed by a car when he darts out between parked vehicles in pursuit of a ball is an example of a homicide that is excusable. **Criminal homicide,** on the other hand, is the unlawful killing of another that includes the crimes of murder and manslaughter.

Murder is considered the most serious crime by society and it is divided into different degrees depending on how the crime is committed. For instance, first degree murder or premeditated murder represents the conscious attempt to take the life of another.

Manslaughter is considered less serious because the killing is committed through gross negligence or under mitigating circumstances such as when a person kills his spouse in a fit of rage after finding her in bed with another man.

The definition of **first degree murder** varies by state but it is generally considered to be the unlawful killing of another human with malice aforethought, and with the specific intent to kill. This type of deliberate homicide is commonly referred to as premeditated murder and involves a killing by such means as torture, ambush, poisoning, or lying in wait. It is this element of a premeditated and deliberate killing that distinguishes first-degree murder from all other types of criminal homicide. A contract killing or an assassination are classic examples of premeditated murder. Specific intent to kill may also be inferred from the surrounding circumstances, such as the use of a deadly weapon upon a vital part of the victim's body. For example, purposely shooting a person in the head or chest would demonstrate a specific intent to kill that individual; shooting the person in the foot would not.

Malice aforethought describes conduct that exhibits a wanton disregard for the safety of others. This legal term has been defined to include not only ill will towards a person, but a wickedness of disposition, hardness of heart, and recklessness of consequences. In other words, malice aforethought includes such things as discharging a gun into a crowd, throwing a rock off the top of a building, cutting a person with a knife or other sharp object, or punching another in the face. These acts show a disregard for the rights of others and demonstrate a wickedness of disposition.

How much time must elapse between forming the intent to kill and the actual act in order to establish premeditation or specific intent to kill? There is no exact time requirement; instead, premeditation may be proven by a person's words or conduct. For instance, premeditation may be inferred by the intentional use of a deadly weapon upon a vital part of the body, regardless of the passage of time between when the shooter formed the intent to pull the trigger and the actual act.

UNITED STATES OF AMERICA v. REJON TAYLOR
2016 WL 537444 (6TH CIR. CT. APPEALS 2016)

Rejon Taylor appeals his convictions and death sentence for carjacking resulting in death while committing carjacking and kidnapping.

Taylor had been responsible for various thefts and burglaries from Guy Luck's house in Atlanta between 2001 and 2003. On August 6, 2003, Taylor, along with Sir Jack Matthews and Joey Marshall, went to Luck's house with the intention of robbing him. After confronting Luck at gunpoint, Marshall guarded Luck while Taylor began looking through Luck's house. Taylor took around $600 or $800. Marshall testified Taylor later told him there was a warrant connected with Taylor's arrest on theft charges in another case, which suggested Luck could be a witness against Taylor.

At gunpoint, Luck was forced outside his house and into his van. Taylor got in the driver's seat, while Matthews guarded Luck in the back. As Taylor drove the van around isolated roads, there was a confrontation in the back of the van, in which Matthews fired a shot, which hit Luck in the arm. Taylor turned around from the driver's seat and fired three shots at Luck. The third bullet hit Luck in the mouth and caused his death. Taylor and Matthews left their guns in the van and walked briskly from the van to the car driven by Marshall. They then drove back to Atlanta. Taylor was subsequently arrested.

There was sufficient evidence to support the jury's finding that Taylor engaged in substantial planning and premeditation before murdering Luck. Taylor's argument is that the evidence shows only that he planned to rob or, at most, kidnap Luck, not that he planned to murder Luck. But the Government introduced several pieces of evidence that support

a finding that Taylor planned to kill Luck. For instance, Taylor arrived at Luck's house the morning of the crime not just with loaded guns, but also without any sort of mask that might conceal his identity—unlike previous burglaries. The jury could reasonably have interpreted the lack of masks as evidence that this was not just another robbery attempt, and that Taylor had no intent of letting Luck out of the van alive, since Luck could otherwise have identified Taylor to the police. While inside Luck's house, Taylor allegedly observed documentation indicating that Luck was helping to procure a warrant for Taylor's arrest. Most significantly, Taylor drove Luck for two hours to a rural area of a different state, all the while not bothering to conceal his identity. The jury could have reasonably concluded that Taylor's conduct suggested that he intended to kill Luck rather than leave him alive to testify against Taylor in the future.

In rejecting Taylor's argument on premeditation, the evidence showed Defendant had been watching Luck and knew when Luck took money from his restaurant to the bank. Defendant picked that time to confront Luck. Luck was then forced into his van, and driven to Tennessee, where Defendant fatally shot Luck. The jury could conclude Defendant killed Luck after substantial planning and premeditation based on the fact that he learned Luck's routine and killed Luck after taking him on a two-hour drive, during which time Defendant would have had substantial time to plan and think about the murder. A rational jury could conclude Defendant had decided to kill Luck sometime before the murder and that the events of the day of the murder were just the culmination of a well thought-out plan.

Precedent does not require that the Government prove that Taylor planned to kill Luck in precisely the manner that he did. Thus, the fact that Luck's struggle may have prompted Taylor to shoot Luck sooner than he might have intended does not mean that Taylor did not engage in substantial planning and premeditation regarding Luck's ultimate demise. The Government provided sufficient evidence of planning and premeditation in this case.

QUESTIONS FOR DISCUSSION:

1. Dudley, Stephens and another sailor were cast adrift in a small boat following a storm with no food or water. Dudley and Stephens discussed sacrificing one of the three so that the remaining two could survive. The two sailors then killed the decedent and fed upon his body for nourishment. The survivors were tried for first degree murder even though all three would have died of starvation. The decedent was chosen because he would have expired first due to his frail and deteriorating health. Are Dudley and Stephens guilty of first degree murder? **Regina v. Dudley and Stephens, 14 Q. B. D. 273 (1884).**

2. Mr. Carrol was selected to attend an electronic's school for nine days. His wife greeted the news with a violent argument. Prior to his departure, and at the request of his wife, Mr. Carrol put a loaded 22 caliber pistol on the window sill, at the head of the bed. Later than evening, the parties engaged in another protracted argument. Carrol's wife proceeded to follow her husband into the bedroom as they continued to argue. Mr. Carrol remembered the gun on the window sill, so he grabbed the pistol, and spontaneously shot his wife twice in the back of the head. Is this a case of premeditated murder? **Commonwealth v. Carrol, 194 A.2d 911 (Pa. 1963).**

3. In the book and movie *Alive*, a plane carrying 15 members of the Uruguay national rugby team crashed in the Andes Mountains. The survivors ate the flesh of their dead friends in order to stay alive until they were rescued. How does this case differ from **Regina v. Dudley and Stephens?**

Second-degree murder or **felony murder,** is the unintentional killing of another committed during the commission of a felony. An example of felony murder is demonstrated by a person who sets fire to a building unaware that the owner is inside. Since the owner died during the commission of an arson, Jones is guilty of felony murder even though he did not know the owner was inside the building. If, however, a criminal specifically kills another during the commission of a felony, such as a robbery, the crime would constitute first-degree murder and not felony murder.

If the crime is committed by more than one person, all participants in the criminal enterprise can be equally found guilty regardless of their involvement. This is called the **co-felons rule**. For instance, the driver of the get-away car in a grocery store robbery is just as liable for the killing of a store clerk as the person who pulls the trigger.

Some states do not make a distinction between first degree and felony murder and treat both crimes the same.

Felony murder is construed very broadly. As long as the defendant's actions were the proximate cause of the death, even if the killing was not planned, the defendant will be convicted of this crime. This is demonstrated by **Robinson v. State** where a co-conspirator was killed by the victim of a robbery and the defendant was convicted of felony murder because it was foreseeable that one of the robbers could be killed during the crime.

ROBINSON V. STATE
2016 WL 462669 (GA. 2016)

Anthony Robinson appeals his convictions for felony murder predicated on criminal attempt to commit armed robbery.

On September 25, 2012, an individual, later identified as Carter from surveillance footage, entered the Coastal Gold Exchange (CGE), a business that bought precious metals. Carter pulled a gun on a CGE employee, Jimmie Skelton, and stole approximately $2,000. No one was ever arrested for this robbery, but there was evidence that Robinson and Carter used their cell phones in the vicinity of CGE around the time that the robbery occurred.

On September 27, 2012, Carter entered CGE while Timothy Johnson, the owner of the business, was working alone. Following the robbery that had occurred two days earlier, Johnson reviewed security footage from the store and studied the features and image of the robber. As a result, Johnson became suspicious when Carter walked into the store. Johnson warned Carter that he knew who he was, and Johnson placed his hand on a gun that he was carrying.

Carter then fled the business, and Johnson pursued. Carter ran behind the shopping center where CGE was located. Johnson testified that, as Carter was fleeing, Carter kept turning and looking back at him. At that time, Johnson noticed that Carter had a gun on his side. Johnson testified that he felt his life was in danger. Based on this belief, Johnson drew his gun and shot Carter in the back. Wounded but still mobile, Carter jumped into the black truck that Robinson had parked in an alley near CGE. Robinson drove the truck away, and Johnson reported the events to a 911 operator. In the area where Carter had fled, Johnson found a loaded gun lying in the grass.

Shortly after the robbery, police in marked vehicles began pursuit of the truck driven by

Robinson. Robinson, however, attempted to elude police and started running stop signs. Eventually, Robinson crashed the truck into a house, exited the vehicle, and ran down the street until he was apprehended. Robinson did not immediately inform police that Carter was still in the truck and needed medical assistance. Carter later died of a gunshot wound to the back.

Proximate cause exists if Robinson's crime of attempted armed robbery "directly and materially contributed to the happening of a subsequent accruing immediate cause of the death, or if ... the homicide [was] committed within the res gestae of the felony ... and is one of the incidental, probable consequences of the execution of the design to commit the [predicate felony]."

Here, it was reasonable to foresee that Carter, who was attempting an armed robbery, could be fatally wounded in attempting such a highly dangerous enterprise. As Robinson was a party to the crime of attempted armed robbery, his acts, therefore, were properly found to be a proximate cause of Carter's death, which flowed directly from the dangerous criminal enterprise.

Judgment affirmed.

Generally, **third-degree murder** is the killing of another with malice aforethought but with no specific intent to kill and not occurring during the commission of a felony. As an illustration, Minnesota law defines third degree murder as "Whomever, without intent to effect the death of any person, causes the death of another by perpetrating an act eminently dangerous to others and evidencing a depraved mind, without regard for human life, is guilty of murder in the third degree."

For example, if an individual is intentionally shot in the foot and dies as a result of medical complications, that action will give rise to third-degree murder. The shooting itself is evidence of malice but no specific intent to kill existed.

COMMONWEALTH OF PENNSYLVANIA V. JOHN KLING
731 A.2D 145 (PA. SUPER. 1999)

John Kling was driving his red Chrysler Conquest near McConnellsburg when he noticed a black Camaro in his rear-view mirror. The Camaro took off, and both automobiles began racing up a curvy mountain road known as Scrub Ridge. At speeds in excess of 80 mpm, both vehicles reached the crest of Scrub Ridge, and with Kling in the lead, the improvident competitors began descending the mountain road.

The first downside mile from the top of Scrub Ridge is riddled with eight substantial curves and five cautionary speed signs. Nevertheless,

Kling maintained his excessive speeds, pulling away from the Camaro and disappearing into the blind curves.

Approaching the eighth major curve on the downslope, Kling swung into the no-passing zone and blew past two pickup trucks traveling in front of him. He then headed into the sharp double curve at nearly 70 mpm, crossed the centerline again, and struck a vehicle driven by Helen Mellott. The collision killed Ms. Mellott instantly.

Third degree murder occurs when a person commits a killing, which is neither intentional nor committed during the perpetration of a felony, but contains the requisite malice. Malice exists where there is a wickedness of disposition, hardness of heart, cruelty, recklessness of consequences, and a mind regardless of social duty, although a particular person may not be intended to be injured. Where malice is based on a reckless disregard of consequences, it is not sufficient to show mere recklessness; rather, it must be shown the defendant consciously disregarded an unjustified and extremely high risk that his actions might cause death or serious bodily injury.

Kling was deliberately racing his high-powered car at speeds of 75-80 mpm on a two and onehalf mile stretch of a curvy mountain road. He passed five cautionary signs warning him to slow down around the treacherous curves. In spite of these warnings, Kling proceeded at high rates of speed and, cutting the curves in order to negotiate the road. Without a doubt, the aggregate of these circumstances plainly warned Kling his conduct was nearly certain to result in disaster.

Kling chose to play Russian roulette with the other drivers on Scrub Ridge. By speeding through the curves, he pulled the trigger four or five times with one near miss; on the last pull, however, he killed a person. This conduct exhibited the sustained recklessness, in the face of warnings, necessary to prove a knowing and conscious disregard that death or serious bodily injury was reasonably certain to occur. We therefore uphold Kling's convictions for third degree murder.

The last category of criminal homicide is **manslaughter** which is divided into voluntary and involuntary manslaughter.

The reader might remember the bizarre case in Germany that gained worldwide attention. Armin Meiwes admitted to slaying and consuming a man's body who had volunteered to be killed after reading an internet message from Meiwes' about his perverted fantasy. The communication by Meiwes read: "Seeking well-built man, 18-30 years old for slaughter." The victim responded: "I offer myself to you and will let you dine on my live body. Not butchery, dining!!" Because the victim had willingly volunteered to be killed, the crime did not fit the German definition of murder, and the act was classified as manslaughter. What then is manslaughter?

Voluntary manslaughter is the intentional killing of another committed in the heat of passion and as a result of provocation that would arouse the passions of an ordinary person beyond the power of his or her control. Courts recognize that these elements will eliminate malice aforethought in what would normally be a first-degree murder case.

Certain types of conduct can provoke a reasonable person to act without consideration for his or her actions. Provocation has been recognized in cases where one spouse finds the partner in bed with another person, or if an assailant learns that a spouse or child has been the victim of a sexual attack.

Words alone, however, are not considered sufficient provocation to cause a person to use deadly force regardless of how insulting or inciteful they might be. This principle will apply in most cases even if the words are spoken just to inform the defendant that a provocative event has occurred. In evaluating the facts of the killing, the courts will use an objective person standard in determining whether sufficient provocation existed to bring about the fit of rage.

To provide an example of a definition for this crime, Ohio provides: "No person, while under the influence of sudden passion or in a sudden fit of rage, either of which is brought on by serious provocation occasioned by the victim that is reasonably sufficient to incite the person into using deadly force, shall knowingly cause the death of another."

Is a person guilty of voluntary manslaughter if she finds her boyfriend in a sexual liaison with another woman? The courts have traditionally ruled that if an accused catches his or her spouse in the act of adultery, the circumstances establishes heat of passion for the crime of voluntary manslaughter.

PEOPLE OF MICHIGAN v. KYLE ALAN WILSON
2016 WL 155770 (MICH. 2016)

This case arises out of the death of defendant's roommate, Brandon Nelson. Defendant admitted to having had an altercation with Nelson in their apartment over defendant's failure to pay rent. Defendant stated to police that Nelson had charged him, causing defendant to duck and hit him with his elbow. Defendant stated that Nelson charged him a second time, that he hit Nelson twice on the side of his head, and that Nelson fell to the ground and began snoring. Defendant denied striking Nelson while Nelson was prone. Defendant told police that he left the apartment, and upon his return found Nelson dead. Defendant stated that, after fruitlessly performing CPR, he took Nelson's telephone and wallet and left the apartment because he was scared. Defendant was later apprehended.

Several experts for the prosecution testified that Nelson's injuries and the crime scene were consistent with him having been struck several times while lying on the ground. A forensic pathologist testified that Nelson sustained at least 7 and as many as 13 blows to the face, and had extensive bruising and lacerations around his eye and cheekbone.

Defendant argues that there was insufficient evidence to prove that the killing was not done in a heat of passion, thus reducing the murder conviction to **voluntary manslaughter.** We disagree. **Voluntary manslaughter** is an intentional killing committed under the influence of passion or hot blood produced by adequate provocation, and before a reasonable time has passed for the blood to cool and reason to resume its habitual control. A fact-finder must examine all the circumstances surrounding the killing to determine whether the homicide was committed in the heat of passion. The determination of what is reasonable provocation is a question of fact for the fact-finder, as is the determination regarding whether "a lapse of time" occurred during which a reasonable person could control his passions.

Defendant claims that Nelson's actions of shoving him in the chest and rushing at him were adequate provocation to make a reasonable person act out of passion rather than reason. However, even if Nelson's actions perhaps provoked defendant's initial response, the evidence indicates that defendant continued to strike Nelson once he fell to the ground. The jury thus could have rationally found that a lapse of time had occurred during which a reasonable person could regain control of his passions. Further, defendant told police that he and Nelson did not get along very well and that Nelson was always trying to boss and push him around. Based on the circumstances of the killing, which involved a roommate dispute, and defendant's actions following the killing, a trier of fact could find that defendant was provoked by the argument, monetary issues, or existing bad blood between him and Nelson, but that he was not adequately provoked so as to reduce his offense to **voluntary manslaughter.** Viewing the evidence in the light most favorable to the prosecution, a trier of fact could find that defendant did not kill Nelson while under the influence of passion produced by adequate provocation.

Involuntary manslaughter lacks an essential element to make the crime murder and it is considered a lesser included offense. This crime is defined as the unintentional killing of another resulting from outrageous conduct or criminal negligence that demonstrates a reckless disregard for the safety of another. For example, an intoxicated driver who causes an accident and kills another person is guilty of this crime which is also called vehicular manslaughter.

The Missouri Criminal Code provides an example of a definition for this crime. That law states: "A person commits the crime of involuntary manslaughter if he: (1) recklessly causes the death of another person; or (2) while in an intoxicated condition operates a motor vehicle with criminal negligence to cause the death of any person.

One of the more publicized cases of involuntary manslaughter, dubbed the "Nanny Murder Trial," involved Louise Woodward. She was the au pair from England who came to the United States to work as a baby sitter. Woodward was in charge of an eight month old infant that died in her care. The case was tried in Massachusetts and the evidence demonstrated that the baby died from being shaken to death. Woodward was initially convicted of murder but the judge reduced the finding to involuntary manslaughter. Following the trial, Woodward returned to Europe, attended law school and is now an attorney in England.

Involuntary manslaughter requires a showing of gross negligence. Ordinary negligence will not suffice. As **Commonwealth of Pennsylvania v. Beatty** notes, this requires that the actor consciously disregards a substantial and unjustifiable risk that will result from his conduct. The risk must be of such a nature and degree that, considering the nature and intent of the actor's conduct and the circumstances known to him, its disregard involves a gross deviation from the standard of conduct that a reasonable person would observe in the actor's situation.

COMMONWEALTH OF PENNSYLVANIA V. BEATTY
2015 WL 6472139 (PA. SUPER. 2015)

On July 4, 2014, a bedroom clothes dresser fell on top of Beatty's two children, Ryeley, age three, and Brooklyn, age two, while they were in their home and caused their death. On October 6, 2014, Beatty was charged with two counts of involuntary manslaughter.

Detective Steven Roberts received a report of two unresponsive children at Beatty's residence. When he arrived, one child was laying on the front porch and the other child was laying in the front yard; both were being treated by firemen, police officers, and paramedics. The children were transported to Heritage Valley Hospital and pronounced dead. Detective Roberts asked Beatty how the children were injured. Beatty told him that he observed the children sitting on a dresser drawer and then he went to the bathroom to prepare a bath for them. While in the bathroom, he heard a crash, returned to the room within seconds, and found the dresser on top of the children. Beatty advised that he then

moved the dresser, placed the children on the bed, and called 911.

Detective Roberts asked Beatty to show him where this incident occurred inside of his home. Beatty showed Detective Roberts the bedroom where the children were injured and the bathroom where he was at the time of the incident. Beatty also showed Detective Roberts the dresser drawer, and demonstrated that it was pulled out approximately three to four inches at the time he observed the children sitting upon it.

Later that evening, Detective Roberts, spoke with Beatty at Children's hospital. During this interview, Beatty stated that he had been using the bathroom when he heard a "bang," he then called out to the children and received no response. Beatty estimated that he checked on the children within one or two minutes of hearing the noise. Upon further questioning, Beatty stated that, after hearing the "bang," he many have remained in the bathroom for up to five minutes before he checked on the children.

Dr. Todd Luckasevic, an expert in forensic pathology, performed an autopsy and found that each child died as a result of asphyxiation due to compression of the chest. Dr. Luckasevic further testified as to the children's likelihood of survival had they received care within thirty seconds of the dresser falling on them. There was a good chance that they would survive with a full recovery.

The Crimes Code defines involuntary manslaughter as follows: A person is guilty of involuntary manslaughter when as a direct result of the doing of an unlawful act in a reckless or grossly negligent manner, or the doing of a lawful act in a reckless or grossly negligent manner; he causes the death of another person.

A person acts recklessly when he consciously disregards a substantial and unjustifiable risk that the material element exists or will result from his conduct. The risk must be of such a nature and degree that, considering the nature and intent of the actor's conduct and the circumstances known to him, its disregard involves a gross deviation from the standard of conduct that a reasonable person would observe in the actor's situation.

The Commonwealth argues that Beatty acted "negligently." A person acts negligently with respect to a material element of an offense when he should be aware of a substantial and unjustifiable risk that the material element exists or will result from his conduct. The risk must be of such a nature and degree that the actor's failure to perceive it, considering the nature and intent of his conduct and the circumstances known to him, involves a gross deviation from the standard of care that a reasonable person would observe in the actor's situation.

The Commonwealth maintains that it produced sufficient evidence that Beatty acted with the above defined *mens rea*. This may be true, but the involuntary manslaughter statute speaks in terms of "gross negligence" rather than mere negligence. The fact that criminal negligence differs from tort negligence does not mean that the negligence is the equivalent of the "gross negligence." If the General Assembly had intended for negligence to be sufficient to establish the *mens rea* necessary for involuntary manslaughter, it need not have added the modifier "gross." We cannot construe the reference to "gross negligence" as requiring mere proof of the "negligent" or "criminally negligent" state of mind.

The law is clear that a showing of mere negligence or "criminal negligence" does not satisfy the Commonwealth's burden of proving the necessary *mens rea* for involuntary manslaughter.

RAPE

Sexual violence affects millions of people a year and is a dramatically unreported crime with only about 39% of the cases being reported to the police. Females are the usual victims but anyone can be a target. Some victims cannot refuse the sexual advances because of threats or intimidation while others are unable to consent because of mental illness, physical disability, age, or because they have been drugged.[5]

The National Institute for Justice reports that one in every six women have been the victim of an attempted or completed rape in their lifetime and about three percent of men have also been the victim of a sex crime. Statistically, 44% of rape victims are under the age of eighteen and 15% have not reached their twelfth birthdays.

The common law definition of **rape** is the unlawful carnal knowledge of a woman by a man through force or the threat of force and without consent. The crime does not require the assailant to complete the act of sexual intercourse. Rape merely requires penetration, no matter how slight.

Is it a defense to rape that the defendant is impotent and unable to perform the act of intercourse? This is the issue in **Arizona v. Kidwell.**

State of Arizona v. Raymond Kidwell
556 P. 2d 20 (Ariz. App. 1976)

KIDWELL, Raymond appeals his conviction of rape.

Kidwell argues that the trial court erred in refusing to direct a verdict on the rape charge. Appellant maintains that the evidence only supports a conviction for attempted rape on the grounds that the proof showed he had no erection at the time of the act and one who is impotent cannot be convicted of rape.

This issue appears to be one of first impression in Arizona. Although we have discovered no case law holding to the contrary, we hold that under Arizona law proof of impotency does not constitute a defense to a charge of rape.

A.R.S. §13—612 provides: The essential guilt of rape consists in the outrage to the person and feelings of the female, and any sexual penetration, however, slight is sufficient to complete the crime.

The critical element of rape is sexual penetration. The slightest penetration of the vulva is sufficient to complete the offense. Whether this penetration is accomplished by an erect or nonerect penis is not, in our opinion, relevant if penetration is established.

In the instant case, it was not disputed that Kidwell was impotent, in that he did not have an erection at the time of the offense. The victim, however, testified that a slight penetration of approximately one inch was accomplished. Kidwell's expert medical witness stressed the difficulty of achieving penetration in light of the victim's position and appellant's lack of an erection, but admitted that penetration as defined by our law could have taken place. This evidence is sufficient to uphold Kidwell's conviction.

The judgment and sentence are affirmed.

The elements of rape are not always easy to ascertain. Courts have struggled with two major questions over the years: (1) what constitutes force?; and (2) did the victim consent to the sexual act? These are especially difficult questions in instances of date rape and where the woman has been psychologically coerced into having sex.

What kind of behavior amounts to a threat, and how vehement must the woman be in resisting the sexual advance? In **Commonwealth v. Rhodes, 510 A.2d 1217 (Pa. 1986),** the Pennsylvania Supreme Court held that force implies more than just physical force; it may also include psychological coercion. Before that ruling, rape convictions were not upheld when the assailant threatened his victim with sending her back to a juvenile detention center if she did not comply with his sexual advances, **(Commonwealth v. Mlinarich, 498 A.2d 395 (Pa. Super. 1985)),** and when a father told his daughter that the Bible commanded her to have sex with him. **Commonwealth v. Biggs, 467 A.2d 31 (Pa. Super. 1983).**

Sex-offense laws have been recently modified to reflect the changing attitudes of society in making it easier to sustain a conviction. Some jurisdictions have made date rape a specific crime and have eliminated the requirement of force as an element of the offense. Pennsylvania is an example of a state that has revamped its law to reflect this change. In **Commonwealth v. Berkowitz, 641 A.2d 1161 (Pa. 1991),** a female college student, who had been drinking, claimed that another student raped her after she entered his dormitory room looking for a mutual friend. The victim testified that although he did not shove her or apply force, she continued to say "no" throughout the encounter. The Pennsylvania Supreme Court found that although the victim established her lack of consent, she did not establish a threat of force or psychological coercion, which is a necessary requirement for rape. The court remanded the case for trial on the charge of indecent assault, which is a misdemeanor, as opposed to rape, which is a felony.

Criticism of this decision prompted the sex offense laws in Pennsylvania to be amended and the crime of **sexual assault** was added. It is now a felony to engage in sexual intercourse with a person who does not consent to the act. What is obviously missing from this definition is the element of force. The result of this legislation is that "no" now means "no."

The legislature further amended the rape statute to afford greater protection to victims by prohibiting sexual conduct where the complainant is unconscious or the person knows that complainant is unaware that sexual intercourse is occurring. Rape also exists where the person has substantially impaired the complainant's power to control his or her conduct by employing, without the knowledge of the complainant, drugs or intoxicants. This change was made in response to those cases in which women have been raped after a drug has been placed in a victim's drink without her knowledge, rendering the victim unconscious.

The following is the current rape statute in Pennsylvania:

A person commits a felony of the first degree when he or she engages in sexual intercourse with a complainant:

1. By forcible compulsion.

2. By threat of forcible compulsion that would prevent resistance by a person of reasonable resolution.

3. Who is unconscious or where the person knows that the complainant is unaware that the sexual intercourse is occurring.

4. Where the person has substantially impaired the complainant's power to appraise or control his or her conduct by administering or employing, without the knowledge of the complainant, drugs, intoxicants or other means for the purpose of preventing resistance.

5. Who suffers from a mental disability which renders the complainant incapable of consent.

6. Who is less than 13 years of age.

The Pennsylvania legislature has addressed the issue of rape between spouses by providing that forcible sex between spouses is rape.

Is it rape when the victim is tricked into having sexual intercourse? The courts make a distinction between cases where the woman does not know that a sexual act is about to occur (fraud-in-factum) and where the victim consents to the sexual act but the permission is obtained through fraud (fraud-in-the-inducement). Fraud-in-factum is rape, but fraud-in-the-inducement is not. For instance, a person who consents to intercourse under the fraudulent promise that the parties will marry knows that a sexual act is to occur so rape has not been committed. A woman, however, who consents to a gynecological examination believing that a metal instrument is being inserting when the doctor is really performing sexual intercourse has been raped.

STATUTORY RAPE

Children are protected by the law in a variety of ways. The reader has already learned that children have a degree of immunity for their torts and they may disaffirm a contract unless it is for a necessity such as food or shelter. These protections are also extended to the voluntary sexual acts of children where adults may be prosecuted for having sexual relations with a child under a certain age. This is the crime of **statutory rape**.

Traditionally, **statutory rape** occurs when a man over the age of 16 has sexual relations with the consent of a female under 16 who is not his spouse. Because of the tender years of the female, she is presumed incapable of giving a meaningful consent, and the man is responsible for statutory rape regardless of his knowledge of her age.

In some states, the required age of the parties will differ. In Pennsylvania, for example, a person is guilty of statutory sexual assault when "that person engages in sexual intercourse with a complainant under the age of 16 years and that person is four or more years older than the complainant and the complainant and that person are not married to each other."

IN RE J.M.
2003 WL 79330 (GA. 2003)

The juvenile court found that sixteen-year-old J.M. violated Georgia's fornication statute, by having sexual intercourse with his sixteen-yearold girlfriend G.D. in her bedroom and adjudicated him delinquent. On appeal, J.M. contends that his constitutional right of privacy prohibits the State from criminalizing his conduct.

G.D. lived with her parents. Between 2 a.m. and 5 a.m. on September 16, 2001, she brought J.M. into her bedroom. She placed a stool next to the closed bedroom door, and she and J.M. engaged in sexual intercourse on the floor. When G.D.'s mother walked in and discovered them having sexual intercourse, J.M. jumped out of the bedroom window and ran.

We begin our analysis by considering whether J.M.'s right to privacy encompassed his sexual liaison with G.D. Both were sixteen years old at the time of the act, and the General Assembly has established sixteen as the age at which a person can legally consent to sexual intercourse. They willingly engaged in sexual intercourse, and there was no force involved.

Finally, J.M. and G.D.'s acts were private. The bedroom was G.D.'s personal bedroom, and she invited J.M. to enter the house and her bedroom. Although G.D.'s mother did not condone her daughter's behavior, she acknowledged that G.D. could reasonably expect privacy in various parts of the family home, including in G.D.'s bedroom. Before beginning her intimacies with J.M., G.D. ensured the bedroom door was closed and placed a stool against the door, further evidencing her and J.M.'s efforts to keep their acts private. Under these facts, we find that they intended to keep their sexual activity private and took reasonable steps to ensure their privacy. Accordingly, Georgia's right to privacy encompassed J.M.'s actions.

We next examine whether the State had a compelling interest that it vindicated through means that were narrowly tailored to accomplish only that compelling interest. Here, the State's interest in "shielding the public from inadvertent exposure to the intimacies of others" is not at issue because the intercourse occurred in a private residence. The State's interests in protecting people from engaging in sexual acts against their will, whether through force or inability to consent, are not implicated because J.M. and G.D. were legally capable of consenting, and they willingly engaged in sexual intercourse. Likewise, the State's interest in restricting commercial sexual activity is not involved.

The State offers its interest in regulating the behavior of "minors" as grounds for prohibiting J.M. and G.D.'s conduct. Whether labeled "minor" or "adult," however, the General Assembly has already determined that persons who are at least sixteen years old are sufficiently old to decide whether to engage in sexual intercourse. Because the State cannot use Georgia's criminal laws to proscribe J.M.'s conduct in this case, we reverse his adjudication as a delinquent.

OPEN LEWDNESS

Society has become much more tolerant in sexual matters between consenting adults. The law, however, remains critical of obscene conduct that is committed in public. For example, streaking and publicly exposing a private body part is not tolerated and fall within the definition of **open lewdness.**

A person is guilty of the crime of open lewdness when he or she commits any lewd act that the individual knows is likely to be observed by others who would be affronted or alarmed.

COMMONWEALTH OF PENNSYLVANIA V. NATHANIEL BROOKS
2016 WL 280416 (PA. SUPER. 2016)

On August 23, 2014, Thérèse McElwee entered the Paoli Public Library. As she sat down at a table, she made eye contact with Appellant and smiled. After a short time, Ms. McElwee noticed Appellant looked at her as he moved to a computer station closer to her table. Ms. McElwee looked up from her work and saw Appellant partially unclothed, with his genitalia exposed as he masturbated. Ms. McElwee immediately gathered her belongings and moved from her seat to report the incident. As she stood, Appellant said "I'll go, I'll go" and left the library.

Ms. McElwee reported the incident to a librarian on duty. Ms. McElwee and the librarian left the library to see if Appellant was still nearby. The women did not see Appellant outside of the building; instead they encountered Officer Jackson, who was investigating a separate incident. Officer Jackson relayed a description of Appellant over the police radio to other officers in the area. While patrolling nearby at the Paoli train station, Officer Gasparo noticed a man who matched Appellant's description. Officer Gasparo notified Officer Jackson, who drove by the train station with Ms. McElwee in his patrol vehicle. Ms. McElwee positively identified Appellant as the man who exposed himself to her in the library.

Meanwhile, Appellant told Officer Gasparo that Appellant had been at the Paoli Public Library earlier in the day. Appellant stated a woman flirted with him while he was there and asked him to expose himself. Appellant admitted he touched himself to please the woman.

The Crimes Code defines open lewdness as follows: A person commits a misdemeanor of the third degree if he does any lewd act which he knows is likely to be observed by others who would be affronted or alarmed.

Appellant exposed himself to Ms. McElwee in a public library. The trial evidence indicates Appellant was looking at Ms. McElwee as he masturbated and said, "I'll go, I'll go" when she reacted with shock. Prior to his arrest, Appellant admitted he had exposed himself in the public library. The Commonwealth's evidence showed Appellant displayed his genitals in a public setting to the shock and alarm of another library patron. Consequently, the evidence was sufficient to sustain Appellant's conviction for open lewdness.

Judgment of sentence affirmed

BURGLARY

According to the FBI, more than two million burglaries occur each year and two-thirds of these offenses are of residential structures. Burglars invade homes primarily during the day through forcible entry while business structures are usually entered at night. The average loss per illegal entry is a little more than $1,700. The Northeast has the fewest number of burglaries while the South has the highest rate for these crimes. As for what month has the highest burglary rate, that distinction goes to July. February has the fewest.

The definition of burglary has changed over time. At common law, **burglary** was defined as the breaking and entering of a building at night with the intent of committing a felony. Since the purpose of this law is to allow people to be secure in their homes, should it matter whether the offense occurs during the day or night? The modern definition of burglary provides that a person is guilty of the crime if he enters a building or occupied structure with the intent to commit a crime unless the premises are open to the public. The distinction of committing the crime between the day or night has been eliminated, as well as the requirement of a breaking and entering.

By way of comparison, England defines burglary as the entry into "any building, part of a building, inhabited vehicle or vessel with the intent to steal, cause grievous bodily harm, criminal damage, or to commit rape."

Burglary is a crime in and of itself and does not require the substantive offense to be committed by the criminal. For example, if a person breaks into a home to steal a rare painting, but the painting is no longer there, the individual is still guilty of burglary.

Does the definition of burglary include a person who enters a tent with the intent to commit a crime? That is the issue in **People v. Wilson.**

People v. John Wilson
15 Cal. Rptr. 2d 77 (Cal. App. 1992)

Wilson appeals his conviction for burglary. We affirm.

The charge arose from Wilson's relationship with Sherry Parsons. Wilson and Parsons met in March of 1991, and Wilson moved into the trailer where Parsons was staying. Parsons discovered that Wilson was aggressive, profane, and dominating, and asked him to move out three or four days later.

On May 1, 1991, Wilson and Parsons were at the grocery store when Wilson grabbed her by the hair, threw her down, and broke the grocery bag. Daniel Brackett, who knew Wilson, drove up with Sean Pray and saw Wilson pulling Parsons by the hair. Brackett calmed Wilson and took Parsons and Wilson to another location. Parsons said she was afraid of Wilson and stayed with Pray and Brackett.

In the early morning of May 11, 1991, Wilson appeared at Pray's tent. He unzipped the tent, stepped inside and said, "I've come to get you. You're going with me. Get up, get your clothes on and get your stuff. You're going to go with me or I'm going to kick your ass."

While Parsons was packing her belongings, Wilson pointed his knife at Pray, who was in his sleeping bag. Wilson threatened to burn Pray and set fire to the tent. Wilson ripped a gold chain off Pray's neck and said, "You're lucky it isn't your throat." Wilson slashed the tires of Pray's car with his knife, and kicked a lantern near his head, shattering glass over the bed.

Wilson argues that a tent is not an inhabited dwelling, house or a building for purposes of burglary. He bases his argument on the common definitions of "house" and "building." We find no merit in this point.

Courts have defined "building" broadly, to include such structures as a telephone booth, a popcorn stand on wheels, and a loading dock constructed of chain link fence. A "house" has also been broadly defined as "any structure, which has walls on all sides and is covered by a roof."

We reject Wilson's claim that a tent does not fall within the dictionary definition of a "building." The term inhabited dwelling house means a structure where people ordinarily live and which is currently being used for dwelling purposes. A place is an inhabited dwelling if a person with possessory rights uses the place as sleeping quarters intending to continue doing so in the future. The place—whether dwelling house or building—must be inhabited.

We conclude that it is the element of habitation, not the nature of the structure that (establishes) the crime of burglary. An "inhabited dwelling house," must be defined as a person's actual place of abode, regardless of the material of which it is built. Applying that conclusion to the instant case, we find that the tent having four sides and a roof and being inhabited by Pray and Parsons and used for sleeping and storage of their possessions, is a dwelling house, for purposes of (burglary).

The judgment is affirmed.

How would you answer the following questions?

1. If a person breaks into a car to steal the radio, does it constitute burglary?

2. If a person enters a mobile home to assault the occupants, is this burglary?

3. If a person enters a department store while it is open in order to steal a coat, is this burglary?

Has a person committed a crime if he or she purposely comes onto the land of another but has no intent to commit a crime? For example, is it a crime if a camper comes upon a home in the woods and enters the structure to take a shower or if one climbs over a fence on someone's property to go hunting on that land? **Criminal trespass** laws have been enacted to protect the unlawful intrusion onto real estate. The crime occurs when a person enters the land of another without permission or with no legal right to be there. For instance, some states make it a crime if a person:

1. Enters, gains entry by subterfuge or surreptitiously remains in any building or occupied structure; or breaks into any building or occupied structure or separately secured or occupied portion thereof, or

2. Knowing that he is not licensed or privileged to do so, enters or remains in any place as to which notice against trespass is given by:

   i. actual communication to the actor;

   ii. posting in a manner prescribed by law or reasonably likely to come to the attention of intruders;

iii. fencing or other enclosure manifestly designed to exclude intruders; or

iv. an actual communication to the actor to leave school grounds as communicated by a school, center or program official, employee or agent or a law enforcement officer.

THEFT RELATED CRIMES

Consider the following cases to ascertain if there is a common thread. Two men rigged the Pennsylvania State Lottery by placing counterfeit balls in the machine insuring that 666 would be the winning number. A bank clerk mistakenly deposited ten thousand dollars into a customer 's checking account which was promptly withdrawn by the recipient. A student gave his ATM card to roommate to withdraw $20 from his checking account as a loan. Instead, the roommate withdrew $500. A person walked into a jewelry store and sold a new $9,000 Rolex watch to the merchant for $100. The common thread in these cases is that they are all examples of theft related offenses.

Larceny is the taking and carrying away of property that belongs to another without the owner's consent and with the intention of depriving the owner of the goods permanently.

Because of the difficulty in distinguishing larceny from embezzlement and other theft-related crimes, these offenses have been consolidated into the crime of theft. No degree of force, however, may be used in taking the property or else the theft will be transformed into robbery.

Robbery consists of all of the elements of larceny with the additional requirement that the taking be accomplished by force or the threat of force.

The Federal Bureau of Investigation reports that most robberies occur on streets and highways and firearms are used almost half of the time. The average dollar value of the items taken per robbery is $1,230.

The force needed to accomplish a pick-pocket is not the type ordinarily required for robbery. If a weapon is used, however, the crime will be considered robbery. For instance, a purse snatch in which the victim is knocked to the ground is considered robbery.

A person commits the crime of **receiving stolen property** if he intentionally obtains or disposes of property of another knowing that it has been stolen, or believing that it has probably been stolen.

As a sign of our dependence on the Internet, states have added the offense of **electronic fencing.** This crime occurs when one uses the Internet to sell property gained through unlawful means. This variation of receiving stolen property is demonstrated by Illinois Public Act No. 94-179 which provides:

> A person commits the offense of electronic fencing when he or she uses or accesses the Internet with the intent of selling property gained through unlawful means knowing that the property was stolen. A person who unknowingly purchases stolen property over the Internet does not violate this provision.

This crime is aimed at penalizing those who take possession of stolen merchandise. The court looks at the circumstances behind the transaction to decide the criminal intent of the person who obtained the goods.

Identity theft is a recent phenomenon that involves using the victim's personal information to obtain a financial advantage such as the misappropriation of a credit card or money from a bank account. Criminals have even assumed the unsuspecting person's identify to obtain a fraudulent driver's license or to apply for a job. In fact, the United States Postal Authority estimates that nearly 10 million people are the victims of identify theft at the cost of about $5 billion dollars.

In 1998, Congress enacted the **Identity Theft and Assumption Deterrence Act** by making it a crime to misuse the personal identifying information of another. A number of states have followed suit by passing similar legislation. For example, Wisconsin provides that: "Whoever intentionally uses or attempts to use any personal identifying information or personal identification documents of an individual to obtain credit, money, goods, services or anything else of value without the authorization or consent of the individual and by representing that he or she is that individual, is guilty of a felony."

It is not necessary to break into someone's home to steal a person's private information. For instance, some thieves engage in "shoulder surfing" which involves watching an unsuspecting victim punch in a password on an automated teller machine or by listening in on a conversation while the person discloses a credit card number over the telephone. Some criminals even engage in "dumpster diving" by looking through discarded trash for copies of checks, or credit card statements. A recent expansion of this crime has occurred with the Internet. People frequently receive spam e-mails requesting personal information under a false pretense and people unwittingly provide that data.[6]

Victims of identify theft need to take four protective steps as quickly as possible after learning of the problem. Contact each of the three major credit reporting agencies and place a fraud alert on your credit card report. Those agencies are as follows:

1. Equifax
P.O. Box 749241
Atlanta, GA 30374-0241

2. Experian
P.O. Box 9532
Allen, TX 75013

3. TransUnion
Fraud Victim Assistance Division
P.O. Box 6790
Fullerton, CA 9283-6790

Once a fraud alert is issued, the credit agency will provide a free copy of your credit report if requested. Review that document carefully and check to see if any inquiries have been made about your credit history from companies that you have not contacted or accounts you did not open. If fraudulent information is discovered, request that it be removed.

The next step in the process of protecting and restoring your credit history is to notify credit card companies and banks in writing about the problem. If you discover an improper entry on an account, file a written dispute with the company and immediately close the account. Also, file a complaint with the police in the location where the identity theft took place and obtain a copy of the police report or report number. Finally, contact the Federal Trade Commission and file a complaint online at www.consumer.gov/idtheft.[7]

CONSPIRACY

Labeled by the court as the "darling of the modern prosecutor 's nursery," **conspiracy** is an all encompassing crime that allows the government to file charges against anyone who has participated in the planning or committing of a crime and to hold each liable for the actions of the other. For example, the following is Pennsylvania's definition of a conspiracy:

A person is guilty of conspiracy with another person or persons to commit a crime if with the intent of promoting or facilitating its commission he or she:

1. agrees with such other person or persons that they or one or more of them will engage in conduct which constitutes such crime or an attempt or solicitation to commit such crime; or

2. agrees to aid such other person or persons in the planning or commission of such crime or of an attempt or solicitation to commit such crime.

3. No person may be convicted of conspiracy to commit a crime unless an overt act in pursuance of such conspiracy is alleged and proved to have been done by him or by a person with whom he conspired.

4. It is a defense that the actor, after conspiring to commit a crime, thwarted the success of the conspiracy, under circumstances manifesting a complete and voluntary renunciation of his criminal intent.

Conspiracy is a separate crime from the actual substance offense that is to be committed. The agreement to commit the crime does not have to be in writing and can be informal. A mere tacit understanding is sufficient and each participant becomes the agent of the other for purposes of criminal responsibility.

ANTHONY HANKINSON v. WYOMING
47 P.3D 623 (WYO. 2002)

Anthony Hankinson was convicted of conspiracy to commit aggravated assault and battery. He submits this appeal contending that there is not sufficient evidence to sustain the conviction.

Hankinson and Lester Poague got drunk on July 25, 2000. They decided to go to the business owned by Daryl Coast and give him a beating, because of grievances against Coast. After drinking most of the day, Hankinson and Poague went to Coast's place of business and broke in the door. Once inside, they looked for Coast because they wanted to "kick his ass." Because Coast was a much bigger man than Poague, Poague had armed himself with an axe handle. However, Coast was not at his business, so the two vandals scattered business papers and poured fingernail polish on a credit card machine. Hankinson subsequently was charged with burglary, attempted assault and conspiracy.

The central thrust of Hankinson's appeal is that he was too drunk to have formed the intent to conspire with Poague and, to the extent they discussed a "plan" to beat up Coast using the axe handle, it did not rise to the level of a conspiracy, as that word is viewed in the context of the criminal law.

In **Jasch v. State**, 563 P.2d 1327, 1332 (Wyo. 1977), we defined a conspiracy as an agreement between two or more persons to do an unlawful act. The crime of conspiracy is complete when an agreement has been made and overt acts are performed to further the unlawful design. A conspiracy is completed when an agreement has been made and some overt act is performed in furtherance of the conspiracy. A mere tacit understanding will suffice, and there need not be any written statement or even a speaking of words, which expressly communicates agreement.

If it is established that a conspiracy existed and that the Defendant was one of its members, then the acts and declarations of any other member of such conspiracy in or out of such Defendant's presence, done in furtherance of the objects of the conspiracy, and during its existence, may be considered as evidence against such Defendant.

Whether or not Hankinson was so drunk that he could not form the requisite intent, and whether Hankinson actually engaged in a conspiracy to commit the crime of assault and battery on Coast, were questions for the jury. There was evidence that suggested that Hankinson was relatively lucid on the night of the crime. During the crimes, Hankinson had to make decisions and take actions that required some presence of mind, even if those actions were only the basest form of stupidity. In light of this evidence, the jury could reasonably have inferred that Hankinson acted with specific intent, even though there was a great deal of evidence to indicate that Hankinson was drunk. Likewise, though the agreement that Poague and Hankinson made to assault Coast was crude and ill conceived, the jury could reasonably have inferred that a conspiracy was present. Hankinson's argument focuses on his own view of the facts, rather than that view which might have been taken by reasonable jurors. The Judgment of the district court is affirmed.

White Collar Crime

From Bernie Madoff to Enron, the news is replete with stories about corporate wrongdoing, improper accounting practices, and stock manipulation. Illegal actions perpetuated in a business setting are generally classified as **white-collar crimes**. It has been estimated that the dollar loss from this offense is larger than all other crimes put together. In fact, the figure has been placed at a staggering $400 billion dollars a year and the crime is on the rise. While there is no one exact definition for this offense, the Federal Bureau of Investigation has defined white collar crime as "...those illegal acts which are characterized by deceit, concealment, or violation of trust and which are not dependent upon the application or threat of physical force or violence." This catch-all phrase includes computer fraud, health care fraud, securities fraud and insider trading, counterfeiting, theft of trade secrets, embezzlement, and tax evasion. The problem is so pervasive that the FBI estimates that white-collar crime accounts for 4% of all reported crime with the majority of these offenses being for fraud, counterfeiting, and forgery. The National White Collar Crime Center has determined that one in every three American households has been victimized by white-collar crimes. While individuals are the largest group of victims, businesses, financial institutions, governments, religious organizations, and other public entities have all been victimized.

Because of the difficulty and expense in uncovering white-collar crime, as well as the public's low tolerance for corporate wrongdoing, the state and federal governments have become more aggressive in prosecuting these cases. Some legislative bodies have even increased the penalty for white collar crime by imposing mandatory jail time. California is an example of a state that now imposes a minimum jail sentence for anyone convicted of economic or white collar crime. The rationale for this mandate is discussed in **People v. Alejandro.**

PEOPLE V. ALEJANDRO
28 CAL. 4TH 481 (CAL. 2002)

On April 18, 1997, a complaint was filed charging defendant with the theft of a trade secret. It was further alleged that the loss exceeded $2.5 million. Defendant pleaded no contest to the theft charge, a charge based upon evidence that he had printed out confidential design specifications for certain computer chips on the last day of his employment as an electrical engineer at Digital Equipment Corporation. Defendant objected to the potential application of **Section 1203.044** to his sentence.

Defendant stands convicted of theft, specifically a violation of **Section 499c**, which provides: "Every person is guilty of theft who, with intent to deprive or withhold the control of a trade secret from its owner, or with an intent to appropriate a trade secret to his or her own use or to the use of another, does any of the following: steals, takes, carries away, or uses without authorization, a trade secret."

The trial court determined that **Section 1203.044** applies to such a theft. This statute, entitled The Economic Crime Law, requires that a defendant who is convicted of certain theft offenses and is granted probation shall be sentenced to at least 90 days in the county jail as a condition of probation.

The Legislature declared in enacting **Section 1203.044:** "Major economic or white collar crime is an increasing threat to California's economy and the well-being of its citizens. The Legislature intends to deter that crime by ensuring that every offender, without exception, serves at least some time in jail. White collar criminals granted probation too often complete their probation without having compensated their victims or society. Probation accompanied by

a restitution order is often ineffective because county financial officers are often unaware of the income and assets enjoyed by white collar offenders. Thus, it is the Legislature's intent that the financial reporting requirements of this act be utilized to achieve satisfactory disclosure to permit an appropriate restitution order. White collar criminal investigation and prosecutions are unusually expensive. These high costs sometimes discourage vigorous enforcement of white collar crime laws by local agencies. Thus, it is necessary to require white collar offenders to assist in funding this enforcement activity."

We observe that the term "white collar crime" is a relatively broad one and is not limited to losses involving cash or cash equivalents. It generally is defined as "a nonviolent crime usually involving cheating or dishonesty in commercial matters. Examples include fraud, embezzlement, bribery, and insider trading." **Black's Law Dict. (7th ed.1999).** The Legislature has applied the term "white collar crime" to fraud and embezzlement in **Section 186.11,** a statute that provides for enhanced prison terms for recidivists committing these offenses when the offense involves a pattern of "taking more than one hundred thousand dollars." Like the crime of theft, fraud and embezzlement are not limited to the unlawful acquisition of cash or cash equivalents. Indeed, frequently fraud and embezzlement simply are methods by which a charged theft is accomplished.

Because the crime of theft includes a wide range of property and the term "white collar crime" has a broad meaning, we find it improbable that the Legislature intended to address only the theft of cash or cash equivalents in adopting The Economic Crime Act.

It is far more reasonable to conclude that the Legislature intended the provision to apply to all thefts of property of a particular value. Any other interpretation would permit many white collar thieves to continue to receive light probationary sentences and to evade strict restitution requirements. From the usual meaning of the terms used in **Section 1202.044**, the purpose of the enactment, and the Legislature's parallel use of the same terms in other statutes, one must conclude that **Section 1203.044** is not limited to thefts of cash or cash equivalents.

We find it clear from the words employed in **Section 1203.044** and the declaration of intent accompanying its enactment, that **Section 1203.044** does not apply solely to thefts of cash or cash equivalents, but rather that it addresses thefts of property, including trade secrets, exceeding specified values.

SECTION 4.2

DEFENSES TO A CRIME

A criminal act may be considered justified or excusable under certain limited circumstances. Defenses in this category include **self-defense** and actions in defense of others. The law recognizes the right of a person unlawfully attacked to use reasonable force in self-defense. However, only a person who reasonably believes there is imminent danger of bodily harm can use a reasonable amount of force under the circumstances.

Some defenses to a crime rest on the defendant's assertion that he or she lacked criminal responsibility for the criminal act. As a general rule, **intoxication** is not a defense unless it negates a specific mental state, such as specific intent to kill, which is required to prove the crime. Some defendants invoke the defense of **insanity** as demonstrating lack of criminal responsibility. Insanity rests on the theory that people who suffer from a mental disease or defect should not be convicted if they fail to appreciate that what they are doing is wrong or if they do not know the difference between right and wrong. The insanity defense only applies if the accused was insane at the time of the crime. Insanity during or after the trial does not affect criminal liability.

In many states, there are at least four possible verdicts: guilty; not guilty; no contest; and not guilty by reason of insanity. **Not guilty by reason of insanity** results in the automatic commitment to a mental institution. States have created another verdict: **guilty but mentally ill**. This option arose from the shooting of President Reagan by John Hinkley. The assailant shot the President in order to impress actress Jodie Foster, with whom he became infatuated after watching the movie *Taxi Driver*. Pennsylvania has adopted the verdict of guilty but mentally ill, which means that a jury that returns with such a finding is saying that the defendant has criminal responsibility for his actions, but it is acknowledged that the defendant suffers from a mental problem.

The following explanation of the insanity defense was offered in **Commonwealth v. Bowers:**

> The verdict of not guilty by reason of legal insanity labels a defendant as a sick person rather than a bad person. It signifies that in the eyes of the law that person, because of mental abnormality at the time of the crime, does not deserve to be blamed and treated as a criminal for what he did.

> The verdict of guilty but mentally ill labels a defendant as both bad and sick. It means that in the law's eyes that person at the time of the crime was not so mentally abnormal as to be relieved from blame and criminal punishment for what he did, but that he was abnormal enough to make a prime candidate for special therapeutic treatment.

Defendants found guilty but mentally ill will be sent to a hospital or mental institution for treatment and will then be transferred to prison after they have recovered.

Entrapment is also a defense to an arrest. This defense is designed to deter impermissible police conduct that entices a person to commit a crime that he or she had no previous inclination to perpetrate. The defense, however, is not available to a party who has no hesitation in committing the crime and the police merely presented the opportunity to act on the impulse. The test for determining entrapment is whether the actions of the police officer are likely to induce a normal law-abiding citizen to commit the crime. Two guiding principles determine whether the defense of entrapment exists. The first deals with the actions of the law enforcement agent and whether those actions would generate in a normal law-abiding citizen a motive to commit the crime. The second inquiry is whether the conduct of the police would make the commission of the crime unusually attractive.

Who saw the movie, American Hustle? This fictional film loosely depicted one of the most amazing scandals in the 20th Century. The film tells the story of several individuals allegedly working for the FBI who enticed several politicians and New Jersey power brokers to accept bribes for helping a business enterprise run by a fake Arab sheik. The illicit activity was filmed by the con artists and the players were then arrested.[8]

In reality, the film received its inspiration from a real life event, known as ABSCAM, the code name adopted by the Federal Bureau of Investigation in relation to undercover "sting" done from the FBI's office in New York, under the supervision of agent John Good.[9]

The theme of the "sting" centered on wealthy Arab interests who had vast amounts of disposable cash available for business opportunities in the United States. Multiple politicians were caught on camera accepted cash in exchange for their help. As the result of the sting operation, a number of prominent politician were criminal charged in federal court for bribery and related offenses. A number of motions were filed by these defendants seeking the dismal of the charges on the basis of entrapment and violations of their due process rights. For instance, they asserted that the "government did not infiltrate or uncover ongoing criminal activity, but instead created such activity; that the government offered overwhelming inducements" to the defendants and that that the techniques employed by the government were "outrageous."[10] Needless to say, the court did not agree and the defendants were convicted. In support of its decisions, the court noted that several Congressmen were captured on videotape accepting money in relation to their official conduct as public servants. The other defendants were found guilty of aiding and abetting in the bribery and "none of the defendants was a "deprived" citizen. All of them occupied honored, well-rewarded, and highly respected positions in our society."[11]

Nickole Nichols v. Indiana involves exotic dancer at a strip club and whether an undercover police officer who offered the dancer money in exchange for certain sexual acts was guilty of entrapment.

NICKOLE NICHOLS V. INDIANA
31 N.E.3D 1038 (IND. APP. 2015)

Nickole Nichols was arrested for prostitution after she agreed to have sex in exchange for money with an undercover detective outside of a strip club. At trial, she raised the affirmative defense of entrapment.

On April 6, 2013, Detective Henry Castor went to the Classy Chassy strip club in Indianapolis as part of an undercover operation. He was dressed in plain clothes and was tasked with determining whether any illegal acts, such as prostitution or drug use, were occurring in the establishment.

After Detective Castor entered the strip club, Nichols approached him, and they engaged in casual conversation. Detective Castor asked

Nichols what private dances were available in the club, and she told him that there was a room where a patron could pay $20 per song for "one on one" time with a dancer. The room itself was open, and multiple dancers used the room at once. Nichols also told Detective Castor that there was a VIP room where a patron could pay $150 to be alone with a dancer for thirty minutes. Detective Castor asked if he could get a "hand job" or get anything "extra ... besides just what would be considered a dance" if he went into the VIP room. Nichols responded "yes," and the two went to the VIP room.

In the VIP room, Nichols began to dance, and Detective Castor asked, "could there be more like sex" and Nichols said "yeah." Detective Castor asked, "Well, what about outside of the establishment?" and Nichols agreed that she would have sex with Detective Castor outside of the establishment for an additional $50.

Shortly thereafter, Detective Castor left the club. There were several undercover officers at the club that night, and after Detective Castor left, other officers entered with a warrant and arrested several people, including Nichols.

Indiana Code § 35–41–3–9 defines entrapment as:

> [a] defense that:
>
> > (1) the prohibited conduct of the person was the product of a law enforcement officer, or his agent, using persuasion or other means likely to cause the person to engage in the conduct; and
> >
> > (2) the person was not predisposed to commit the offense.

Conduct merely affording a person an opportunity to commit the offense does not constitution entrapment. Once a defendant indicates that she intends to rely on the defense of entrapment and establishes police inducement, the burden shifts to the State to rebut the inducement element, or demonstrate the defendant's predisposition to commit the crime.

To rebut the first element of the entrapment defense, inducement, the State must prove police efforts did not produce the defendant's prohibited conduct because those efforts lacked a persuasive or other force.

Detective Castor's was the first to mention sexual conduct. In addition, he was already in the process of exchanging money with Nichols for a legitimate business purpose when he mentioned the sexual conduct. However, we do not find that his policing efforts produced Nichols' criminal conduct. Detective Castor merely asked Nichols questions and "did not exert a persuasive or other force" over her. Nichols readily responded "yeah," both when Detective Castor asked if "fondling" and sex were a possibility. Then, when Detective Castor asked if they could have sex outside of the establishment, Nichols readily proposed a price for that activity. Accordingly, we conclude that Detective Castor merely afforded Nichols an opportunity to commit the offense, which does not constitute entrapment.

Because we determine that Detective Castor did not induce Nichols' conduct, we need not address her arguments regarding her predisposition. The State produced sufficient evidence to rebut Nichols' entrapment defense and, thus, we conclude that the trial court did not err in denying Nichols' motion to dismiss.

SECTION 4.3
POLICE INVESTIGATION

Most crimes require the police to conduct an investigation in order to ascertain the identity of the perpetrator. This process requires the police to examine the crime scene, and to question witnesses.

While justice demands that the culprit be apprehended, the government must not violate the constitutional rights of the suspect in their zest to solve the crime. Over the years, the police have developed a number of tools and procedures to help identify the criminal. Suspects will be questioned and search warrants will be issued. Several of these police methods are discussed in the following sections.

SECTION 4.4
THE POLYGRAPH

The police will frequently ask suspects and complainants to submit to a **polygraph** or "lie detector" examination. No one can be forced to take the test, and the results are generally not admissible in court since the polygraph is subject to error.

The machine itself fits into a small case and consists of devices to measure skin temperature, blood pressure, and respiration. The person to be tested is told of the questions that will be asked in advance of the examination. The test is then administered with the questions being repeated and the responses recorded on graph paper.

The scientific community remains divided over the accuracy of the lie detector. The advocates of the test praise the machine's ability to detect deception with an accuracy rate of at least 85%. The critics of the polygraph place the accuracy of the test at less than 50%. For the most part, state and federal courts continue to question the validity of the polygraph, and the results of the test are not admitted into court as accurate scientific evidence.

In **United States v. Scheffer,** the Supreme Court was asked to decide whether an individual who had passed a polygraph examination concerning his use of drugs but had tested positive on his urine analysis could use the test results of the lie detector in the defense of his case. In excluding the polygraph evidence, the Court reconfirmed the inadmissibility of the test results because of the lack of uniform scientific opinion concerning the validity of the test.

UNITED STATES OF AMERICA v. EDWARD SCHEFFER
118 S. CT. 1261 (1999)

In March 1992, Edward Scheffer volunteered to work as an informant on drug investigations for the Air Force Office of Special Investigations (OSI). In early April, one of the OSI agents supervising respondent requested that he submit to a urine test. Shortly after providing the urine sample, but before the results of the test were known, respondent agreed to take a polygraph test administered by an OSI examiner. In the opinion of the examiner, the test "indicated no deception" when respondent denied using drugs since joining the Air Force.

On April 30, Scheffer was absent without leave until May 13, when an Iowa State patrolman arrested him following a routine traffic stop and held him for return to the base. OSI agents later learned that respondent's urinalysis revealed the presence of methamphetamine.

Scheffer was tried by general court-martial on charges of using methamphetamine.

Scheffer sought to introduce the polygraph evidence in support of his testimony that he did not knowingly use drugs. The military judge denied the motion, relying on **Military Rule of Evidence 707**, which provides, in relevant part:

> (a) Notwithstanding any other provision of law, the results of a polygraph examination, the opinion of a polygraph examiner, or any reference to an offer to take, failure to take, or taking of a polygraph examination, shall not be admitted into evidence.

A defendant's right to present relevant evidence is not unlimited, but rather is subject to reasonable restrictions. A defendant's interest in presenting such evidence may thus bow to accommodate other legitimate interests in the criminal trial process.

Rule 707 serves several legitimate interests in the criminal trial process. These interests include ensuring that only reliable evidence is introduced at trial, preserving the jury's role in determining credibility, and avoiding litigation that is collateral to the primary purpose of the trial.

The contentions of Scheffer notwithstanding, there is simply no consensus that polygraph evidence is reliable. To this day, the scientific community remains extremely polarized about the reliability of polygraph techniques. Some studies have concluded that polygraph tests overall are accurate and reliable. See, e.g., S. Abrams, *The Complete Polygraph Handbook* 190-191 (1968) (reporting the overall accuracy rate from laboratory studies involving the common "control question technique" polygraph to be "in the range of 87 percent"). Others have found that polygraph tests assess truthfulness significantly less accurately and that scientific field studies suggest the accuracy rate of the "control question technique" polygraph is "little better than could be obtained by the toss of a coin," that is, 50 percent. See Iacono & Lykken, *The Scientific Status of Research on Polygraph Techniques: The Case Against Polygraph Tests*, in 1 Modern Scientific Evidence, supra, § 14-5.3, p. 629.

The approach taken by the President in adopting **Rule 707**–excluding polygraph evidence in all military trials–is a rational and proportional means of advancing the legitimate interest in barring unreliable evidence. Although the degree of reliability of polygraph evidence may depend upon a variety of identifiable factors, there is simply no way to know in a particular case whether a polygraph examiner's conclusion is accurate, because certain doubts and uncertainties plague even the best polygraph exams. Individual jurisdictions therefore may reasonably reach differing conclusions as to whether polygraph evidence should be admitted. We cannot say, then, that presented with such widespread uncertainty, the President acted arbitrarily or disproportionately in promulgating a rule excluding all polygraph evidence.

For the foregoing reasons, Military Rule of Evidence 707 does not unconstitutionally abridge the right to present a defense. The judgment of the Court of Appeals is reversed.

SECTION 4.5 **QUESTIONING** **OF A SUSPECT**	Nearly everyone has seen a movie or television show in which a police officer reads a suspect his rights as the person is being handcuffed. Is this something that has been added to the film for drama or is a law enforcement agent really mandated to tell the suspect that he has the right to remain silent? **Custodial interrogation** by the police is considered inherently coercive so the Supreme Court has mandated specific

procedures to be followed in obtaining statements. More specifically, the Fifth Amendment provides that no person may be compelled to be a witness against himself. This fundamental guarantee is the basic cornerstone for the **Miranda Warnings.** If a person is the subject of custodial interrogation, the police must inform the suspect that he or she has the right to remain silent, that anything said can and will be used against the individual in court, and the accused has the right to have a lawyer present during the questioning. If the accused cannot afford counsel, the government will supply an attorney for free.

Custodial interrogation has been defined as "questioning initiated by law enforcement officers after a person has been taken into custody or otherwise deprived of his or her freedom of action in any significant way." Custody is much broader than being incarcerated for purposes of the Miranda Warnings. A suspect must be told of his right to remain silent if his freedom of movement or liberty is significantly restricted. In practical terms, the issue is whether the suspect is free to walk away from the interrogation. If not, the suspect must be read his rights. For example, a suspect is considered in custody while in the back of a police car or while in bed and surrounded by the police. Interrogation, on the other hand, involves more than merely asking the suspect questions about routine information such as the person's name and address. The questions must focus on the crime to trigger the reading of the warnings.

How broad is the Fifth Amendment right against self-incrimination? The courts have ruled that this guarantee does not protect an individual from being fingerprinted or photographed, since these procedures are not testimony.

Do the results of a breathalyzer for suspicion of driving under the influence of alcohol violate the driver's Fifth Amendment right? The United Supreme Court has expressly stated that a defendant does not have a constitutional right to refuse blood tests. While blood test evidence may be incriminating, this evidence does not implicate an accused's testimonial capacities and its admission does not violate the privilege against self-incrimination embodied in the Fifth Amendment. After all, the Fifth Amendment privilege relates to testimony or communication from an accused. It does not prevent the police from using the accused's blood as physical evidence when it is relevant.[12]

Commonwealth of Pennsylvania v. Foster provides an application of this doctrine.

COMMONWEALTH OF PENNSYLVANIA V. SAMUEL FOSTER
2016 WL 104528 (PA. SUPER. 2016)

Samuel Foster appeals from the judgment of sentence imposed in this road-rage incident after the trial court found him guilty of driving under the influence ("DUI").

Trooper Gibson was uniformed and on duty while operating a marked State Police vehicle in a southbound direction on the Media bypass. At the trooper's vantage point, he observed a white Chevy minivan proceeding southbound when it drove off the roadway and onto the left hand berm. Believing the minivan had just crashed, he activated his vehicle's overhead emergency lights and siren and drove to where the white vehicle was located. Immediately behind the minivan was a black truck, also on the left shoulder of the road. Upon his arrival at the scene, the Trooper exited his vehicle and heard shouting voices as he proceeded around the back of the truck. After rounding the truck, he saw Appellant exiting his truck shouting at the driver of the minivan, who was also out of his vehicle.

The Trooper saw Appellant reaching into Appellant's right rear pants pocket with his right hand while advancing towards the minivan driver. The Trooper believed that if he did not intercede a physical assault was imminent. All the while the Trooper was repeating orders for the two men to disengage, which went ignored. The Trooper had to finally draw his weapon to get the two drivers to comply, and get down on the ground before the Trooper hand cuffed both men.

While Appellant was informing the trooper of how the minivan driver was driving, the trooper noticed a strong odor of alcohol emanating from Appellant's breath. The Trooper also noticed that Appellant's speech was slurred, and while standing unrestrained Appellant was swaying with unsure footing.

After failing the field tests, Appellant was offered a portable breath test, which Appellant consented to and performed the test as instructed. The test results indicated he was over the limit.

Thereafter, Appellant was placed under arrest.

Pennsylvania courts have long recognized that police are justified in investigating a situation, so long as the police officer reasonably believe that criminal activity is afoot. When Trooper Gibson smelled a strong odor of alcohol on Appellant's breath, observed Appellant's slurred speech and unsure footing, there is no question that he had sufficient probable cause to believe Appellant was operating his vehicle under the influence of alcohol.

As a condition of maintaining a driver's license in Pennsylvania, all drivers are subject to the implied consent requirements of the Motor Vehicle Code and must submit to blood and breath tests under appropriate circumstances. Where an officer has reasonable grounds to believe that a motorist is driving while under the influence of alcohol, the driver may properly be requested to submit to a chemical test of blood, breath or urine to determine the alcoholic content of the blood. The Fifth Amendment privilege against self-incrimination [does not] prevent the Commonwealth from requiring a driver to submit to a breathalyzer test.

In the instant case Trooper Gibson had reasonable suspicion that Appellant was operating his vehicle while under the influence, accordingly, his request for field sobriety tests, breathalyzer test and blood analysis were appropriate as a matter of law. Further, in addition to the implied consent to submit to testing, Appellant freely gave actual consent to submit to the requested tests.

Accordingly, all the test results were properly admissible.

SECTION 4.6
COMMONWEALTH
v. CHRISTOPHER

PROBLEM FOUR

PARK, BROWN & SMITH, P.C.
ATTORNEYS AT LAW
MEMORANDUM

To: All Students

FROM: Peter Smith, Esquire

RE: Commonwealth v. Peter Christopher
In Court Identification

Kathy Roberts often stayed after school to workout. The wrestling team was usually there practicing but they were away at a match on the evening in question.

Kathy was so busy exercising that she didn't notice the presence of a stranger—at least not until it was too late. Kathy first realized that she wasn't alone when she looked up and saw what appeared to be a shark staring back at her. When she looked again, she realized it was a man with a tattoo of a shark on his left shoulder. The strange thing was that he was wearing a ski mask. Before she had time to realize what was happening, she was assaulted and her pocketbook was stolen.

Afterward, Kathy was extremely troubled by the incident. She could not stop thinking about the tattoo, since she knew she had seen the image before. To her shock and amazement, Kathy soon realized that she knew her assailant. It was her next door neighbor, Peter Christopher. He had a tattoo of a shark on his shoulder, and he intensely disliked the family.

Ms. Roberts reported her suspicions to the police and their investigation lead to the arrest of Peter Christopher on a variety of criminal charges. During the second day of trial, the District Attorney requested Peter Christopher to stand before the jury and remove his shirt so the panel could ascertain whether the defendant had a tattoo of a shark on his shoulder. The defense vigorously objected to this in-court identification, claiming that it would violate Christopher's Fifth Amendment rights against self-incrimination. The issue before the court concerns these identifying marks on the defendant's shoulder. The Fifth Amendment guarantees that no person shall be compelled to testify against himself. According to **Morgan v. State**, can the District Attorney compel Christopher to remove his shirt to show the jury his shoulder? Why would this type of in-court identification violate (or not violate) the Constitution?

GLENMORE MORGAN V. STATE OF MARYLAND
558 A.2D 1226 (MD. APP. 1989)

We are called upon to decide whether requiring a defendant to don an article of clothing in the courtroom in front of the jury so that the jury may see if the article of clothing fits violates his privilege against self-incrimination under the 5th Amendment.

In the case before us, Glenmore Morgan, defendant, was charged with possession of cocaine with intent to distribute, possession of cocaine and possession of controlled paraphernalia. During a jury trial, the court required the defendant to put on a jacket seized by officers of the Montgomery County Police Department pursuant to a search warrant.

At the time the search warrant was executed, defendant and two other men were present in the living room of the residence. After the two other men retrieved their coats, Morgan queried, "What about my jacket?" When asked by the police if a jacket located on the loveseat in the living room was his, Morgan hesitated before responding, "No." Police search of the jacket revealed a small quantity of cocaine, a beeper, keys to the residence and a key to a safe in the kitchen. During a search of the safe, the police discovered bottles of inositol powder, several baggies, razor blades, measuring spoons, a box containing a grinder, and twenty-three grams of cocaine. Morgan was convicted on all charges.

The Fifth Amendment of the United States Constitution provides: "No person... shall be compelled in any criminal case to be a witness against himself." Defendant contends that the court's order requiring him to put on the jacket in front of the jury violated his constitutional right against compelled self-incrimination.

The Court of Appeals in **Andrews v. State** upheld a trial court order restraining Andrews from shaving his head or facial hair until the conclusion of this trial. Purportedly, he had changed his appearance immediately after the crime in question by shaving his head and beard. The trial court order was designed to prevent the defendant from defeating "legitimate avenues of identification" by disguising his appearance.

In **Schmerber v. California, 384 U.S. 757 (1966)**, the Supreme Court stated that the privilege against compelled self-incrimination "protects an accused only from being compelled to testify against himself or otherwise provide the State with evidence of a testimonial or communicative nature..." Requiring a defendant to put on an article of clothing, simply does not constitute an act compelling a testimonial or communicative response. The fact that an article of clothing fits may give rise to a inference of ownership, which under the facts of any given case could be incrimination, is not a communicative response from the defendant.

By granting the prosecutor 's request to order the defendant to don the coat in the presence of the jury, the trial court compelled the defendant to disclose nothing of his personal knowledge. This is not communication within the meaning of the Fifth Amendment. Moreover, it is of no consequence that the defendant declined to take the stand to testify on his own behalf; his physical display simply does not constitute "testimony."

In this case, the trial court order requiring defendant to don a coat, which admittedly contained incriminatory evidence, to determine whether it fit him did not constitute a compulsion to elicit communicative or testimonial evidence from the defendant.

Judgment affirmed.

**ANSWER SHEET
PROBLEM FOUR**

Name   **Please Print Clearly**

1. According to **Morgan v. State,** can the District Attorney compel Christopher to remove his shirt to show the jury his tattoo? Explain your answer.

2. Why would this type of in court identification violate or not violate Christopher's constitutional rights? Explain your answer.

_____

_____

_____

_____

_____

_____

_____

_____

_____

_____

_____

_____

_____

_____

_____

_____

_____

_____

_____

_____

_____

SECTION 4.7
SEARCH AND SEIZURE

Roy Caballes' car was stopped by the police for a traffic violation. A drug-detecting dog was then walked around the vehicle while another officer wrote the traffic ticket. The canine soon became agitated alerting the police to the presence of drugs. A search of the car's trunk yielded several hundred pounds of marijuana. Is there anything wrong with allowing a police dog to randomly walk around a person's car? The court found that the canine sniff was an illegal search and seizure. What exactly is a search and seizure?

The **Fourth Amendment** prohibits unlawful **search and seizure** and requires that all warrants be issued upon probable cause. This protection against overzealous police conduct usually requires a police officer to appear before a judge to establish probable cause for the issuance of a search warrant. Probable cause, however, is not defined in the Constitution. Over the years, the courts have determined probable cause to exist when the information on which the warrant is based is such that a reasonable person would believe that what is being sought will be found in the location to be examined. The judge, however, may consider the opinion of an experienced law enforcement officer in making the probable cause determination for a search warrant. An affidavit based on mere suspicion, or stating a conclusion with no supporting facts, however, is insufficient. If the court is satisfied that sufficient evidence exists to issue a warrant, that document must be specific as to the location and evidence that is the subject of the search warrant.

The general test to determine whether a warrant is needed by the police to conduct a lawful search and seizure is to ascertain whether the person had a reasonable expectation of privacy. If the individual enjoyed a reasonable expectation of privacy, a warrant must be obtained before the search can be undertaken. For example, a person has an expectation of privacy while at home, but the police would not need a warrant to seize a gun that a person is brandishing while walking down the street.

The police may also seize property that has been discarded or abandoned by a person since there is no longer an expectation of privacy.

Police generally need to obtain a **search warrant** when there is a reasonable expectation of privacy. There are, however, a number of exceptions to this rule. The police are not required to obtain a search warrant in the following situations:

1. **Plain View:** If the subject of the search is readily observable, in other words, in plain view, there is no reasonable expectation of privacy. For instance, if marijuana is growing in one's backyard and is visible from the sidewalk, the police do not need a search warrant to seize the plants. An improper search, however, will occur

if the police peer into a basement window, and with the aid of a flashlight uncover contraband, since the homeowner would have a reasonable expectation of privacy against this type of intrusion.

2. **Emergency:** If the time delay in obtaining the warrant will defeat the ends of justice, the police can engage in the search without the warrant. Car searches generally fall within this exception since vehicles are mobile and can avoid the police by merely being driven away. The police, however, must still have probable cause for the search. If the vehicle is towed to the police station and impounded, a search warrant will have to be obtained in order to conduct a lawful search since the vehicle is no longer mobile. The emergency situation would no longer be present, since the car would be in the possession of the authorities.

3. **Search Incident to an Arrest:** Police officers can search a defendant and the area within that person's immediate reach for weapons and other contraband. This exception was established to protect the public from possible harm.

4. **Hot Pursuit:** If the police are pursuing a suspect who is fleeing the scene of a crime, they may make a reasonable search of the area looking for the suspect.

5. **Consent:** The police are not required to obtain a search warrant when a suspect consents to a search. The consent, however, must be freely and voluntarily given, and not be coerced by law enforcement officials. Certain third parties may also consent to a search. For instance, parents may allow the police to search a child's room, and a school principal is authorized to allow the police to search student lockers at the educational institution. While a roommate may allow the police to search the common areas in an apartment, a landlord does not have the authority to allow the police to search the leased premises without a search warrant.

6. **Search Incident to a General Police Measure:** Border and custom searches are allowed to prevent the entry of illegal aliens and contraband. Custom agents can check everyone's luggage regardless of the existence of probable cause. Other examples include searches of passengers at the airport, and individuals can be required to pass through a metal detector before being allowed to enter a courtroom. Both of these measures are designed to protect the safety of the public. The police, however, may not selectively discriminate against a particular racial group under the auspices of conducting a search incident to a general police measure. For example, the police may not stop young African-American males on the New Jersey Turnpike merely because the individual may match a racial profile.

7. **Stop and Frisk:** Police officers may conduct "pat-down" searches when there is probable cause to believe that a crime is about to occur and the suspect may possess a weapon. If the police find contraband during the "pat-down" that is instantly recognizable by feel, it may be seized without a warrant. This seizure is called **plain feel**. This exception has the potential for abuse, so courts generally require that the officers present very specific facts that lead to a conclusion of probable cause.

DAVID RILEY V. CALIFORNIA
134 S. CT. 2473 (2014)

David Riley was stopped by a police officer for driving with expired registration tags. In the course of the stop, the officer learned that Riley's license had been suspended. The officer impounded Riley's car, and another officer conducted an inventory search of the car. Riley was arrested for possession of concealed and loaded firearms when that search turned up two handguns under the car's hood.

An officer searched Riley incident to the arrest and found items associated with the "Bloods" street gang. He also seized a cell phone from Riley's pants pocket. The phone was a "smart phone," a cell phone with a broad range of other functions based on advanced computing capability, large storage capacity, and Internet connectivity. The officer accessed information on the phone and noticed that some words were preceded by the letters "CK"—a label that, he believed, stood for "Crip Killers," a slang term for members of the Bloods gang.

At the police station, a detective specializing in gangs further examined the contents of the phone. The detective testified that he "went through" Riley's phone "looking for evidence, because ... gang members will often video themselves with guns or take pictures of themselves with the guns. The police found photographs of Riley standing in front of a car they suspected had been involved in a shooting a few weeks earlier.

Riley was ultimately charged, in connection with that earlier shooting. The State alleged that Riley had committed those crimes for the benefit of a criminal street gang. Prior to trial, Riley moved to suppress all evidence that the police had obtained from his cell phone. He contended that the searches of his phone violated the Fourth Amendment, because they had been performed without a warrant and were not otherwise justified by exigent circumstances.

The Fourth Amendment provides: "The right of the people to be secure in their persons, houses, papers, and effects, against unreasonable searches and seizures, shall not be violated, and no Warrants shall issue, but upon probable cause, supported by Oath or affirmation, and particularly describing the place to be searched, and the persons or things to be seized." As the text makes clear, the ultimate touchstone of the Fourth Amendment is reasonableness. Our cases have determined that where a search is undertaken by law enforcement officials to discover evidence of criminal wrongdoing, reasonableness generally requires the obtaining of a judicial warrant.

The case before us concerns the reasonableness of a warrantless search incident to a lawful arrest. It has been well accepted that such a search constitutes an exception to the warrant requirement. Indeed, the label "exception" is something of a misnomer in this context, as warrantless searches incident to arrest occur with far greater frequency than searches conducted pursuant to a warrant.

When an arrest is made, it is reasonable for the arresting officer to search the person arrested in order to remove any weapons that the latter might seek to use in order to resist arrest or effect his escape. Otherwise, the officer's safety might well be endangered, and the arrest itself frustrated. In addition, it is entirely reasonable for the arresting officer to search for and seize any evidence on the arrestee's person in order to prevent its concealment or destruction.

This case requires us to decide how the search incident to arrest doctrine applies to modern cell phones, which are now such a pervasive and insistent part of daily life. A smart phone of the sort taken from Riley was unheard of ten years ago; a significant majority of American adults now own such phones.

[Searches incident to an arrest are generally allowed to] protect the officers and destruction of evidence. There are no comparable risks when the search is of digital data. In addition, cell phones place vast quantities of personal information literally in the hands of individuals. We therefore decline to extend [the law of a search incident to an arrest] to searches of data on cell phones, and hold instead that officers must generally secure a warrant before conducting such a search.

Digital data stored on a cell phone cannot itself be used as a weapon to harm an arresting

officer or to effectuate the arrestee's escape. Law enforcement officers remain free to examine the physical aspects of a phone to ensure that it will not be used as a weapon—say, to determine whether there is a razor. The term "cell phone" is itself misleading; many of these devices are in fact minicomputers that also happen to have the capacity to be used as a telephone. They could just as easily be called cameras, video players, rolodexes, calendars, tape recorders, libraries, diaries, albums, televisions, maps, or newspapers.

One of the most notable distinguishing features of modern cell phones is their immense storage capacity. The storage capacity of cell phones has several interrelated consequences for privacy. First, a cell phone collects in one place many distinct types of information—an address, a note, a prescription, a bank statement, a video—that reveal much more in combination than any isolated record. Second, a cell phone's capacity allows even just one type of information to convey far more than previously possible. The sum of an individual's private life can be reconstructed through a thousand photographs labeled with dates, locations, and descriptions; the same cannot be said of a photograph or two of loved ones tucked into a wallet.

The United States concedes that the search incident to arrest exception may not be stretched to cover a search of files accessed remotely—that is, a search of files stored in the cloud. Such a search would be like finding a key in a suspect's pocket and arguing that it allowed law enforcement to unlock and search a house. But officers searching a phone's data would not typically know whether the information they are viewing was stored locally at the time of the arrest or has been pulled from the cloud.

Our answer to the question of what police must do before searching a cell phone seized incident to an arrest is accordingly simple—get a warrant.

To deter the police from pursuing illegally obtained evidence within the ambit of the Fourth Amendment, the court has implemented an **"exclusionary rule."** This prophylactic measure prohibits the use of any fruits of an illegal search to be used by the government in court. If, however, the police have a reasonable and good faith belief that they were acting within the law pursuant to a search warrant butd a court subsequently determines that the warrant was defective, the illegally obtained evidence by the police will still be admissible in court.

The first application of this rule occurred in **Herring v. United States** when the Supreme Court ruled that a honest mistake by the police resulting in an unlawful search, instead of a systemic error or reckless disregard of constitutional requirements, will not bar the use of the evidence at trial. The following case provides an example of this exception as it applies to a search of the cell phone of a drug dealer which revealed inappropriate pictures of a young girl.

United States of America v. Ernest Taylor
2016 WL 633890 (D. OR. 2016)

Ernest Taylor is charged with using a minor to produce visual depictions of sexually explicit conduct. Defendant now moves to suppress photos and videos found during a search of his cell phone.

Police Officer Newell investigated Defendant on suspicion that he was manufacturing and delivering psilocybin mushrooms. An anonymous informant told Newell that Defendant was growing psilocybin mushrooms in a storage shed in Central Point, Oregon. In January 2014, an officer arranged a buy of marijuana from Defendant at Defendant's house. The buyer purchased marijuana from Defendant, and said that Defendant had a grocery bag of loose marijuana in his house.

Newell prepared an affidavit for a search warrant stating that Defendant was growing psilocybin mushrooms in the storage unit, transporting the psilocybin mushrooms to his house and delivering them to customers.

Newell stated that based on her experience and training, drug dealers often keep records of their transactions with customers. Newell sought a warrant to search for evidence of possession and manufacture of psilocybin mushrooms and marijuana. Included among the items to be seized were "Recipes," "Drug Records," and "Cell Phones."

On February 18, 2014, officers executed the search warrant at Defendant's residence. Among the items seized was a cell phone. The police examined the contents of Defendant's cell phone and discovered eighteen images of a prepubescent girl partially undressed. Several images showed an adult male touching the girl and pulling down her top.

The Fourth Amendment provides that "no warrants shall issue, but upon probable cause, supported by Oath or affirmation, and particularly describing the place to be searched, and the persons or things to be seized." To comply with the Fourth Amendment, a search warrant must describe the place to be searched and things to be seized with particularity, and there must be probable cause to seize the things specified in the warrant.

Defendant contends that the search warrant did not show a sufficient connection between the cell phone and the crimes of drug manufacturing and dealing. Defendant also contends that the search of the contents of his cell phone was beyond the scope of the warrant.

As the Supreme Court has noted, "modem cell phones ... are now such a pervasive and insistent part of daily life that the proverbial visitor from Mars might conclude they were an important feature of human anatomy." Because cell phones have become so common, and so powerful, able to record, store, and potentially reveal every aspect of a person's life, courts must now confront Fourth Amendment issues that would have been difficult to imagine only ten years ago.

The exclusionary rule prohibits the government from using illegally seized evidence against the victim of the unlawful search. There is a good faith exception to the exclusionary rule, however, for searches "conducted in good faith reliance upon an objectively reasonable search warrant." I con-clude that the good faith exception applies to the search and seizure here.

Defendant argues that Newell's affidavit "provided no information regarding drug dealing activities and a cell phone." The [search warrant] affidavit did establish probable cause that Defendant was manufacturing and distributing psilocybin mushrooms and marijuana. A reasonable officer could conclude there was at least a "fair probability" that a cell phone belonging to Defendant would contain evidence of his drug manufacturing or transactions. It is reasonable to believe that a drug dealer might have records of transactions on his cell phone. I conclude that no "'reasonably well trained officer would have known that the search was illegal in light of all the circumstances.'"

While searching Defendant's cell phone for evidence of drug dealing, the officer inadvertently encountered evidence of child abuse and child pornography. I agree with the government that the doctrine of plain view applies here. For the plain view doctrine to apply, "(1) the officer must be lawfully in the place where the seized item was in plain view; (2) the item's incriminating nature was 'immediately apparent'; and (3) the officer had a 'lawful right of access to the object itself.'" Because the good faith exception applies to the search of Defendant's cell phone, the motion to suppress is denied.

SECTION 4.8
CRIMINAL TRIAL

Once the defendant is arrested, he or she will be brought before a judge for a **Preliminary Arraignment**. This is usually done within six hours of the person's arrest at which time the suspect is informed of the charges, a decision will be made about whether to grant **bail** and the date for a **Preliminary Hearing** will be set. The police or district attorney makes the sole determination about whether to arrest a person but that does not mean that there is sufficient evidence to warrant the defendant going to trial on the charges. The idea behind a Preliminary Hearing is for a judge to decide early on in a criminal prosecution if there is enough evidence to warrant the defendant proceeding to trial. If the government cannot make out a prima facie case at this time, the charges will be dismissed. If the evidence satisfies the court that the suspect may have committed the crime, the case will proceed to trial.

The Constitution guarantees that the defendant has the right to a speedy trial so the government cannot permit the suspect to languish in jail by failing to call the case to trial because of the possibility of a not guilty verdict. A constitutional violation of the speedy trial rule is usually done on a case by case basis and the defendant must convince the court that he or she has been prejudiced by the lengthy delay. Some states, such as Pennsylvania, use a fixed time table for an unreasonable delay such as a one year period. If the defendant has not been brought to trial within one year of the arrest or indictment though no fault of his own, the court can dismiss the charges.

At the completion of a criminal trial, the fact finder may return with a variety of verdicts, including: **(1)** Not guilty; **(2)** Guilty; **(3)** Not guilty by reason of insanity; and **(4)** Guilty but Insane.

The verdicts of **not guilty** and **guilty** are easy to understand. If the defendant is found innocent, the case is over and the accused may not be prosecuted again for the same crime.

This result is mandated by the **double jeopardy** clause contained in the Fifth Amendment which provides: "nor shall any person be subject for the same offense to be twice put in jeopardy of life or limb." This concept is such a basic tenant of civilized law whose origins can be traced back to the ancient Roman Empire where it was proclaimed that the "governor should not permit the same person to be again accused of a crime of which he has already been acquitted."

The premise of the double jeopardy is to protect people against three distinct risks: (1) a second prosecution for the same offense after acquittal, (2) a second prosecution for the same offense after conviction, and (3) multiple punishments for the same offense.

As the reader may remember from Chapter Two, it is not a violation of the double jeopardy clause if both criminal charges and a civil lawsuit are brought against a person for the same event. On rare occasions, a person may even be prosecuted in both federal and state courts for the same act based on the logic that the state and federal governments are separate sovereigns.

The idea of a defendant being found insane in response to a crime is not a novel idea. It was first introduced in England during the late 1800's and it continues to be a viable verdict. The fact finder is the ultimate judge of a person's mental capacity, and if the jury is convinced that the defendant was mentally ill at the time of the commission of the crime, they may return with a verdict of **not guilty by reason of insanity** or **guilty but mentally ill.** A person will be found not guilty by reason of insanity if he or she does not know the difference between right and wrong because of a defective thought process caused by mental illness. If a jury concludes that a person is insane at the time of the crime, the defendant will be sent to a mental institution instead of prison. Once the individual regains his sanity, he will be released from the mental facility.

Guilty but mentally ill offers the jury an "in-between" verdict. The defendant is still responsible for his criminal conduct, but is provided treatment for the mental illness. Only a minority number of states have adopted this approach including Pennsylvania and Delaware. Juries who determine that the accused suffered from a psychiatric disorder that left him with insufficient willpower to choose whether to commit the act or refrain from doing it, may return with a verdict of guilty but mentally ill.

The distinction between "not guilty by reason of insanity" and "guilty but mentally ill" lies in the degree of mental illness. The verdict of not guilty by reason of insanity reflects a finding that the defendant is so mentally impaired that he lacks the ability to appreciate the wrong-fulness of his criminal conduct. A person who is guilty but mentally ill appreciates the inappropriateness of his conduct but due to a psychiatric disorder, lacks sufficient willpower to choose whether to do a particular act or refrain from doing it.

Perhaps the reader may remember John DuPont and his killing of an Olympic wrestler who trained at the DuPont estate. The accused admitted that he shot the athlete but claimed that he was insane at the time. The defendant introduced evidence to show that his paranoia resulted in his installing razor wire in the walls to prevent people from hiding there, and he had excavators dig on his property in search of underground tunnels that he thought led to his home. On the day of the incident, DuPont walked up to the wrestler, asked the athlete if he had a problem with the defendant, and then shot the man three times with a .44 Magnum revolver. The jury found that the multimillionaire suffered from a mental disease process but it was not severe enough to prevent DuPont from understanding the difference between right and wrong. He was found guilty but mentally ill and sentenced to thirteen to thirty years in jail.

If the defendant is found not guilty, the case is concluded. The government can generally not appeal an adverse determination because of the concept of double jeopardy. If the defendant is found guilty, however, the case proceeds to the sentencing phase of the trial which phase rarely takes place immediately following conviction.

There is usually a short delay to allow counsel to file post-trial motions and for the court to conduct a background check on the defendant. Rarely, does the jury participate in the sentencing aspect of the trial except in capital murder convictions.

The idea of punishment for a crime is not novel and can be traced back to historical times. Most people are aware of the biblical reference by Matthew of "an eye for an eye and a tooth for a tooth." This quote is often used as the justification for retribution against a criminal which punishment is also thought to be a deterrent. That famous quote, however, is not the only reference in the bible for punishment. For instance, the bible also states that "he that killeth any man shall surely be put to death" or "he that killeth a beast shall make it good; beast for beast."

The Bureaus of Justice Statistics estimates that nearly 2.2 million people are confined in prisons across the United States and this figure represents a 33-year continuous rise in the prison population which makes this country number one in the world in people that are incarcerated at any given time. In fact, 1 out of every 136 people in this country is incarcerated despite a falling crime rate.[15]

Judges have a degree of discretion in the types and lengths of sentences that may be imposed in order for the penalty to fit the crime.

Punishment can range from incarceration to non-reporting probation or community service. Jail time remains the most frequent penalty with 72% of defendants being incarcerated for serious felonies while 25% receive probations.[16]

Prison sentences are usually indeterminate with a minimum and maximum term of incarceration. For instance, a defendant will be sentenced to five to ten years in a state penitentiary. This range allows the prisoner to be paroled after the minimum time period if he has been a model prisoner and has shown evidence of rehabilitation.

Mandatory sentencing is the legislature's attempt to take away the sentencing decision from the judge so that people who commit certain types of crimes will be treated the same. For example, committing a crime with a gun, selling drugs within a school zone, and the commission of three separate felonies will result in the imposition of mandatory jail time. Proponents of mandatory sentencing believe that it acts as a deterrent since it sends a clear message to criminals that they will face real prison time if they commit certain types of crimes. Not everyone, however, is sold on the idea since it removes the discretion from the judge in cases with extenuating circumstances and it does not consider the role of a particular defendant in the crime.

Judges can be creative in their sentences, and the newspapers occasionally contain stories about the more unusual punishments. For instances, novel penalties have included sex offenders being castrated, defendants having to put bumper stickers on their cars advertising their crimes, and a rap fan who was forced to listen to Wayne Newton's music for violating a sound ordinance.

Regardless of whether the penalty seems excessively harsh or whimsical, they involve the same issue. Does the punishment violate the person's constitutional rights on the basis that is it humiliating or barbaric?

The **Eighth Amendment** prohibits punishment that is cruel and unusual. This guarantee is frequently asserted by a defendant in response to a prison term that seems excessively harsh, or a penalty that seems a little too creative. The Constitution does not define what constitutes cruel and unusual punishment but is clear that the guarantee is intended to limit those entrusted with the sentencing power. Courts have interpreted the clause to mean that the penalty must be proportionate to the crime. That determination changes with evolving standards of decency but it is directed to punishments that *shock the conscious of civilized man*. The Eighth Amendment encompasses more than barbarous physical punishment. It also includes the unnecessary infliction of pain and those sentences that are grossly disproportionate to the severity of the crime.

Much litigation exists over what is and is not an appropriate sentence. Incarceration does deprive inmates of a number of life's pleasures but the courts hold that these restrictive and harsh conditions are part of the penalty that offenders must pay for their offenses against society.

Constitutional violations, however, have been found in cases of prison overcrowding, insufficient bathroom facilities, serving insect infested food, and in not supplying toothpaste, shampoo, and shaving cream.

The death penalty has had a varied course before the United States Supreme Court. Between 1930 and 1965, almost four thousand people were executed. In the 1960's, the death penalty was considered cruel and unusual punishment. About ten years later, the Supreme Court in **Furman v. Georgia** invalidated the death penalty statutes in forty states citing to the law's arbitrary nature since the jury had too much discretion in the process. Within a few years, thirty-five states reinstituted the death penalty with legislation that provided guidelines for the jury in deciding when a sentence of death is the appropriate penalty. These guidelines allow for the examination of aggravating and mitigating factors.

The death penalty was routinely carried out through the 1990's and beginning of the twenty-first century. Nevertheless, controversy continues to surround the death penalty. Amnesty International has determined that more than half of the countries in the world have abolished the death penalty and eighty percent of recent executions have taken place in the United States, China, Iran, and Vietnam.

Court decisions no longer focus on the constitutionality of the death penalty but on specific aspects of this ultimate penalty. For example, the death penalty for rape has been found unconstitutional because the sentence is disproportionate to the crime. The Supreme Court has found it improper to execute a person who is insane but it did not prohibit the killing of a mentally handicapped individual found guilty of capital murder. The court also ruled it to be unconstitutional to execute a person who was under the age of 18 at the time of committing the crime. The justices felt that the death penalty is "disproportionate punishment for juveniles."

The United States ended the twentieth century with a great deal of dissatisfaction over use of the electric chair. This controversy has now abated since lethal injection has supplanted the electric chair as the method of choice for execution. A lethal injection is administered in a variety of ways using one, two, or three drugs. The three-drug approach utilizes an anesthetic or sedative, usually followed by drug to paralyze the criminal and potassium chloride to stop the inmate's heart. The one or two-drug set-ups generally use a fatal dose of an anesthetic or sedative.[13] It is claimed that this new procedure is painless and humane.

Death row inmates, however, have started to attack lethal injection as cruel and unusual punishment. For instance, a prisoner in Tennessee challenged that state's procedure for administering the lethal dose of medicine. Apparently, Tennessee prohibits a health care professional from administering the injection and the defendant maintained that safeguards are not in place to insure that mistakes will not cause inhumane deaths. An inmate in Alabama received a stay from the Supreme Court moments before his execution in order to appeal his sentence on the basis that his execution would be unconstitutional harsh. The inmate is a former drug addict whose damaged veins make it difficult to inject him without cutting into his muscle to administer the fatal injection. Another prisoner in Indiana contended that letha was cruel and unusual because his obesity resulted in the locate a suitable vein. Regardless of the merits of these as long as the death penalty is legal in the United State be challenges to the sentence regardless of how the p carried out.

RICHARD GLOSSIP V. KEVIN GROSS
135 S. CT. 2726 (2015)

Prisoners sentenced to death in Oklahoma filed an action contending that the method of execution now used by the State violates the Eighth Amendment because it creates an unacceptable risk of severe pain. They argue that midazolam, the first drug employed in the State's current three-drug protocol, fails to render a person insensate to pain.

The death penalty was an accepted punishment at the time of the adoption of the Constitution and the Bill of Rights. In that era, death sentences were usually carried out by hanging. While methods of execution have changed over the years, this Court has never invalidated a State's chosen procedure for carrying out a sentence of death as the infliction of cruel and unusual punishment. And the Court did not retreat from that holding even when presented with a case in which a State's initial attempt to execute a prisoner by electrocution was unsuccessful. Our decisions in this area have been animated in part by the recognition some risk of pain is inherent in any method of execution, we have held that the Constitution does not require the avoidance of all risks of pain. After all, while most humans wish to die a painless death, many do not have that good fortune. Holding that the Eighth Amendment demands the elimination of essentially all risks of pain would effectively outlaw the death penalty altogether.

[Prior court cases] have cleared any legal obstacle to use of the common three-drug protocol that had enabled States to carry out the death penalty in a quick and painless fashion. But a practical obstacle soon emerged, anti-death-penalty advocates pressured pharmaceutical companies to refuse to supply the drugs used to carry out death sentences. After other efforts to procure sodium thiopental proved unsuccessful, States sought an alternative, and they eventually replaced sodium thiopental with pentobarbital, another barbiturate.

The Eighth Amendment prohibits the infliction of "cruel and unusual punishments." Prisoners cannot successfully challenge a method of execution unless they establish that the method presents a risk that [will] very likely cause serious illness and needless suffering, and give rise to sufficiently imminent dangers. To prevail on such a claim, there must be a substantial risk of serious harm, an objectively intolerable risk of harm that prevents prison officials from pleading that they were subjectively blameless for purposes of the Eighth Amendment.

Numerous courts have concluded that the use of midazolam as the first drug in a three-drug protocol is likely to render an inmate insensate to pain that might result from administration of the paralytic agent and potassium chloride. Petitioners argue that even if midazolam is powerful enough to induce unconsciousness, it is too weak to maintain unconsciousness and insensitivity to pain once the second and third drugs are administered. Midazolam is capable of placing a person at a sufficient level of unconsciousness to resist the noxious stimuli which could occur from the application of the second and third drugs. If States cannot return to any of the "more primitive" methods used in the past and if no drug that meets with the principal dissent's approval is available for use in carrying out a death sentence, the logical conclusion is clear. But we have time and again reaffirmed that capital punishment is not *per se* unconstitutional.

SECTION 4.9
ETHICS

Enron and Bernard Madoff Investment Securities are two examples of scandals that rocked the business world and resulted in criminal and civil charges, as well as raising a host of ethical issues. However, corporations are abstract entities separate and apart from their owners. They have no minds to form intentions, nor brains in which to conceive a guilty intent. They only act through the company's officers, board of director and employees. How then can these entities be criminal liable for the actions of their agents?[14] Also, how can good ethical practice reduce these types of white collar crimes?

SECTION 4.10
PROBLEM CASES

1. Three packages containing more that $500,000 fell out of the back of an armored truck. Morant, an individual walking down the street, retrieved and carried away the bags. The money was not returned immediately nor were the police notified that the money had been located. A couple of days later, the armored truck company posted a $75,000 reward, and Morant came forward with the money in order to claim the reward. Has this individual committed the crime of theft by retaining the money until a reward was posted?

2. Anthony Saduk filled a muzzleloader rifle with gun powder, cigarette butts, and paper-towel wadding. As a practical joke, he shot the gun in the direction of his roommate, but three of the cigarette butts penetrated his friend's chest causing death. Since Saduk had no intention of hurting his friend, and was merely carrying out a practical joke, did he have the necessary intent to be found guilty of any type of criminal homicide?

3. The police suspected that Gindlesperger was growing marijuana in his basement. An officer aimed a thermal detection device at the home from the street in order to measure the heat emissions coming from the defendant's house. The temperature of the home was felt to be consistent with marijuana production activities. Did the warrantless search of the house, with a thermal detection device, constitute an unlawful Search and Seizure? **Commonwealth of Pennsylvania v. Gregory Gindlesperger, 706 A.2d 1316 (Pa. Super. 1997).**

4. The police set up a road block as part of a program to interdict drunk drivers. Schavello, who was driving towards the road block, made a U-turn in order to avoid police contact. He was then stopped by the police a short distance away, and alcohol was detected on his breath. Schavello failed a field sobriety test and was arrested for driving under the influence of alcohol. Is avoiding a road block

sufficient probable cause to stop a motor vehicle when it makes a U-turn without any further suspicion by the police of illegal activity? **Commonwealth of Pennsylvania v. Schavello, 734 A.2d 386 (Pa. 1999).**

5. The manager of an apartment building was making yearly repairs and maintenance inspections. The date of these inspections were posted throughout the building. During his examination of one of the units, the manager observed drugs on the kitchen table and immediately contacted the police. The manager then led the officers into the apartment with a pass key. The police observed five plastic bags containing crack cocaine on the kitchen table. Based upon their observations, one officer left the apartment in order to obtain a search warrant. The other officer remained behind and arrested Davis when he entered the apartment. The lease agreement provided: "Landlords and anyone allowed by the landlord, may enter the leased unit after first notifying tenant." Was the entry by the police into the apartment without a search warrant legal? **Commonwealth of Pennsylvania v. Curtis Davis, 743 A.2d 946 (Pa. Super. 1999).**

6. Booth disregarded a stop sign while he was driving and collided with the car of Nancy Boehm. She was 32 weeks pregnant at the time and lost the fetus as a result of the trauma. Booth's alcohol level was .12, and he was charged with involuntary manslaughter or homicide by vehicle. The Motor Vehicle Code provides that any person who unintentionally causes the death of another individual as the result of driving under the influence of alcohol or controlled substances has committed the crime of involuntary manslaughter. Is an unborn fetus, a person for the purposes of involuntarily manslaughter? **Commonwealth of Pennsylvania v. Jeffrey Booth, 2001 WL 166998 (Pa. 2001).**

Footnotes:

1. U.S. Department of Justice –Office of Justice Programs, *Homicides Trends in the United States; Long Term Trends and patterns.*

2. "CDC: Newborns Face Highest Murder Risk," http://usgovinfo.about.com/-library/weekly/aa031202a.htm.

3. "Murder Victims-Circumstances and Weapons Used or Cause of Death," U. S. Census Bureau, Statistical Abstract of the United States: 2000, page 206.

4. Hallinan, "California Leads in Justifiable Killings, http://www.trosch.org/tro/mpr-7g30.htm.

5. "Sexual Violence," National Center for Injury Prevention and Control, http://www.cdc.gov/ncipc/factsheets/svoverview.htm.

6. Identify Theft and Identify Fraud, www.usdoj/gov/criminal/fraud/idtheft.html.

7. Fighting Back Against Identify Theft: Deter, Detect, Defend, www.ftc.gov/bcp/edu/microsites/idtheft/consumers/defend.html.

8. "American Hustle," IMBd, http://www.imdb.com/title/tt1800241/ (last visited February 15, 2016).

9. *United States of America v. Michael Myers*, 527 F. Supp. 1206 (E.D. N.Y. 1981).

10. *Id.*

11. *Id.*

12. *Commonwealth of Pennsylvania v. Graham*, 703 A.2d 510 (Pa. Super. 1997).

13. "Lethal Injection," Death Penalty Information Center, http://www.deathpenaltyinfo.org/lethal-injection (last visited February 15, 2016).

14. John Hasnas, "Over criminalization: The Politics of Crime," 54 Am. U. L. Rev. 579, February 2005.

KEY TERMS

Arraignment

Arrest

Arson

Bail

Burglary

Carnal Knowledge

Conspiracy

Crime

Criminal Complaint

Criminal Homicide

Criminal Trespass

Cruel and Unusual Punishment

Custodial Interrogation

Date Rape

Eighth Amendment

Electronic Fencing

Entrapment

Exclusionary Rule

Excusable Homicide

Expectation of Privacy

Federal Rule of Criminal
  Procedure

Felony Murder

Fifth Amendment

First Degree Murder

Fourth Amendment

General Police Measure

Grand Jury

Gross Negligence

Guilty

Guilty but Insane

Heat of Passion

Homicide

Hot Pursuit

Identity Theft

Indictment

Innocent

Insanity

Intentional Killing

Involuntary Manslaughter

Justifiable Homicide

Larceny

Malice Aforethought

Mandatory Sentencing

Miranda Warnings

Murder

Not Guilty by Reason of Insanity

Open Lewdness

Overt Act

Plain View

Plain Feel

Polygraph

Preliminary Arraignment

Preliminary Hearing

Premeditation

Pre-Sentence Investigation

Probable Cause

Rape

Receiving Stolen Property

Robbery

Search and Seizure

Search Incident to an Arrest

Search Incident to a General
  Police Measure

Search Warrant

Second Degree Murder

Self-defense

Sentencing

Speedy Trial Act

Statutory Rape

Stop and Frisk

Theft

Third Degree Murder

Trial

Voluntary Manslaughter

White Collar Crime

CHAPTER 5

CONSUMER PROTECTION

Doubtless the government and lawsuits should not always protect us from our own foolishness, but costly consumer fraud and other forms of consumer abuse (invasion of privacy, dangerous products, identity theft, false advertising, and so on) are not unusual in our consumption-driven lives. Historically, we relied on the market to address those problems; but in recent decades legislatures, courts, and administrative agencies have developed laws and rulings to protect us where the market arguably has failed. This chapter surveys some of those legal interventions.

FOR-PROFIT SCHOOLS

For-profit schools like the University of Phoenix and Kaplan enroll nearly 2 million students, but the government is concerned that deceptive marketing practices, fraudulent claims about job placement, and huge student loan burdens are denying many of those students the better future they are seeking. Chelsi Miller was managing a burger joint when she saw an ad for Everest University promising a better life. The single mother in a small town near Salt Lake City wanted an associate's degree as a first step toward medical school. She said she chose Everest, a for-profit college, after a recruiter guaranteed that she could apply her credits toward a higher degree at the University of Utah.[1]

Once Miller graduated in 2008, she learned that her credits would not transfer. After two years of school and $30,000 in student loans, Miller says she was sold "a lemon." Miller's experience was not unusual. Although public and private nonprofit colleges typically achieve graduation rates around 65 percent, the comparable number at the for-profits often falls below 30 percent, and those students are more likely to default on their student loans and have greater difficulty securing jobs than their nonprofit counterparts.[2] Indeed, government figures show that for-profits have twice the federal student loan default rate of public colleges.[3] Further, the for-profits are routinely accused of using high-pressure sales tactics and false promises to lure students. In response, the federal government imposed "gainful employment" regulations designed to cut off aid to colleges with poor job placement rates. After a federal court held in 2012 that the government had failed to provide a clear rationale for its new rules, new regulations were released in 2014, based in part on the mortgage industry's standard for sustainable levels of debt.[4] Meanwhile, the market seems to be asserting itself as for-profit enrollment has been falling and the industry leader, the University of Phoenix, has closed many of its locations. The schools defend themselves, in part, by saying that the students have more "risk factors" than traditional college students. Do you think higher education admissions practices are best left to the market, or is more aggressive government oversight needed?

Later in this chapter, we will explore government efforts to protect consumers from dangerous products, unfair lending practices, and the like. Before turning to that legislation, we need to appreciate the common law (judge-made law) that preceded and, in some respects, provided the foundation for the many federal, state, and local initiatives of recent years. In addition to the product liability protection, injured consumers can look to several common-law protections, including actions for fraud, misrepresentation, and unconscionability. [For an extensive menu of consumer law sites, see www.lectlaw.com/tcos.html]

FRAUD AND INNOCENT MISREPRESENTATION

If the market is to operate efficiently, the buyer must be able to rely on the truth of the seller's product claims. Regrettably, willful untruths appear to be common in American commerce. A victim of **fraud** is entitled to rescind the contract in question and to seek damages, including, in cases of malice, a punitive recovery. Although fraud arises in countless situations and is difficult to define, the legal community has generally adopted the following elements, each of which must be proved:

1. Misrepresentation of a material fact.

2. The misrepresentation was intentional.

3. The injured party justifiably relied on the misrepresentation.

4. Injury resulted.

In identifying a fraudulent expression, the law distinguishes between statements of objective, verifiable facts and simple expressions of opinion. The latter ordinarily are not fraudulent even if erroneous. Thus, normal sales **puffing** ("This baby is the greatest little car you're ever gonna drive") is fully lawful, and consumers are expected to exercise good judgment in responding to such claims. If a misleading expression of opinion comes from an expert, however, and the other party does not share that expertise (such as in the sale of a diamond engagement ring), a court probably would offer a remedy.

QUESTION FOR DISCUSSION

1. Vitt, an Apple iBook G4 laptop purchaser, sued Apple, claiming that advertising words including "mobile," "durable," "rugged," "reliable" and "high value" allegedly constituted a misrepresentation of the durability, portability, and quality of the laptop. Vitt's laptop failed soon after the expiration of its one-year warranty. Vitt argued that it should be expected to last for "at least a couple of years." In Vitt's view, Apple's ads caused buyers to believe the computer was of better quality than it turned out to be. Was Vitt a victim of a misrepresentation? Explain.

Of course, fraud can involve false conduct as well as false expression. A familiar example is the car seller who rolls back an odometer with the result that the buyer is misled.

A variation on the general theme of fraud is **innocent misrepresentation,** which differs from fraud only in that the falsehood was unintentional. The wrongdoer believed the statement or conduct in question to be true, but he or she was mistaken. In such cases, the wronged party may secure rescission of the contract, but ordinarily damages are not awarded. The following case involves a fraud claim against Harley-Davidson.

TIETSWORTH V. HARLEY-DAVIDSON
677 N.W. 4D 233 (WIS. S. CT. 2004)

Plaintiff Steven C. Tietsworth and the members of the proposed class own or lease 1999 or early-2000 model year Harley motorcycles equipped with Twin Cam 88 or Twin Cam 88B engines. Harley's marketing and advertising literature contained the following statement about the TC-88 engines:

Developing [the TC-88s] was a six-year process. . . . The result is a masterpiece. We studied everything from the way oil moves through the inside, to the way a rocker cover does its job of staying oil-tight. Only 21 functional parts carry over into the new design. What does carry over is the power of a Harley-Davidson™ engine, only more so.

Harley also stated that the motorcycles were "premium" quality, and described the TC-88 engine as "eighty-eight cubic inches filled to the brim with torque and ready to take you thundering down the road."

On January 22, 2001, Harley sent a letter to Tietsworth and other owners of Harley motorcycles informing them that "the rear cam bearing in a small number of Harley-Davidson's Twin Cam 88 engines has failed. While it is unlikely that you will ever have to worry about this situation, you have our assurance that Harley-Davidson is committed to your satisfaction." The letter went on to explain that the company was extending the warranty on the cam bearing from the standard one-year/unlimited mileage warranty to a five-year/50,000 mile warranty. Separately, Harley developed a $495 "cam bearing repair kit" and made the kit available to its dealers and service departments "to expedite rear cam bearing repair."

The amended complaint alleges that the cam bearing mechanism in the 1999 and early-2000 model year TC-88 engines is inherently defective, causing an unreasonably dangerous propensity for premature engine failure. [T]he amended complaint alleged that Harley's failure to disclose the cam bearing defect induced the plaintiffs to purchase their motorcycles by causing them to reasonably rely upon Harley's representations regarding the "premium" quality of the motorcycles.

The amended complaint further alleges that if the plaintiffs had known of the engine defect, they either would not have purchased the product or would have paid less for it. The amended complaint does not allege that the plaintiffs' motorcycles have actually suffered engine failure, have malfunctioned in any way, or are reasonably certain to fail or malfunction. Nor does the amended complaint allege any property damage or personal injury arising out of the engine defect. Rather, the amended complaint alleges that the plaintiffs' motorcycles have diminished value, including diminished resale value, because Harley motorcycles equipped with TC-88 engines have demonstrated a "propensity" for premature engine failure and/or fail prematurely.

The plaintiffs' common-law fraud claim is premised on the allegation that Harley failed to disclose or concealed the existence of the cam bearing defect prior to the plaintiffs' purchases of their motorcycles. It is well established that a nondisclosure is not actionable as a misrepresentation tort unless there is a duty to disclose. **Ollerman v. O'Rourke Co., Inc.,** 94 Wis.2d 17, 26, 288 N.W.2d 95 (1980). Our decision in Ollerman outlined the three categories of misrepresentation in Wisconsin law— intentional misrepresentation, negligent misrepresenta-

tion, and strict responsibility misrepresentation—and described the common and distinct elements of the three torts.

All misrepresentation claims share the following required elements: (1) the defendant must have made a representation of fact to the plaintiff; (2) the representation of fact must be false; and (3) the plaintiff must have believed and relied on the misrepresentation to his detriment or damage. The plaintiffs here allege intentional misrepresentation, which carries the following additional elements: (4) the defendant must have made the misrepresentation with knowledge that it was false or recklessly without caring whether it was true or false; and (5) the defendant must have made the misrepresentation with intent to deceive and to induce the plaintiff to act on it to his detriment or damage.

Ollerman reiterated the general rule that in a sales or business transaction, "silence, a failure to disclose a fact, is not an intentional misrepresentation unless the seller has a duty to disclose." The existence and scope of a duty to disclose are questions of law for the court. Ollerman held that "a subdivider– vendor of a residential lot has a duty to a 'noncommercial' purchaser to disclose facts which are known to the vendor, which are material to the transaction, and which are not readily discernible to the purchaser." We specified that this was a "narrow holding," premised on certain policy considerations present in noncommercial real estate transactions.

The transactions at issue here, however, are motorcycle purchases, not residential real estate purchases, and it is an open question whether the duty to disclose recognized in Ollerman extends more broadly to sales of consumer goods. Ollerman also held that damages in intentional misrepresentation cases are measured according to the "benefit of the bargain" rule, "typically stated as the difference between the value of the property as represented and its actual value as purchased.". . .

[W]e have generally held that a tort claim is not capable of present enforcement (and therefore does not accrue) unless the plaintiff has suffered actual damage. . . . Actual damage is harm that has already occurred or is "reasonably certain" to occur in the future. . . . Actual damage is not the mere possibility of future harm. . . . [T]he amended complaint must adequately plead an actual injury—a loss or damage that has already occurred or is reasonably certain to occur—in order to state an actionable fraud claim.

The injury complained of here is diminution in value only— the plaintiffs allege that their motorcycles are worth less than they paid for them. However, the amended complaint does not allege that the plaintiffs' motorcycles have diminished value because their engines have failed, will fail, or are reasonably certain to fail as a result of the TC-88 cam bearing defect. The amended complaint does not allege that the plaintiffs have sold their motorcycles at a loss because of the alleged engine defect. The amended complaint alleges only that the motorcycles have diminished value—primarily diminished potential resale value—because Harley motorcycles equipped with TC-88 engines have demonstrated a "propensity" for premature engine failure and/or will fail as a result of the cam bearing defect. This is insufficient to state a legally cognizable injury for purposes of a fraud claim.

Diminished value premised upon a mere possibility of future product failure is too speculative and uncertain to support a fraud claim. The plaintiffs do not specifically allege that their particular motorcycles will fail prematurely, only that the Harley product line that consists of motorcycles with TC-88 engines has demonstrated a propensity for premature engine failure. An allegation that a particular product line fails prematurely does not constitute an allegation that the plaintiffs' particular motorcycles will do so, only that there is a possibility that they will do so.

We certainly agree with the court of appeals that the damage allegations in a fraud complaint are not evaluated against a standard of "absolute certainty" for purposes of a motion to dismiss for failure to state a claim. But an allegation that a product is diminished in value because of an event or circumstance that might—or might not—occur in the future is inherently conjectural and does not allege actual benefit-of- the-bargain damages with the "reasonable certainty" required to state a fraud claim.

QUESTIONS FOR DISCUSSION

1. According to the Wisconsin Supreme Court, under what circumstances might the nondisclosure by a seller of a defect constitute misrepresentation? Did the court find that Harley-Davidson had a duty to disclose in this case? Explain.

2. What injury, if any, do the plaintiffs claim they suffered in this episode?

3. According to the Wisconsin Supreme Court, must a plaintiff in a fraud action prove that he or she has suffered actual damages prior to bringing a claim? Explain. What is the "benefit of the bargain" rule?

4. Why did the Wisconsin Supreme Court rule for the defendant Harley-Davidson in this case?

5. Robert McGlothlin, an employee of Thomson Consumer Electronics in Bloomington, Indiana, was injured while loading televisions into a semitrailer when the trailer's "landing gear" (retractable legs that support the front of the trailer when it is not attached to the semitractor) collapsed. McGlothlin sued the owner of the trailer, among others, claiming that the defendants' repair and inspection procedures for latent (hidden) defects were inadequate. Should the court treat latent defects differently than patent (observable) defects in determining when a legal duty exists? Explain.

DOCTRINE OF UNCONSCIONABILITY

The **doctrine of unconscionability** emerged from court decisions where jurists concluded that some contracts are so unfair or oppressive as to demand intervention. (Unconscionability is also included in state statutory laws via the Uniform Commercial Code 2—302.) The legal system intrudes on contracts only with the greatest reluctance. Mere foolishness or want of knowledge does not constitute grounds for unconscionability, nor is a contract unconscionable and hence unenforceable merely because one party is spectacularly clever and the other is not. Unconscionability can take either or both of two forms:

1. **Procedural unconscionability.** The bargaining power of the parties was so unequal that the agreement, as a practical matter, was not freely entered. Procedural unconscionability usually arises from lack of knowledge (e.g., fine print) or lack of choice (e.g., urgent circumstances).

2. **Substantive unconscionability.** The clause or contract in question was so manifestly one-sided, oppressive, or unfair as to "shock the conscience of the court." A contract that does not provide a remedy for a breach, or contract terms completely out of line with the relative risks assumed by the parties are among the conditions that might lead to a finding of substantive unconscionability.

SECTION 5.3 THE CONSUMER AND GOVERNMENT REGULATION OF BUSINESS

Having looked at the common-law foundation of consumer protection, we turn to some of the many governmental measures that provide shelter in the marketplace. Many states have enacted comprehensive **consumer protection statutes.** States also have specific statutes addressing such problems as door-to-door sales, debtor protection, and telemarketing fraud. We will look at a pair of high-interest consumer loan situations as well as state "lemon laws," which address the particularly frustrating problem of a hopelessly defective vehicle.

PAYDAY LOANS

When Jeffrey Smith of Phoenix needed money quickly to pay a medical bill, he took out a string of payday loans (short-term, high-interest loans to be paid back with the borrower's next pay check) and fell into a downward spiral that found him calling in sick to work to give himself time to drive all over the city taking out new loans to cover those coming due. The result was bankruptcy along with thoughts of suicide by his despondent wife. Annual interest rates on those loans were as high as 459 percent.

At least 15 states now ban these loans and others cap interest rates. Loan volume is down considerably, but customers are estimated to number about 12 million annually. Looking for new profit centers, a few of the most mainstream of big banks, such as Wells Fargo and U.S. Bancorp, have begun offering a payday loan variant labeled direct deposit advance loans. The banks lend to current customers and repay themselves by deducting the amount due from the customer's account after the next paycheck has been deposited. Other big banks have established new payday profit lines by joining with smaller online lending operations sometimes operated by offshore entities or Native Americans. Payday lenders make the online loans and the big banks provide service for those loans. Interest to the online lenders and service fees to the big banks mount up and borrowers are quickly buried in debt.

Federal rules, in 2013, would require big banks, among other things, to consider ability to pay before making payday-style, short-term loans. Whether more federal rules and existing state laws advance fairness, or simply reduce the availability of loans and increase interest rates is the subject of debate.

LEMON LAWS

New car purchases are covered by **warranty laws.** In addition, all 50 states have some form of law designed to provide recourse for consumers whose new vehicles turn out to be defective such that they cannot be repaired after a reasonable effort. The quarrel, of course, is about when a car is truly a lemon. **Lemon laws** differ significantly from state to state, but they often cover new cars for one to two years or up to 24,000 miles after purchase. Typically, state laws provide that the vehicle must have been returned to the manufacturer or dealer three or four times to repair the same defect and that defect must substantially impair the value or safety of the vehicle, or the vehicle must have been unavailable to the consumer for a total of at least 30 days in a 12-month period. A vehicle meeting either or both of those tests often would be a lemon, and the purchaser would be entitled to a replacement vehicle or full refund of the purchase price. In some states, used cars may also be treated as lemons. In almost all states, the determination about whether a car is a lemon is handled by an arbitration panel. If dissatisfied with the ruling, the consumer may then file suit.

The case that follows examines Minnesota's lemon law requirements. [For lemon laws in all 50 states, see www.lemonlawusa.com]

PAUL SIPE V. WORKHORSE CUSTOM CHASSIS
572 F.3D 525 (8TH CIR. 2009)

On September 18, 2004, Paul Sipe purchased a motor home manufactured by Fleetwood Motor Homes of Pennsylvania, Inc. ("Fleetwood"), from Brambillas, Inc. ("Brambillas"), an authorized Fleetwood motor home dealer and repair facility located in Minnesota. Workhorse manufactured the motor home's chassis, which included the motor home's supporting frame, engine, transmission, and certain electrical components. Sipe purchased the motor home for $105,616.75, and Brambillas delivered it to Sipe on October 21, 2004. Sipe received an owner's manual with the motor home that contained Workhorse's limited warranty for the chassis.

Sipe began experiencing problems with the motor home's engine shortly after he bought it. The engine stalled on three occasions while being driven by Sipe, once in October 2004, once in May 2005, and once in June 2005. Sipe brought the Brambillas conducted diagnostic tests but made no repairs because it found no defect in the engine. Sipe testified in his deposition that after the second and third incidents, Brambillas claimed it performed diagnostic tests and found no defect but that the work order he received contained no indication that Brambillas performed any such tests. Sipe further testified that the last time the engine stalled was in June 2005 and that the engine

problem has not prevented him from taking trips in the motor home.

In February 2006, Sipe listed the motor home for sale for the price of $94,900. After receiving only two offers at lower prices, Sipe reduced the listing price to $84,900, the Kelley Blue Book value of the motor home. Sipe testified that he ultimately decided to reduce the price because of a crack in the kitchen counter and that he did not recall any other defects that contributed to his decision to reduce the asking price. Sipe did not sell the motor home.

In January 2007 and December 2007, Sipe experienced problems with the motor home's transmission when he discovered that transmission fluid had leaked. Sipe testified that Brambillas refused to diagnose or repair the transmission after both incidents of fluid leakage.

Sipe brought this action against Workhorse and Fleetwood in the District Court for Hennepin County, Minnesota, alleging violations of Minnesota's lemon law. The court dismissed Sipe's lemon law claims, finding that Sipe presented no evidence that the alleged engine defect required repair or that the defect substantially impaired the motor home and concluding that Sipe's claim regarding the transmission was time-barred.

Sipe contends that the district court erred in granting summary judgment to Workhorse on his lemon law claim because Workhorse failed to repair his motor home's engine and transmission. Minnesota's lemon law provides: If the manufacturer, its agents, or its authorized dealers are unable to conform the new motor vehicle to any applicable express warranty by repairing or correcting any defect or condition which substantially impairs the use or market value of the motor vehicle to the consumer after a reasonable number of attempts, the manufacturer shall either replace the new motor vehicle with a comparable motor vehicle or accept return of the vehicle from the consumer and refund to the consumer the full purchase price.

The manufacturer must make the required repairs if "the consumer reports the nonconformity to the manufacturer, its agents, or its authorized dealer during the term of the applicable express warranties or during the period of two years following the date of original delivery of the new motor vehicle to a consumer, whichever is the earlier date."

After thoroughly reviewing the record, we conclude that Sipe failed to present evidence showing a genuine issue of material fact about whether the engine stalls "substantially impaired the use or market value of the motor [home]," as required by Minnesota's lemon law. In response to being asked if the engine defect "ever prevented [him] from going somewhere [or] taking a trip with [his] motor home," Sipe replied "no." In fact, Sipe traveled over 11,000 miles in the motor home since the first time the engine stalled. As Sipe explained, "I don't know if [the engine problem] affect[s] my use now because I know how to deal with it." Sipe also stated that he had not experienced an engine stall since June 2005. Thus, Sipe's own testimony shows that the engine defect has not impaired his use of the motor home; it follows that the defect has not substantially impaired his use.

With respect to the effect of the engine defect on the market value of the motor home, Sipe argues that the low number of offers he received for the motor home shows that its market value was substantially impaired. However, Sipe cannot avoid summary judgment by merely relying on his conclusory allegation that the engine defect caused the low number of offers. Sipe presented no evidence to suggest that his receipt of only two offers was in any way caused by the engine stalls and not some other factor, such as market conditions for used motor homes. He offered no evidence that potential buyers were even aware of the engine stalls, given that he described the motor home as being in "excellent condition" when he originally listed it for sale in February 2006. Sipe testified that he only reduced the original asking price to the Kelley Blue Book value because of a crack in the kitchen counter and that he did not recall any other defects "that played a role in reducing the price." Further, Sipe submitted no other evidence suggesting that the value of the motor home was impaired, such as expert testimony or an appraisal of the motor home. As with his testimony regarding his use of the motor home, Sipe's own testimony shows that the engine defect has not impaired, substantially or otherwise, the motor home's market value.

When he received the motor home in October 2004, Sipe received a three-year limited warranty from Workhorse. Thus, to bring an actionable lemon law claim, Sipe must have reported any nonconformities within two years of the date of the original delivery of the motor home. See Minn. Stat. Section 325 F. 665, subdiv. 2 (requiring consumers to report a nonconformity "during the term of the applicable express warranties or during the period of two years following the date of original delivery of the new motor vehicle . . ., whichever is the earlier date"). Sipe first reported the transmission fluid leak to Brambillas in January 2007, which was more than two years after the delivery of the motor home. As such, we agree with the district court that Sipe's lemon law claim with respect to the transmission leaks is barred by statute.

Much of the federal government's authority to protect consumers rests with some powerful agencies including a new one approved in 2010 when Congress and President Obama concluded that our financial markets had failed in some important respects.

CONSUMER FINANCIAL PROTECTION BUREAU

Placing a bold bet on the capacity of the federal government to protect consumers, Congress and President Obama approved the creation of the **Consumer Financial Protection Bureau** (CFPB) as a direct response to the financial calamity of recent years. The new agency, authorized by the 2010 **Dodd–Frank Wall Street Reform and Consumer Protection Act,** is charged with writing and enforcing rules covering consumer financial products and services including mortgages, credit cards, payday loans, loan servicing, check cashing, debt collection, and others. Another important element of the Bureau's charge is to provide financial education, thereby promoting Americans' financial literacy. [For the Consumer Financial Protection Bureau home page, see: www.consumerfinance.gov/]

Rather than counting on market forces to ensure financial transparency and fair treatment for consumers, new rules are being created in an effort to mandate those results. Broadly, the Bureau will be expected to prohibit and prevent the commission of "an unfair, deceptive, or abusive act or practice" in conjunction with a consumer financial product or service. The expectation is that the Bureau will protect us from a wide array of dishonest practices such as hidden credit card fees and misleading "teaser" rates for mortgages.

The Act generally accords the Bureau authority over financial service firms, including banks, thrifts, and credit unions, though it specifically excludes real estate brokerages, accountants, lawyers, and those selling nonfinancial goods and services, among others. The Bureau's new rules must be subjected to cost–benefit reviews, and those rules can be set aside by a two-thirds vote of the new Financial Stability Oversight Council (created as part of the Dodd–Frank bill) if the rule would threaten the nation's financial system.

Having broad authority over federal consumer finance law, the Bureau is consolidating consumer finance programs currently residing in other agencies, and it is responsible for enforcing the finance laws outlined later in this chapter, including the Electronic Fund Transfer Act, the Equal Credit Opportunity Act, the Fair Credit Billing Act, and many more. The CFPB quickly asserted its regulatory authority. In 2013, the Bureau began addressing the mortgage problems that led to the recent financial meltdown. For example, one new rule spells out standards for ensuring that borrowers will be able to afford their mortgages, and another new rule requires lenders to provide borrowers with direct and ongoing access to loan servicing personnel. And in 2012, the CFPB set up an online portal where consumers can file complaints about credit cards, mortgages, banking, student loans, and more (see www.consumerfinance.gov/complaint). Those complaints are easily accessible to the public, thus imposing pressure on financial institutions to improve customer service.

Of course, the Bureau has many doubters and outright enemies. A primary fear is that increased government regulation is likely to reduce the availability of credit or raise the cost of that credit, thereby potentially damaging consumers and the economy. Some of the critics simply want the government to leave the finance market alone while others suggest, for example, that government resources should be limited to consumer education and counseling rather than more rules. [For a "one-stop shop for the American people to learn how to protect themselves from fraud and to report it wherever—and however—it occurs," see the Federal Financial Fraud Task Force's website: www.stopfraud.gov]

THE FEDERAL TRADE COMMISSION

The **Federal Trade Commission** (FTC) was created in 1914 to prevent "unfair methods of competition and unfair or deceptive acts or practices in and affecting commerce." The FTC operates as a miniature government with powerful quasi-legislative (rule-making) and quasi-judicial (adjudication) roles. [For the FTC's Bureau of Consumer Protection home page, see www.ftc.gov/bcp/ index.shtml]

A. RULE MAKING

The FTC's primary legislative direction is in issuing **trade regulation rules** to enforce the intent of broadly drawn congressional legislation. That is, the rules specify particular acts or practices that the commission deems deceptive. The FTC's quasi-legislative (rule-making) power is extensive, as evidenced by the following examples:

The Federal Trade Commission's **Do Not Call Registry** forbids telemarketers, with certain exceptions, from placing calls to the more than 200 million Americans who have added their phone numbers to the Federal Trade Commission's list. Although some violations continue, the rule has clearly been a success for annoyed consumers. The FTC also issued a 2009 rule banning many types of so-called robocalls (prerecorded telemarketing solicitations). Under the rule, sellers and telemarketers who transmit prerecorded messages to consumers who have not agreed in writing to accept those messages will face penalties of up to $16,000 per call. [Those wanting to be added to the Do Not Call list and those wanting to file complaints can visit www.donotcall.gov]

In 2009, the Los Angeles Times asked: "Does a moment pass when Kim Kardashian isn't selling? If she's not hyping her workout video, she's touting her online shoe club, her new book or her sisters' 'reality' TV spin-off, a gripping look inside their high-end Miami boutique."[5]

Kardashian and all others hyping products and services on the Internet are now subject to penalties for false or misleading advertising if they fail to comply with the FTC's **"Guides Concerning Use of Endorsements and Testimonials in Advertising."** The rules, among other things, require those offering endorsements on new media sites (blogs, Twitter, Facebook, etc.) to disclose any connection they have (including in most cases, receiving cash or gifts) in exchange for their testimonials.

B. ADJUDICATION

On its own initiative or as a result of a citizen complaint, the FTC may investigate suspect trade practices. At that point, the FTC may drop the proceeding, settle the matter, or issue a formal complaint.

Where a formal complaint is issued, the matter proceeds essentially as a trial conducted before an administrative law judge. The FTC has no authority to impose criminal sanctions.

C. FEDERAL TRADE COMMISSION—FRAUD AND DECEPTION

Unfair and deceptive trade practices, including those in advertising, are forbidden under Section 5 of the Federal Trade Commission Act. The FTC test for deception requires that the claim is (1) false or likely to mislead the reasonable consumer and (2) material to the consumer's decision making. Deception can take many forms, including, for example, testimonials by celebrities who do not use the endorsed product or do not have meaningful expertise. Product quality claims are an area of particular dispute.

D. QUALITY CLAIMS

Under the FTC's ad substantiation program, advertisers are engaging in unfair and deceptive practices if they make product claims without some reasonable foundation for those claims. Skechers, for example, agreed to pay $50 million in 2012 to settle FTC and state charges that it misled the public by making unsupported claims that its toning sneakers allow buyers to, among other things, "Shape Up While You Walk" and "Get in Shape without Setting Foot in a Gym." According to the FTC, a Skechers' ad said that its fitness claims were backed by a chiropractor study. The study, however, did not produce the claimed results, and Skechers failed to disclose that the chiropractor was married to a Skechers executive and that the chiropractor was paid for doing the study.[6] Skechers denied the FTC allegations. Shoe purchasers are eligible for refunds ranging from $20 to $84 per product purchased. An FTC survey found that nearly 11 percent of American adults were victims of fraud in 2011.[7] Weight-loss products and prize promotions were the most common types of fraudulent products.

E. Federal Trade Commission—Consumer Privacy

Kellie Droste, a Maricopa, Arizona, resident was shocked in March 2013 when she learned that an identity thief had stolen her personal information and filed a tax return in her name to claim her tax refund.[8] According to the federal Justice Department, credit card data theft grew 50 percent from 2005 to 2010.[9] Millions of stolen card numbers are for sale at a price of perhaps $10 to $50 each, and a no-limit American Express card issued to a consumer with a high credit rating might sell for hundreds of dollars.[10] When businesses are hacked, millions of credit records may be compromised at a cost of an estimated $150 to $250 for each number stolen.[11] Of course, those costs are passed on to consumers. Despite these staggering numbers and the prospect for even greater losses in the future, identity theft expert Adam Levin reminds us that we don't seem to pay much attention:

> Despite considerable coverage and legislative initiatives, identity theft, cyber warfare, and the death of privacy at the hands of hackers and hyper-marketers are barely on the public radar. People say they care about identity theft but they don't really understand it.[12]

A 2013 federal government study found that 1 in 14 Americans age 16 and older were either targets of identity theft or actually experienced identity theft. The resulting financial losses for 2012 totaled nearly $25 billion.[13] [For a privacy database and links, see www.privacyrights.org].

F. Privacy Law

The Federal Trade Commission's authority to stop unfair methods of competition along with unfair and deceptive acts and practices gives the agency considerable power in policing **consumer privacy** breaches. The FTC also enforces the privacy provisions in a number of other federal laws, including those addressing the use of consumer credit reports, children's online privacy, identity theft, personal health information, personal financial information, and others. In 2011, the FTC began enforcing its "Red Flags Rule" that is designed to slow **identity theft.** Under the rule, all "financial institutions" and "creditors" must establish a written program to prevent identity theft in their organizations and then mitigate whatever losses may come from identity theft. The FTC identifies "Red Flags" as, for example, suspicious documents, financial account activities, or IDs.

As needed, the FTC has been aggressive in privacy enforcement, having recently reached agreements with both Google and Facebook to settle Commission charges of privacy violations. Furthermore, the FTC in 2012 called for Congress to enact additional general privacy legislation along with several other new laws to address expanding threats in our technology-driven culture. In addition, the Obama administration in 2012 issued a **Consumer Privacy Bill of Rights,** which addresses how businesses collect and use consumers' personal information and outlines core principles such as the expectation that consumers should control how their information will be used in the market. The administration expects to work with the various stakeholders in developing voluntary, but legally enforceable, codes of conduct that implement the Consumer Privacy Bill of Rights. Of course, rule-enhanced privacy comes with significant costs because constricted information flow risks reduced efficiency and increased costs.

The Federal Trade Commission recognizes the need for active engagement, especially in hot-button areas, such as a global "Do Not Track" standard that would strengthen users' ability to control when and how their online information is collected. In 2013, FTC Chair Edith Ramirez made it very clear, however, that the Commission should use its authority "very judiciously."[14] Speaking of the FTC's power to police unfairness in the market, Ramirez said, "I want to just emphasize that that's not a blank check for the FTC in going after privacy violations."[15] The market and self-regulation, from the FTC point of view, must remain the core methods for assuring consumer privacy.

THE CONSUMER PRODUCT SAFETY COMMISSION

Another reason to avoid sleeping with an ex: fear of contracting lead poisoning. Just ask Barbie, who got it from Ken. That's according to "Toxic Toys: A Poisonous Affair," a YouTube attack on the Consumer Product Safety Commission produced by the nonprofit Campaign for America's Future.[16]

The **Consumer Product Safety Commission** (CPSC) is the federal agency charged with protecting us from "unreasonable risks of injury and death" from consumer products. The YouTube attack was a product of frustration with the CPSC's response to a 2007 wave of toy recalls, largely because of dangerous levels of lead. Tens of millions of toys and children's items, most of them made in China, have been recalled in recent years. Widespread outrage over the lead risk led to the **Consumer Product Safety Improvement Act** that, among other things, lowered permissible levels of lead in children's (up to age 12) products. Critics, however, argued that the bill created excessive, unnecessary, and unintended costs, especially for small businesses. Responding to those concerns, Congress and President Obama in 2011 approved new legislation giving the CPSC greatly expanded latitude to grant exceptions to the Consumer Product Safety Improvement Act in situations where risk to human health does not exist.

A. CRIBS

After more than 30 infant and toddler deaths and millions of recalls in the past decade, the CPSC unanimously voted to ban, effective June 28, 2011, the manufacture, sale, and resale (including yard sales) of the traditional drop-side baby crib that has cradled millions. The new standard requires fixed sides.[17] [For an ABC News visit to the Consumer Product Safety Commission Testing Lab, see http://abcnews.go.com/GMA/video/consumer-product-safety-commission-test-lab-13827984]

B. REDUCING RISK

The CPSC, created in 1972, is responsible for reducing the risks in using consumer products such as toys, lawn mowers, washing machines, bicycles, fireworks, pools, portable heaters, and household chemicals. The CPSC pursues product safety, initially, by collecting data and issuing rules. The commission conducts research and collects information as a foundation for regulating product safety. Via its rule-making authority, the CPSC promulgates mandatory consumer product safety, performance, and labeling standards.

To enforce its policies and decisions, the CPSC holds both compliance and enforcement powers. In seeking compliance with safety expectations, the commission can exert a number of expectations. Manufacturers must certify before distribution that products meet federal safety standards. Manufacturing sites may be inspected, and specific product safety testing procedures can be mandated. Businesses other than retailers are required to keep product safety records. In cases of severe and imminent hazards, the CPSC has the power to enforce its decisions by seeking a court order to remove a product from the market. In less-urgent circumstances, the commission may proceed with its own administrative remedy. Preferring voluntary compliance, the commission may negotiate with companies to recall dangerous products. **Product recalls** issued in 2011 by the CPSC, the Food and Drug Administration, and the Department of Agriculture totaled 2,363 (up from 1,460 in 2007).[18] The result presumably is improved consumer safety, but we have some evidence of "recall fatigue." A 2009 study found 40 percent of Americans indicating they have never looked for recalled products in their home.[19] [For the federal government recall site, see www.recalls.gov/]

Where voluntary negotiations fail, the commission may proceed with an adjudicative hearing before an administrative law judge or members of the commission. That decision may be appealed to the full commission and thereafter to the federal court of appeals. Civil or criminal penalties may result. Only a few products, such as the drop-side cribs, have actually been banned from the market by the Commission. The CPSC launched a public database in 2011 that allows all of us to report dangerous products and to search com- plaints entered by others. [See http://saferproducts.gov/]

THE FOOD AND DRUG ADMINISTRATION

A. TOBACCO

The **Food and Drug Administration** announced in 2013 that it had begun exercising its authority over tobacco; power conferred by Congress and President Obama in 2009. For the first time, the FDA can keep tobacco products off the market if they pose public health risks beyond comparable products already on the market. Prior to the 2009 legislation, the FDA could not regulate tobacco, a process that was left to the limited authority of the states. The FDA can also regulate tobacco ingredients, including nicotine, but the agency is not yet exercising that power.

B. DRUG SAFETY

The FDA monitors much of America's health landscape with responsibility for assuring the safety, effectiveness, and security of food, drugs (prescription and over- the-counter), medical devices, cosmetics, tobacco products, and more. Perhaps the biggest FDA duty is to decide when drugs should be approved for marketing. Companies must subject a new drug to laboratory, animal, and eventually human testing before the FDA will consider approval. FDA physicians and scientists review the scientific evidence, and thereafter the FDA approves a drug for marketing only if it is safe and effective. The FDA is empowered to impose fines and remove dangerous drugs from the market. Thus, arthritis drug Vioxx, approved by the FDA in 1999, was pulled from the market in 2004 because the estimated 25 million Americans who took the drug faced a nearly-doubled risk of heart attack and stroke. An FDA study linked Vioxx to as many as 140,000 injuries and 56,000 deaths in the United States.[20] Merck, the drug's manufacturer, has paid billions of dollars to settle many civil lawsuits and, in 2011, Merck agreed to pay $950 million and pleaded guilty to a criminal charge over Vioxx marketing and sales practices.[21] Lawsuits continue, but at this writing no person has been penalized for the Vioxx wrongs.

C. FOOD SAFETY

In 2013, the FDA has announced a preliminary determination that artificial trans fats are not safe in foods. After public comment and further review, the FDA may effectively banish trans-fats from processed foods by allowing them only with scientific proof of safety. In recent years, food safety has climbed the list of FDA worries following a series of massive food poisoning scares. Vegetables, peanut products, eggs, and other foodstuffs have been contaminated by salmonella and E. coli. The 2010 salmonella outbreak in eggs (primarily regulated by the FDA, but assisted by the Agriculture Department and other agencies) sickened more than 1,600 people and led to the recall of 550 million eggs.[22] A 2012 salmonella outbreak in peanut butter prompted the FDA to force the closure of Sunland Inc.'s New Mexico production facility. FDA data show that one in six Americans suffers from a foodborne illness annually resulting in 3,000 deaths and 130,000 hospitalizations.[23]

The 2011 **Food Safety and Modernization Act** gave the FDA greatly expanded food safety power. With about one in six Americans suffering from eating contaminated food each year, the FDA has proposed new rules to implement the 2011 Act. The rules would require farmers to make sure, for example, that irrigation water is clean and that animals are kept out of fields. Food manufacturers will be expected to submit food safety plans to the government. Imported food would be subjected to the same standards as domestic production with importers being required to prove that their foreign suppliers have careful safety measures in place. Since the FDA is able to inspect only 1 to 2 percent of all imported food, the food safety burden will lie primarily with suppliers. The food industry has responded by, among other things, improving worker training and employing technological advances, including high-tech labels, which allow monitoring of food from the fields to the supermarket checkout.

TRUST THE MARKET OR STRENGTHEN THE FDA

Perhaps because of its crucial safety role in American life, the FDA is one of the most criticized divisions of the federal government. As

---

PLAN B

At this writing in 2013, the FDA is considering several new consumer rules including protection for children and adolescents from added caffeine in products such as Cracker Jack and a warning against tanning bed use for those under 18. The most controversial decision, however, has to do with the morning-after birth control pill, popularly known as Plan B. In early 2013, a federal judge ordered the FDA to make Plan B available without prescription to girls and women of all ages. The Obama administration announced that it would appeal the federal judge's order, but soon thereafter the appeal was dropped and the FDA was expected to approve Plan B for sale over the counter without restrictions.

noted, food safety worries, or at least publicity about them, seem to have spiraled in recent years. The drug approval process has been the subject of particularly fierce criticism. New drug approvals (39) in 2012 reached their highest level in 15 years despite tightened safety standards following several drug scandals—Vioxx in particular.[24] Nevertheless, critics argue that lifesaving new products could reach consumers much more quickly if we relied less on government rules and more on market forces. Reduced regulation, of course, carries its own risks. For example, during a recent five-year study period, more than 70 percent of 113 recalled medical devices (such as defibrillators and insulin pumps) had been approved by the FDA under an expedited system.[25] The devices were approved for sale more quickly because they were deemed sufficiently similar to products already on the market. Beyond safety concerns, experts Tomas Philipson and Andrew von Eschenbach argue that reduced and more efficient regulation could double medical innovation and sharply boost the American GDP.[26] Thus, to some critics, the FDA imposes too many rules; to others, too few.

SECTION 5.5
CREDIT REGULATIONS

According to The New York Times, Angelique Trammel, a single mother and telephone operator, decided to buy a laptop for her son on a "low weekly payment plan." She paid $99 down and agreed to have $41 per week withdrawn from her bank account. After six months, a broken computer arrived. Having spent well over $1,000 and after having received two nonworking computers, she demanded a refund from the retailer, Blue Hippo. Under her agreement, Ms. Trammel allegedly would have paid more than $2,000 for a computer worth much less. Describing sales schemes directed to the poor, Better Business Bureau spokesman Steve Cox said: "The way these companies operate is simply another form of predatory lending."[27] Blue Hippo, on the other hand, said that, "before, during and after the sales transaction we fully disclose the total price and all shipping guidelines" to customers.[28]

Situations like Trammel's and broad fears of abuse in credit and lending led Congress and the state legislatures to supplement the market's powerful messages with a substantial array of protective legislation. We will turn now to a look at several particularly important pieces of federal lending practices law. [For a debtor/creditor law database, sewww.law.cornell.edu/topics/debtor_creditor.html]

A. DODD–FRANK WALL STREET REFORM AND CONSUMER PROTECTION ACT

In addition to creating the **Consumer Finance Protection Bureau** (CFPB), the 2010 Dodd–Frank bill provides increased legislative oversight of the nation's financial processes. Broadly, the bill's consumer protection provisions move away from the old system that mandated disclosure to consumers of critical financial information (e.g., interest rates) to a more prescriptive regime that requires lenders to affirmatively protect borrowers.

B. TRUTH IN LENDING ACT (TILA)

Consumers often do not understand the full cost of buying on credit. The **TILA** is designed primarily to assure full disclosure of credit terms. Having been designed for consumer protection, the TILA does not cover all loans. The following standards determine the TILA's applicability:

1. The debtor must be a "natural person" rather than an organization.

2. The creditor must be regularly engaged in extending credit and must be the person to whom the debt is initially payable. Dodd–Frank expressly amends the definition of creditor to include mortgage originators.

3. The purpose of the credit must be "primarily for personal, family, or household purposes" not in excess of $25,000, but "consumer real property transactions" are covered by the act. Hence home purchases fall within TILA provisions.

4. The credit must be subject to a finance charge or payable in more than four installments.

The TILA and **Regulation Z** interpreting the act were designed both to protect consumers from credit abuse and to assist them in becoming more informed about credit terms and costs so they could engage in comparison shopping. Congress presumed the increased information would stimulate competition in the finance industry. The heart of the act is the required conspicuous disclosure of the amount financed, the finance charge (the actual dollar sum to be paid for credit), the annual percentage rate (APR—the total cost of the credit expressed at an annual rate), and the number of payments. The finance charge includes not just interest but service charges, points, loan fees, carrying charges, and other costs. The TILA covers consumer loans generally, including credit cards and auto purchases. [For consumer information on "abusive lending," see www.ftc.gov/bcp/menu-lending.htm]

TILA amendments in the Dodd–Frank bill give extensive, new attention to residential mortgages, a recognition of our ongoing subprime mortgage crisis and its destructive impact on the entire American economy. Creditors, for example, are prohibited from making a residential mortgage loan without a good faith determination that the consumer has a reasonable "ability to repay" the loan. Likewise mortgage service providers must, for example, respond to error notices within a specified period of time.

The case that follows examines the application of TILA to a credit card interest rate dispute.

BARRER v. CHASE BANK USA
566 F.3D 883 (9TH CIR. 2009)

We must decide whether a credit card company violates the Truth in Lending Act when it fails to disclose potential risk factors that allow it to raise a cardholder's Annual Percentage Rate.

Walter and Cheryl Barrer held a credit card account with Chase. The Barrers received and accepted the Cardmember Agreement ("the Agreement") governing their relationship at the relevant time in late 2004. In February 2005, Chase mailed to the Barrers a Change in Terms Notice ("the Notice"), which purported to amend the terms of the Agreement, in particular to increase the Annual Percentage Rate ("APR") significantly. It also allowed the Barrers to reject the amendments in writing by a certain date. They did not do so, and continued to use the credit card. Within two months, the new, higher, APR became effective.

According to the Barrers' First Amended Complaint, they enjoyed a preferred APR of 8.99% under the Agreement. In a section entitled "Finance Charges," the Agreement provided a mathematical formula for calculating preferred and non-preferred APRs and variable rates. In the event of default, the Agreement stated that Chase might increase the APR on the balance up to a stated default rate. The Agreement specified the following events of default: failure to pay at least a minimum payment by the due date; a credit card balance in excess of the credit limit on the account; failure to pay another creditor when required; the return, unpaid, of a payment to Chase by the customer's bank; or, should Chase close the account, the consumer's failure to pay the outstanding balance at the time Chase has appointed.

Another section entirely, entitled "Changes to the Agreement," provided that Chase "can change this agreement at any time. . . by adding, deleting, or modifying any provision. [The] right to add, delete, or modify provisions includes financial terms, such as APRs and fees." The next section, entitled "Credit Information," stated that Chase "may periodically review your credit history by obtaining information from credit bureaus and others." These sections appeared five and six pages, respectively, after the "Finance Charge" section.

Around April 2005, the Barrers' noticed that their APR had "skyrocketed" from 8.99% to 24.24%, the latter a rate close to a non-preferred or default rate. None of the events of default specified in the Agreement, however, had occurred. When the Barrers contacted Chase to find out why their APR had increased, Chase responded in a letter citing judgments it had made on the basis of information obtained from a consumer credit reporting agency. In particular, Chase wrote that: "outstanding credit loan(s) on revolving accounts . . . [were] too high" and there were "too many recently opened installment/revolving accounts." The Barrers do not dispute the facts underlying Chase's judgments.

Despite the Barrers' surprise, the Notice they had received in February contained some indication of what would be forthcoming. Specifically, it disclosed that Chase would shortly increase the APR to 24.24%, a decision "based in whole or in part on the information obtained in a report from the consumer reporting agency."

The Barrers paid the interest on the credit account at the new rate for three months before they were able to pay off the balance. Then they sued Chase in federal district court.

The Barrers filed a class action lawsuit on their own behalf and on behalf of all Chase credit card customers similarly harmed and similarly situated. The complaint asserted one cause of action under the Truth in Lending Act ("the Act"), and Regulation Z. The Barrers claim to have been the victims of a practice they now call "adverse action repricing," which apparently means "raising . . . a preferred rate to an essentially non-preferred rate based upon information in a customer's credit report." Though the Barrers do not claim that the practice itself is illegal, they do claim that it was illegal for Chase not to disclose it fully to them or to the other members of the putative class.

The Truth in Lending Act is designed "to assure a meaningful disclosure of credit terms so that the consumer will be able to compare more readily the various credit terms available to him and avoid the uninformed use of credit." Rather than substantively regulate the terms creditors can offer or include in their financial products, the Act primarily requires disclosure.

In general, the Act regulates credit card disclosures at numerous points in the commercial arrangement between creditor and consumer: at the point of solicitation and application, at the point the consumer and the creditor consummate the deal, at each billing cycle, and at the point the parties renew their arrangement. Specifically, creditors must disclose "[t]he conditions under which a finance charge may be imposed," "[t]he method of determining the amount of the finance charge," and, "[w]here one or more periodic rates may be used to compute the finance charge, each such rate . . . and the corresponding nominal annual percentage rate."

Regulation Z, 12 C.F.R. Section 226, provides the precise regulations that the Barrers claim Chase violated. In general, these regulations establish two conditions a creditor must meet. "First, it must have disclosed all of the information required by the statute." That is, disclosures must be complete. "And second, [they] must have been true—i.e., accurate representation[s] of the legal obligations of the parties at [the] time [the agreement was made]."

Section 226.6 lists the initial disclosures required of a creditor under a new credit agreement. The list includes "each periodic rate that may be used to compute the finance charge . . . and the corresponding annual percentage rate."

Just as section 226.6 states what must be disclosed, so section 226 describes how to disclose it. Among other things, creditors must make the required disclosures "clearly and conspicuously in writing."

The Board has also recognized that creditors may reserve the general right to change the credit agreement, as Chase did in this case. Should the creditor make changes in these ways, it may have to disclose anew under Section 226.9(c).

The Barrers argue that . . . Chase failed to disclose completely under the Act why it would change the APRs of its cardholders, in violation of subsection 226.6(a)(2) of Regulation Z.

The Barrers do not argue that either the Agreement or the Notice failed to disclose the APR, which their complaint puts at 8.99% under the Agreement and 24.24% under the Notice. Rather, the gravamen of the Barrers' complaint is that Chase did not disclose that if a cardholder's credit report revealed certain information, what Chase calls "risk factors," the APR might go up.

Regulation Z requires that creditors disclose any APR "that may be used to compute the finance charge," and that they do so "clearly and conspicuously."

We are persuaded that Chase adequately disclosed the APRs that the Agreement permitted it to use simply by means of the change-in-terms provision. That provision reserved Chase's right to change APRs, among other terms, without any limitation on why Chase could make such a change. The provision thus disclosed that, by changing the Agreement, Chase could use any APR, a class of APRs that logically includes APRs adjusted on the basis of adverse credit information. Apart from the gloss of Comment 11, neither the Act nor Regulation Z require Chase to disclose the basis on which it would change or use APRs. Therefore the failure to disclose the reason for the change to the Barrers' APR—adverse credit information—and that Chase would look up their credit history to acquire that information does not undermine the adequacy of Chase's disclosure.

Even so, such disclosure must be clear and conspicuous. Neither the Act nor Regulation Z define clarity and conspicuousness in this context. The Staff Commentary explains only that "[t]he clear and conspicuous standard requires that dis- closures be in a reasonably understandable form."

Clear and conspicuous disclosures, therefore, are disclosures that a reasonable cardholder would notice and under- stand. No particular kind of formatting is magical, but, in this case, the document must have made it clear to a reasonable cardholder that Chase was permitted under the agreement to raise the APR not only for the events of default specified in the "Finance Terms" section, but for any reason at all.

[T]he change-in-terms provision appears on page 10–11 of the Agreement, five dense pages after the disclosure of the APR. It is neither referenced in nor clearly related to the "Finance Terms" section. This provision, as part of the APRs allowed under the contract, is buried too deeply in the fine print for a reasonable cardholder to realize that, in addition to the specific grounds for increasing the APR listed in the "Finance Charges" section, Chase could raise the APR for other reasons.

Therefore, the Barrers have stated a claim because Chase cannot show that, as a matter of law, the Agreement made clear and conspicuous disclosure of the APRs that Chase was permitted to use.

QUESTIONS FOR DISCUSSION

1. a. How did Chase violate Regulation Z and the TILA?
    b. According to this decision, what is a "clear and conspicuous" disclosure?

2. Green Tree Financial financed Randolph's mobile home purchase. Randolph sued, claiming that Green Tree's financing document contained an arbitration clause that violated TILA because it did not provide the same level of protection as TILA accords. If the arbitration clause provided lesser protection than that provided for by TILA, as Randolph claimed, should the arbitration go forward? Explain. See **Randolph v. Green Tree Financial Corp.,** 531 U.S. 79 (2000).

3. Sarah Hamm sued Ameriquest Mortgage Company claiming a violation of the Truth in Lending Act (TILA). Hamm borrowed money secured by a 30-year mortgage from Ameriquest. She signed a "Disclosure Statement" specifying, among other things, that she was responsible for 359 payments at a specified amount and one payment for the last month of a slightly smaller amount. The Statement did not, however, explicitly specify, as required by the TILA, the total payments due (360). Was the TILA violated? Explain. See **Hamm v. Ameriquest Mortgage,** 506 F.3d 525 (7th Cir. 2007).

SECTION 5.6
CREDIT AND CHARGE
CARDS

College students are burying themselves in debt. As of 2013, student loan debt (about $1 trillion) exceeded the total amount owed by all Americans on their credit cards.[29] Student credit card use, on the other hand, declined to 35 percent in 2012 from 42 percent in 2010.[30] That decline apparently was partially attributable to the 2009 federal **Credit Card Accountability, Responsibility, and Disclosure Act** (CARD Act). Among other things, CARD forbids lenders from issuing credit cards to those under age 21 without a parent as cosigner or without proof the applicant can make payments. Many colleges and universities that have allowed credit marketing on campus have profited handsomely from deals with card companies. While federal rules have significantly curbed campus credit card marketing, about 900 colleges maintain card partnerships with banks, and other commercial relationships are common.[31] For example, Ohio State University, while not allowing credit card marketing to students, reportedly receives $25 million from Huntington Bank in return for allowing branches and ATMs on campus. The deal allows Huntington the exclusive opportunity to directly tailor products and services to more than 600,000 students, faculty, staff, and alumni.[32]

QUESTION FOR DISCUSSION

1. How would you argue that government intervention in the credit card market is not in the best interest of consumers generally and college students in particular?

A. TILA PROTECTIONS

The law offers substantial protections for credit card users. The TILA provides that credit cards cannot be issued to a consumer unless requested. Cardholder liability for unauthorized use (lost or stolen card) cannot exceed $50, and the cardholder bears no liability after notifying the issuer of the missing card. In general, issuers must disclose key cost features, including APR, annual membership fees, minimum finance charges, late payment fees, and so on.

B. CARD

The aforementioned CARD Act of 2009 provides extensive additional protection for credit card holders. Some of the key provisions:

Credit card companies are barred from increasing the annual percentage rate on existing account balances except when the cardholder's minimum payment is 60 days overdue.

- Issuers cannot charge interest on bills paid on time.

- Without specific agreement by the consumer, banks cannot accept charges where doing so puts creditors over their limits.

- Interest rates, with some exceptions, cannot be raised in the first year.

A WIN FOR CONSUMERS?

Debit card interchange fees (the charges paid by merchants to banks for providing debit processing services) had reached an average of 44¢ per transaction prior to the passage of the 2010 Dodd–Frank Act. By contrast, the median variable cost of each transaction was estimated at 7¢. Retailers and consumers argued that the two primary debit card processing services, Visa and MasterCard, were operating what amounted to a shared monopoly that permitted supra competitive pricing.

Following a battle by armies of lobbyists, Congress approved new rules allowing the Federal Reserve (The Fed) to cap the interchange fees. The Fed in 2011 settled on a maxi- mum charge of 21¢ per transaction with some additional small fees and a cap exemption for smaller banks. Following six months of transactions under the new rules, the Fed found that banks subject to the cap saw a 45 percent drop in their average fees—down to 24¢— whereas fees at smaller banks with an exemption stayed steady at about 43¢. The big banks say the fee cap merely shifts revenue to the big box retailers who are failing to pass on the fee savings to consumers. The banks also say the rule will force them to cut back on perks for customers while requiring new or increased fees on various services. At this writing, a federal district court judge has ruled that the 21¢ fee is higher than Congress intended in enacting Dodd–Frank. That decision has been appealed. [See **NACS v. Board of Governors of the Federal Reserve System**, 2013 U.S. Dist. LEXIS 107581]

CREDIT CARDS GOOD FOR THE WORLD?

By 2025 or so, Chinese residents are expected to expand their credit card holdings from 331 million at the end of the 2012 million to 1.1 billion and thereby pass the United States (536 million cards) as the world's biggest credit card market by number of cards. Credit cards are becoming a commonplace shopping tool in the developing world. As a result, those consumer are joining Americans and other Westerners in struggling to repay their credit card debt. For example, consumers in Turkey in recent years have embraced credit cards with enthusiasm, but having so, they increasingly find themselves in a "debt trap" built by high interest rates (nearly 29 percent in 2011). Turkey has imposed some regulatory restraints, but consumer rights advocate, Turhan Cakar, foresees continuing problems." Critics are concerned that consumers around the globe will be caught up in a debt cycle they often do not understand and that they cannot escape.

QUESTION

Is the consumer credit path embraced by Americans a wise course for consumers in developing nations around the world? List some of the competing arguments.

Sources: Bloomberg News, "Credit-Card Companies Battle in China," Bloomberg Businessweek, May 2, 2013 [www.businessweek.com/]; and Carol Matlack and Steve Byrant, "Turkey's Credit-Card Crunch," Bloomberg Businessweek, October 27, 2011 [www.businessweek.com].

Beyond the CARD Act, other recent federal credit card rule changes have provided additional consumer shelter. Those rules cap fees for late payments, banish penalties for inactive accounts (although those accounts can still simply be closed), and allow merchants to set a $10 minimum for credit card purchases.

Skepticism is often the response to new rules, but the early evidence suggests that the federal government's credit card measures have been good for consumers. A 2011 Pew study found that penalty fees have dropped, over limit fees (for charges beyond the credit limit) are now rare, and annual fees have not proliferated as some critics expected.[33] Furthermore, government officials have praised the industry itself for going even further than the law requires, although some banking officials believe the law has increased credit costs while decreasing credit availability.[34]

Section 5.7
Consumer Credit
Reports

Do you want to borrow money for a new car or a house? Want to get a better job? Success in each of those efforts may depend to a considerable extent on your credit score. A favorable credit rating is a vital feature of consumer life, and having reliable credit information is essential to efficient business practice. Thus, the three national credit information giants, Equifax, Experian, and TransUnion, as well as local credit bureaus, provide retailers, employers, insurance companies, and others with consumers' detailed credit histories. From those credit histories, a credit score is computed and sold to lenders. The federal Fair Credit Reporting Act (FCRA) affords consumers the following credit reporting protections, among others:

- Anyone using information from a credit reporting agency (CRA), such as Equifax, to take "adverse action" against you (denying you credit, a job, and insurance) must notify you and tell you where it secured the information.

- At your request, a CRA must give you the information in your file and a list of all those who have recently sought information about you.

- If you claim that your credit file contains inaccurate information, the CRA must investigate your complaint and give you a written report. If you remain unsatisfied, you can include a brief statement in your credit file. Notice of the dispute and a summary of your statement normally must accompany future reports.

- All inaccurate information must be corrected or removed from the file, usually within 30 days.

- In most cases, negative information more than seven years old must not be reported.

- You must provide written consent before a CRA can provide information to your employer or prospective employer.

- You can sue for damages if your rights under the act have been violated.

- Lenders are required to provide a consumer's credit score as well as any factors that affected that score if the lender took any adverse action based on that score.[35]

The FCRA provides useful consumer protection, but serious weaknesses remain. The Federal Trade Commission released a 2013 study showing that 20 percent of consumers have a material error on at least one of their credit reports. At least 5 percent of consumers suffer errors serious enough that they may pay more than they should for products.[36] Thus, millions of Americans have been injured, including some who may have been denied jobs because of inaccurate credit reports.

(Several states have limited the use of credit histories in making employment decisions.) When consumers try to correct their credit reports by filing complaints with the ratings agencies, the FTC found that the files are modified in about 80 percent of the cases.[37] In an effort to bring increased fairness to consumers, the Consumer Financial Protection Bureau now has supervisory authority over 30 of the largest credit bureaus, including the three biggest. Consumers can file credit report complaints with the CFPB. [For an extensive set of practical questions and answers about consumer rights under the Fair Credit Reporting Act, see www.ftc.gov/os/statutes/fcrajump.shtm]

**Section 5.8
Electronic Fund Transfers**

The **Electronic Fund Transfer Act** (EFTA) provides remedies for lost or stolen cards, billing errors, and other such problems involving ATMs, point-of-sale machines, electronic deposits, and the like. Under the EFTA, liability for misuse of missing cards is capped at $50 if the consumer provides notice within two business days after learning of the loss. The loss could reach $500 if notice is provided within 60 days and could be unlimited thereafter. The Dodd–Frank Act amended the EFT to impose limits on debit card interchange fees. [For consumer information on electronic banking, see www.ftc.gov/bcp/edu/pubs/consumer/credit/cre14.shtm]

**Section 5.9
Equal Credit Opportunity**

The **Equal Credit Opportunity Act** is designed to combat bias in lending. ECOA was in large part a response to anger over differing treatment of women and men in the financial marketplace. Credit must be extended to all creditworthy applicants regardless of sex, marital status, age, race, color, religion, national origin, good-faith exercise of rights under the Consumer Credit Protection Act, and receipt of public assistance (like food stamps).

LUCAS ROSA V. PARK WEST BANK & TRUST CO.
214 F.3D 213 (1ST CIR. 2000)

On July 21, 1998, Lucas Rosa came to the Park West Bank to apply for a loan. A biological male, he was dressed in traditionally feminine attire. He requested a loan application from Norma Brunelle, a bank employee. Brunelle asked Rosa for identification. Rosa produced three forms of photo identification: (1) a Massachusetts Department of Public Welfare Card; (2) a Massachusetts Identification Card; and (3) a Money Stop Check Cashing ID Card. Brunelle looked at the identification cards and told Rosa that she would not provide him with a loan application until he "went home and changed." She said that he had to be dressed like one of the identification cards in which he appeared in more traditionally male attire before she would provide him with a loan application and process his loan request.

Rosa sued the Bank. Rosa charged that "by requiring [him] to conform to sex stereotypes before proceeding with the credit transaction, [the Bank] unlawfully discriminated against [him] with respect to an aspect of a credit transaction on the basis of sex." He claims to have suffered emotional distress.

Without filing an answer to the complaint, the Bank moved to dismiss. . . . The district court granted the Bank's motion. The court stated, "The issue in this case is not [Rosa's] sex, but rather how he chose to dress when applying for a loan. Because the Act does not prohibit discrimination based on the manner in which someone dresses, Park West's requirement that Rosa change his clothes does not give rise to claims of illegal discrimination. Further, even if Park West's statement or action were based upon Rosa's sexual orientation or perceived sexual orientation, the Act does not prohibit such discrimination."

PriceWaterhouse v. Hopkins, which Rosa relied on, was not to the contrary, according to the district court, because that case "neither holds, nor even suggests, that discrimination based merely on a person's attire is impermissible."

On appeal, Rosa says that the district court "fundamentally misconceived the law as applicable to the Plaintiff's claim by concluding that there may be no relationship, as a matter of law, between telling a bank customer what to wear and sex discrimination."

The Bank says that Rosa loses for two reasons. First, citing cases pertaining to gays and transsexuals, it says that the ECOA does not apply to cross-dressers. Second, the Bank says that its employee genuinely could not identify Rosa, which is why she asked him to go home and change.

The ECOA prohibits discrimination, "with respect to any aspect of a credit transaction on the basis of race, color, religion, national origin,

sex or marital status, or age." Thus to prevail, the alleged discrimination against Rosa must have been "on the basis of...sex."

While the district court was correct in saying that the prohibited bases of discrimination under the ECOA do not include style of dress or sexual orientation that is not the discrimination alleged. It is alleged that the Bank's actions were taken, in whole or part, "on the basis of...[the appellant's] sex."... Whatever facts emerge, and they may turn out to have nothing to do with sex-based discrimination, we cannot say at this point that the plaintiff has no viable theory of sex discrimination consistent with the facts alleged.

The evidence is not yet developed, and thus it is not yet clear why Brunelle told Rosa to go home and change. It may be that this case involves an instance of disparate treatment based on sex in the denial of credit... It is reasonable to infer that Brunelle told Rosa to go home and change because she thought that Rosa's attire did not accord with his male gender; in other words, that Rosa did not receive the loan application because he was a man, whereas a similarly situated woman would have received the loan application. That is, the Bank may treat, for credit purposes, a woman who dresses like a man differently than a man who dresses like a woman. If so, the Bank concedes, Rosa may have a claim. Indeed, under PriceWaterhouse, "stereotyped remarks [including statements about dressing more 'femininely'] can certainly be evidence that gender played a part." It is also reasonable to infer, though, that Brunelle refused to give Rosa the loan application because she thought he was gay, confusing sexual orientation with cross-dressing. If so, Rose concedes, our precedents dictate that he would have no recourse under the Federal Act. It is reasonable to infer, as well, that Brunelle simply could not ascertain whether the person shown in the identification card photographs was the same person that appeared before her that day. If this were the case, Rosa again would be out of luck. It is reasonable to infer, finally, that Brunelle may have had mixed motives, some of which fall into the prohibited category.

It is too early to say what the facts will show; it is apparent, however, that, under some set of facts within the bounds of the allegations and nonconclusory facts in the complaint, Rosa may be able to prove a claim under the ECOA.

We reverse and remand

QUESTIONS FOR DISCUSSION

1. a. Did the court of appeals find that Park West Bank has violated the ECOA? Explain.
    b. If a trial, the facts reveal that the bank employee thought Rosa was gay and demanded that he change clothes for that reason, who will win this case? Explain.
    c. According to the court of appeals, how did the lower court misunderstand this case?

2. a. Does federal law protect bank customers based on their style of dress? Explain.
    b. Should it offer that protection? Explain.

SECTION 5.10
DEBTOR PROTECTION

Our ongoing financial crisis, one of the most destructive of modern times, has thrown millions of Americans deeply in debt. Wages can be garnished. Debts pile up on one another. Then the debt collection process continues the nightmare. The New York Times in 2010 recounted the story of Ruth M. Owens, a disabled Cleveland woman who was sued by Discover Bank in 2004 for an unpaid credit card bill. In six years, Ms. Owens had paid nearly $3,500 on her original balance of $1,900, but Discover sued her for $5,564 that had accumulated from late fees, compound interest, penalties, and charges even though she had not used the card to buy anything more. The judge called Discover's behavior "unconscionable" and threw out the case. Discover said that it turned the case over to a lawyer only after repeated unsuccessful efforts to reach Ms. Owens.[38]

Debtors are properly expected to repay what they owe, but critics claim debtors often are wrongly pursued. U.S. Senator Sherrod Brown (D-OH) explained:

It's hard enough when families aren't able to make enough to pay their bills, but it's tragic that families who are struggling to make ends meet are hounded to make payments on debts that they have already paid off or that they never owed in the first place.[39]

Furthermore, collectors reportedly call at all hours of the night, spewing obscenities, contacting family members or employers and falsely threatening property seizures or imprisonment.[40] Perhaps not surprisingly, the big banks—so broadly criticized for their roles in the financial meltdown—are likewise accused of involvement in unlawful debt-collection practices. At this writing in 2013, the state of California has sued the nation's largest bank, J P Morgan Chase, for having run a "massive debt collection mill" seeking wage garnishments and default orders against about 100,000 credit cardholders from 2008 to 2011. The complaint also accuses J P Morgan of practicing "sewer service" where the bank claims to have properly provided notice to the defendant-consumer of a debt-collection lawsuit when, in fact, notice was not provided.[41] Since about one in ten Americans is dealing with debt collectors,[42] and the consequences can be so destructive, both state and federal governments have developed extensive legal protections for debtors.

Debt Collection Law

The (FDCPA) is designed to shield debtors from unfair debt collection tactics by debt collection agencies and attorneys who routinely operate as debt collectors. FDCPA does not extend to creditors who are themselves trying to recover money owed to them. Often employing very aggressive tactics, several thousand debt collection agencies nationwide pursue those who are delinquent in their debts.

The FDCPA protects consumers by forbidding, among others, the following practices:

- Use of obscene language.

- Contact with third parties other than for the purpose of locating the debtor. (This provision is an attempt to prevent harm to the debtor's reputation.)

- Use of or threats to use physical force.

- Contact with the debtor during "inconvenient" hours. For debtors who are employed during "normal" working hours, the period from 9 pm to 8 am would probably be considered inconvenient.

- Repeated phone calls with the intent to harass.

- Contacting the debtor in an unfair, abusive, or deceptive manner.

The Federal Trade Commission and the Consumer Financial Protection Bureau jointly enforce the FDCPA. The CFPB also has supervisory authority over the largest debt collectors—about 175 firms. Under that authority, the CFPB provides a consumer complaint– dispute resolution process and determines whether debt collectors have harassed or deceived consumers along with assuring that debt collectors provide accurate information and fully disclose who they are and how much the consumer owes. In addition to federal and state regulatory protection, wronged consumers may sue for damages. [For more details about the FDCPA, see www.ftc.gov/os/statutes/fdcpajump.shtm].

The case that follows suggests some of the confusion that can arise in the debt collection process.

WILLIAMS V. OSI EDUCATIONAL SERVICES
505 F.3D 675 (7TH CIR. 2004)

Sandra Williams . . . sought relief under the Fair Debt Collection Practices Act ("FDCPA"). The district court granted the defendant, OSI Educational Services, Inc., ("OSI"), summary judgment. Ms. Williams then filed a timely appeal to this court.

Ms. Williams is a consumer whose debt was incurred for personal, family or household purposes. OSI is a debt collection agency; it was hired by Great Lakes Higher Education Guaranty Corp. ("Great Lakes") to collect its debts. OSI sent Ms. Williams a letter and a debt validation notice, dated March 28, 2005. The letter sought to collect a sum of $807.89 labeled as "Total Due," which was the outstanding balance owed to Great Lakes. The letter breaks down the amount owed as follows:

Date:	03/28/05
Principal:	$683.56
Interest:	16.46
Fees:	107.87
Total Due:	$807.89

The letter further states: The balance may not reflect the exact amount of interest which is accruing daily per your original agreement with your creditor. Contact us to find out your exact payout balance.

The district court . . . determined that the letter apprised Ms. Williams of the total amount due, including the amount of the principal, interest and fees due. The district court stated that, the letter clearly advises that additional interest is accruing on a daily basis and that, therefore, additional interest may be added. Comparing this case to **Taylor v. Cavalry Investment, L.L.C.,** the district court took the view that the letter complied with the statute because OSI's "letter states the amount of the debt clearly enough so that an unsophisticated recipient would not misunderstand it."

Ms. Williams submits that there is an issue of material fact as to whether OSI's letter clearly states the amount of the debt, as required by the FDCPA. In examining that contention, we begin with the wording of the statute. The FDCPA requires that debt collectors state "the amount of the debt" that they are seeking to collect from the consumer. The debt collector's letter must state the amount of the debt "clearly enough that the recipient is likely to understand it." **Chuway v. Nat'/Action Fin. Servs. Inc.** To ensure that this statutory command is implemented properly, we must evaluate the letter to determine whether it causes any "confusion" or "misunderstanding" as to the amount due. In making this determination, we evaluate the letter from the perspective of an "unsophisticated consumer or debtor." The unsophisticated consumer is "uninformed, naive, [and] trusting," but possesses "rudimentary knowledge about the financial world, is wise enough to read collection notices with added care, possesses 'reasonable intelligence,' and is capable of making basic logical deductions and inferences." **Pettit v. Retrieval Masters Creditors Bureau, Inc.** Notably, we have rejected explicitly the notion that we should employ the least sophisticated debtor standard, the "very last rung on the sophistication ladder" Pettit.

Our past cases indicate that summary judgment may be avoided by showing that the letter, on its face, will "confuse a substantial number of recipients." We also have said that, absent a showing that the face of the letter will precipitate such a level of confusion, the "plaintiff must come forward with evidence beyond the letter and beyond [her] own self-serving assertions that the letter is confusing in order to create a genuine issue of material fact for trial." **Durkin v. Equifax Checking Servs** (noting that evidence may consist of "carefully designed and conducted consumer survey[s]" or expert witnesses).

Ms. Williams chooses to base her case on the first of these options. She focuses on the following language from OSI's letter:

> The balance may not reflect the exact amount of interest which is accruing daily per your original agreement with your creditor. Contact us to find out your exact payout balance.

In her view, there are three reasons why OSI's letter would confuse a substantial number of recipients. We shall examine each.

First, Ms. Williams argues that the language in OSI's letter is more confusing than that in Chuway, which we held could "confuse a substantial number of recipients." Chuway. In that case, the letter stated the "balance" and also contained the following language: "Please remit the balance listed above in the return envelope provided. To obtain your most current balance information, please call [phone number]." We held that the letter violated the FDCPA. There, the confusion arose because the letter did not state why the "current balance" would be different than the stated "balance." The plaintiff could have thought that "the reference to the 'current balance' meant that the defendant was trying to collect an additional debt [without] telling her how large an additional debt and thus violating the statute." In contrast, the language in OSI's letter links the difference between the "total due" and the "exact payout balance" to the "interest which is accruing daily per your original agreement with your creditor." OSI's letter thus provides the information that created the confusion in the Chuway letter.

Ms. Williams' second and third arguments are best treated together. She submits that the letter's language leaves open the possibility that the actual amount due is less than the amount stated on the letter. She further suggests that the sentence's use of the present tense makes it possible to conclude that the stated amount due was not accurate on the date that the letter was written. In our view, both these contentions are based on a strained reading of the sentence. It would be "unrealistic, peculiar, [and] bizarre" to read OSI's letter in this way. The common sense reading of the letter is that the balance is accurate as of the date the letter is written, but that the amount due will increase because of interest that is accruing daily. This construction is supported by the letter's itemization of "PRINCIPAL," "INTEREST," "FEES" and "TOTAL DUE" in a box with, and immediately below, the "DATE." Under a natural reading, the language conveys, even to an unsophisticated consumer, that interest will accrue after the letter is sent and therefore that the consumer should call to find out the "exact payout balance."

As we said in Chuway, "It is impossible to draft a letter that is certain to be understood by every person who receives it; only if it would confuse a significant fraction of the persons to whom it is directed will the defendant be liable."

We believe that the language in this letter is closer to the language in Taylor than to the language in Chuway. In Taylor, the letter similarly set forth the total due and broke down that total into principal and interest. If further stated: "[I]f applicable, your account may have or will accrue interest at a rate specified in your contractual agreement with the original creditor." Three plaintiffs in Taylor had submitted affidavits stating that this sentence confused them about the amount of debt that the debt collector was trying to collect. We held that the language was "entirely clear on its face."

As we noted earlier, in opposing summary judgment, Ms. Williams relied solely on OSI's letter. She submitted no other evidence to support her view that OSI's letter is confusing. Without more, Ms. Williams' unsupported assertion that OSI's letter is confusing is insufficient to create a genuine issue of fact as to confusion.

The letter set forth the amount of the debt with sufficient clarity and accuracy to comply with the requirements of the statute. Affirmed.

QUESTIONS FOR DISCUSSION

1. A debt collection letter must be evaluated to determine whether it causes confusion or misunderstanding for the consumer. What level of consumer sophistication was employed by the court to determine whether the debt Collection letter to Williams caused confusion or misunderstanding?

2. Miller owed $2,501.61 to the Star Bank of Cincinnati. Payco attempted to collect the debt by sending a one-page collection form to Miller. The front side of the form included, among other words, in very large capital letters a demand for IMMEDIATE FULL PAYMENT, the words PHONE US TODAY, and the word NOW in white letters nearly two inches tall against a red background. At the bottom of the page in the smallest print on the form was the message: NOTICE: SEE REVERSE SIDE FOR IMPORTANT INFORMATION. The reverse side contained the validation notice required under the FDCPA. Does the form conform to FDCPA requirements? Explain. See **Miller v. Payco-General American Credits, Inc.,** 943 F.2d 482 (4th Cir. 1991).

3. Why shouldn't debt collectors be able to use aggressive tactics to encourage payment of legitimate bills?

FORECLOSURE FRAUD?

The mortgage industry, already buried in bad loans and worse publicity, faced another scandal in 2010 when the news emerged that some or perhaps many banks and individuals had not followed proper legal procedures in pursuing foreclosure orders against borrowers (commonly, the situation in which a homeowner fails to make mortgage payments and loses the home). Broadly, the scandal involved allegations that lenders bent rules to speed up the foreclosure process. Sloppy record keeping and outright errors apparently were routine. In a process now called "robo-signing," bank employees sometimes signed thousands of foreclosure affidavits in a single day, clearly never carefully examining them as expected. Critics now believe banks often cannot prove the facts necessary to achieve a lawful foreclosure. In some instances, the sloppy and perhaps negligent record keeping may even prevent banks from proving they are the legal owners of the properties being foreclosed on. Foreclosure proceedings were halted all over the country as bank and government officials reviewed records to see how common these problems were. Hundreds of thousands of homeowners now believe they were foreclosed on unlawfully.

State and federal officials and the five biggest mortgage servicing banks (e.g., JPMorgan Chase, Citigroup, and Ally Financial) reached a 2012 settlement totaling $25 billion in penalties to compensate for robo signing, faulty loan processing, and wrongful mortgage foreclosure practices. At least $17 billion of the settlement will go directly to homeowners. Many, many complaints remain, however, and at this writing, the New York state attorney general has indicated that he intends to sue Bank of America and Wells Fargo for failing to fulfill the settlement requirements.

Sources: Associated Press, "Foreclosure Class Actions Pile Up Against Banks," The Des Moines Register, November 18, 2010, p. 7B; Associated Press, "Iowa Attorney General: Mortgage Industry Problems Broad," The Des Moines Register, November 17, 2010, p. 7B; and Editorial, "Banks Still Behaving Badly," The New York Times, May 8, 2013 [www.nytimes.com/].

SECTION 5.11
BANKRUPTCY

A. FRESH START

Should we lend a hand to those subprime borrowers and others who are down on their luck? **Bankruptcy** law was specifically designed to provide a fresh start for those whose financial problems were insurmountable. We believed that both the debtor and society benefited from the new beginning. As bankruptcy filings skyrocketed, however, we down-sized the fresh start by reforming federal bankruptcy law in 2005 to force more bankrupt parties to repay their creditors. Following the reform, bankruptcies did fall somewhat in 2006 to about 618,000, then rose to a recession-era high of 1.6 million in 2010 before falling back in 2012 to about 1.2 million.[43] Of course, those tough times are often of our own making. At this writing in 2013, American consumers owed $2.8 trillion in non-mortgage debt, an average of $8,900 for every person in the nation.

Thus, we have millions of Americans deep in debt and facing a troubled economy. Does our bankruptcy system provide the rescue we intend for those people? A recent study concludes that the system falls short. Just one year following a declaration of bankruptcy, one in four debtors continues to struggle to pay routine bills and one in three reports a financial condition much the same or worse than was the case prior to the bankruptcy filing.[45] Without steady, sufficient income, the study finds that "bankruptcy is an incomplete tool to rehabilitate those in financial distress."[46]

B. BANKRUPTCY RULES

Bankruptcy in the United States is governed exclusively by federal law; the states do not have the constitutional authority to enact bankruptcy legislation, but they do set their own rules within the limits provided by Congress. Our attention will be limited to the principal federal statute, the Bankruptcy Reform Act of 1978, as amended. Bankruptcy is an adjudication relieving a debtor of all or part of his/her/its liabilities. Any person, partnership, or corporation may seek debtor relief. Three forms of bankruptcy action are important to us:

Liquidation (Chapter 7 of the Bankruptcy Act), is used by both individuals and businesses. Most debts are forgiven, all assets except exemptions are fairly distributed to creditors, and debtors receive a "fresh start."

Reorganization (Chapter 11), used by both individuals and businesses, keeps creditors from the debtor's assets while the debtor, under the supervision of the court, works out a financial reorganization plan and continues to pay creditors.

Adjustment of debts of an individual with regular income (Chapter 13), in which individuals with limited debts are protected from creditors while paying their debts in installments. [For frequently asked bankruptcy questions and links to bankruptcy sites on the Internet, see www.lawtrove.com/bankruptcy]

A. LIQUIDATION

A Chapter 7 liquidation petition can be voluntarily filed in federal court by the debtor, or creditors can seek an involuntary bankruptcy judgment. Chapter 7 liquidation is commonly called a "straight" bankruptcy.

In a voluntary action, the debtor files a petition with the appropriate federal court. The court then has jurisdiction to proceed with the liquidation, and the petition becomes the order for relief. The debtor need not be insolvent to seek bankruptcy.

Creditors often can compel an involuntary bankruptcy. The debtor may challenge that bankruptcy action. The court will enter an order for relief if it finds the debtor has not been paying his or her debts when due or if most of the debtor's property is under the control of a custodian for the purpose of enforcing a lien against that property.

After the order for relief is granted, voluntary and involuntary actions proceed in a similar manner. Creditors are restrained from reaching the debtor's assets. An interim bankruptcy trustee is appointed by the court. The creditors then hold a meeting, and a permanent trustee is elected. The trustee collects the debtor's property and converts it to money, protects the interests of the debtor and creditors, may manage the debtor's business, and ultimately distributes the estate proceeds to the creditors. Debtors are allowed to keep exempt property, which varies from state to state but typically includes a car, a homestead, some household or personal items, life insurance, and other "necessities." Normally a dollar maximum is attached to each.

The debtor's nonexempt property is then divided among the creditors according to the priorities prescribed by statute. Secured creditors are paid first. If funds remain, "priority" claims, such as employees' wages and alimony/child support, are paid. Then, funds permitting, general creditors are paid. Each class must be paid in full before a class of lower priority will be compensated. Any remaining funds will return to the debtor.

When distribution is complete, the bankruptcy judge may issue an order discharging (relieving) the debtor of any remaining debts except for certain statutorily specified claims. Those include, for example, taxes and educational loans. Thus, as noted above, the debtor is granted a "fresh start."

B. Reorganization

Under Chapter 11, the debtor may voluntarily seek reorganization, or the creditors may petition for an involuntary action. When a reorganization petition is filed with the court and relief is ordered, one or more committees of creditors are appointed to participate in bankruptcy procedures. Typically in the case of a business, the debtor continues operations, although the court may appoint a trustee to replace the debtor if required because of dishonesty, fraud, or extreme mismanagement. The company, its bankers, and its suppliers will meet to work out a method for continuing operations. A plan must be developed that will satisfy the creditors that their interests are being served by the reorganization. Perhaps new capital is secured, or perhaps creditors receive some shares in the company. The plan must be approved by the creditors and confirmed by the court. The company is then required to carry out the plan.

C. Adjustment of Debts

Under Chapter 13, individuals (not partnerships or corporations) can seek the protection of the court to arrange a debt adjustment plan. Chapter 13 permits only voluntary bankruptcies and is restricted to those with steady incomes and somewhat limited debts. The process can begin only with a voluntary petition from the debtor. Creditors are restrained from reaching the debtor's assets. The debtor develops a repayment plan. If creditors' interests are sufficiently satisfied by the plan, the court may confirm it and appoint a trustee to oversee the plan. The debtor may then have three to five years to make the necessary payments. [For an extensive bankruptcy law database, see www. law.cornell.edu/wex/Bankruptcy]

D. Bankruptcy Critique

The stigma that had historically attached to filing for bankruptcy dissipated somewhat in the "greed is good" 1980s, and bankruptcy became a more acceptable way of dealing with debts.[47] In an effort to benefit all by reducing unjustified and sometimes fraudulent bankruptcy filings, the federal Bankruptcy Abuse Prevention and Consumer Protection Act of 2005 has forced many debtors to seek bankruptcy through the challenging Chapter 13 process rather than the more forgiving Chapter 7. Debtors found to have some money (according to a means test) to apply to debts are required to take the Chapter 13 route, which requires a repayment plan rather than the much more attractive "fresh start" of Chapter 7. Supporters of the 2005 reform argue that it reduces the cost of credit for all Americans, but opponents see the changes as a punitive assault on those already down on their luck.

For individuals, the reform made the process much more complicated, and the average cost of filing more than doubled to more than $2,000.[48] During the recession, homeowners be- hind on their house payments often found mortgage foreclosure more attractive than bankruptcy. Thus, many borrowers simply walked away from their "underwater" homes, leaving lenders with mountains of troubled properties. (Rising home values and banks' mortgage modification decisions have recently reduced the number of underwater homes.)

SECTION 5.12
ETHICS

Is bankruptcy ethical? It depends upon what side of the fence you are on with respect to the financial crisis and how you define right and wrong. The creditor, who will have its debt extinguished, finds bankruptcy criminal and morally wrong. After all, the debtor is being "let off the hook" while the failure to receive the money can cause the creditor to suffer great financial difficulties and lost profits. To the debtor who has lost his or her job while using up the family savings, bankruptcy is the last hope and provides relief and a fresh start.[49]

Some will look at the Bible and presume that bankruptcy is unethical because it represents the failure to satisfy an obligation. However, the discharging of a debt was first referenced in the bible where the scriptures allowed for the release of a financial obligation every seven years.[50] Others will say that bankruptcy comes with a price. The debtor must liquidate much of his or her remaining property to give the proceeds to the creditor and there is a negative stigma that attaches to the insolvency. It makes it very difficult to obtain credit and buying a house or car is a very daunting task.[51]

Some facing financial collapse take advantage of the system. For instance, a financially strapped company will keep soliciting orders and advanced payments even though the business knows that it has no intention of fulling the orders or the restaurant will keep selling gift certificate when it is going to close its business operations.

How do you view the ethics of bankruptcy? Are you in favor or against it?

SECTION 5.13
PROBLEM CASES

1. DeSantis sued a debt collection agency, Computer Credit. DeSantis apparently owed $319.50 to Dr. Jeffrey A. Stahl, who assigned the debt to CC for collection. On April 27, 2000, CC sent the following collection letter to DeSantis: This notice will serve to inform you that your overdue balance with Dr. Jeffrey A. Stahl has been referred to Computer Credit, Inc., a debt collector. [The] doctor insists on payment or a valid reason for your failure to make payment. The law prohibits us from collecting any amount greater than the obligation stated above. Unless you notify us

to the contrary, we will assume the amount due is correct. This communication is sent to you in an attempt to collect this debt. Any information obtained will be used for that purpose in the absence of a valid reason for your failure to make payment, pay the above debt or contact the doctor to settle this matter. Payment can be sent directly to the doctor. The Fair Debt Collection Practices Act specifies that the consumer may dispute the alleged debt, in which case the debt collector must desist from collection until the debt collector obtains verification regarding the amount of the debt, if any. Given that statutory requirement, was the FDCPA violated by the italicized sentences in the collection letter? Explain. See **DeSantis v. Computer Credit, Inc.,** 269 F.3d 159 (2d Cir. 2001).

2. A New York Times editorial argued that college students are taken advantage of by credit card companies: The credit card industry has made a profitable art of corralling consumers into ruinous interest rates and hidden penalties that keep even people who pay their bills permanently mired in debt. The companies are especially eager to target freshly minted college students, who are naïve in money matters and especially vulnerable to credit card offers that are too good to be true.[49, 52]

   a. Do you think beginning college students are often "vulnerable" to manipulation by credit card companies?
   b. Are you vulnerable to that alleged manipulation?
   c. Should the federal government provide more protection against credit card deception? Explain.

3. Phusion Projects was accused by the Federal Trade Commission of mislabeling its flavored malt drink Four Loko. The FTC investigated the company's implied claims that consumers could safely drink one 23.5-ounce can at a sitting and that each can contained the alcoholic equivalent of one to two 12-ounce beers and concluded that those claims were misleading. The FTC found that a single Four Loko can had as much alcohol as four to five beers and that drinking one can on a single occasion would amount to binge drinking. Several states banned the drink and Phusion removed the caffeine and other stimulants. In 2013, the FTC ordered Phusion to put on the back of Four Loko cans containing more than two servings (a "serving" equals 0.6 ounces of alcohol) an "Alcohol Facts" panel that discloses alcohol content, serving size and the number of servings per can. Resealable containers are required for Four Loko drinks containing more alcohol than the equivalent of two and one-half servings.

   a. Many public comments to the FTC called for banning Four Loko from the market. Should the FTC do so? Explain.

b. From the FTC point of view, what consumer benefit was achieved by the order?

c. How would you have handled the Four Loko situation?

d. Millions of Americans are "underwater" on their home mortgages; that is, they owe more than their homes are worth. Many of those families could simply walk away from their mortgage, rent a similar home, and save thousands of dollars per year. Doubtless many decline to abandon their mortgages because they fear the consequences for their credit records and they want to avoid the cost of changing homes, but surely some continue to make payments simply because they believe defaulting would be immoral. While serving as U.S. Treasury Secretary, Henry Paulson said that anyone who walks away from his or her mortgage is "simply a speculator—and one who is not honoring his obligation."50 Make the argument that deliberately walking away from an underwater home morgage situation is immoral. Make the argument that walking away is not immoral.

e. What would you do? Explain. See Richard H. Thaler, "Underwater, but Will They Leave the Pool?" The New York Times, January 24, 2010 [www.nytimes.com]; and Brent T. White, "Buyers Have No Moral Duty to Lenders," Arizona Republic, April 25, 2010 [www.azcentral.com/arizonarepublic/viewpoints/articles/2010/04/25/2 0100425white25.htm].

4. William Cohan, writing in The New York Times, objected to the federal government's consumer protection efforts in the Dodd–Frank Wall Street Reform and Consumer Protection Act, including the creation of the Consumer Financial Protection Bureau. Explain why Cohan and other critics would object to the government's efforts to protect consumers from "devious credit-card companies" and "dishonest mortgage lenders." See William D. Cohan, "The Elizabeth Warren Fallacy," The New York Times, September 30, 2010 [http://opinionator.blogs.nytimes.com/].

5. Playtex manufactured the market-leading spill proof cup for children, which a child uses by sucking on a spout to cause a valve to open. Gerber introduced its own version and ran ads showing an unnamed competitor's product and claiming that "Gerber's patented valve makes our cup more than 50 percent easier to drink from than the leading cup." Gerber's claims for the superiority of its cup were backed by tests from an independent laboratory. Playtex said the unnamed cup obviously was its brand and that the superiority claims were false and misleading. Playtex sought an injunction to block the Gerber ads. Would you grant that injunction? Explain. See **Playtex Productsv. Gerber Products,** 981 F. Supp. 827 (S.D.N.Y. 1997).

6. Maguire, a credit card holder at Bradlees Department Store, fell behind in her payments. She received a series of dunning letters from Citicorp, which managed Bradlees' accounts, demanding that she pay the overdue amount. Later Maguire received a letter from "Debtor Assistance," which said that "your Bradlees account has recently [been] charged off." Debtor Assistance is a unit of Citicorp, but was not identified as such in the letter, beyond the phrase "a unit of CRS." The back of each Bradlees' account statement includes a notice that Citicorp Retail Services was the creditor that handled Bradlees' accounts. In general, creditors are not subject to the requirements of the Fair Debt Collections Practices Act, but Maguire sued claiming the Debtor Assistance letter violated the FDCPA. Is she correct? Explain. See **Maguire v. Citicorp Retail Services, Inc.,** 147 F.3d 232 (2d Cir. 1998).

7. A door-to-door salesman representing Your Shop at Home Services, Inc., called on Clifton and Cora Jones, who were welfare recipients. The Jones couple decided to buy a freezer from the salesman for $900. Credit charges, insurance, and so on were added to that $900 base so that the total purchase price was $1,439.69. Mr. and Mrs. Jones signed a sales agreement that accurately stipulated the price and its ingredients. The Joneses sued to reform the contract on unconscionability grounds. They had paid $619.88 toward the total purchase price. At trial, the retail value of the new freezer at the time of purchase was set at approximately $300.

    a. What is the issue in this case?
    b. Decide. Explain. **See Jones v. Star Credit Corp.,** 298 N.Y.S.2d 264 (1969).

8. Roseman resigned from the John Hancock Insurance Company following allegations of misuse of his expense account. He reimbursed the account. Subsequently he was denied employment by another insurance firm after that firm read a Retail Credit Company credit report on him. The credit report included accurate information regarding Roseman's resignation. Was Retail Credit in violation of the Fair Credit Reporting Act in circulating information regarding the resignation? Explain. See **Roseman v. Retail Credit Co., Inc.,** 428 F. Supp. 643 (Pa. 1977).

9. Consumers sometimes abuse sellers. One familiar technique is shoplifting. Of course, shoplifting is a crime. However, the criminal process is cumbersome and often does not result in monetary recoveries for sellers. As a result, at least 43 states now have laws permitting store owners to impose civil fines, the collection of which is usually turned over to a lawyer or collection agency with a threat to sue in civil court, file criminal charges, or both if payment is not forthcoming. Fines may range from $50 to $5,000 or more, depending on the value of the item stolen.

a. Defense lawyers say this civil fine system is unfair. Why?

b. On balance, is the civil fine approach to shoplifting a good idea? Explain.

c. Cite some other examples of consumers abusing business people.

10. Goswami failed to pay her $900 credit card bill. A collection agency, ACEI, mailed her a collection letter with a blue bar across the envelope saying "Priority Letter." The letter did not, in fact, constitute priority mail. The purpose of the bar was to encourage Goswami to open the envelope. Was the bar a deceptive practice in violation of the Fair Debt Collection Practices Act? Explain. See **Goswami v. American Collections Enterprise, Inc.,** 377 F.3d 488 (5th Cir. 2004); cert. den. 2005 U.S. LEXIS 5511.

*Reprinted with permission from "Consumer Protection," Law, Business and Society, by McAdams, Nesland and Nesland, Copyright 2015 by McGraw-Hill Companies.

Footnotes:

1. Walter Hamilton, "For-Profit Colleges Face Federal Crackdown," latimes.com, February 6, 2011 [www.latimes.com/business/la-fi-for-profit-colleges-20110206,0,1109616.story].

2. "Community College Funding Shrinks, For-Profit Enrollment Grows," Huff Post College, December 26, 2012 [www.huffington.com/].

3. Justin Pope, "Enrollment Falls at For-Profit Colleges, after Years of Growth," Des Moines Register, October 20, 2012, p. 8A.

4. Amer Madhani, "New Federal Rules Target For-Profit Colleges," USA Today, March 17, 2014 [http://www.usatoday.com/story/news/politics/2014/03/13/obama-for-profit-college-regulations/6386565/]. For a journalistic account of the 2012 federal court ruling and a broader discussion of the "gainful employment" rules, see Tamar Lewin, "Judge Strikes Main Element of For-Profit College Rules," The New York Times, July 1, 2012 [www.nytimes.com/].

5. James Rainey, "Truth in Advertising Meets the Blogosphere," latimes.com, October 7, 2009 [www.latimes.com/].

6. Brent Kendall, "Skechers to Pay $50 Million to Settle Ad Suit," The Wall Street Journal, May 17, 2012, p. B3.

7. Jeffrey D. Knowles et al., "FTC Survey Estimates Fraud Affected 25.6 Million Americans in 2011," LEXOLOGY, April 25, 2013 [www.lexology.com/].

8. J. Craig Anderson, "Identity Theft Growing, Costly to Victims," The Arizona Republic, April 14, 2013 [www.azcentral.com/business/consumer/articles/20130401identity-theft-growing-costly.html].

9. *Id.*

10. *Id.*

11. *Id.*

12. Levin, "Identity Theft in 2013: The Battle for Your Data," ABC News, December 23, 2012 [http://abcnews.go.com/].

13. Pete Yost, "Gov't: 1 in 14 Fell Prey to Identity Theft in 2012," boston.com, December 12, 2013 [www.boston.com/].

14. Alex Byers, "Privacy Issues at Top of Edith Ramirez's Federal Trade Commission Agenda," Politico, March 11, 2013 [http://dyn.politico.com/].

15. *Id.*

16. Monica Hesse, "Barbie Tells CPSC to Get the Lead Out in Viral Video," Washington Post, November 24, 2007, p. C01.

17. Associated Press, "New Crib Rules Toughest in World," The Des Moines Register, June 30, 2011, p. 7B.

18. Christopher Doering, "Surge in Products Being Recalled May Be Numbing Consumers," USA TODAY, June 20, 2012 [usatoday30.usatoday.com].

19. *Id.*

20. Jonathan V. O'Steen and Van O'Steen, "The FDA Defense: Vioxx and the Argument Against Federal Preemption of State Claims for Injuries Resulting from Defective Drugs," 48 Arizona Law Review 67 (2006).

21. Duff Wilson, "Merck to Pay $950 Million over Vioxx," The New York Times, November 22, 2011 [www.nytimes.com/].

22. P. J. Huffstutter, "Amid Mounting Safety Concerns, Technology Helps Track Food from Farm to Table," latimes.com, October 3, 2010 [www.latimes.com].

23. Neela Banerjee and Alana Semuels, "FDA Proposes Sweeping New Food Safety Rules," Los Angeles Times, January 4, 2013 [http://articles.latimes.com/].

24. Anna Edney and Catherine Larkin, "Drug Approvals Reach 15-Year High on Smoother FDA Reviews," Bloomberg, January 2, 2013 [www.bloomberg.com].

25. Andrew Zajac, "Most Recalled Medical Devices Received Speedy FDA Review," latimes.com, February 15, 2011 [latimes.com/health/la-na-medical-devices-20110215,0,4206876.story].

26. Thomas Philipson and Andrew von Eschenbach, "FDA Reform Can Lift U.S. Economy," Bloomberg, February 28, 2013 [www.bloomberg.com/].

27. *Id.*

28. *Id.*

29. JP, "Are Student Loans Ruining the Economy?" U.S. News & World Report, May 29, 203 [money.usnews.com/].

30. Joshua Eferighe, "College Students More Wary of Credit Card Debt," Washington Times, April 1, 2013 [www.washingtontimes.com/].

31. Andrew Martin, "On Campus, New Deals with Banks," The New York Times, May 30, 2012 [www.nytimes.com/].

32. *Id.*

33. Associated Press, "Positive Results Seen from Credit Card Law," Waterloo/Cedar Falls Courier, May 10, 2011, p. B7.

34. Jennifer Liberto, "Bank Critic Praises Credit Card Companies," CNNMoney.com, February 22, 2011 [http://money.cnn.com/fdcp?1298396190777].

35. This summary of FCRA requirements was drawn largely from the FTC document, "A Summary of Your Rights under the Fair Credit Reporting Act" [www.ftc.gov/bcp/conline/edcams/fcra/summary.htm].

36. Editorial Board, "Taking Credit Scores Seriously," The Washington Post, February 16, 2013 [www.washingtonpost.com/].

37. *Id.*

38. John Collins Rudolf, "Pay Garnishments Rise as Debtors Fall Behind," The New York Times, April 1, 2010 [www.nytimes.com] and Washington Post, "Punitive Charges Dog Credit Card Users," Waterloo/Cedar Falls Courier, March 7, 2005, p. A1.

39. "Brown Calls on CFPB to Enact Rules to Rein in Debt Collection Agencies and End Consumer Abuses," press release, June 5, 2013 [www.brown.senate.gov/].

40. Editorial, "When a Stranger Calls," The New York Times, July 9, 2006 [www.nytimes.com].

41. Danielle Douglas, "California Suing JPMorgan Over Debt-Collection Practices," The Washington Post, May 9, 2013 [www.washingtonpost.com/].

42. Susan Tompor, "Reining in Debt Collectors," USA TODAY, November 1, 2012, p. 5B.

43. "Latest Bankruptcies for the 12 Months Ended December 31, 2012," BankruptcyAction.com, June 11, 2013 [www.bankruptcyaction.com/].

44. "Average American Owes $8,900 in Consumer Debt and Does Not Use a Budget," The Central Banker, March 20, 2013 [www.thecentralbanker.com/].

45. Katherine Porter and Deborah Thorne, "The Failure of Bankruptcy's Fresh Start," 92 Cornell Law Review 67 (2006).

46. *Id.*

47. "Bankruptcy and Ethics," Experienced Bankruptcy Representation, http://chapter7-11.com/is%20it%20wrong%20to%20file%20bankruptcy.html (last visited February 23, 2016).

48. *Id.*

49. "Ethics of Bankruptcy," Baylor Business Review, http://bbr.baylor.edu/bankruptcy/ (last visited February 23, 2016).

50. John Greenya, "Bankruptcy Reform's Poor Legacy," Pacific Standard, October 2, 2008 [www. psmag.com/].

51. John Collins Rudolf, "Pay Garnishments Rise as Debtors Fall Behind," The New York Times, April 1, 2010 [www.nytimes.com/2010/04/02/].

52. Editorial, "The College Credit Scam," The New York Times, August 27, 2007 [www.nytimes. com].

53. Richard H. Thaler, "Underwater, but Will They Leave the Pool?" The New York Times, January 24, 2010 [www.nytimes.com].

KEY TERMS

Adjustment of debts

Bankruptcy

Chapter 7 of the Bankruptcy Act

Chapter 11 of the Bankruptcy Act

Chapter 13 of the Bankruptcy Act

Consumer Product Safety
  Commission

Doctrine of Unconscionability

Electronic Fund Transfer Act

Equal Credit Opportunity Act

Fair Credit and Charge Card
  Disclosure Act

Fair Credit Reporting Act

Fair Debt Collection Practices Act

Federal Trade Commission

Food and Drug Administration

Fraud

Identity Theft

Innocent Misrepresentation

Lemon Law

Liquidation

Puffing

Reorganization

Regulation Z

Truth in Lending Act

Unfair Practice and Consumer
  Protection Law

Unfair and Deceptive Trade
  Practices

CHAPTER 6

INTERSECTION OF RACE/ETHNICITY, LAW & REALITY

By: Vanessa J. Lawrence, Esq.

SECTION 6.1
INTRODUCTION

"Give me your tired, your poor, Your huddled masses yearning to breathe free, The wretched refuse of your teeming shore. Send these, the homeless, tempest-tossed to me, I lift my lamp beside the golden door!"

Statue of Liberty

The United States of America is an extremely diverse nation. A country whose foundation is composed of three groups: Native Americans, the original inhabitants; people who came here by choice; and people who were brought here by force. From the first settlement in Jamestown, Virginia in 1619 to the present, America's diversity continuously increases. This includes diversity of race, ethnicity, religion, economics and so many other areas: too many to discuss in a chapter or even a book. This chapter will provide an overview of some of the current race and ethnicity issues, specifically as it relates to Hispanic immigration and an historical overview of the impact law has had on race issues as it relates to African Americans.

"Give me your tired, your poor." This group came here by choice and they continue to come to the "land of opportunity." Historically, the majority within this group came from various parts of Europe and is classified as "white." During the later portion of the 20th and currently in the 21st centuries, there has been a vast increase in immigration by other races/ethnicities; particularly Asian and Hispanic. In 2014, Whites composed 62% of the U.S. population, Blacks 12%, Hispanics 18%, and Asians 6%. Predictions are that by 2042 the majority, white Americans, will become the minority.[1]

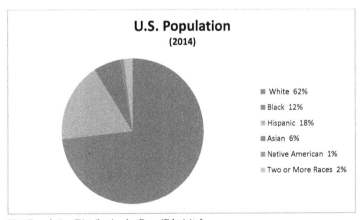

2014 Population Distribution by Race/Ethnicity[2]
Persons of Hispanic origin may be of any race; all other racial/ethnic groups are non-Hispanic.

According to U.S. Census Bureau projections, by 2050, the Black population is expected to increase to 15% and the Asian population is projected to increase to 9%. Hispanics are projected to nearly double to 30% of the total U.S. population. Thus, nearly one in three residents will be Hispanic.[3]

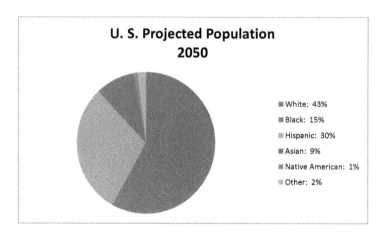

U. S. Projected Population 2050

- White: 43%
- Black: 15%
- Hispanic: 30%
- Asian: 9%
- Native American: 1%
- Other: 2%

SECTION 6.2
IMMIGRATION

A current issue with the existing and anticipated increase in the Hispanic population is that even though a portion is documented and in the U.S. legally, there is a large, undocumented segment that is here illegally. This raises an outcry by some for correction.

As a result of this changing diversity, race was and race and ethnicity currently are a part of many aspects of American society. It is involved in business, politics, education and it overlaps religion, gender, economic status, and so many other areas.

"Law" has been defined as "rules and regulations that governs one's conduct within a society." There are a plethora of laws regulating issues of race. However, law cannot and does not try to regulate all aspects of conduct within society. There are competing rights and interests that have to be balanced. Action and/or words that may be offensive to some, or even many, may be protected by the law.

As an example, during the 2016 primaries, statements were made by Presidential candidate Donald Trump in reference to Mexico that he would "build a wall, a great big beautiful wall, with a great big door in it," in reference to the illegal immigration issue with Mexico. Even though this statement is protected by the First Amendment, it remains very offensive to some. Others consider it a welcomed solution to a problem because estimates are that approximately one-half of the illegal immigrants in the U.S. are from Mexico. Illegal immigration is a controversial issue that intersects with race/ethnicity.

The Pew Research Center reported that in 2014 there were 11.3 million illegal immigrants in this country representing 3.5% of our nation's population.[4] The peak of unauthorized immigrants in the U.S. occurred in 2007, at 12.2 million, representing 4% of the national population.[5] It is difficult to accurately determine this number because this is a population with a vested interest to remain undocumented. There are estimates as high as 20 million for the number of people in the United States illegally. Laws and policies have been proposed, passed, implemented, and enjoined that affect the immigrant population.

The discussion has ranged from providing amnesty and a path to citizenship for some or even all immigrants who are here illegally; to the other extreme of deporting all individuals who are in this country illegally; to various proposals somewhere in between. Each branch of the Federal Government has weighed in on the issue. Recently, the executive branch has issued policies, Congress has debated the problem, and the judicial branch has ruled upon the question.

In an attempt to address the illegal alien issue, Congress debated the **Comprehensive Immigration Reform Act of 2007**. This bill offered citizenship to the millions of illegal aliens currently residing in the U. S. The proposed legislation created a new class of visa (Z visa) that would be given to anyone who was living illegally in the U. S. on January 1, 2007. This visa would provide its holder with the right to remain in this country for the rest of his or her life, and have access to a Social Security number. After eight years, those individuals would be eligible for a "green card" if they paid a $2,000 fine and back taxes for some of the period in which they worked. Based upon the existing immigration rules concerning green cards, five years later these illegal immigrants could begin the process of becoming U. S. citizens. The bill created another new category of visa (Y visa) that would let temporary guest workers stay in the U. S. for two years, after which they would have to return home. The proposed legislation also contained **The Dream Act** which would provide a fast-track to citizenship for illegal-immigrant minors who either go to college or serve in the U. S. military. It would also guarantee minors lower, in-state tuition rates if they attended a public university in their home state. Finally, the bill had provisions for added enforcement of the United States-Mexico border by increasing the number of border patrol agents to 20,000 and by adding another 370 miles of fencing. On June 28, 2007, the Immigration Reform Act of 2007 effectively died due to the inability of Congress to garner the necessary votes to end the debate on the bill.

In June 2012, the executive branch responded. President Obama's administration enacted a new immigration policy called **"Deferred Action for Childhood Arrivals"** (DACA). This program allows certain undocumented immigrants who entered the country before their

16th birthday and before June 2007 to receive a renewable two-year work permit and exemption from deportation. This policy confers legal status but does not provide a path to citizenship.[6]

In November 2014, the executive branch took additional action. President Obama announced DAPA, **Deferred Action for Parents of Americans** and **Lawful Permanent Residents**, and also announced an expansion of the DACA immigration policy. DAPA is another immigration policy that grants deferred status on undocumented immigrants. It applies to parents. It pertains to those who have been in the U.S. since 2010 and who have children who are U.S. citizens or lawful permanent residents. The parent, who is unlawfully in the U.S., may receive deferred action under DAPA and be able to temporarily stay in the U.S. without fear of deportation. Also under DAPA, that parent will be considered for employment authorization that would allow them to work legally in the U.S. for a three year period.[7]

In February 2015, the judicial branch of the federal government weighed in on this issue. A federal court issued a temporary injunction that halted the implementation of both DAPA and the expanded DACA immigration policies but did not affect the original DACA policy of 2012.[8] The United States Supreme Court granted the writ of certiorari in that case, **United States v. Texas**, and oral argument was scheduled for April 18, 2016. The court may determine, among other issues, whether the actions of the executive branch exceeded its authority under the "take care clause" of Article II of the U. S. Constitution.[9]

SECTION 6.3 STATE AND LOCAL INVOLVEMENT IN IMMIGRATION

Issues of race and/or ethnicity are not only addressed by each branch of the federal system, but at times the state system steps in. When challenged, these attempts are scrutinized carefully because immigration is generally a national concern but it clearly can have an impact at the state or even the local level.

In 1982, the United States Supreme Court ruled in **Plyler v. Doe** that Texas violated the Equal Protection Clause of the Fourteenth Amendment of the United States Constitution by "...deny[ing] to undocumented school-age children the free public education that it provides to children who are citizens of the United States or legally admitted aliens."[10] This case successfully challenged a revision made by the Texas Legislature to its education laws wherein the state withheld from local school districts any state funds for the schooling of children who were not "legally admitted" into the United States. The Texas law also authorized local school districts to deny enrollment in their public schools to children not "legally admitted" to the country. This case addressed school-age children of Mexican origin living in a local Texas school district who were in the U.S. illegally. Texas's efforts to have local school districts not enroll or provide public education to children in the U.S. illegally was unsuccessful.

Advancing the clock to 2006, a local government regulated immigration. In Hazelton, a small Pennsylvania town with population less than 30,000, the City Council passed an ordinance entitled "**Illegal Immigration Relief Act.**"[11] Section 2 states:

> *The People of the City of Hazleton find and declare:*
>
> A. *That illegal immigration leads to higher crime rates, contributes to overcrowded classrooms and failing schools, subjects our hospitals to fiscal hardship and legal residents to substandard quality of care, contributes to other burdens on public services, increasing their cost and diminishing their availability to lawful residents, and destroys our neighborhoods and diminishes our overall quality of life.*[12]

The ordinance imposed fines and denied business permits to any person or entity that hired or attempted to hire, rented, leased, or provided goods and services to illegal aliens.[13] The ordinance also contained an English only clause:

> *SECTION 6.   ENGLISH ONLY*
>
> A. *The City of Hazleton declares that English is the official language of the City.*
>
> B. *Unless explicitly mandated by the federal government, the state of Pennsylvania or the City of Hazleton, all official city business, forms, documents, signage will be written in English only.*[14]

Hazelton was the start: other local and state governments have passed laws that attempt to control illegal immigration. These local and state actions were in response to federal inaction. Prior to DACA and DAPA, during 2006 and 2007 at the federal level, heated, but ultimately fruitless, congressional debates took place over immigration reform, such as the Comprehensive Immigration Reform Act of 2007 and The Dream Act. However, the perception, particularly within some communities experiencing rapid immigration growth, was that the federal government was unable to address the issue of the estimated 12 million unauthorized immigrants. Locales such as Riverside, New Jersey, Valley Park, Missouri, and Farmers Branch, Texas, adopted ordinances similar to Hazelton's.[15] "...there is no comprehensive database of all local-level immigration enforcement laws considered post-Hazleton, estimates suggest that between July 2006 and July 2007, U.S. towns and counties actively considered 118 immigration enforcement proposals. And between 2000 and 2010, 107 U.S. towns, cities, and counties had approved local immigration enforcement ordinances."[16]

QUESTION FOR DISCUSSION:

1. What are the arguments for and against local government regulating immigration?

After the inaction during 2006 and 2007 by the federal government to pass any laws to address the illegal immigration problem, states increased their actions. In 2007, Arizona was the first state to enact a law that required all businesses to use the federal **E-Verify** system to determine whether new employees were authorized to work. A business could lose its business licenses if shown that it knowingly hired unauthorized immigrants. Three years later, Arizona enacted **S.B. 1070,** followed by five other states enacting similar laws (Utah, South Carolina, Indiana, Georgia, and Alabama) allowing local and/or state police officers to inquire about immigration status if there was reasonable suspicion that the person they stopped was an unauthorized immigrant, made it a state crime if an immigrant did not carry proof of immigration status, and a crime for an immigrant to apply for or get a job in the state if there illegally.

The U.S. Supreme Court spoke in both of these situations. In 2011, the Supreme Court in **Chamber of Commerce of The United States v. Whiting** (563 U.S. 582), upheld Arizona's E-Verify requirement for all employers and permitted the state to use its licensing authority to penalize businesses that knowingly hired unauthorized immigrants.

In 2012, the Supreme Court in **Arizona v. United States** (132 S. Ct. 2492), determined that the state statute operated in areas solely controlled by federal policy or interfered with federal enforcement efforts. Specifically, the Supreme Court found unconstitutional the parts of Arizona's statute that made it a crime for an immigrant to be in Arizona without legal papers, made it a crime to apply for or obtain a job in the state, and allowing police to arrest individuals who had committed crimes that could lead to their deportation. The Supreme Court left intact for possible future lower court challenges the most controversial provision of S.B. 1070 that required police to make reasonable attempt to determine the immigration status of a person stopped, detained or arrested if there is reasonable suspicion that person is in the country illegally and holding that person until their immigration status could be checked with federal officials. It must be noted that various civil rights groups also challenged Arizona's S.B. 1070 statute as a form of racial bias, but that issue was not considered by the U.S. Supreme Court.

Following the Supreme Court rulings in **Whiting** and **Arizona** and the Supreme Court's refusal to grant certiorari in the appeal of the **Hazleton** case, in 2013 the United States Court of Appeals for the Third Circuit re-affirmed its previous decision concerning the Hazleton ordinance holding "...that both the employment and housing provisions of the Hazleton ordinances are preempted by federal immigration law."[17] Additionally, Hazleton was ordered to pay $1.4 million in attorney's fees.

There are other state efforts to regulate immigration. Under DACA unauthorized immigrant youth can obtain a two-year reprieve from deportation however, two states, Nebraska and Arizona, state policies prohibit these youth from obtaining driver's licenses. In 48 states, these same youth can lawfully obtain a driver's license. Florida's highest court recently held that unauthorized immigrants are ineligible for admission to the state bar to practice law. California has enacted legislation providing for the opposite outcome.

QUESTION FOR DISCUSSION:

1. What concerns exist when states take completely opposite positions on issues involving illegal immigrants?

SECTION 6.4
RACE AND OTHER ISSUES

"We the People of the United States, in Order to form a more perfect Union, establish Justice, insure domestic Tranquility, provide for the common defense, promote the general Welfare, and secure the Blessings of Liberty to ourselves and our Posterity, do ordain and establish this Constitution for the United States of America."

Preamble to the U. S. Constitution

"...nor shall any State ...deny to any person within its jurisdiction the equal protection of the laws."

U.S. Constitution
XIV Amendment

Issues of race and law are a part of most, if not all, aspects of life in America. They can overlap with issues of color, ethnicity, culture, and class; can intersect with economic, political, social and religious issues; and run parallel to issues involving gender, age, and disability. Due to this intertwining, it is often difficult to identify and it is almost impossible to isolate the race component. Is every citizen included in "We" of "We the people"? Is every citizen equally protected?

In 2015, in Flint, Michigan, it was determined that lead was in the drinking water, poisoning the residents. This lead laden water has greater impact on children under the age of six. It can cause brain damage, learning disabilities, and motor coordination problems among other issues. This is a prime example of the intersection of so many issues: race, law, economics, federal, state, and local government, and politics, to name a few. How did this happen? The state government ordered the take-over of the local government and an appointment of a manager to govern Flint because the city was experiencing an economic crisis. Flint was on the brink of bankruptcy. The manager, appointed by the governor, as one of his efforts to defray costs, changed the source of the water supply from Lake Huron (one of the five Great Lakes of North America) to the Flint River. The Flint residents complained that their drinking water was discolored, contained an odor, and questioned its quality. The city of Flint is 25% black, 10 % Hispanic and a vast majority of households are below the poverty line. Some residents experienced health issues including rashes, hair loss, fever… The Flint residents were assured by government officials at various levels that there were no issues with the quality of the water. After over a year of residents' complaints and over a year of reassurance by government, it was determined, by an outside entity, that the water from the Flint River source had caused excessive amounts of lead to leach into the water; poisoning the Flint residents. This determination was made in February 2015.

Over one year later, the residents continue to receive their water from the same source and no permanent remedy has been implemented. The residents that are able to do so are required to drive to water distribution locations to receive two cases of bottled water each day. This water is to be used for all water needs: drinking, cooking, bathing, washing hair… On the federal level, in 2016, Congress held hearings questioning the Republican Governor and the Director of Environmental Services, a Democratic appointee. But the federal government has not issued any funding to remedy this issue. The Michigan state budget has a $1.1 billion excess, but it has not appropriated any funds. The control of the government has been returned to local officials. Two class action lawsuits have been filed by the Flint residents against the Governor and the City.[18] The water that flows through the Flint waterlines still contains lead and this situation is awaiting a solution.

The Michigan Governor commissioned the "Flint Water Advisory Task Force," an independent body, to investigate the Flint water crisis and to make findings and recommendations. On March 21, 2016, the Task Force issued its final report wherein it made numerous findings including one that the Government failed the residents of Flint at every single level. The report references race, ethnicity, economics,

> *The facts of the Flint water crisis lead us to the inescapable conclusion that this is a case of environmental injustice. Flint residents, who are majority Black or African American and among the most impoverished of any metropolitan area in the United States, did not enjoy the same degree of protection from environmental and health hazards as that provided to other communities. Moreover, by virtue*

of their being subject to emergency management, Flint residents were not provided equal access to, and meaningful involvement in, the government decision-making process.

The occurrence of environmental injustice in the Flint water crisis does not indict or diminish other public and private efforts to address Flint's many challenging circumstances. However, irrespective of the intent of the parties involved, the simple reality is that the Flint water crisis is a case of environmental injustice.[19]

THE TASK FORCE REPORT ALSO STATED THAT:

Among African American seniors, the protracted Flint water crisis echoes the tragic Tuskegee syphilis study and the decision not to treat smallpox among freedmen in the aftermath of the American Civil War. From this perspective, it is noted that measuring blood lead levels without removing the sources of lead from the environment—in this case, lead-tainted water—appears the equivalent of using Flint's children (and adults) as human bioassays.[20]

QUESTIONS FOR DISCUSSION:

1. What is the current situation with the toxic water in Flint, Michigan?

2. Has a permanent solution been found and implemented?

3. Discuss other situations were issues of race are intertwined with other factors.

4. What are those factors?

5. Discuss the role that race, economics, politics played in the initial decision to change the water sources.

6. What, if any, role did race, economics, politics play in remedying the situation?

7. What legal remedies do you think the residents are seeking in their class action lawsuits?

For a better understanding of the Task Force's report, there is a need to rewind. An historical examination of the intertwining factors may shed additional light on the issue of race as it relates to African Americans.

**SECTION 6.5
HISTORICAL
EXAMINATION**

"We hold these truths to be self-evident, that all men are created equal, that they are endowed by their Creator with certain unalienable Rights, that among these are Life, Liberty and the pursuit of Happiness."

Declaration of Independence

When that statement was made, did "all" include all? Despite the noble statement espoused in the Declaration of Independence and the Constitutional mandate of "equal protection of the laws," those concepts did not apply to the race of people that were brought here by force. When these historic documents were written, slavery not only existed but was protected by the Constitution. The migration and importation of Africans was left up to the individual states and Congress was prohibited from amending that clause until 1808. The original Constitution also counted African Americans as only 3/5 of a person for purposes of determining taxation and representation. On the other hand, Native Americans were not counted on the premise they were not taxed. Census figures from 1790 determined that African Americans composed 19.3% of this country's population and 92.15% of these individuals were slaves. Race was, therefore, an issue.

Advancing the clock seventy years to 1857, race continued to be an issue in this country. This is demonstrated by the plight of Dred Scott, a slave who sued for his freedom after he returned with his master from residing in a free state. The United States Supreme Court ruled against Mr. Scott. The Court's ruling went well beyond the plight of Dred Scott. This country's highest Court expanded its review and held that African Americans were not citizens of the United States. The Court's ruling extended well beyond Mr. Scott, to include not only all African American slaves, but also to include all African Americans who were free. In 1857, a little over one hundred fifty years ago, the highest court in this country determined that an entire race of people, who had been a part of this country since its first continuous settlement in Jamestown, Virginia in 1619, were not citizens and therefore had no rights or protection provided by the U.S. Constitution. Race for the group of people that was forced to come here was an issue.

The **Dred Scott** decision affords a reader in the 21st century excellent, written documentation of how African Americans were viewed in this country for over two and one half centuries; from 1619-1857. An excerpt of the **Dred Scott** decision follows.

DRED SCOTT V. SANDFORD
19 HOW. 393 (1857)

The question is this: Can a negro become a member of the community formed and brought into existence by the Constitution of the United States, and become entitled to all the rights, and privileges guaranteed by that instrument to the citizens?

This plea applies to that class of persons only whose ancestors were Negroes of the African race, imported into this country, and sold and held as slaves. The only issue is, whether the descendants of such slaves, when they shall be emancipated, or who are born of parents who had become free before their birth, are citizens of a State, in the sense the word citizen is used in the Constitution.

The question then arises, whether the provisions of the Constitution embraced the African race, at that time in this country, or who might afterwards be imported, who had then or should afterwards be made free in any State?

The court thinks the affirmative of these propositions cannot be maintained. And if it cannot, the plaintiff could not be a citizen, within the meaning of the Constitution.

It becomes necessary to determine who were citizens of the States when the Constitution was adopted. In order to do this, we must refer to the Governments and institutions of the thirteen colonies, when they separated from Great Britain. We must inquire who, at that time, were recognized as citizens of a State, whose rights and liberties had been outraged by the English Government; who declared their independence, and assumed the powers of Government to defend their rights by force of arms.

In the opinion of the court and the language used in the Declaration of Independence, neither the class of persons who had been imported as slaves, nor their descendants, were intended to be included in the general words used in that memorable instrument.

It is difficult to realize the state of public opinion in relation to that unfortunate race, which prevailed in the civilized and enlightened portions of the world at the time of the Declaration of Independence. But the public history of every European nation displays it in a manner too plain to be mistaken.

They had for more than a century before been regarded as beings of an inferior order, and unfit to associate with the white race, either in social or political relations;

and so far inferior, that they had no rights which the white man was bound to respect; and that the Negro might justly and lawfully be reduced to slavery for his benefit. He was bought and sold, and treated as an ordinary article of merchandise. This opinion was at that time fixed and universal in the civilized portion of the white race.

And in no nation was this opinion more firmly fixed or more uniformly acted upon than by the English Government and English people. They not only seized them off the coast of Africa, and sold them in slavery for their own use; but they took them as ordinary articles of merchandise to every country where they could make a profit on them, and were far more extensively engaged in this commerce than any other nation in the world.

(Colonial laws and the state of feeling toward blacks) show that a perpetual and impassable barrier was intended to be erected between the white race and the one which they had reduced to slavery, and governed as subjects with absolute and despotic power, and which they then looked upon as so far below them in the scale of created beings, that intermarriages between white persons and negroes or mulattoes were regarded as unnatural and immoral, and punished as crimes, not only in the parties, but in the person who joined them in marriage. And no distinction in this respect was made between the free Negro or mulatto and the slave, but this stigma, of the deepest degradation, was fixed upon the whole race.

The Declaration of Independence proceeds to say: "We hold these truths to be self-evident: that all men are created equal; that they are endowed by their Creator with certain unalienable rights; that among them is life, liberty, and the pursuit of happiness; that to secure these rights, Governments are instituted, deriving their just powers from the consent of the governed."

The general words above quoted would seem to embrace the whole human family. But it is too clear for dispute that the enslaved African race were not intended to be included, and formed no part of the people who framed and adopted this declaration; for if the language would embrace them, the conduct of the distinguished men who framed the Declaration of Independence would have been utterly inconsistent with the principles they asserted.

Yet the men who framed this declaration were great men, and incapable of asserting principles inconsistent with those on which they were acting. They perfectly understood the meaning of the language they used, and how it would be understood by others; and they knew that it would not in any part of the civilized world be

supposed to embrace the Negro race, which had been excluded from civilized Governments and the family of nations and doomed to slavery. The unhappy black race were separated from the white by indelible marks, and laws long before established, and were never thought of or spoken of except as property.

The court is of opinion, that Dred Scott was not a citizen within the meaning of the Constitution of the United States.

Mr. Justice McLean dissenting.

In the argument, it was said that a colored citizen would not be an agreeable member of society. This is more a matter of taste than of law. Several of the States have admitted persons of color to the right of suffrage, and in this view have recognized them as citizens; and this has been done in the slave as well as the free States...

QUESTION FOR DISCUSSION:

1. Relying upon at least two passages from the Supreme Court's majority opinion, discuss how each provides insight into how African Americans were viewed in 1857.

The Chief Justice of the Supreme Court stated in the majority opinion that "[a black man] had no rights which the white man was bound to respect." This was how African Americans were viewed by society at the time. The court also stated, "...that the Negro might justly and lawfully be reduced to slavery for his benefit." These statements and others in the **Dred Scott** decision demonstrate that an individual's race was an issue.

SECTION 6.6
THE FIRST STEPS
TOWARDS CHANGE

Steps to eradicate these perceptions were taken by the legislative branch of the federal government following the Civil War. Three Constitutional Amendments were added that are collectively known as the **Civil War Amendments: Amendment Thirteen** abolished slavery, **Amendment Fourteen** made all persons born or naturalized in the United States citizens of the United States, determined that each person would be counted as a whole person (but excluded Native Americans), established the equal protection and due process clauses, and prohibited any state from assuming or paying any debt based on the loss or emancipation of any slave. **Amendment Fifteen** gave the right to vote to all citizens regardless of race, color, or previous condition of servitude.

During this same period, Congress passed the first two Civil Rights Acts. The **Civil Rights Act of 1866** was enacted over the veto of President Andrew Jackson and provided that all persons born in the United States must be considered citizens, without regard to race, color, or previous condition of slavery. The Native American, however, was not protected by this legislation. It also gave citizens of every race the right to make contracts, sue, purchase, sell, and convey real and personal property and to have full and equal benefits of the laws as enjoyed by white citizens. A violation of this law was a crime and carried a fine not to exceed $1,000, or imprisonment of up to one year.

The **Civil Rights Act of 1875** mandated that all public accommodations and facilities be made available to all people regardless of race and there must be equality in the use of transportation, theaters, and other places of public amusement.

QUESTIONS FOR DISCUSSION:

1. The Fifteenth Amendment states: "(t)he right of citizens of the United States to vote shall not be denied or abridged by the United States or by any State on account of race, color, or previous condition of servitude." Does this Amendment guarantee the right to vote?

2. Does the Civil Rights Act of 1866 apply to individual or private discrimination against another based on race?

3. What do you think is the current status of the CRA 1875? Support your response.

4. Congress passed the Civil War Amendments and Civil Rights Acts in an attempt to bring about equality following the abolition of slavery. Do you think the U. S. Supreme Court's decisions that were rendered after the passage of those laws continued the march towards equality?

SECTION 6.7
THE SUPREME COURT

In reality, the Civil Rights Act of 1875 was largely ignored. The judicial branch of the federal government also weighed in on this issue. The Supreme Court was asked to pass upon the constitutionality of this legislation. Not only did the Justices find the Civil Rights Act of 1875 unconstitutional but it also ruled that the Fifteenth Amendment did not guarantee all people the right to vote, only a right not to be discriminated against in voting. The legislative branch took steps forward towards change but the judicial branch took steps to maintain the status quo.

Many of the southern states seized upon these court pronouncements to support the enactment of various ways to dilute the African American's right to vote. Methods such as poll taxes, literacy tests, and **Grandfather Clauses** were enacted that were either administered in a discriminatory fashion or had a disparate impact upon African Americans. Out of all of the impediments enacted, Grandfather Clauses had the greatest impact. Eleven states had such statutes or clauses in their constitution. For example, Louisiana's Grandfather Clause stated that "you could vote, if your father and grandfather could vote as of January 1, 1867." On its face, this type of clause appears to be fair, and to apply to all people regardless of race. However, it had a desperate impact on the African American race. Remember, it was not until 1870 that the Fifteenth Amendment was ratified giving African Americans the right to vote. In 1896, there were 130,344 African Americans registered to vote in Louisiana, thereby constituting a majority in 26 parishes in that state. By 1900, or just two years after the adoption of that state's new constitution, only 5,320 African Americans were on the voter registration books. Of 181,471 African American males of voting age in Alabama in 1900, only 3,000 registered after the new constitutional provision went into effect.[21] Race was an issue.

SECTION 6.8
SEPARATE BUT EQUAL

Once the federal troops left the south following the end of the Civil War, barriers were erected to maintain the discriminatory practices against African Americans. Known as **Jim Crow Laws**, states passed legislation that required businesses to maintain separate facilities for people based upon race. This practice came to a head in 1892 when Homer Plessy refused to sit in a railroad car designated for African Americans. This act of defiance found its way to the Supreme Court where the court sanctioned the ill conceived concept of **separate but equal**. Arguably, that principle is still having lingering effects on race relations today.

PLESSY V. FERGUSON
163 U.S. 537 (1896)

This case turns upon the constitutionality of an act of the General Assembly of Louisiana, providing for separate railway carriages for the white and colored races.

The statute enacts "that all railway companies carrying passengers in their coaches, shall provide equal but separate accommodations for the white, and colored races. No person shall be admitted to occupy seats in coaches other than the ones assigned to them on account of the race they belong to."

The information filed in the criminal District Court charged that Plessy, was assigned to the coach used for the race to which he belonged, but he insisted upon going into a coach used by the race to which he did not belong.

Plessy was seven-eighths Caucasian and one-eighth African blood; that the mixture of colored blood was not discernible, and that he was entitled to every right, privilege and immunity secured to citizens of the United States of the white race; and he took possession of a vacant seat in a coach where passengers of the white race were accommodated, and was ordered by the conductor to vacate said coach and take a seat in another assigned to persons of the colored race, and having refused to comply with such demand he was forcibly ejected with the aid of a police officer, and imprisoned to answer a charge of having violated the above act.

The constitutionality of this Act is attacked upon the ground that it conflicts both with the Thirteenth Amendment abolishing slavery, and the Fourteenth Amendment which prohibits certain restrictive legislation on the part of the States.

A statute which implies merely a legal distinction between the white and colored races and which must always exist so long as white men are distinguished from the other race by color has no tendency to destroy the legal equality of the two races, or reestablish a state of involuntary servitude. Indeed, we do not understand that the Thirteenth Amendment is strenuously relied upon by the plaintiff in error in this connection.

By the Fourteenth Amendment, the object of the Amendment was undoubtedly to enforce the absolute equality of the two races before the law, but in the nature of things it could not have been intended to abolish distinctions based upon color, or to enforce social equality, or a commingling of the two races upon terms unsatisfactory to either. Laws permitting, and even requiring, their separation in places where they are liable to be brought into contact do not necessarily imply the inferiority of either race to the other, and have been generally, if not universally, recognized as within the competency of the state legislatures in the exercise of their police power.

So far, then, as a conflict with the Fourteenth Amendment is concerned, the case reduces itself to the question whether the statute of Louisiana is a reasonable regulation. In determining the question of reasonableness the legislature is at liberty to act with reference to the established usages, customs and traditions of the people, and the preservation of the public peace and good order. Gauged by this standard, we cannot say that a law which authorizes or even requires the separation of the two races in public conveyances is unreasonable.

We consider the underlying fallacy of the plaintiff's argument to consist in the assumption that the enforced separation of the two races stamps the colored race with a badge of inferiority. If this be so, it is not by reason of anything found in the act, but solely because the colored race chooses to put that construction upon it. If the two races are to meet upon terms of social equality, it must be the result of natural affinities, a mutual appreciation of each other's merits and a voluntary consent of individuals. If one race be inferior to the other socially, the Constitution of the United States cannot put them upon the same plane.

The judgment of the court below is, therefore, *Affirmed.*

This decision provided the legal authorization for maintaining two separate societies within the United States. While slavery was abolished in 1865, the segregation of the races was now authorized by the highest court in this country.

QUESTIONS FOR DISCUSSION:

1. What do you think may have been the relationship between the races if the Supreme Court had reached the opposite decision from the one rendered in **Plessy?**

2. What are some reasons why the separate but equal standard announced in **Plessy** should not be maintained?

3. Does separation of a race stamp a race with a badge of inferiority?

SECTION 6.9
THE JAPANESE AMERICAN
EXPERIENCE

From a historical perspective, most of the legal issues involving race focused on whites, Native Americans and African Americans. This changed during World War II when the court examined certain discriminatory practices directed to those of Japanese descent residing in this country.

As a result of the attack on Pearl Harbor, President Roosevelt authorized directives that placed a curfew and another that excluded Japanese people from certain military zones in the United States irrespective of whether they were American citizens.

Hirabayshi was a Japanese student at the University of Washington, and he refused to obey a curfew imposed against the Japanese. His disobedience resulted in a criminal conviction. The Supreme Court considered the constitutionality of that conviction in **Hirabayashi v. United States,** 320 U.S. 81 (1943). The order in question required all persons of Japanese ancestry to be confined to their home between the hours of 8 p.m. to 6 a.m. The Court concluded that this curfew was a constitutional exercise of power by the government to take steps necessary to prevent espionage and sabotage in an area threatened by Japanese attack.

A short time later, the Supreme Court was again called upon to determine the constitutionality of an even more restrictive executive order.

KOREMATSU v. UNITED STATES
323 U.S. 214 (1944)

The petitioner, an American citizen of Japanese descent, was convicted for remaining in San Leandro, California, a "Military Area," contrary to Civilian Exclusion Order No. 34, which directed that all persons of Japanese ancestry be excluded from that area. No question was raised as to petitioner's loyalty to the United States.

Exclusion Order No. 34, which the petitioner knowingly and admittedly violated, was one of a number of military orders issued after we were at war with Japan, declaring that the successful prosecution of the war requires every possible protection against espionage and sabotage to national-defense material, national-defense premises, and national-defense utilities.

One of the series of proclamations, a curfew order, which like the exclusion order here was promulgated pursuant to Executive Order 9066, subjected all persons of Japanese ancestry in prescribed West Coast military areas to remain in their residences from 8 p.m. to 6 a.m. As is the case with the exclusion order here, that prior curfew order was designed as a "protection against espionage and against sabotage."

Exclusion from the area in which one's home is located is a far greater deprivation than constant confinement to the home from 8 p.m. to 6 a.m. Nothing short of apprehension by the proper military authorities of the gravest imminent danger to the public safety can constitutionally justify either. The military authorities, charged with the primary responsibility of defending our shores, concluded that curfew provided inadequate protection and ordered exclusion. They did so in accordance with Congressional authority to the military to say who should, and who should not, remain in the threatened areas.

We uphold the exclusion order and in doing so, we are not unmindful of the hardships imposed by it upon a large group of American citizens. But hardships are part of war, and war is an aggregation of hardships. All citizens alike feel the impact of war in greater or lesser measure. Citizenship has its responsibilities as well as its privileges, and in time of war the burden is always heavier. Compulsory exclusion of large groups of citizens from their homes, except under circumstances of direst emergency and peril, is inconsistent with our basic governmental institutions. But when under conditions of modern warfare our shores are threatened by hostile forces, the power to protect must be commensurate with the threatened danger.

It is said that we are dealing here with the case of imprisonment of a citizen in a concentration camp solely because of his ancestry, without evidence or inquiry concerning his loyalty and good disposition towards the United States. Our task would be simple were this a case involving the imprisonment of a loyal citizen in a concentration camp because of racial prejudice. Regardless of the true nature of the assembly and relocation centers—and we deem it unjustifiable to call them concentration camps with all the ugly connotations that term implies—we are dealing with nothing but an exclusion order. To cast this case into outlines of racial prejudice, without reference to the real military dangers which were presented, merely confuses the issue. Korematsu was not excluded from the Military Area because of hostility to him or his race. He was excluded because we are at war with the Japanese Empire, because the properly constituted military authorities feared an invasion of our West Coast and felt constrained to take proper security measures, because they decided that the military urgency of the situation demanded that all citizens of Japanese ancestry be segregated from the West Coast temporarily. There was evidence of disloyalty on the part of some, the military authorities considered that the need for action was great, and time was short. We cannot—by availing ourselves of the calm perspective of hindsight—now say that at that time these actions were unjustified. *Affirmed.*

Mr. Justice Roberts, dissenting.

I dissent, because I think the indisputable facts exhibit a clear violation of Constitutional rights.

This is not a case of temporary exclusion of a citizen from an area for his own safety or that of the community, nor a case of offering him an opportunity to go temporarily out of an area where his presence might cause danger to himself or to his fellows. On the contrary, it is the case of convicting a citizen as a punishment for not submitting to imprisonment in a concentration camp, based on his ancestry, and solely because of his ancestry, without evidence or inquiry concerning his loyalty and good disposition towards the United States. If this be a correct statement of the facts disclosed by this record, and facts of which we take judicial notice, I need hardly labor the conclusion that Constitutional rights have been violated.

Mr. Justice Murphy, dissenting.

This exclusion of "all persons of Japanese ancestry from the Pacific Coast on a plea of military necessity in the absence of martial law ought not to be approved. Such exclusion goes over "the very brink of constitutional power" and falls into the ugly abyss of racism.

Being an obvious racial discrimination, the order deprives all those within its scope of the equal protection of the laws. It further deprives these individuals of their constitutional rights to live and work where they will, to establish a home where they choose and to move about freely.

That this forced exclusion was the result in good measure of this erroneous assumption of racial guilt rather than bona fide military necessity is evidenced by the Commanding General's Final Report on the evacuation from the Pacific Coast area. In it he refers to all individuals of Japanese descent as "subversive," as belonging to "an enemy race" whose "racial strains are undiluted," and as constituting "over 112,000 potential enemies." In support of this blanket condemnation of all persons of Japanese descent, however, no reliable evidence is cited to show that such individuals were generally disloyal, or had generally so conducted themselves in this area as to constitute a special menace to defense installations or war industries, or had otherwise by their behavior furnished reasonable ground for their exclusion as a group.

Similar disloyal activities have been engaged in by many persons of German, Italian and even more pioneer stock in our country. But to infer that examples of individual disloyalty prove group disloyalty and justify discrimina-

tory action against the entire group is to deny that under our system of law individual guilt is the sole basis for deprivation of rights.

I dissent from this legalization of racism. Racial discrimination in any form and in any degree has no justifiable part whatever in our democratic way of life.

Mr. Justice Jackson, dissenting.

Korematsu was born on our soil, of parents born in Japan. The Constitution makes him a citizen of the United States and a citizen of California by residence. No claim is made that he is not loyal to this country. There is no suggestion that apart from the matter involved here he is not law-abiding and well disposed. Korematsu, however, has been convicted of an act not commonly a crime. It consists merely of being present in the state whereof he is a citizen, near the place where he was born, and where all his life he has lived.

Even more unusual is the series of military orders which made this conduct a crime. They forbid such a one to remain, and they also forbid him to leave. They were so drawn that the only way Korematsu could avoid violation was to give himself up to the military authority. This meant submission to custody, examination, and transportation out of the territory, to be followed by indeterminate confinement in detention camps.

A citizen's presence in the locality, however, was made a crime only if his parents were of Japanese birth. Had Korematsu been one of four—the others being, say, a German alien enemy, an Italian alien enemy, and a citizen of American-born ancestors, convicted of treason but out on parole—only Korematsu's presence would have violated the order. The difference between their innocence and his crime would result, not from anything he did, said, or thought, different than they, but only in that he was born of different racial stock.

In 1988, Congress enacted the **Civil Liberties Act** formally recognizing the injustice done to those of Japanese ancestry in the United States by the evacuation, relocation, and internment of civilians during World War II.

Congress found that the internments by the government were carried out without adequate security reasons and were motivated primarily by racial prejudice, wartime hysteria, and failure of political leadership.

Because the excluded individuals suffered incalculable losses in education and job training, surviving internees were eligible to receive restitution of $20,000 each from the federal government.

QUESTIONS FOR DISCUSSION:

1. Which opinion of the court in **Korematsu v. United States** do you agree with and why?

2. Do you believe the American government in 1988 should have compensated the survivors of the internment camps for the actions that took place during World War II? What is your opinion on the amount of money that was awarded?

3. How did the actions taken by the U. S. Government during WWII deprive its Japanese citizens of their "due process rights" guaranteed by the 14th Amendment?

4. Is there any way that the U. S. Government could have protected itself from espionage and sabotage and at the same time afforded its Japanese citizens their Constitutional guaranteed rights.

SECTION 6.10
EQUALITY IN EDUCATION

In 1954, the Supreme Court was again called upon to decide an issue involving the segregation of the races. This time the question was whether segregation in public schools is constitutional? Now that the composition and judicial philosophy of the Supreme Court had changed since **Plessy v. Ferguson** and the separate but equal doctrine had come under increasing criticism, the time for change was in the wind. This occurred in **Brown v. Board of Education**, (Brown I) when the court ruled that segregation in public education was inherently unconstitutional.

This case has been declared one of the most important rulings during the twentieth century since it reversed many years of legally authorized segregation and disparate treatment of African Americans.

Brown v. Board of Education
347 U.S. 483 (1954)

These cases come to us from the States of Kansas, South Carolina, Virginia, and Delaware.

In each, minors of the Negro race seek the aid of the courts in obtaining admission to the public schools of their community on a non-segregated basis. In each instance, they had been denied admission to schools attended by white children under laws requiring or permitting segregation according to race. This segregation was alleged to deprive the plaintiffs of the equal protection of the laws under the Fourteenth Amendment.

The doctrine of "separate but equal" did not make its appearance in this Court until 1896 in *Plessy v. Ferguson* involving not education but transportation. American courts have since labored with the doctrine.

In the instant cases, there are findings that the Negro and white schools involved have been equalized with respect to buildings, curricula, qualifications and salaries of teachers, and other "tangible" factors. Our decision, therefore, cannot turn on merely a comparison of these tangible. We must look instead to the effect of segregation on public education.

Education is perhaps the most important function of state and local governments. Compulsory school attendance laws and the great expenditures for education both demonstrate our recognition of the importance of education to our democratic society. In these days, it is doubtful that any child may reasonably be expected to succeed if he is denied the opportunity of an education.

We come to the question presented: Does segregation of children in public schools solely on the basis of race, even though the physical facilities and other "tangible" factors may be equal, deprive the children of the minority group of equal educational opportunities? We believe that it does.

Segregation of white and colored children in public schools has a detrimental effect upon the colored children. The impact is greater when it has the sanction of the law; for the policy of separating the races is usually interpreted as denoting the inferiority of the Negro group. A sense of inferiority affects the motivation of a child to learn. Segregation with the sanction of law, therefore, has a tendency to [retard] the educational and mental development of Negro children and to deprive them of some of the benefits they would receive in a racially integrated school system.

We conclude that in the field of public education, the doctrine of "separate but equal" has no place. Separate educational facilities are inherently unequal. Therefore, we hold that the plaintiffs and others similarly situated are, by reason of the segregation complained of, deprived of the equal protection of the laws guaranteed by the Fourteenth Amendment.

The Supreme Court in **Brown v. Board of Education** (**Brown 1**) did not fashion a remedy so the court revisited the case in 1955, (**Brown II**) and noted that the school districts needed to desegregate with "all deliberate speed." Did the public school systems, particularly some of the ones in the southern states, desegregate with all deliberate speed?

There was massive resistance to the Court's ruling. Many saw this as an issue involving states' rights v. federal law. Local school districts in states such as Virginia closed school districts to avoid desegregation. They did not want white and African American children to go to school together. In Little Rock, Arkansas, Governor Faubus used the National Guard to prevent nine African American students, who had been selected by the school board, from desegregating Central High School. Upon the intervention of President Dwight Eisenhower, the Governor withdrew the National Guard leaving the local police to handle the volatile situation. The President had to summon the elite 101st Airborne Division of the United States Army to Little Rock, thus removing the issue of desegregation from the Governor's control. Race was still an issue in this country

SECTION 6.11 CIVIL RIGHTS LEGISLATION

Congress continued in its struggle to pass remedial legislation that would bring about racial equality. After an 82 year gap in legislation, the Civil Rights Acts of 1957, 1960, and 1964 were enacted. Each built upon the other and provided additional legal tools to fight unequal treatment solely because of the color of one's skin.

The **Civil Rights Act of 1957** established the Commission on Civil Rights and gave this organization the power to investigate allegations of discrimination and deprivation of the right to vote. The Act also established the Civil Rights Division within the Justice Department with an Assistant Attorney General to head that special division and imposed fines if convicted of unlawful conduct.

The **Civil Rights Act of 1960** strengthened existing laws on obstruction of court orders and imposed criminal penalties for violence and destruction. It also provided for court appointed referees to monitor voting rights.

In 1963, President Kennedy was instrumental in the introduction of a bill to ban discrimination in the work place regardless of one's racial makeup. Because of his assassination, however he never saw his idea come to fruition. Instead, the **Civil Rights Act of 1964** became the law under the guidance of President Lyndon Johnson. The purpose of this progressive legislation was multifaceted including the enforcement of the constitutional right to vote, to confer jurisdiction upon the federal courts, to provide injunctive relief against discrimination in public accommodations, to authorize the Attorney General to institute suits to protect the constitutional rights in public facilities and public education, to prevent discrimination in federally assisted programs, to establish the **Equal Employment Opportunity Commission (EEOC)**, and for other purposes.

There are three sections of the Civil Rights Act of 1964 that are of particular relevance. **Title IV** addresses public education and calls for desegregation within public education at all levels; elementary, secondary and college. **Title VI** focuses on federally assisted programs and provides for nondiscrimination within those federal programs. In fact, federal funds will be terminated if the party receiving the money refuses to voluntarily comply with the statute. Of the three titles, however, **Title VII** is the most commonly recognized section. Its purpose is to eliminate job discrimination in employment by making it illegal to discriminate in employment based on race, color, religion, sex or national origin. It also created the Equal Employment Opportunity Commission to enforce the law.

Relying upon the Civil Rights Acts as its foundation, Congress passed the **Elementary and Secondary Education School Act of 1965** which provided for federal school aid for the first time to insure that the poor received a proper education. In order to receive federal funds, the local school districts must abide by the requirements of the Civil Rights Acts. Local districts had to choose between whether to maintain segregation or receive the massive federal funding that had been made available. Needless to say, they opted for the money, thereby bringing statutorily mandated, de jure segregation in public education to an end. In some districts, however, de facto segregation continues due to factors such as housing patterns, neighborhood school systems, and economics.

**SECTION 6.12
EEOC**

On the federal level, the U.S. Equal Employment Opportunity Commission (EEOC) is the administrative agency responsible for enforcing federal laws that make it illegal to discriminate against a job applicant or an employee because of the person's race, color, religion, sex (including pregnancy), national origin, age (40 or older), disability or genetic information. It is also illegal to discriminate against a person because that individual complained about discrimination, filed a charge of discrimination, or participated in an employment discrimination investigation or lawsuit. EEOC laws cover most employers with at least 15 employees, most labor unions, and employment agencies. This governmental agency has the authority to investigate charges of discrimination against a covered employer, make findings, and attempt to settle if the agency finds that discrimination has occurred. The EEOC also can file a lawsuit to protect the rights of individuals or the interests of the public. However, lawsuits are not filed in all cases where discrimination is found. The EEOC has other responsibilities that relate to its covered areas including providing leadership and guidance to other federal agencies. Their headquarters is in Washington, D.C. with 53 field offices serving the United States.[22]

In February 2007, the Equal Employment Opportunity Commission (EEOC) "launched a national initiative to bring a fresh, 21st century approach to combating racism, which remains the most frequent claim filed with the agency." In an effort to identify and implement new strategies that will strengthen its enforcement of Title VII of Civil Rights Act of 1964 and advance the statutory right to a workplace free of race and color discrimination, the EEOC instituted the **E-RACE Initiative** (Eradicating Racism and Color in Employment).[23]

New forms of discrimination are emerging based on race and color. Recent studies have shown that employees with lighter colored skin are paid more or favored over a darker skinned employee even though the darker skinned employee had higher educational credentials.[24] Facially neutral employment criteria are significantly disadvantaging applicants and employees on the basis of race and color. Practices such as employers using names as a basis for making selection decisions, employment and personality tests, use of credit scores or video resumes can all have a disparate impact. With a growing number of interracial marriages and families and increased immigration, racial demographics of the workforce have changed and the issue of race discrimination in America is multi-dimensional.[25]

E-Race is a multi-faceted approach. It involves outreach, education, and an enforcement campaign. EEOC chairperson stated "new times demand new strategies to stay ahead of the curve. These old evils are still around in new forms and we intend to act vigorously to eradicate them."[26]

Title VII of the Civil Rights Act of 1964 created the EEOC and is one of the most important federal statutes that the EEOC is responsible for enforcing. In 2014, race discrimination remained the most frequent ground for discrimination alleged under Title VII, comprising 35% of the charges filed with the Commission under all the statutes the agency enforces. African Americans filed 25,482 of these charges.[27] National origin discrimination comprised 11% of charges filed with EEOC in 2014 under all the statutes the agency enforces. Of these charges, Hispanics filed 4,469.[28] In 2014, race and national origin discrimination comprised 45% of the complaints filed with EEOC under all the statutes the agency enforces. Of these race or national origin charges, Asian-Americans files 1,213.[29]

**SECTION 6.13
RACE AND
INTER-PERSONAL
RELATIONSHIPS**

In 1967, the Supreme Court reviewed one of the most sensitive areas in race relations; inter-racial marriage. The court was called upon in **Loving v. Virginia**, 388 U.S. 1, to determine the constitutionality of **miscegenation statutes**; laws that regulate interracial relationships including dating and marriage. The law in question provided: "If any white person intermarries with a colored person, or any colored person intermarries with a white person, he shall be guilty of a felony and shall be punished by confinement in the penitentiary for not less than one nor more than five years." At the time, Virginia and fifteen other states had statutes that prevented marriages between persons solely on the basis of race. In declaring these laws unconstitutional on the basis of the Equal Protection Clause, the court stated that "there can be no question but that Virginia's miscegenation statutes rest solely upon distinctions drawn according to race." Further, "there is patently no legitimate overriding purpose independent of invidious racial discrimination which justifies this classification."

QUESTIONS FOR DISCUSSION:

1. Why do you think the area of inter-racial relationships was one of the last to be addressed by the Supreme Court?

2. Is there any justifiable area in our daily existence when racial segregation does not violate the Constitution?

3. Is it ever "o.k." to discriminate based upon race?

SECTION 6.14
AFFIRMATIVE ACTION

An outgrowth of the Civil Rights Acts is the concept of **affirmative action**. This phrase was not mentioned in any previous legislation. Affirmative action as it applies to race has become controversial. This concept attempts to achieve racial equality by recognizing that certain employers and educational facilities need to create affirmative goals so that disadvantaged groups are placed upon a level playing field with other candidates when employment and admission decisions are made. The term was first coined by President Kennedy in Executive Order 10925. Among other things, that Order required projects financed with federal funds to "take affirmative action" to ensure that hiring and employment practices are free of racism.

President Johnson outlined the premise for "affirmative action" in a speech at Howard University, when he stressed that civil rights laws are not enough to fix years of discrimination. He stated:

You do not wipe away the scars of centuries by saying: now, you are free to go where you want, do as you desire, and choose the leaders you please. You do not take a man who for years has been hobbled by chains, liberate him, bring him to the starting line of a race, saying, you are free to compete with all the others, and still justly believe you have been completely fair. This is the next and more profound stage of the battle for civil rights. We seek not just freedom but opportunity—not just legal equity but human ability—not just equality as a right and a theory, but equality as a fact and as a result.

Subsequently, he issued an Executive Order mandating affirmative action for the first time. It required government contractors to "take affirmative action" toward minorities in all aspects of hiring and employment. Also, contractors must take and document all measures to ensure equality in hiring. A few weeks later, the Order was amended to cover discrimination on the basis of gender as well.

In 1969, President Nixon implemented the **Philadelphia Order** which is the most forceful program to guarantee fair hiring practices in construction jobs. Philadelphia was selected as the test case because, as Assistant Secretary of Labor Arthur Fletcher proclaimed, "The craft unions and the construction industry are among the most egregious offenders against equal opportunity laws . . . openly hostile toward letting blacks into their closed circle." This order also included specific goals and timetables which had to be followed. President Nixon said, "We would not impose quotas, but would require federal contractors to show affirmative action to meet the goals of increasing minority employment."

Affirmative action is a polarizing subject in many circles. Opponents maintain that affirmative action is nothing more than reverse discrimination and allows for the admission or employment of less qualified persons. Advocates argue that it is merely an attempt to level the playing field. What is often missed in these arguments it that affirmative action, or preferential treatment, is not limited to African Americans, but applies equally to other minorities, women, and in many instances to other subgroups such as military veterans and the handicapped.

It must be acknowledged that the idea of affirmative action existed long before the 1960's and continues to this day. It just was not labeled affirmative action nor was it applied to minorities. For example, legacy preferences in college admissions, in-state tuition reduction, free college tuition to employees, spouses, and children, and the "old boy network" are just some examples of preferential treatment afforded to certain classes of people.

The **legacy preference**, as it is known, is as widespread as the affirmative action programs based on race and ethnicity. Colleges like these preferences because it keeps alumni happy and more inclined to donate. But overwhelmingly, the legacy preference benefits Caucasians. It has a disparate impact.

For example, 91% of the legacy applicants at the University of Virginia accepted on an early-decision basis for the fall of 2003 were white; 1.6% were black, 0.5% were Hispanic, and 1.6% were Asian. Among applicants whose parents were not alumni of the University, the pool of those accepted was more diverse: 73% were Caucasians, 5.6% African American, 9.3% Asian and 3.5% Hispanic. About half of the legacy applicants accepted at Virginia were children of out-of-state alumni. Virginia gives these applicants a break by grouping them with its in-state applicants. The SAT scores of accepted state residents averaged about 30 to 35 points lower than those of accepted out-of-state applicants.[30]

It must not be overlooked, however, that elimination of this form of preferential treatment would have serious financial implications for colleges and universities. Alumni provide approximately 28% of the private donations to higher education.

At most Ivy League schools, it is estimated that sons and daughters of graduates make up 10% to 15% of the student body and enjoy a sharply higher rate of acceptance. For instance, Harvard accepts 40% of legacy applicants, compared with an 11% overall acceptance rate of its applicants. Princeton accepts 35% of the children of alumni who apply, but only 11% of the overall applicant pool. The University of Pennsylvania accepts 41% of legacy applicants, compared with an admission rate of 21% overall.[31]

Acceptance based upon legacy is not always as clear cut as awarding additional points or placement in a different applicant pool. It may include favoritism based on social class or a specific high school. President George W. Bush attended Yale. While the University did not have an explicit point system in 1964, Bush received preferential treatment. After all, he was the product of an exclusive prep school, the son and grandson of alumni, and a member of a politically influential family. His admission to this prestigious University was not based solely upon his SAT scores: 566 verbal and 640 math.[32] These forms of affirmative action programs continue; they just have a different label.

Affirmative action programs stemming from the civil rights movement focus primarily on education and employment. These policies require that active measures or affirmative steps, be taken to ensure that women, African Americans, and other minorities and subgroups enjoy the same opportunities for employment, promotions, salary increases, career advancement, school admissions, scholarships, and financial aid that had been the nearly exclusive province of Caucasians in this country.

These initiatives have met with resistance on many levels. For instance, the Supreme Court considered the issue of reverse discrimination in **Regents of the University of California v. Bakke,** 438 U.S. 265 (1978). Bakke is a white male, who had been rejected two times by a medical school in California. The institution had two separate admissions pools, one for standard applicants, and another for minority students. The school maintained a quota in which it reserved 16 of its 100 places for minority students. Bakke was refused admission while minority applicants with lower scores were granted admission. The Supreme Court ruled that a fixed quota system was unlawful. However, it upheld affirmative action by ruling that it was lawful to consider race as a factor in school admissions.

In 1995, the Supreme Court refined its affirmative action position in **Adarand Constructors, Inc. v. Pena** by imposing a "strict scrutiny" test in determining whether discrimination exists before a federal affirmative action program may be implemented. This meant that an affirmative action program must fulfill a "compelling governmental interest," and it has to be "narrowly tailored" to fit the particular situation. The Court's majority held that "the unhappy persistence of both the practice and the lingering effects of racial discrimination against minority groups" justified the use of race-based correctional measures only under particular circumstances.

The following month, President Clinton acknowledged this new standard for affirmative action programs and stated "it actually reaffirmed the need for affirmative action and reaffirmed the continuing existence of systematic discrimination in the United States." On the same day, he issued a White House memorandum that called for the elimination of any program that creates a quota, establishes preferences for unqualified individuals, mandates reverse discrimination, or continues after its equal opportunity purposes have been achieved.

The up and down history of affirmative action continued when in 1996, a United States Court of Appeals in **Hopwood v. University of Texas Law School**, suspended the University of Texas' affirmative action admissions program and opined that the **Bakke** decision was invalid. The appellate court rejected diversity as a goal, asserting that "educational diversity is not a compelling state interest." The U. S. Supreme Court did not hear the appeal so the decision was allowed to stand.

In 1997, the Texas Attorney General announced that all "Texas public universities (should) employ race-neutral criteria." In that same year, California enacted "**Proposition 209**" which banned all forms of affirmative action. That mandate provided: "The state shall not discriminate against, or grant preferential treatment to, any individual or group on the basis of race, sex, color, ethnicity, or national origin in the operation of public employment, public education, or public contracting."

The pendulum continued to swing away from affirmative action at a state level in several other jurisdictions. For instance, in 1998, the State of Washington enacted Initiative 200 making it the second state to completely abolish state affirmative action measures. In 2000, the Florida legislature approved the education component of Gov. Jeb Bush's "One Florida" initiative. This ended admission programs based on affirmative action in all of Florida's colleges and universities.

The United States Supreme Court, however, spoke again in 2003 on affirmative action. The University of Michigan's undergraduate and law school affirmative action policies were called into question in **Gratz v. Bollinger** and **Grutter v. Bollinger** respectively. The highest court determined that modification was needed to the undergraduate policy of awarding additional points to minorities during the admission process. The law schools' admission policy of merely taking race into account as one of many factors considered in the process was upheld because it furthered "a compelling interest in obtaining the educational benefits that flow from a diverse student body." Unlike the undergraduate program that utilized a formula, the law school's affirmative action program provided "individualized consideration" which the U.S. Supreme Court allowed. This decision effectively over ruled the **Hopwood** case from Texas.

In June of 2007, in **Parents Involved in Community Schools v. Seattle School District**, the Supreme Court reexamined the issue of race in a case involving integration in the public school systems of Seattle and Louisville. The Court rejected the integration plans that had been implemented but left the door open for using race to assign students in limited circumstances. As the court stated, "A district may consider [race] a compelling interest to achieve a diverse student population... Race may be one component of that diversity."

In 2013, the Supreme Court in **Fisher v. University of Texas**, ruled that an affirmative action program that mirrored the one approved in the **University of Michigan** case must be able to meet a "strict scrutiny" test and remanded the case for a review of the facts in view of that test. The **Fisher** case had a second trip back to the Supreme Court where arguments were heard at the end of 2015. In 2016, the Supreme Court is posed to issue its decision, but lacking the presence of the most ultra conservative view on the court. Justice Antonin Scalia died in 2016, before the Supreme Court rendered its decision.

Following the U.S. Supreme Court's ruling in the **University of Michigan** case, the voters of Michigan approved a referendum that barred publicly funded colleges from granting "preferential treatment to any individual or group on the basis of race, sex, color, ethnicity or national origin." In 2014, in the **Schuette v. Coalition to Defend Affirmative Action**, the Supreme Court did not rule on the constitutionality of affirmative action in college admissions but did uphold the Michigan voter's right to ban the use of race as one of many factors in determining admissions to public universities.

Affirmative action continues to be constitutional while race continues to be an issue. A decision in **Fisher** is pending as of the writing of this chapter. The Supreme Court in 2016, just like they did in 1875, holds in the balance whether laws or policy can address issues of race because there is not only a recognized need but also a benefit or rule that race is no longer an issue that is appropriately addressed in an affirmative manner.

SECTION 6.15
OTHER REMEDIES:

The EEOC is not the only available avenue to address issues of race in the workplace. Employees who believe they have been discriminated against have other recourses. Venues range from the media to the courts and all options in between. With the increased availability and use of technology and the speed of numerous social media platforms, events involving race are being documented and disseminated at an ever increasing pace resulting in greater societal awareness and education, providing documentary evidence, and a place to afford exposure and apply pressure.

A recent situation at a Michigan hospital evidences the use of these various forums. In 2012, a father requested that no African Americans care for his baby who was hospitalized in the Neonatal Intensive Care Unit. The hospital honored this discriminatory request. Hospital representatives placed a note on the assignment clipboard that read "Please, No African American Nurses to care for [redacted] Baby per Dad's request. Thank you."[33] The African American nurse, who had previously cared for the baby, was reassigned by her supervisor. Various avenues were employed to disseminate and remedy this race issue including the print and broadcast media, news conferences, various social media platforms, and filing a civil lawsuit.[34]

QUESTIONS FOR DISCUSSION:

1. What are the rights and interests of all persons/entities involved including the father, nurse/employee, and the hospital/employer?

2. Was the hospital right or wrong in granting the father's request?

3. Should the law be involved in a matter of personal preference of who provides medical care to your child?

4. Discuss the legal and equitable remedies you think the plaintiff requested in her complaint.

SECTION 6.16
ADDITIONAL CURRENT
ISSUES

Issues concerning race, ethnicity, law, and reality are continuously a part of American society. In 2016, 35 people were killed and over 300 wounded in Brussels, Belgium by two attacks at the airport and another bombing at the metro subway station: each within minutes of the other. ISIS, an Islamist extremist group claimed credit for these attacks. Various reactions followed, including Republican Primary Presidential Candidate Donald Trump who reaffirmed his previous stance on how to deal with ISIS. Prior to the attacks in Belgium, in December 2015, Mr. Trump issued a press release wherein he called for "…a total and complete shutdown of Muslims entering the United States until our country's representatives can figure out what is going on."[35] Republican Primary Presidential Candidate Ted Cruz provided an even stronger reaction following the Brussels attack stating: "We need to empower law enforcement to patrol and secure Muslim neighborhoods before they become radicalized."[36]

There were other terroristic events prior to Brussels that had a tremendous impact on the United States including 2015 attack in Paris, shootings in San Bernardino, California, and in a Dallas, Texas suburb, and the Boston Marathon bombings in 2013. Each attack had a common element; ISIS, an ISIS sympathizer, or committed by persons who had pledged allegiance to ISIS. This terrorist group, which consists of extremist Muslims, perpetrates heinous acts that have been successful in instilling fear throughout the world. There is a desire to prevent this terror from further infecting the United States and an aspiration to completely eliminate their deadly activities. But how should this be done? Who are these terrorist? The easy answer is to say they are Muslim thereby painting all of this faith as potential terrorists. Identification of these potential threats to our safety becomes easier based on the difference in dress, some Muslim women wear the hijab, and distinctive daily religious practices. There are communities with higher concentration of Muslims and a portion of the immigrant population is Muslim. The majority of Muslims in the U.S. are minorities with only 38% being white.[37]

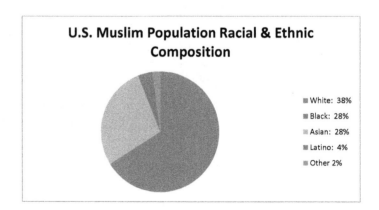

U.S. Muslim Population Racial & Ethnic Composition

■ White: 38%
■ Black: 28%
▨ Asian: 28%
■ Latino: 4%
■ Other 2%

Three states and the District of Columbia have the largest concentration of Muslims. Arkansas, District of Columbia, and New York each have 2% of their total population classified as Muslim. New Jersey population consists of 3% who are Muslim.[38] In all other states, Muslims compose 1% or less of the total state population. In 2015, the Pew Research Center estimated that there were about 3.3 million Muslims living in the United States; representing approximately 1% of the total U.S. population of about 322 million people.[39] The Pew Center further determined that by 2050, the number of Muslim in this country will double to 2.1% of the total population.[40] Further, it must be noted that based on Pew's first-ever nationwide survey of Muslim Americans in 2007, it was estimated that the total population of Muslims in the U.S. was 2.35 million;[41] representing .78% of total U.S. population. Therefore, it is estimated that the U.S. Muslim population will almost triple between 2007 and 2050.

Is this a matter of race, ethnicity, religion or any of the other factors or is this purely an issue of security? The question may be answered by an examination of the totality of the circumstances followed by an analysis of the response. In reality, the actual and anticipated increase of the U.S. Muslim immigrant population, concentrated living locales, easily identified, and majority minority, causes concern and even fear within a segment of the population. ISIS, a terrorist organization, is Muslim. The resulting proposals are over-arching, discriminatory responses. In current society, frequently there are so many factors that play an integral part that it is very easy to deny that race or ethnicity is one of them.

QUESTIONS FOR DISCUSSION:

1. What are the similarities with the current, suggested treatment of Muslims and the treatment of the Japanese during WWII? What are the differences?

2. Discuss the intersection of issues including race, religion, ethnicity and politics.

    "This refusal to accept the stark reality that race matters is regrettable. The way to stop discrimination on the basis of race is to speak openly and candidly on the subject of race, and to apply the Constitution with eyes open to the unfortunate effects of centuries of racial discrimination."

    Justice Sotomayor's dissent in *Schuette*

Footnotes:

1. Jet Magazine, Sept. 1, 2008 issue, p. 8, "Minorities to Become the Majority by 2042-" Associated Press.

2. http://kff.org/other/state-indicator/distribution-by-raceethnicity/Downloaded 3-21-16. Kaiser Family Foundation estimates based on the Census Bureau's March 2015 Current Population Survey (CPS: Annual Social and Economic Supplement).

3. Jet Magazine, *Id*.

4. http://www.pewresearch.org/fact-tank/2015/11/19/5-facts-about-illegal-immigration-in-the-u-s/. "5 Facts about illegal immigrants in the U.S." Published Nov. 19, 2015. Downloaded 3-10-16.

5. *Id*.

6. https://www.uscis.gov/humanitarian/consideration-deferred-action-childhood-arrivals-daca. Downloaded 3-8-16

7. https://www.uscis.gov/sites/default/files/USCIS/ExecutiveActions/EAFlier_DAPA.pdf downloaded 3-15-16

8. https://www.uscis.gov/humanitarian/consideration-deferred-action-childhood-arrivals-daca. Downloaded 3-8-16

9. https://www.dhs.gov/news/2015/02/17/statement-secretary-jeh-c-johnson-concerning-district-courts-ruling-concerning-dapa downloaded 3-15-16

10. **Plyer v. Doe,** 457 U.S. 202 (1982)

11. "City of Hazleton Illegal Immigration Relief Act Ordinance," Ordinance 2006-10 http://www.ojjpac.org/illegal_immigration_relief_act.asp Downloaded 3-24-16

12. *Id* at Section 2A.

13. *Id*. See Section 4.

14. *Id*. Section 6.

15. http://www.migrationpolicy.org/article/hazleton-immigration-ordinance-began-bang-goes-out-whimper Downloaded 3-24-16

16. *Id*.

17. **Lozano v. City of Hazleton,** in the U.S. Court of Appeals for the Third Circuit, No: 07-3531, date filed 07/26/2013.

18. **Melisa Mays v. Governor Rick Snyder,** in the U.S. District Court Eastern District of Michigan, Document #15-160202-003C and In the State of Michigan Court of Claims, Document #15-160202-002C.

19. http://www.michigan.gov/documents/snyder/FWATF_FINAL_REPORT_21March2016_517805_7.pdf, p. 55. Accessed 3-26-16

20. *Id* p. 56.

21. See *From Slavery to Freedom: A History of Negro America*, 5th edition, by John Hope Franklin, Alfred A. Knoph, Inc, 1980 at page 265.

22. See http://www.eeoc.gov/eeoc/index.cfm Downloaded 3-21-16

23. www.eeoc.gov/initiatives/e-race/why_e-race.html, United States Equal Employment Opportunity Commission, *The E-Race Initiative*, February 28, 2007.

24. *Id.*

25. *Id.*

26. *Id.*

27. http://www.eeoc.gov/eeoc/statistics/reports/american_experiences/african_americans.cfm Downloaded 3-21-16

28. http://www.eeoc.gov/eeoc/statistics/reports/american_experiences/hispanics.cfm Downloaded 3-21-16

29. http://www.eeoc.gov/eeoc/statistics/reports/american_experiences/asian_americans.cfm Downloaded 3-21-16

30. See The Wall Street Journal, *Admissions Preferences for Alums' Kids Draw Fire*, by Daniel Golden, January 2003.

31. *Id.*

32. See CNN.com/inside politics, *How Affirmative Action Helped George W.*, by Michael Kinsley, January 20, 2003.

33. http://gma.yahoo.com/blogs/abc-blogs/no-black-nurses-request-draws-lawsuit-173026275--abc-news-health.html Downloaded 2-21-13. ABC News, "No Black Nurses Request Draws Lawsuit," Feb. 20, 2013.

34. **Tonya L. Battle v. The Board of Hospital Managers of Hurley Medical Center et. al., State of Michigan,** In the Circuit Court County of Genesse, 13-99763

35. https://www.donaldjtrump.com/press-releases/donald-j.-trump-statement-on-preventing-muslim-immigration. Press release dated Dec. 7, 2015. Downloaded 3-8-16

36. http://www.nytimes.com/politics/first-draft/2016/03/22/ted-cruzs-call-to-secure-muslim-neighborhoods-stirs-a-backlash/?_r=0 Accessed 3-26-16

37. http://www.pewforum.org/religious-landscape-study/religious-tradition/muslim/Downloaded 3-26-16

38. http://www.pewforum.org/religious-landscape-study/religious-tradition/muslim/Accessed 3-26-16

39. http://www.pewresearch.org/fact-tank/2016/01/06/a-new-estimate-of-the-u-s-muslim-population/Accessed 3-26-16

40. *Id.*

41. http://www.pewresearch.org/2007/05/22/muslim-americans-middle-class-and-mostly-mainstream/Accessed 3-26-1

KEY TERMS

Affirmative Action

Amendment Thirteen

Amendment Fourteen

Amendment Fifteen

Civil Liberties Act

Civil Rights Act of 1866

Civil Rights Act of 1875

Civil Rights Act of 1957

Civil Rights Act of 1960

Civil Rights Act of 1964

Civil War Amendments

Comprehensive Immigration Reform Act of 2007

Deferred Action for Childhood Arrivals (DACA)

Deferred Action for Parents of Americans and Lawful Permanent Residents (DAPA)

E-RACE Initiative

E-Verify

Elementary and Secondary Education School Act of 1965

Equal Employment Opportunities Commission (EEOC)

Equal Protection

Grandfather Clauses

Illegal Immigration Relief Act

Jim Crow Laws

Legacy Preference

Miscegenation Statutes

Philadelphia Order

Proposition 209

S.B. 1070

The Dream Act

Title IV

Title VI

Title VII

PART TWO

THE PROCEDURAL LAW

CHAPTER 7

THE JUDICIAL SYSTEM

"A Court is only as sound as its jury, and a jury is only as sound as the men who make it up."

Harper Lee
"To Kill a Mockingbird," 1960

Article III of the Constitution provides that "the judicial power of the United States shall be vested in one Supreme Court, and in such other inferior courts as Congress may from time to time establish."

The court is the last branch of the government to be addressed by the Constitution and very little direction is provided by the framers in that historic document. Article III merely creates the **Supreme Court** of the United States and it glaringly fails to set forth that Court's powers, composition or jurisdiction. In what one may call a lack of respect, the framers also gave Congress the power to create the remaining courts thereby making the court system seem subservient to the legislature.

The First Congress of the United States accepted this grant of power when it enacted the Judiciary Act of 1787. Through the efforts of Senator Oliver Ellsworth of Connecticut, the legislature created thirteen judicial districts and three circuit courts throughout the country. Initially, the Supreme Court consisted of one chief justice and five other jurists who met twice a year in the Nation's Capital, the initial session commencing on the first Monday of February, and the other on the first Monday in August.

The Supreme Court was given exclusive jurisdiction over all controversies of a civil nature in which a state is a party and it has exclusive jurisdiction over proceedings against ambassadors or other public ministers consistent with the law of nation. The Supreme Court is also given appellate jurisdiction or the ability to hear cases on appeal from the federal circuit courts and courts of the states.

During its first few years, the Supreme Court heard very few cases and was viewed as the weakest branch of the government. This perception changed dramatically in 1801 when John Marshall became the Chief Justice and issued the landmark ruling in **Marbury v. Madison**. This case established the fundamental principle that the Supreme Court uniquely has the power to declare a law of Congress unconstitutional. It is also the final arbiter of the meaning of the Constitution. With these powers, the Supreme Court became an equal partner in the government, and it has enjoyed that status ever since.[1]

Presently, the court of **original jurisdiction** or trial court in the federal system is the District Court, and appeals are entertained by the Circuit Court of Appeals. On rare occasion, the Supreme Court of the United States will review a lower court's decision if it presents a compelling national question that needs to be answered.

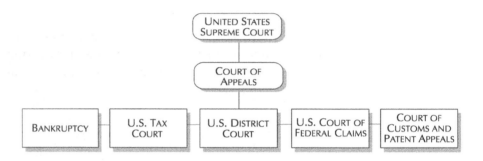

The **United States District Court**, or trial court, is in direct contact with the parties, hears the evidence, and applies the appropriate law to the facts of a case. There are ninety-four district courts in the United States and its territories. A state may have one or more district courts within its boundaries depending on its population. For example, the state of New York has four district courts within its boundaries, whereas Maine only has one.

The type of cases the federal court may hear are limited to questions involving federal law, the United States Constitution, and disputes between citizens of different states where the amount in controversy exceeds $75,000. Congress has also created several specialized courts that hear cases involving very narrow issues, such as tax matters and customs or patent appeals.

The **Court of Appeals** is the intermediate appellate court within the federal court system. There are thirteen circuit courts throughout the United States. Eleven of the circuit courts hear cases on appeal from the district courts. The twelfth circuit is devoted to hearing cases from the District of Columbia. Congress has also created one specialized court called the United States Court of Appeals for the Federal Circuit. This Federal Circuit hears appeals involving tort claims against the United States government, patent cases, and appeals from the United States Court of Federal Claims and the Court of International Trade. Parties may appeal to the Circuit Courts of Appeal as a matter of right.

Because the Supreme Court's decision to hear a case is discretionary, the Courts of Appeal are usually the last place that a party will appeal a federal case. When a Court of Appeals decides a case, that decision is binding over all of the district courts within that circuit.

The **Supreme Court of the United States** is the final arbiter of all legal disputes. As a result, it often decides very controversial issues that affect our daily lives. Supreme Court decisions establish precedent and bind all other courts. Commentators and constitutional scholars analyze each word of an opinion and predict how a particular holding will impact society.

The **Supreme Court of the United States** is the highest judicial body in the land. It is made up of a chief justice and other members as Congress shall deem appropriate. The President has the authority to appoint the Justices for life subject to the advice and consent of the Senate. The Constitution further provides that "[t]he Judges, both of the supreme and inferior courts, shall hold their offices during good behavior, and shall, at stated times, receive for their services, a compensation, which shall not be diminished during their continuance in office."[2] At its inception, the salary of the Chief Justice was $4,000. Today, that salary is pegged at $260,700.[3]

The operational aspects of the Supreme Court reveal that its term starts on the first Monday in October and ends when the list of scheduled cases is reached during the summer. Before World War II, the Supreme Court had 1,300 docketed cases. Today, about 8,000 cases are appealed each year and an additional 1,200 applications are filed that can be acted upon by a single Justice.[4] The Supreme Court is also a court of both original and appellate jurisdiction. Cases involving Ambassadors, Consuls, litigation between the federal government and a state as well as suits between states may be heard directly by the Supreme Court. There are no appeals of these decisions. Most cases, however, reach the Supreme Court on appeal of a lower court's decision. These appeals are originated by the filing of a **writ of certiorari** which is Latin for "we wish to be informed."[5]

History demonstrates that few appeals are actually heard by the court, even though it takes a mere four of nine jurists to agree to hear the appeal. This has become known as the **"Rule of Four."** The Justices meet on Wednesdays and Fridays to review recent appeals and the junior most Justice acts as the "doorkeeper" when it is necessary to retrieve materials. Their deliberations are secret and what is said among the justices is not available for public consumption.[6]

Supreme Court Rule 10 governs these petitions and provides that the acceptance of a case on a Writ of Certiorari is not a matter of right but within the sound discretion of the court and the appeal will only be entertained for compelling reasons. Some of the factors the court considers in determining whether to grant an appeal include:

A. A conflict in United States Court of Appeal decisions on the same issue;

B. A state's highest court has issued a ruling on an issue that conflicts with a decision of another state's highest court or with a United States Court of Appeal; or

C. A state court or a United States Court of Appeal has decided an important question of federal law that has not been, but should be, settled by the Supreme Court.

A Petition for a Writ of Certiorari is rarely granted when the alleged error merely consists of factual mistakes or the misapplication of a properly stated rule of law.

For additional reading about the workings of the United States Supreme Court, see *Gideon's Trumpet* by Anthony Lewis and *The Brethren* by Bob Woodward and Scott Armstrong.

The official web address for the United States Supreme Court is:

- **www.supremecourtus.gov**
  This site provides information about the high court, including biographies of the current Court members, an overview of how the court works, Supreme Court Rules, and Supreme Court decisions.

**SECTION 7.2
THE STATE
COURT SYSTEM**

We are a nation of states with each maintaining its own independent court system. While the configuration of the court system will vary from state to state, each will have a trial court and at least one appellate court.

The state court system in Pennsylvania is provided as an illustration. The court of original jurisdiction in Pennsylvania is the **Court of Common Pleas** and they were established as part of the Pennsylvania Constitution in 1776. It is subdivided into the following three divisions: (1) The Trial Court; (2) the Family Court; and (3) Orphan's Court.

The Trial Division will hear both civil and criminal cases. Orphan's Court is concerned with matters involving estates, such as will contests, trusts, and incompetence hearings. Family Court decides juvenile cases and matters involving the family unit such as divorce, custody, support, paternity, and domestic violence.

To reduce the backlog of cases, a specialized court has been created to handle small disputes. In Philadelphia, this court is called the Municipal Court and is divided into civil and criminal divisions. It handles all landlord/tenant problems, civil disputes of $10,000 or less, criminal cases where the penalty involves five years or less imprisonment, and code violations. In the surrounding counties, magesterial district justices who have offices in the various townships throughout the Commonwealth handle these matters. Parties appearing in Municipal Court do not enjoy the right to a jury trial, so most cases can be appealed directly to the Court of Common Pleas at which time the person will receive a new trial equipped with a jury if so desired.

PENNSYLVANIA STATE JUDICIAL SYSTEM

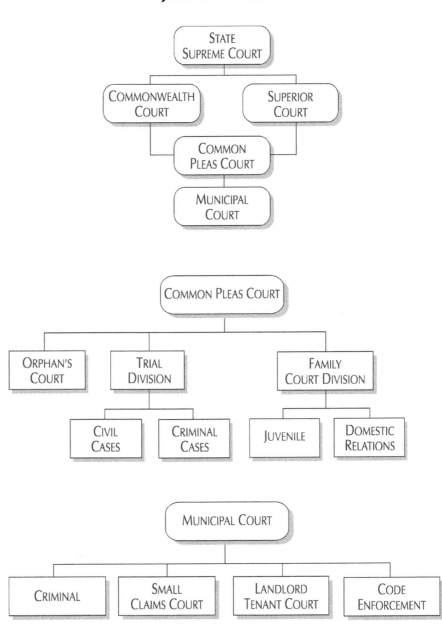

SECTION 7.3
THE JURY SYSTEM

The right to a trial by one's peers is a basic building block of American democracy guaranteed by the United States Constitution. In fact, it has been estimated that this country accounts for 95% of all jury trials in the world.[7] As the Supreme Court noted, "The guarantees of a jury trial reflect a profound judgment about the way in which the law should be enforced and justice administered. Providing an accused with the right to be tried by a jury of his peers gives him an inestimable safeguard against the corrupt or overzealous prosecutor and against the compliant, biased, or eccentric judge."[8]

While the right to a jury trial is firmly engrained in our system of jurisprudence, it was not conceived by the founders of this country. Jury trials have been in existence in England for centuries and some scholars contend that the concept originated in thirteenth-century England as an outgrowth of the *Magna Carta*.

During the founding days of this country, the right to a jury trial was brought to America by the English colonists. In fact, it was adopted by the First Congress of the American Colonists in 1765 with the declaration that "trial by jury is the inherent and invaluable right of every British subject in these colonies."

The founding fathers considered the concept to be so fundamental that it is contained in two different Amendments to the United States Constitution. The Sixth Amendment guarantees the defendant in a criminal case the right to a speedy and public trial by an impartial jury. The Seventh Amendment entitles citizens to a jury trial in civil cases involving a dispute of more than twenty dollars.

In application, a judge presides over the trial and decides questions-of-law. The jury, on the other hand, is the ultimate arbiter of the facts. They decide which party should win a controversy based upon the evidence presented at trial.

To better understand the distinction between a question of law and a question of fact, consider the following hypothetical situation:

> Joe Roberts is driving his car south on Broad Street and enters the intersection on what he maintains is a green light. Bill Smith is proceeding east on Montgomery Avenue and enters the same intersection on what he too alleges is a green light. The vehicles collide on Broad Street, and Roberts maintains that he is injured. Joe institutes suit against Smith for personal injuries.

The judge will inform the jury that a party who enters an intersection against a red light is negligent and responsible for the injuries caused by that negligence. This is a statement of law. On the other hand, it is up to the jury to decide which party entered the intersection after the light turned red. This is a determination of fact.

A jury in a criminal trial generally consists of twelve people whose decisions must be unanimous. The origin of this number is not clear. Some say it represents the number of apostles from the bible, Solomon's officers which numbered twelve, or twelve was a favorite number in mid-evil times. The Supreme Court, however, has noted that the number is an historical accident that became fixed in the fourteenth century. The essential feature of a jury lays in the collective judgment of a group of people, and in the community participation that results from that group's determination of innocence or guilt. The performance of this role is not dependent on a specific number of citizens that make up the jury.[9] Jury requirements, therefore, vary by state and type of proceeding. For instance, Pennsylvania requires that a defendant in a criminal trial be provided with twelve jurors and all must agree on the verdict. In a civil case, however, the verdict need not be unanimous, and the jury will consist of eight members unless a litigant specifically demands a trial by twelve.

More than 120,000 jury trials a year are conducted in the United States. In contrast, only about one-percent of trials in England are conducted with the help of a jury. France utilizes juries for only the most serious crimes, and Italy uses panels of three judges. Germany, Finland and Sweden have mixed tribunals of a professional judge and several laymen.[10] Russia has only recently reinstituted the use of jury trials in serious criminal matters, and Japan started using six-person juries in 2009.

Mark Twain stated in a 1873 speech that: "We have a criminal jury system which is superior to any in the world; and its efficiency is only marred by the difficulty of finding twelve men every day who don't know anything and can't read."

Is the jury system the best way of having a matter decided in a court of law? The verdict in the O.J. Simpson case left many people questioning the validity of the jury system, and who can forget the two-million dollar award against McDonald's for the coffee that spilled on a woman's leg as she rode in a car or the $55 million dollar verdict awarded to sports announcer, Erin Andrews, in a peeping tom case against a hotel. Most legal experts however, agree that it is the best system available despite certain recognized short comings and occasional erroneous verdicts. After all, it is better to be tried by the collective judgment of one's peers than by the wisdom of a single individual. This is the backbone of a democracy.

The jury system does have inherent weaknesses. The law is very complicated, and a trial is an intimidating proceeding. Jurors are thrust into the role of deciding complex cases without the proper legal training or experience.

An analysis of civil jury verdicts by the United States Department of Justice determined that in 53% of the cases, the jury found in favor of plaintiffs and awarded a total of $3.9 billion dollars in compensatory and punitive damages during the one-year period under review. The average finding was $37,000 and juries awarded punitive damages in 6% of the cases with a median punitive damage award of $50,000.[11]

On the other hand, some scholars have found the very weaknesses of the jury system to be its strength. In a speech given by Oliver Wendell Holmes on January 17, 1899, he stated:

> *"I confess that in my experience I have not found juries especially inspired for the discovery of truth…they will introduce into their verdict a…large amount…of popular prejudice, and thus keep the administration of the law in a court with the wishes and feelings of the community."*[12]

SECTION 7.4
VOIR DIRE

Voir Dire is French for *"to speak the truth"* and refers to the jury selection process. Many lawyers consider jury selection one of the most important parts of the trial. It is through this procedure that prospective members of the jury are questioned by the judge or attorneys to ascertain whether they are suitable to serve at the trial. Issues of prejudice, conflicts of interest, and philosophies on life will be explored.

In theory, the attorneys are trying to find objective and unbiased citizens who can render a fair decision. In reality, the individual attorneys are trying to find prospective jurors who are most sympathetic to his or her cause.

Percy Foreman, a famed criminal attorney, once noted:

> The classic adversary system in the United States not only encourages, it demands that each lawyer attempt to empanel the jury most likely to understand his argument or least likely to understand that of his opponent. You don't approach the case with the philosophy of applying abstract justice. You go in to win.[13]

The O.J. Simpson trial, dubbed as the trial of the twentieth century, generated a great deal of controversy regarding the actual fairness of jury trials and whether the process of voir dire is a successful means of obtaining a fair and impartial jury. Indeed, a Gallup Poll showed that public interest in serving on juries dropped more than 50 percent during the duration of the Simpson trial.[14]

A prominent concern is that juries do not reflect the racial make-up of the community. Voter rolls don't always reflect minority participation, and some minority communities feel alienated from the process. Minnesota has taken direct action by posting billboards in predominately minority communities encouraging jury participation. New

York has added unemployment and welfare participants to its jury lists. Some jurisdictions obtain their jury pools from both the voter registration lists and the drivers license records in order to have a better cross-section of the population.

There are also concerns that jurors feel underappreciated. While most states have laws that prohibit employers from firing people who are called for jury duty, only a handful of states require employers to keep paying the person while on jury duty. According to surveys, however, jurors are more concerned about inconvenience than a lack of adequate compensation.[15] Jurors are often left sitting around for days waiting to be called. To help solve this problem, many states have switched to a one-day, one-trial jury process where a person is summoned to appear only on one day. If not chosen for service that day, the individual's jury duty is over.

As for the jury selection process, judges in England summon the first twelve potential jurors and ask a very basic question: "Can you give a fair hearing to both the Crown and the defense?" If the potential jurors respond in the affirmative, they are impaneled as part of the jury. The jury selection process in the United States, however, is much more complicated.[16]

In this country, a prospective juror may be challenged on two grounds. Counsel may challenge a juror for cause or exercise a peremptory challenge. A **challenge for cause** is utilized when an individual is biased or unable to render a fair verdict. For instance, the court will exclude a relative of the victim or a person that has a preconceived opinion on the defendant's innocence or guilt. The number of challenges for cause is unlimited, and the judge is the final arbiter as to whether the juror can be fair and impartial. **Peremptory challenges** are discretionary with the attorney and are used to exclude those who are perceived to be least sympathetic to a litigant's position. These individuals are dismissed without reason or justification. The number of peremptory challenges will vary. In a civil suit, an attorney generally receives a modest number of peremptory challenges such as three. In a criminal case, the number will be significantly higher and will increase with the severity of the crime.

For instance, North Carolina provides both the government and the defense with fourteen peremptory challenges in murder cases, and eight in other criminal trials. In a civil case, such as a malpractice lawsuit or car accident, each side is given eight discretionary challenges. Georgia allows twelve peremptory challenges in criminal cases and twenty in matters where the prosecution seeks the death penalty.

The length of jury duty will vary depending upon the jurisdiction. Jury duty in federal court ranges between two and three weeks unless an individual is selected to serve on a case that extends beyond this time period. While the length of jury duty in state courts vary by jurisdiction, a number of courts utilize the "One Day or One Trial" program. Under this system, a person who is not selected to serve on a jury during the first day of jury duty is discharged. If a person is selected to sit on a panel, that individual's civic obligation is fulfilled upon completion of the one case.

SECTION 7.5
COMMONWEALTH
v. CHRISTOPHER

SELECTION
OF THE JURY

PROBLEM SEVEN—A

PARK, BROWN & SMITH, P.C.
ATTORNEYS AT LAW
MEMORANDUM

To: All Students

From: Peter Smith, Esquire

Re: Jury Selection

The selection of a jury is not an exact science and requires an attorney to make quick decisions about the suitability of a potential juror based upon a short conversation with that individual. The ultimate goal of counsel is not to find a jury that will be fair and unbiased but to select jurors that will favor the client.

To gain an appreciation for this important trial task, the following case is presented so that the reader may experience firsthand the jury selection process. You will learn the background of the case by reviewing the following news broadcast.

TRANSCRIPTION OF NEWS BROADCAST

In local news, a 16-year-old student was assaulted at her high school gym last night and her handbag was stolen. The student, whose name is not being released because of her age, was confronted around 8:00 p.m. while working out in the nautilus room. The victim is unable to identify the thief, since he was wearing a green and white ski mask. She did, however, notice a tattoo of a shark on his bare left shoulder. According to police, the suspect is 5' 10" and weighs approximately 160 pounds. He was last seen wearing a red and white striped shirt, denim pants, and sneakers.

The police eventually arrested an individual who lived near the school who matched the thief's description. The suspect even had a tattoo of a shark on his shoulder. The suspect was charged with theft and other related offenses. The criminal case is about to commence and twenty-one potential jurors are sitting in the courtroom. Biographical sketches are provided of the individual members of the jury pool to assist you in selecting a jury of twelve people.

You should review the biographical data for each prospective juror to see which individuals should be challenged for cause and which people should be considered for use of a peremptory challenge. When reviewing the sketches, first analyze the problem as though you represent the defendant and make your selections. You should then examine the biographical sketches and assume that you represent the prosecution.

For the purposes of this exercise, each side is given three peremptory challenges. The goal is to select twelve jurors suitable to both the prosecution and defense. A worksheet is provided for your selections following the biographical sketches.

Sample questions have also been provided and will be used by the defense and prosecution at the time of the jury selection process. They will give you an idea of the types of issues that are of concern to each side.

QUESTIONS FOR DEFENSE COUNSEL TO ASK THE PANEL:

1. Is anyone familiar with any of the parties, counsel, or the judge in this case?

2. Does anyone know anything about this case?

3. Has anyone ever been the victim of a crime?

4. Is anyone a member of the police force, or does anyone have a close family member on the police force?

5. Has anyone heard or read anything about this case?

6. Does anyone believe that the testimony of a police officer should be given more credence than any other witness?

7. The government has the burden of proving the defendant guilty. Would anyone draw an adverse inference if the defendant didn't testify?

QUESTIONS FOR THE DISTRICT ATTORNEY TO ASK THE PANEL:

1. Has anybody ever been accused of committing a crime?

2. Does anyone believe that they cannot be fair and impartial in the hearing of this matter?

3. Does anyone believe that he or she will have a difficult time in finding the defendant guilty if he could go to jail as a result of the conviction?

4. Will serving on this jury be a hardship or an inconvenience?

BIOGRAPHICAL SKETCHES OF PROSPECTIVE JURORS:

Our consultant service has provided us with 21 biographical sketches of the jurors that we may encounter at trial. Please review the sketches and make your decision on jury selection for both the prosecution and defense.

JUROR 1   *Marilyn Trainer*—Female, 40-year-old mother with three daughters, ages 18, 15 and 12. She claims that she can be fair in the case, even though she has three daughters. She is an unemployed housewife.

JUROR 2   *John McNamara*—Male, 35 years old, married, no children. He is a police sergeant.

JUROR 3   *Hans Forrestor*—Male, single, 30-year-old philosophy professor at Penn who has been mugged on the subway. The police never found his attacker. He claims that he can be fair in the rape case.

JUROR 4   *Star Jackson*—Female, 26-year-old rock singer, single, and a member of Women Organized Against Rape.

JUROR 5   *Chip Wright*—Male, 22 years old, single, college student who resides in fraternity house.

JUROR 6   *Jeanette Williams*—Female, 29-year-old civil litigation paralegal, married, no children. Her husband is a doctor (gynecologist).

JUROR 7   *Duke Septa*—Male, 50-year-old, divorced bus driver with four sons. His marriage represented the "worst years of his life." He believes women should not work and should only take care of the household.

JUROR 8   *Vincent Serino*—Male, 60-year-old gym teacher, not married. Teaches at a girls' Catholic school.

JUROR 9   *Lola Thomas*—Female, 21-year-old exotic dancer. Single, lives with her boyfriend.

JUROR 10   *Alice B. Davis*—Female, 58-year-old housewife with two sons, ages 28 and 30. She has never worked because her household duties keep her busy enough. Her husband is a traveling salesman for an encyclopedia company.

JUROR 11   *Andrew Hoffman*—Male, 23 years old and single. He has heard about the case from the neighborhood, and believes that the defendant has a bad reputation. He does not think he can be impartial.

JUROR 12   *Joseph Hammer*—Male, 23-year-old, unemployed construction worker who lives at home with family. He has two sisters and a brother.

JUROR 13   *Louis Waterman*—Male, 40-year-old, retired sailor who was in the Navy for 20 years. He is single.

JUROR 14   *Anna Klein*—Female, 43-year-old, widowed fashion designer with no children.

JUROR 15   *Desmond Lovejoy*—Male, 28-year-old florist. He is not married.

JUROR 16   *Aileen Wheeler*—Female, 33-year-old, divorced cab driver. She has one 16-year-old son.

JUROR 17   *Elizabeth Addis*—Female, college student at Princeton. She is awaiting trial for a streaking incident.

JUROR 18   *Thomas Bradford*—Male, 50-year-old, disabled veteran on Social Security. He is married with eight children and ten grandchildren.

JUROR 19   *Rose Kelly*—Female, 45-year-old, married waitress whose husband is a roofer. She was convicted of prostitution when she was 18 years old.

JUROR 20   *Margaret Jones*—Female, 35-year-old, single, psychiatrist. Her practice involves drug therapy. She was in the Peace Corps.

JUROR 21   *Jane Sullivan*—Female, 28-year-old lawyer who works for the Office of the Public Defender. She is single.

JURY SELECTION WORKSHEET

Juror Number (For Government)		Juror Number (For Defense)	
1. Yes/No	12. Yes/No	1. Yes/No	12. Yes/No
2. Yes/No	13. Yes/No	2. Yes/No	13. Yes/No
3. Yes/No	14. Yes/No	3. Yes/No	14. Yes/No
4. Yes/No	15. Yes/No	4. Yes/No	15. Yes/No
5. Yes/No	16. Yes/No	5. Yes/No	16. Yes/No
6. Yes/No	17. Yes/No	6. Yes/No	17. Yes/No
7. Yes/No	18. Yes/No	7. Yes/No	18. Yes/No
8. Yes/No	19. Yes/No	8. Yes/No	19. Yes/No
9. Yes/No	20. Yes/No	9. Yes/No	20. Yes/No
10. Yes/No	21. Yes/No	10. Yes/No	21. Yes/No
11. Yes/No		11. Yes/No	

Record of Peremptory Challenges:		Record of Challenges For Cause:	
Government:	Defendant:	Government:	Defendant:
1.	1.	1.	1.
2.	2.	2.	2.
3.	3.	3.	3.

SECTION 7.6 DISCHARGE OF AN EMPLOYEE FOR JURY SERVICE

Employers are often confronted with the difficult problem of what to do when an employee announces that he or she has been selected for jury duty. The worker's absence can have a disruptive influence on production schedules and cause economic hardship. Can the employer discharge the worker and hire a replacement to minimize the impact of the juror's absence?

Federal law prohibits the discharge, intimidation, or coercion of any permanent employee because of jury service **(28 U.S.C.A. § 1875)**. Penalties for a violation of the statute include reinstatement of the worker, recovery of lost wages, other loss of benefits suffered by the employee, and attorney's fees.

An individual claiming that the employer has violated this law may file an application with the Federal District Court in the locale where the employer maintains a place of business. Upon a finding of probable merit in the claim, the court will appoint counsel to represent the employee in any federal court action necessary to resolve the dispute.

Court cases that have dealt with this legislation have prohibited the recovery of mental pain and suffering for the employer's actions and have based the recovery of attorney's fees on a per-hour basis rather than on a percentage of recovery. A court has even granted a discharged employee a preliminary injunction reinstating him to his job pending the outcome of the trial for wrongful discharge.

SECTION 7.7 JURISDICTION

Jurisdiction refers to the power of a court to determine the merits of a dispute and to grant an aggrieved party relief. In order for a court to properly entertain an action, it must have jurisdiction over the subject matter in dispute and jurisdiction over the parties involved.

Subject matter jurisdiction is quite simple. The particular court where the dispute is heard must have the power to hear the kind of case that is in controversy. The courts are very specialized, and the plaintiff must institute suit before the proper court. For instance, a divorce proceeding may not be instituted in tax court. The court's power to hear these specific types of cases is usually granted by the legislature.

Jurisdiction over the person requires the court to have power to exercise its authority over the defendant. Traditionally, suit was instituted where the defendant could be found. This was either in the state where he resided or where he worked. Now, a court is considered to have jurisdiction over the parties when the defendant has "minimum contacts" with the state where the court is located (the **forum state**). **Minimum contacts** are generally deemed to exist when the defendant takes actions that are purposefully directed toward the forum state.

The rule of serving a defendant where the defendant can be found was expanded over time by the passage of long arm statutes that allow a jurisdiction to reach beyond the state boundaries to serve a defendant with the lawsuit. The most common **long arm statutes** deal with a non-resident who commits a tort within a state, a party who owns property in a state, and one doing business in a state.

In order to satisfy the requirements of due process, the Supreme Court has ruled that a state court may exercise personal jurisdiction over a non-resident defendant as long as there are *minimum contacts* between the defendant and the state in which the suit has been filed. The concept of minimum contacts protects defendants against the burdens of litigating in a distant or inconvenient court. Usually, a defendant will have some kind of presence in the forum. In the case of transacting business within a state, however, it is not necessary to have an office in that jurisdiction. Soliciting business through sales representatives or by placing an advertisement in a local newspaper have been held to constitute minimum contacts.

MICHAEL MATOS V. SETON HALL UNIVERSITY
102 F. SUPP. 3D 375 (D. CT. MASS. 2015)

Seton Hall University is incorporated under the laws of New Jersey as an educational corporation. Plaintiff is a resident of Massachusetts and a former Seton Hall student. On December 27, 2011 Seton Hall mailed an admission package to Plaintiff, offering him a place in Seton Hall's incoming class. The package included the offer of a four-year scholarship totaling $90,000. Plaintiff accepted the offer and enrolled for the Fall 2012 semester.

In February of his freshman year, Plaintiff experienced a depressive episode and was diagnosed with Major Depressive Disorder. To deal with his depression, Plaintiff voluntarily withdrew from the University for the remainder of the school year. He re-enrolled for the Fall 2013 semester. On October 21, 2013, a Seton Hall employee found marijuana and drug paraphernalia in Plaintiff's dorm room. Plaintiff denied that the contraband belonged to him. He was summoned to a meeting with the Dean of Students. According to Plaintiff, the Dean stated that because she believed Plaintiff to be bipolar, he would be stripped of his standing as a student. On October 22, the Dean instructed Plaintiff that he had one day to submit an application for medical withdrawal. Plaintiff refused, and the Dean placed Plaintiff on interim suspension. At the behest of his parents, Plaintiff withdrew from the university one month later.

Seton Hall has moved to dismiss [this case] for lack of personal jurisdiction. Plaintiff asserts that this Court may exercise specific personal jurisdiction over Seton Hall because the university recruited him in Massachusetts.

Jurisdiction exists over an out-of-state defendant where the cause of action arises directly out of, or relates to, the defendant's forum-based contacts. To determine whether the Constitution permits the exercise of jurisdiction, [the court] uses a three-part inquiry. First, the legal claims must relate to or arise out of the defendant's contacts in the forum. Second, the defendant's contacts must constitute "purposeful availment of the benefits and protections" of the forum's laws. Third, the exercise of jurisdiction must be consistent with principles of justice and fair play.

Seton Hall does not dispute that it sent an admission and scholarship offer to Plaintiff at his home in Massachusetts. This type of contact provides a basis for specific jurisdiction on a contract claim. Further, through its recruiting activity and national advertising campaigns, Seton Hall could reasonably anticipate that Massachusetts students like Plaintiff would apply for and accept offers of admission.

Seton Hall's activities in Massachusetts constitute a purposeful availment of the benefits and protections of Massachusetts law. The University voluntarily recruits in Massachusetts and advertises in national publications that are seen by Massachusetts residents. Seton Hall also acted voluntarily when it sent an admission and scholarship offer to Plaintiff at his home in Massachusetts. Reaching into Massachusetts to recruit students in general and Plaintiff in particular, made it foreseeable that Seton Hall could be hauled into Massachusetts courts. Therefore, the Court concludes that the purposeful availment requirement is satisfied.

While Seton Hall will incur some burden in defending itself in this Court, that burden is not "onerous in a special, unusual, or other constitutionally significant way." Massachusetts has a strong interest in protecting citizens from being lured to and suffering harm in another state, and in offering its residents a convenient forum for adjudicating claims. This is especially true where, as here, a plaintiff would be unable to pursue the claims elsewhere. There is no advantage to be had in an alternative forum for the effective administration of justice, and Seton Hall raises no pertinent policy arguments that would counsel against jurisdiction in this Court. Accordingly, the Court finds that exercising jurisdiction over Seton Hall is reasonable and consistent with principles of justice and fair play.

With the advent of websites and their ability to convey information to people around the world, additional jurisdictional issues arise. For instance, is a business that places information about itself on the internet subject to lawsuits in any place where an individual can access the site even if the business has no presence in that state and has not solicited business in that state? In **Michael Hurley v. Cancun Playa Oasis International Hotels**, a federal count in Pennsylvania determined that a website by itself is not sufficient contact to confer jurisdiction in a state just because a person may be able to access the site from that state. The plaintiff must still establish that the defendant has maintained continuous, systematic, and substantial business contacts within the state where the lawsuit has been filed.

Anita Ford v. Mentor Worldwide
2 F. Supp. 3d 898 (E.D. La. 2014)

This case arises out of injuries Anita Ford allegedly suffered after a failed breast augmentation procedure. Plaintiff, a Louisiana resident, alleges that she learned about Dr. Revis through the website www.justbreastimplants.com ("JBI"), which Dr. Revis used "to solicit patients from across the country to come to Florida for breast augmentation surgery." According to plaintiff, she e-mailed Dr. Revis to "inquire about breast augmentation," and the two exchanged approximately twenty-two e-mails over the next several weeks. Dr. Revis allegedly knew that plaintiff was a Louisiana resident while he was corresponding with her.

Dr. Revis performed breast augmentation surgery on plaintiff in Fort Lauderdale. Plaintiff alleges that she began feeling pain in her breast and corresponded with Dr. Revis about that pain. Plaintiff alleges that after Dr. Revis removed the implants from plaintiff, he discovered that one of the implants was leaking saline. According to plaintiff, the leaking saline in her breast implant caused her to experience pain and to require another surgery.

Dr. Revis [does not] regularly does business in Louisiana, and Dr. Revis has never lived or practiced medicine there. While plaintiff alleges that "about 50% of Dr. Revis' patients are out of state or international patients," Dr. Revis's affidavit reflects that less than 0.001% of his patient base comes from Louisiana.

Plaintiff filed suit against Dr. Revis in Louisiana. Dr. Revis moves to dismiss plaintiff's claim for lack of personal jurisdiction. Jurisdiction exists when a nonresident defendant "has purposefully directed its activities at the forum state and the litigation results from alleged injuries that arise out of or relate to

those activities." Minimum contacts may be established by actions, or even just a single act, by the nonresident defendant whereby it "purposefully avails itself of the privilege of conducting activities within the forum State, thus invoking the benefits and protections of its laws."

Plaintiff argues that defendant made contacts with Louisiana through JBI, which she characterizes as an "interactive website." Second, she contends that, by agreeing to perform breast augmentation on plaintiff while plaintiff was living in Louisiana, Dr. Revis "entered into a contract in the state of Louisiana" and thereby availed himself of the benefits and protections of the state. A court, in determining whether it can exercise personal jurisdiction over a nonresident defendant based on the defendant's online presence, "looks to the nature and quality of commercial activity that an entity conducts over the Internet." The court categorizes Internet use into a spectrum of three areas as follows: At one end of the spectrum, there are situations where a defendant clearly does business over the Internet by entering into contracts with residents of other states which "involve the knowing and repeated transmission of computer files over the Internet...." In this situation, personal jurisdiction is proper. At the other end of the spectrum, there are situations where a defendant merely establishes a passive website that does nothing more than advertise on the Internet. With passive websites, personal jurisdiction is not appropriate. In the middle of the spectrum, there are situations where a defendant has a website that allows a user to exchange information with a host computer. In this middle ground, the exercise of jurisdiction is determined by the level of interactivity and commercial nature of the exchange of information that occurs on the Website.

Plaintiff contends that Dr. Revis does business through JBI, or, alternatively, because users of the website can post questions on the website and have them answered by physicians such as Dr. Revis. Plaintiff's argument is unavailing, because there is no indication that physicians and patients actually "do business" through the websites. The cases that plaintiff cites in support of her argument are distinguishable, because they all involve sites that allowed individuals to make purchases online. Here, plaintiff has not alleged or shown that she or any other user of JBI purchased breast augmentation services through the website.

This would be a different case if, say, Dr. Revis had given plaintiff erroneous medical advice through the website while she was in Louisiana, and she had suffered injury as a result of following that advice. But plaintiff used the site merely to obtain Dr. Revis' e-mail address and initiate contact with him. Under such circumstances, Dr. Revis' presence on a website, even one with interactive features, does not constitute purposeful availment. True, plaintiff allegedly engaged with Dr. Revis by e-mail several times in the weeks leading up to her surgery, and entered into a contract with him regarding that surgery while she was located in Louisiana. But the court has made clear that actions of this kind, without more, do not constitute sufficient minimum contacts that will subject the nonresident defendant to the jurisdiction of the forum state's courts.

The Court finds that defendants do not have minimum contacts with Louisiana such that this Court can exercise personal jurisdiction over them consistent with the Due Process Clause.

SECTION 7.8
VENUE

Venue is the place where a case should be heard. The plaintiff decides where to institute suit. This decision will rarely be disturbed unless the defendant can demonstrate a compelling reason to remove the matter to another jurisdiction. This will occur if the defendant cannot obtain a fair trial in the location where the lawsuit was filed because of prejudice or bias. For instance, in the case of the Oklahoma City bombing, Timothy McVeigh requested a change of venue because of the potential bias of the jury pool. The 1995 bombing destroyed a large part of the Alfred P. Murrah Federal Building and left 169 people dead and 500 injured. The original judge was removed from the trial because of doubts about his impartiality since the bombing had destroyed his office. The defense also asserted that the trial should take place outside of Oklahoma to insure an unbiased jury because of the intense pre-trial publicity surrounding the heinous crime, and the effect the criminal activity had on the people in Oklahoma. The trial was eventually moved to Denver, Colorado.

The second reason for requesting a change of venue derives from the concept of **forum non-conveniens**. This Latin term means that the place of the trial is inconvenient for the parties and the witnesses involved in the litigation. A court may refuse to exercise jurisdiction over the parties if it would be more convenient for a court in another jurisdiction to hear the case. For example, suppose Joe is injured in a car accident because of the negligence of Pete in going through a red light. The accident occurred in New York and the witnesses, investigating police officer and the majority of the evidence is also located in that state. Joe lives in New York and both vehicles involved in the accident were registered and insured in that state. Pete originally lived in New York but moved to Oregon about six months ago. Joe files suit in Oregon since that is where the defendant can be found. Even though the Oregon court has jurisdiction, it can transfer the case to New York on the basis of forum non-conveniens because having the trial in Oregon would be very difficult and the suit in New York would be more convenient for the evidence and witnesses. Since the accident happened in New York, that state also has jurisdiction.[17]

SECTION 7.9
STANDING

In accordance with the United States Constitution, courts are only permitted to hear actual cases or controversies. That is, courts cannot offer advisory opinions to people who are not actually involved in a dispute. The plaintiff in a lawsuit must have a direct and substantial interest in the outcome of the case that he or she intends to bring. This concept is referred to as **standing**. To meet this requirement, the plaintiff must show that he or she has actually been injured by the action that is the subject of the lawsuit. The injury can be physical, economic, environmental, or aesthetic, but must injure the plaintiff in fact. To have standing to have a case heard, it is also necessary that the relief sought by the plaintiff either correct or compensate for the harm alleged in the lawsuit.

Consider this example: Estelle was in the process of researching the environmentally fragile nature of the Nevada mountains when she discovered that someone planned to build an amusement park in that area. The park would have a detrimental effect on the environment in the mountain region. If Estelle makes no allegation of the way in which the building of the park would cause an actual injury to her personally, she will be denied standing to bring that case.

Elton John authored the composition *Can You Feel the Love Tonight* as the featured song in the Disney film, *The Lion King*. Subsequently, two publishing companies instituted suit over the composition, claiming it infringed on their copyright to a previous work, *Listen to Your Heart*. Since only one company may be the proper owner of the song, the court had to ascertain which publisher had standing to maintain the action for copyright infringement.

Halwill Music, Inc. v. Elton John
2000 U.S. Dist. LEXIS 7067 (S.D. N.Y. 2000)

Two different companies seek to assert the same copyright against the same purported infringers; but only one has the right to do so, and the other must be dismissed.

The first suit was brought by plaintiff GoldRhyme Music Company ("GoldRhyme") against The Walt Disney Company and other defendants, alleging that the Elton John composition *Can You Feel the Love Tonight*, featured in connection with the film *The Lion King*, infringed the copyright on a previous work, *Listen To Your Heart*, composed by Glenn Medeiros. Subsequently, however, Halwill Music, Inc. ("Halwill") filed suit, making essentially the same claim against essentially the same defendants and further alleging that Medeiros had conveyed to Halwill the sole and exclusive right to sue for copyright infringement with respect to *Listen To Your Heart.*

The Court hereby grants Halwill's motion and dismisses the action brought by GoldRhyme for lack of standing.

Under the **Copyright Act of 1976,** "the legal or beneficial owner of an exclusive right under a copyright is entitled…to institute an action for any infringement of that particular right committed while he or she is the owner of it."

It is undisputed that in 1988, as part of an agreement conveying to Halwill an undisputed half-interest in certain of Medeiros' musical compositions (including *Listen to Your Heart)*,

Medeiros agreed that Halwill shall have the sole and exclusive right to administer and protect the Musical Compositions on behalf of both parties throughout the world. Pursuant to that 1988 agreement, Halwill registered a claim for copyright in *Listen To Your Heart* in 1993.

In 1996, Medeiros entered into a separate agreement with GoldRhyme that gave GoldRhyme the exclusive right to initiate all actions for infringements of any Medeiros compositions covered by that agreement. This 1996 agreement, however, was limited to compositions "that have not been assigned in writing to any third party as of the date hereof." Therefore, the 1996 agreement does not in any way pertain to *Listen To Your Heart* which was covered by the 1988 agreement.

Although GoldRhyme attempts to attack the validity of the 1988 agreement between Halwill and Medeiros, its arguments in this regard are without merit. For example, GoldRhyme contends that the 1988 agreement is not signed and is therefore invalid. In fact, however, the signed amended agreement between Halwill and Medeiros specifically refers to and incorporates prior agreements,

Accordingly, the Court hereby grants plaintiff Halwill's motion and dismisses with prejudice GoldRhyme's action against defendants for lack of standing.

SECTION 7.10
FULL FAITH AND CREDIT

Full Faith and Credit is a constitutional mandate that requires each state to uphold the laws and decrees of every other state. As the Supreme Court noted in **Sherrer v. Sherrer**, 334 U.S. 343, the Full Faith and Credit Clause "is one of the provisions incorporated into the Constitution by its framers for the purpose of transforming an aggregation of independent sovereign states into a nation." This guarantee is contained in **Article Four** of the United States Constitution which provides that Full Faith and Credit shall be given in each state to the public acts, records, and judicial proceedings of every other state. Essentially, this means that a judgment in one state will be enforced in another state as long as the first state has jurisdiction. Without this provision, the legal system would become uncertain and chaotic. People would never know if a different state would enforce a validly obtained judgment in another jurisdiction. How does this concept work in reality?

Assume that John Smith, a New Jersey resident and college student, goes to Florida for spring break. Upon his arrival in Florida, he rents a car, but unfortunately Smith runs over the clerk as he is pulling away from the rental agency. He is so distraught by the incident that he takes the next plane back to Newark International Airport in New Jersey. The clerk files suit in Florida for her injuries. John ignores the lawsuit since he has no plans of ever returning to Florida, and a judgment is rendered against him in the amount of $100,000. Is Smith correct in assuming that nothing can be done to him as long as he stays out of Florida? Pursuant to the "Full Faith and Credit Clause" of the Constitution, the Florida judgment can be transferred to New Jersey and be enforced in that jurisdiction. Florida had jurisdiction over the New Jersey resident since he committed a tort in that state.

Are traffic tickets that are received in another jurisdiction enforceable in the state of domicile of the driver under the doctrine of Full Faith and Credit? The answer depends upon the jurisdiction. Forty-five states and the District of Columbia have entered into the **Driver's License Compact,** which governs the enforcement of motor vehicle violations committed by a driver in another jurisdiction. Based upon this agreement, a traffic ticket received in a sister state will be enforced in the state where the driver is licensed. The only jurisdictions that do not belong to the Compact are Georgia, Massachusetts, Michigan, Tennessee, and Wisconsin. The purpose of the Compact is to maximize law enforcement efforts nationwide and to create a "one driver record" concept which requires that the complete driving record of an individual be maintained in one location–the state of licensing. The benefits enjoyed by the member states are varied and include the following: (a) law enforcement officers are not burdened with traffic ticket procedures and are able to devote more time to highway patrol, surveillance, and apprehension; (b) court revenues are increased because non-residents cannot ignore member state's citations without facing driver licenses penalties at home; and (c) there is a decrease in the number of "Failure to Appear" cases.

The Compact requires that member states report all traffic convictions which occur within its boundaries to the state where the violator was licensed. This report must describe the violation and the disposition of the charges. In return, the licensing state shall give the same effect to "serious" motor vehicle violations, as though the offense had occurred in the state of licensing in cases of vehicular manslaughter, driving under the influence, using a motor vehicle to commit a felony, or failure to stop and render aid in the event of a motor vehicle accident. Minor traffic violations, such as speeding, disregarding a stop sign, or going through a red light will be reported to the licensing state, but the conviction will not appear on the individual's driving record nor will points be assigned.

A driver will also not be detained in another jurisdiction if that state is a member of the Compact. Instead, the individual will merely receive a traffic ticket. If the operator fails to pay the fine, the licensing state will be notified of the non-compliance, and the driver's license will be suspended until the ticket is paid. Notice of non-compliance is reported to the home jurisdiction within six months from the date of the issuance of the ticket. If a traffic violation is committed in a state that is not a member of the Compact, the driver will be brought before a judge for an emergency hearing and will be required to make arrangements for the payment of the fine before being allowed to leave the jurisdiction.

SECTION 7.11
ROBERTS v. COMMONWEALTH

PROBLEM SEVEN—B

PARK, BROWN & SMITH, P.C.
ATTORNEYS AT LAW
MEMORANDUM

To: All Students

From: Peter Smith, Esquire

Re: Joe Roberts' Trip to Arizona

Joe Roberts recently visited Arizona for a white-water rafting adventure on the Colorado River. The weather was hot and Joe was in the sun for hours. Joe and the other rafters consumed several alcoholic beverages while shooting the rapids. At the end of the day, he drove back to Phoenix for his return flight home. Unfortunately, the excitement of the day caught up with him. About an hour outside of Phoenix, Joe fell asleep at the wheel and his vehicle became stuck in a ditch along the side of the road.

A police officer arrived and asked Joe what had happened. Mr. Roberts could not remember. Joe then exited the car but became dizzy when he stood up. The officer grabbed Joe to prevent him from falling, and smelled liquor on Joe's breath. The policeman suspected that Joe was intoxicated so he administered a breathalyzer which registered a bloodalcohol level of 0.06%. Joe was charged with violating Arizona's laws on DUI since the cop suspected that Joe was an "impaired driver" as defined by Arizona state law.

Following a contentious hearing, Mr. Roberts was convicted of the charges. The judge believed that Joe's consumption of alcohol contributed to Roberts' falling asleep behind the wheel making him an impaired driver. Joe paid the fine and returned to Pennsylvania thinking that the matter was over. Mr. Roberts received the shock of his life when he opened the mail. The Arizona Department of Transportation sent notice of his DUI conviction to the Pennsylvania authorities under the Driver's License Compact. The Pennsylvania Department of Transportation has demanded that Joe immediately surrender his license and attend a hearing next month on whether he should go to jail as a repeat DUI offender.

Joe wishes to fight the suspension by the Pennsylvania Department of Transportation. Joe insists that he did nothing wrong since his blood-alcohol level of 0.06% demonstrated that he was not intoxicated. Even using the new Pennsylvania law for intoxication of a blood-alcohol of 0.08%, Joe was not legally intoxicated.

I have located the Arizona law under which Joe was convicted. *A.R.S. §28-692(A) (1)* provides that it is unlawful for a person to drive:

1. While under the influence of intoxicating liquor, the person is *impaired to the slightest degree.*

2. If there was at the time of driving a blood-alcohol content in excess of 0.05% but less than 0.10% alcohol concentration in the defendant's blood, that fact shall not give rise to a presumption that the defendant was or was not under the influence of intoxicating liquor, but that fact may be considered with other competent evidence in determining the guilt or innocence of the defendant.

Pennsylvania's law on driving under the influence provides that:

1. An individual may not operate a vehicle after imbibing a sufficient amount of alcohol that the individual is *rendered incapable of safely driving.*

2. An individual may not operate a vehicle after imbibing a sufficient amount of alcohol such that the alcohol concentration in the individual's blood or breath is at least 0.08% but less than 0.10% within two hours after the individual has driven.

Joe maintains that it is not fair that he will lose his license because the law in Arizona is more rigid than that in Pennsylvania. Joe's conviction resulted from that part of Arizona's law that provides for a conviction if the driver is *impaired to the slightest degree*. Pennsylvania requires that the operator be rendered incapable of safely driving.

Read **Kline v. Commonwealth of Pennsylvania** and let me know whether we can successfully challenge the actions of the Department of Transportation. Keep in mind that the laws in Pennsylvania when the **Kline** case was decided required a blood-alcohol content of 0.10% for conviction. Pennsylvania has now lowered the blood-alcohol level requirement to 0.08% in order to sustain a conviction. That change in the law, however, does not affect the court's holding.

JOHN KLINE v. COMMONWEALTH OF PENNSYLVANIA
725 A.2D 860 (CMWLTH. COURT 1999)

On July 9, 1997, Kline, a Pennsylvania resident, pled guilty in Virginia, to a charge of violating Virginia's "Driving under the Influence" (DUI) statute. By pleading guilty, he admitted to driving a motor vehicle while having a blood-alcohol concentration of 0.08 percent.

The Pennsylvania Department of Motor Vehicles suspended Kline's operating privilege for one year as a result of the Virginia conviction. The Department's notice advised that the Pennsylvania Motor Vehicle Code requires the Department to treat certain out-of-state convictions as though they had occurred in Pennsylvania.

The Drivers License Compact provides that the licensing authority in the home state, shall give the same effect to the conduct reported as it would if such conduct had occurred in the home state. If the laws of the home state do not provide for the offenses described in precisely the words employed in laws of the state in which the offense occurred, such home state shall construe the law as being applicable only to violations of a *substantially similar nature*.

Kline filed an appeal with the trial court, which found that he was not convicted on the basis of conduct that would have constituted the offense of DUI in Pennsylvania. Rather, the trial court found that Kline's conviction was predicated solely upon a blood-alcohol content level below that proscribed for an adult driver in Pennsylvania which is 0.10%. The trial court concluded that Kline's Virginia conviction was not for an offense substantially similar to a violation of the Motor Vehicle Code of Pennsylvania.

Virginia's statutory provision proscribing various forms of driving while intoxicated reads as follows:

> It shall be unlawful for any person to drive or operate any motor vehicle, engine or train *(i) while such person has a blood alcohol concentration of 0.08 percent or more by weight by volume.*

Pennsylvania's DUI statute states:

> A person shall not drive, operate or be in actual physical control of the movement of a vehicle *while the amount of alcohol by weight in the blood of an adult is 0.10%.*

In determining whether a reported offense from another state may serve as a basis for suspending a Pennsylvania licensee's operating privilege, the other state's offense need only be *"substantially similar"* to the Pennsylvania Vehicle Code in order to mandate a suspension under the Compact.

Here, Kline was convicted of driving with a blood-alcohol concentration level of 0.08% or more. Looking at the offense for which he was convicted, we agree with the trial court that Kline's conduct would have no consequences under Pennsylvania law.

Similarly, in **Eck v. Department of Transportation, Bureau of Driver Licensing, 713 A.2d 744 (Pa.Cmwlth.1998),** the court confined its analysis to the language of the specific provision of the party state's DUI statute under which the licensee was convicted. The licensee in **Eck** was convicted under a subsection of Maryland's DUI statute prohibiting a person from driving under the influence of alcohol. The **Eck** court observed that the use of any amount of alcohol would support a conviction, while a conviction under Pennsylvania's law requires evidence that the licensee was under the influence of alcohol to a degree that renders him incapable of driving safely. The court concluded that the two offenses were not substantially similar. A person violates the Vehicle Code of Pennsylvania if such person has a blood-alcohol content level of 0.10% or higher, *or* if such person is under the influence of alcohol to a degree that renders the person *incapable of safe driving.* While a driver in Pennsylvania need not have a blood alcohol level of 0.10% in order to be convicted of DUI, where there is no evidence to this effect, the Department must prove that the licensee was influenced by alcohol to a degree that he could not drive safely. A person driving with a blood alcohol level of 0.08% will suffer no consequences under of the Vehicle Code of Pennsylvania if he is still capable of being a safe driver in any case.

We decline to hold that a twenty-percent difference between the two statutes' threshold blood-alcohol levels is insignificant. As it currently exists, the Vehicle Code of Pennsylvania does not prohibit the conduct for which Licensee was convicted in Virginia. Therefore, the Compact does not authorize the Department to suspend driver's operating privilege based on that conduct.

Please analyze the **Kline** decision and let me know if we will be successful in an appeal of Joe's license suspension.

ANSWER SHEET
PROBLEM SEVEN—B

Name   **Please Print Clearly**

1. What is the difference between the laws in Pennsylvania and Arizona on driving a motor vehicle after consuming acholic beverages?

2. What arguments would you make on behalf of Joe to overturn his suspension?

3. Will we win an appeal of Joe's suspension? Please explain.

_____

_____

_____

_____

_____

_____

_____

_____

_____

_____

_____

_____

_____

_____

_____

_____

_____

_____

_____

_____

_____

Section 7.12
Comity

Comity is derived from the Latin "comitas" which means courteous. In the arena of international law, this principle allows for the courteous recognition of the rules and laws of a foreign jurisdiction. States are not mandated to enforce the laws and judgments of another country. Rather, each determines on its own the extent to which it will provide courtesy and respect to a foreign sovereign taking into consideration the state's international obligations and rights of its own citizens.[18] Generally, as long as the laws of another country are not contrary to public policy or prejudicial to the interests of the forum jurisdiction, the law will be upheld.

The death penalty is not uniformly supported around the world. This issue of philosophical differences can strain relations between countries–even those sovereignties otherwise maintain good relations. This fact is evident in two cases in which the United States sought the return of a person from a foreign country in order to face murder charges in which the death penalty could be imposed in those jurisdictions.

A new generation has learned the name of Ira Einhorn. This 1960's activist was charged with the Philadelphia murder of Holly Maddux, whose mummified body was found in a steamer trunk in Einhorn's closet. Shortly before his criminal trial, the defendant disappeared. Nevertheless, the trial went on in his absence, and Einhorn was found guilty of first-degree murder and was sentenced to death. After twenty years on the run, Einhorn was located in France. That country, however, refused to return him to the United States because of its opposition to the death penalty. It was only after the Pennsylvania legislature agreed that Einhorn would not face the death penalty and that he would be granted a new trial that the French court ordered the fugitive's return to Philadelphia.

A similar situation occurred in Canada where two young men who were residents of that country were accused of killing three people in the state of Washington. Despite requests by the United States government to return the suspects, Canada had refused because of their opposition to the death penalty. This case went before the Canadian Supreme Court, which ruled that the suspects would not be returned until the United States guaranteed that they would not face the death penalty.

Badawi v. Alesawy deals with whether New York will recognize a divorce obtained by the plaintiff in Abu Dhabi. This case provides an example of comity.

SANDY MOHAMED BADAWI v. WAEL MOUNIR ALESAWY
135 A.D.3D 792 (N.Y. 2016)

In May 1998, the parties were married in New York in a civil ceremony, and, thereafter, were married in New York in a religious ceremony under Islamic law. As part of the religious ceremony, the parties signed a mahr agreement requiring the defendant to make an advanced payment to the plaintiff in the amount of $5,000 and, in the event of divorce, a deferred payment of $250,000. The parties' mahr agreement is a marriage agreement in accordance with Islamic law wherein the defendant pledged to pay the plaintiff a "deferred dowry" in the event of a divorce.

While the parties were living in Abu Dhabi, United Arab Emirates, the plaintiff obtained a judgment of divorce against the defendant in the Abu Dhabi courts. The judgment of divorce awarded the plaintiff custody of the parties' children and financial relief, including an award of $250,000 pursuant to the mahr agreement.

The plaintiff commenced this action for a judgment declaring that the foreign judgment of divorce is valid and enforceable in New York. Thereafter, she moved, among other things, to enforce the judgment of divorce and for an attorney's fee with respect to the prosecution of the motion.

Although not required to do so, the courts of this State generally will accord recognition to the judgments rendered in a foreign country under the doctrine of comity which is the equivalent of full faith and credit given by the courts to judgments of our sister States." Comity should be extended to uphold the validity of a foreign divorce decree absent a showing of fraud in its procurement or that recognition of the judgment would do violence to a strong public policy of New York. Moreover, in extending comity to uphold the validity of a foreign divorce decree, New York courts will generally recognize all the provisions of such decrees, including any agreement which may have been incorporated therein, unless modification is required by reason of some compelling public policy.

Here, the mahr agreement, although not acknowledged in accordance with Domestic Relations Law § 236(B)(3), was signed by the parties and two witnesses, as well as the Imam of the Islamic Cultural Center of New York. Under the circumstances presented, the Supreme Court properly recognized so much of the foreign judgment of divorce as incorporated the mahr agreement under the principles of comity, as no strong public policy of New York was violated thereby. Accordingly, the court properly granted the plaintiff's motion which was to enforce so much of the judgment of divorce in the sum of $250,000 pursuant to the mahr agreement.

SECTION 7.13
ALTERNATIVE
DISPUTE RESOLUTION

Controversies may be resolved in ways other than by using the state and federal court systems, which may be too time-consuming or expensive. Parties may agree to submit to any of a number of alternative methods for resolving their disputes. In considering an **alternative dispute resolution** mechanism, the parties will focus on factors such as cost, who will represent them, who will arbitrate the dispute, and whether the alternative method will lead to a more helpful or fair resolution.

Arbitration is often used in a commercial setting where both parties agree to have a third party or arbitrator resolve the controversy. When the parties agree to abide by the arbitrator's decision, they are involved in binding arbitration, and the court will automatically enforce the arbitrator's award. Both parties must agree on who the impartial arbitrator will be. Arbitration proceedings are usually informal, and the parties are not bound by the rules of evidence that control court cases.

Became of the binding nature of arbitration, the courts will rarely overturn an award. Courts will refuse to uphold an arbitration award if it is the product of fraud, gross misconduct corruption, or serious misconduct by the arbitrator.[19]

The following is sample language from an arbitration statute on when an award may be vacated:

> The Federal Arbitration Act specifies the following grounds for vacating an arbitration award:
>
> (a) Where the award was procured by corruption, fraud, or undue means.
>
> (b) Where there was evident partiality or corruption in the arbitrators, or either of them.
>
> (c) Where the arbitrators were guilty of misconduct in refusing to postpone the hearing ... or in refusing to hear evidence pertinent and material to the controversy; or of any other misbehavior by which the rights of any party have been prejudiced.
>
> (d) Where the arbitrators exceeded their powers, or so imperfectly executed them that a mutual, final and definite award upon the subject matter submitted was not made.[20]

Several high profile cases involving arbitrations between professional athletes and the National Football League has resulted in a challenge to the award being contested in court. The following case involves future Hall of Fame running back Adrian Peterson and his suspension by the NFL over an incident involving the discipline of Peterson's son. The court vacated a suspension levied by the league because the arbitrator improperly applied a new conduct policy retroactively in determining the player's punishment.

ADRIAN PETERS V. NATIONAL FOOTBALL LEAGUE
88 F. SUPP.3D 1084 (D. MINN. 2015)

This matter is before the court upon the petition to vacate the arbitration award [filed on behalf] of Adrian Peterson. This arbitration dispute arises out of the discipline imposed by NFL Commissioner Roger Goodell on Minnesota Vikings running back Adrian Peterson following Peterson's corporal punishment of his son.

The parties' relationship is governed by the Collective Bargaining which authorizes the Commissioner to impose discipline on NFL players for "conduct detrimental to the integrity of, or public confidence in, the game." Article 46 allows a player to appeal the Commissioner's disciplinary decision to a hearing officer appointed by the Commissioner. The NFL Player Contract, which is part of the CBA, further provides that on a finding of conduct detrimental to the league, the Commissioner "will have the right, but only after giving Player the opportunity for a hearing ... to fine Player in a reasonable amount; to suspend Player for a period certain or indefinitely; and/or to terminate this contract." The Policy provided that the NFL may impose discipline when the player has committed a criminal offense. The Policy did not set forth the presumed length of suspension for particular types of conduct, but noted that the disciplinary response "will be based on the nature of the incident, the actual or threatened risk to the participant and others, any prior or additional misconduct and other relevant factors."

In response to a well-publicized domestic violence incident involving Baltimore Ravens running back Ray Rice, the Commissioner issued an enhanced Personal Conduct Policy (New Policy), increasing the sanctions for domestic violence and sexual assault incidents.

A grand jury indicted Peterson on a charge of felony negligent injury of a child, as a result an incident involving his son. Peterson pleaded nolo contendere to a reduced misdemeanor charge of reckless assault. Two days later, the NFL acknowledged Peterson's plea and advised him that the "matter warrants review for potential disciplinary action under the Personal Conduct Policy." The NFL requested that Peterson provide certain information regarding the criminal case and notified him that he would have the opportunity to participate in a hearing before the Commissioner imposed any discipline. The NFL notified Peterson that he was expected to attend a hearing at the NFL's offices in New York. The NFLPA responded on Peterson's behalf with several questions regarding the agenda and process for the proposed hearing. The NFL answered that Peterson would be permitted to present "any information or evidence in support of his position" and that the NFL would determine the appropriate discipline, if any, under "the policies." The NFL further explained that it had invited "some outside people" to the hearing to "broaden [the NFL's] perspective" but did not indicate what role those individuals would play.

The NFLPA then asked to reschedule the hearing to early the following week to accommodate Peterson's and his representatives' schedules. The NFLPA complained that holding a formal hearing violated the parties' "long-standing custom and practice regarding such meetings." Concerned with the proposal to include outside people, the NFLPA requested further clarification about the role of each attendee.

Not having received a response from the NFL, the NFLPA inquired as to the status of the proceedings and offered the following week as a possible meeting date. The NFL responded that Peterson elected not to attend or participate as requested, leaving the league to move forward. The next day, the NFLPA notified the NFL that Peterson would submit his position to the Commissioner in writing. The NFL did not give him the chance to do so. The Commissioner then applied the New Policy to Peterson and suspended Peterson without pay for "at least the remainder of the season.

The NFLPA immediately appealed the discipline. The NFLPA specifically challenged the application of the New Policy to conduct occurring before its implementation. The NFL responded by setting the arbitration for December 2 and appointing Harold Henderson as the designated hearing officer. The NFLPA asked Henderson to recuse himself given his "inextricable ties to Commissioner Goodell" and evident partiality. Henderson declined and upheld the Commissioner's discipline in its entirety.

Courts give decisions by labor arbitrators "substantial deference." Therefore, as long as the arbitrator is even arguably construing or applying the CBA and acting within the scope of his authority, and he committed an error does not suffice to overturn his decision. Arbitration awards, however, are not inviolate, and the court needs not merely rubber stamp the arbitrator's interpretations and decisions. The court must vacate the award if it fails to "draw its essence" from the agreement, such that the arbitrator imposed "his own brand of industrial justice."

The essence of the CBA is derived not only from its express provisions, but also from the industrial common law." The common law includes "past practices of the industry and the shop," The NFLPA argues that the award fails to draw its essence from the CBA because it ignores established law of the shop, namely, that the New Policy may not be retroactively applied. There is no dispute that the Commissioner imposed Peterson's discipline under the New Policy.

It is not seriously contested that the Commissioner understood he was constrained to apply the New Policy prospectively. [Nevertheless] Henderson simply disregarded the law of the shop and in doing so failed to meet his duty under the CBA. As a result, the arbitration award fails to draw its essence from the CBA and vacatur is warranted.

Mediation is used primarily in disputes between labor and management, but also is suited to disputes between neighbors and family members. Mediation is different from arbitration because it is advisory in nature. A mediator makes recommendations to the parties in order to aid them in solving their differences. Successful mediation will keep the parties out of court. Mediation is gaining popularity in divorce cases in helping the parties work out their differences.

Private judging is used when both sides are constrained by time and can afford to hire a private judge, usually a retired judge. Private judging proceeds as a normal trial would be conducted.

Non-binding or **mini-trials** are another form of private dispute resolution in which the parties may or may not be represented by a lawyer.

The parties usually submit their case to a panel of experts and a neutral advisor, who aids both sides. The panel and advisor suggest the likely outcome if the case were to go to court. This method is helpful for business disputes involving long processes of fact-finding.

Neighborhood Justice Centers derive from a program initiated in the 1970s. The centers receive their cases from local police or magistrates' offices. The cases usually involve neighborhood or family disputes, in which the two sides represent themselves before a panel of local residents. The aim is to avoid having the disputes escalate to the point where the criminal court system takes over.

SECTION 7.14
ETHICS

Certain members of Congress want to pass a law requiring Justices on the Supreme Court to comply with the same rules of ethics that apply to other federal judges. Under the bill, the Justices would be barred from engaging in political activity and fundraising endeavors along with other forms of conduct that would raise a concern about their impartiality. The Supreme Court Justices indicate that they look at the ethics rules that apply to other members of the federal judiciary for guidance, but they are not mandated to follow them. Chief Justice Roberts commented on this issue when he said:

> "The Code of Conduct, by its express terms, applies only to lower federal court judges." That reflects a fundamental difference between the Supreme Court and the other federal courts. Article III of the Constitution creates only one court, the Supreme Court of the United States, but it empowers Congress to establish additional lower federal courts that the Framers knew the country would need. Congress instituted the Judicial Conference for the benefit of the courts it had created. Because the Judicial Conference is an instrument for the management of the lower federal courts, its committees have no mandate to prescribe rules or standards for any other body."[21]

At the present time, each Justice decides on his or her own was is proper. Do you think this proposal should be adopted? How would it be enforced since a question arises as to whether Congress can constitutionally regulate the actions of the highest court in the land?

SECTION 7.15
PROBLEM CASES

1. Francis Thomas received an envelope at his New Jersey home with a return address from the Philadelphia Chamber of Commerce. Upon opening the letter, he discovered two tickets to a Philadelphia 76ers game. Mr. Thomas could not believe his good fortune and took his son to the contest at the First Union Center. During the second period, the Sheriff tapped Thomas on the shoulder and served him with a lawsuit concerning a motor vehicle accident that

had happened one year earlier in New Jersey. Does the Philadelphia Court have jurisdiction over this New Jersey resident because Thomas was served with the lawsuit within its boundaries? See: **M. H. Eastburn v. Saul Turnoff, 147 A.2d 353 (Pa. 1959).**

2. Robert DeLuca had a long history of being involved in violent crimes. During his criminal trial for extortion, the trial judge empaneled an anonymous jury in order to safeguard the panel members' identity and to prevent jury tampering. Spectators were also screened and had to produce identification before being allowed into the courtroom. DeLuca claimed that his Sixth Amendment right to a public trial were violated by the judge's unusual actions. Do you agree? **United States v. Robert DeLuca, 96-1173, (1st Cir. Ct. 1998).**

3. A franchise agreement between Charles Jones and General Nutrition Companies, Inc., required that all disputes concerning the agreement be litigated in a Pennsylvania venue. Jones operated a GNC store in California. Following a dispute, he sued GNC in his home state where his store is located, the contracts were entered into in California, and the majority of witnesses are in that state. GNC requested a change of venue so that the case could be removed to Pennsylvania based upon the forum selection clause in the contract even though California does not favor this type of clause. Where should the case be heard? **Charles Jones v. GNC Franchising, Inc., CV-98-10611-DMT (9ᵗʰ Cir. Ct. 2000).**

4. Beer Across America sold beer to a minor via the internet. The liquor was shipped from the store's location in Illinois to the child's home in Alabama. After the parents returned home from vacation, they discovered the beer in the refrigerator. This prompted the parents to file a suit in Alabama against the Illinois company for the unlawful sale of liquor to a minor. Beer Across America was not registered to do business in Alabama, and it owned no property within the state. Is a passive Internet site that can be accessed from anywhere in the world sufficient to confer jurisdiction over a nonresident defendant for doing business in Alabama? **Lynda Butler v. Beer Across America, 83 F. Supp. 2d 1261 (2000).**

Footnotes:

1. *Marbury v. Madison* http://usinfo.state.gov/usa/infousa/facts/democrac/9.htm.

2. "A Brief Overview of the Supreme Court," Supreme Court of the United States, http://www.supremecourt.gov/about/briefoverview.aspx (last visited on February 16, 2016).

3. *Id.*

4. Supreme *Court of the United States,* Supreme Court Historical Society, http://www.supremecourthistory.org/.

5. *How the Court Works,* The Supreme Court Historical Society, www.suprme-courthistory.org.

6. *Id.*

7. *Williams v. Florida,* 399 U.S. 78 (1970).

8. *Duncan v. Louisiana,* 88 S. Ct. 1444 (1968).

9. *American Bar Association Points: Trial by Jury,* www.abanet.org.

10. See: *Criminal Justice across Europe,* www.crimeinfo.org.uk.

11. Civil Justice Statistics, U.S. Department of Justice Bureau of Justice Statistics, http://www.ojp.usdoj.gov/bjs/civil.htm.

12. Shrager and Frost, "The Quotable Lawyer," Facts on File, at 152.

13. New York Times, February 3, 1969 as cited in the "Quotable Lawyer" at 154.

14. American Bar Association Journal, November 1995, page 72.

15. *Id.*

16. See: *Lesson 7-9: Voir Dire,* American Bar Association.

17. "Forum Non Conveniens Example," Legal Information Institute, Cornell University Law School, https://www.law.cornell.edu/ (last visited on March 10, 2016).

18. *Judgment of the Court of Foreign Countries as Entitled to Enforcement of Extraterritorial Effect in State Court,* 13 A. L R. 4th 1109.

19. "Can An Arbitration Award Be Overturned By A Court?," FreeAdvice, http://law.freeadvice.com/litigation/arbitration/arbitration_overturned.htm (last visited on February 17, 2016).

20. *O.R. Securities, Inc. v. Professional Planning Associates, Inc.,* 857 F.2d 742 (11th Cir. Ct. App. 1988).

21. Martha Neil, "Can Congress impose ethics rules on the US Supreme Court?," August 5, 2013, ABA Journal, http://www.abajournal.com/news/article/is_proposed_bill_to_impose_ethics_rules_on_us_supreme_court_constitutional/ (last visited on February 20, 2016).

KEY TERMS

Activist
Alternative Dispute Resolution
American Arbitration
  Association
Appellate Court
Arbitration
Article III
Article IV
Certiorari
Challenge for Cause
Circuit Court of Appeals
Comity
Commonwealth Court
Court of Common Pleas
Court of Federal Claims
District Court
Driver's License Compact
Federal Court
Federal Mediation and
  Conciliation Service
Forum Non-Conveniens
Full, Faith and Credit
Judicial Restraint Oriented
Jurisdiction
Jurisdiction over the Person
Jury

Long Arm Statute
Magna Carta
Mediation
Minimum Contacts
Municipal Court
Neighborhood Justice Centers
One-Day or One-Trial
Original Jurisdiction
Peremptory Challenge
Private Judging
Questions-of-Facts
Questions-of-Law
Rule of Hour
Service
Seventh Amendment
Sixth Amendment
Standing
State Court
State Supreme Court
Subject Matter Jurisdiction
Superior Court
Supreme Court Rule 10
United States Supreme Court
Venue
Voir Dire

CHAPTER 8

CIVIL PROCEDURE

We live in a litigation oriented society whose members seem to institute suit over every conceivable problem. "You will be hearing from my lawyer" seems to be a frequent refrain. Cases range from class action lawsuits against the tobacco industry to suits against McDonald's for causing obesity in children.

Rules have been established to govern the conduct of these lawsuits from the filing of the claim to the verdict. These regulations are called the **Rules of Civil Procedure** and vary depending upon the type of proceeding and court. Matters before a Justice of the Peace or Municipal Court judge will be informal since they involve small amounts of money and the litigants are encouraged to represent themselves. Jury trials are more formal and the rules are complex. Failure to follow these court mandates may result in an adverse finding or dismissal of the lawsuit.

Civil litigation involves three distinctive but equally important parts:

1. Pleadings;
2. Discovery; and
3. Trial.

The **Pleadings** consist of the initial documents filed with the court that set forth the theories of liability and damages requested by the plaintiff and the defenses of the parties being sued. These documents include the Complaint, Answer, New Matter or Affirmative Defenses, and Counterclaim. The pleadings also establish the boundaries of the lawsuit, since matters not asserted are generally waived. For instance, the defense of assumption of the risk or payment of a loan must be raised at this time or it will be lost as a defense.

Discovery allows each party to find out more information about the opponent's case. It is during this stage that witnesses can be questioned, and counsel can obtain copies of an opponent's documents and trial exhibits. In addition, medical or psychological examinations of a party may be ordered if relevant to the case.

The **Trial** is the final stage of the litigation. It is at this judicial proceeding that evidence will be presented, witnesses cross-examined, and factual disputes resolved by the rendering of a verdict in favor of one of the parties.

SECTION 8.2
PETER CHRISTOPHER
v. JOSEPH ROBERTS

The news is filled with stories about odd lawsuits or unusual court results. For instance, Satan was the subject of a civil rights lawsuit filed by a person who lost his home in mortgage foreclosure claiming that the devil had violated his constitutional rights. Even Bill Gates is not immune from creative lawsuits. The founder of Microsoft was sued by a person who believed that Mr. Gates and others had conspired to murder him through the Windows operating system that was hooked up to the claimant's mind.

Any number of lawsuits may be utilized to creatively illustrate the civil litigation process. The lawsuit against Joe Roberts by his next-door neighbor over Joe's choice of a pet rivals any for its unusual facts so it will be used to demonstrate the civil litigation process.

SECTION 8.3
FACTS

Peter Christopher v. Joseph Roberts deals with the liability attached for Joe's keeping a pet bear in his backyard. Joe purchased this unusual animal when it was a cub from a bankrupt circus. Roberts raised the animal to full maturity and the black bear is named "Harry." The animal weighs a little more than 300 pounds, stands five feet tall and is able to do any number of tricks. Mr. Roberts kept Harry at his house in a residential neighborhood much to the dismay of the other homeowners.

The events leading up to the lawsuit occurred on Labor Day weekend when the bear was left unattended in Joe's backyard. It was late in the afternoon and the Roberts family went inside to eat dinner. The bear had fallen asleep by the portion of the fence that borders Mr. Christopher's property.

Peter Christopher, however, did not view the bear with quite the same admiration as the Roberts family. Christopher found the odors emanating from Joe's backyard offensive and the conditions unsanitary. Christopher's complaints to the township were being investigated, but no formal action had been taken to remove the black bear from the neighborhood.

On this particular weekend, Christopher had invited 50 guests to his home for a barbecue. As Christopher was setting up his lawn area for the party, he was becoming more and more agitated by the bear's close proximity to his backyard. Brazened with the consumption of alcohol, Christopher picked up a long metal pole that was normally used to clean his pool. He then walked over to the fence and started poking the animal with the instrument to relocate the sleeping bear to the opposite side of Joe's yard. The bear, however, awakened in an agitated state and mauled the next door neighbor.

Christopher was injured in the fracas and instituted suit claiming that Roberts had been negligent for keeping a non-domesticated animal in his backyard.

SECTION 8.4
FEE ARRANGEMENTS

An attorney may be hired under a variety of fee arrangements including a fixed price, a per-hour billing, a retainer, and a contingent fee agreement.

In a limited number of cases, an attorney knows exactly how much time will be involved in the handling of a matter and can quote a specific price. These matters include a simple uncontested divorce, the drafting of a will, or the incorporation of a business. Most cases, however, are handled on a per-hour basis. An attorney will charge for the time spent on the file and the per-hour fee will vary depending upon the sophistication of the problem and expertise of counsel. Average rates range from $150 to $500 per hour. All case work is recorded on a time sheet, and the client is billed for that time on a periodic basis. Billable time includes telephone conferences and the writing of letters on a client's behalf. Anyone who hires an attorney on a per-hour basis should ask for an itemized bill setting forth the time spent by the attorney by date and services rendered. Bills should be sent on a periodic basis, such as each month or quarterly.

Personal injury claims are frequently handled on a contingent fee basis. This means that the attorney will take a percentage of the recovery as the fee. If counsel is unsuccessful in recovering money for a claimant, no legal fee is due. The contingent fee agreement varies in percentage from one-third to one-half of the recovery. The average arrangement is forty percent, but some firms will offer a staggered rate depending upon the amount of work expended to create the fund. For instance, if a case is settled before suit, an attorney may take thirty percent of the recovery; if the settlement is achieved after the institution of suit, the percentage may increase to thirty-five percent; and if the case is tried, the fee will increase to forty percent.

SECTION 8.5
CONTINGENT FEE
AGREEMENT

In the case of **Peter Christopher v. Joseph Roberts,** Mr. Christopher signed a contingent fee agreement. The following is a sample of that document and provides for a 40 percent recovery from the gross settlement.

The undersigned hereby constitutes and appoints the law firm of London and Flanigan, P.C., as his attorney to prosecute all causes of action on account of an accident or incident which occurred on September 3, involving an assault by a non-domesticated animal.

I hereby agree that the compensation of my attorney for services shall be determined as follows:

Out of whatever sum which is secured by either my said attorney or by me from the defendant, or from anyone else, either by way of voluntary payment, settlement or verdict, my said attorney, for and in consideration of the professional services rendered in the investigation and general conduct of the said case or claim, including the institution of suit, if necessary, shall retain or be entitled to forty percent (40%) of the gross amount of any recovery.

I understand and agree that my attorney is under no obligation to represent or continue to represent me on any appeal from an adverse verdict or decision. I reserve the right to decide on the acceptability of any settlement offer that may be made and to decide whether an appeal from an adverse verdict or decision will be taken. Should no money be recovered by verdict or settlement by either my attorney, or by me, my said attorney is to have no claim against me of any kind for services rendered by him.

Peter Christopher (SEAL)
_____
Peter H. Christopher

SECTION 8.6
HOURLY BILL

Joseph Roberts is being defended on a per-hour basis. The time expended on his case is recorded on a timelog broken down into six-minute intervals. For instance, one-tenth of an hour or ".1" is the equivalent of six minutes.

PARK, BROWN & SMITH, P.C.
1515 MARKET STREET, 6TH FL.
PHILADELPHIA, PA 19100

Joseph A. Roberts
39 Royal Court
Rydal, Pennsylvania 19000   **Invoice:** 1010101
                                 Page: 1

RE: **Christopher v. Roberts**
For Professional Services Rendered:

Date	Description of Service	Hours	Rate Per Hour
1/5	Conference with client	0.5	$125
1/5	Letter to opposing counsel	0.3	$125
1/7	Legal research	3.0	$125

Total Hours: 3.8

Total Amount of Bill: ***$475.00***

What happens when a client hires a lawyer on a contingent fee basis and then fires that lawyer before the case is completed? Is the attorney entitled to the full fee even though he is no longer working on the file? The courts generally award the discharged attorney a fee based on the value of services rendered to the date of discharge, or in legal terms, on a **"quantum meruit"** basis. Quantum meruit is an equitable remedy that provides for a form of restitution when one person has been unjustly enriched at the expense of another.

Some states, such as New Jersey and New York, regulate the percentage that an attorney may charge in handling a contingency fee case. Pennsylvania does not have such a restriction unless the claim involves the representation of a child.

SECTION 8.7
SERVICE OF PROCESS

Procedural due process requires that a defendant be notified of any legal proceeding that has been filed against him. This is called **service of process**. In a criminal case, this occurs when the defendant is arrested or indicted. In a civil matter, however, the defendant must be served with a copy of the lawsuit. This task is usually accomplished by having a representative of the court, such as the Sheriff, personally hand a copy of the lawsuit to the defendant. Frequently, the defendant is not at home when the Sheriff attempts to serve the legal papers. When this occurs, is the Sheriff mandated to continue the search for the defendant or may the judicial officer serve another person, such as the defendant's spouse or business partner?

Court rules allow service of a legal document upon someone other than the defendant as long as the service is reasonably calculated to notify the defendant that he or she is the subject of a claim. For example, *Pennsylvania Rule of Civil Procedure 402* provides that the defendant must be handed a copy of the legal document personally, or the Sheriff may serve an adult member of the household of the defendant at the residence.

What happens if the defendant is lured or tricked into entering a state solely for purposes of serving that individual with the lawsuit? Will this type of conduct be allowed? That is the issue in **Gatte v. Dohm.**

TAMMY GATTE V. JUDY DOHM
574 FED. APPX. 327 (5TH CT APP. 2014)

This case arises out of the death of Phillip Gatte, a Louisiana citizen, at a hospital in Cancun, Mexico. Gatte allegedly died from complications following post-weight-loss body-sculpting surgery. Gatte's family, sued R4C, a Minnesota-based medical tourism company that had arranged the surgery, and Judy Dohm, a Minnesota citizen and co-owner of R4C.

The plaintiffs sued in Louisiana. Typically, personal service of process on a defendant who is voluntarily present in a state will give rise to personal jurisdiction in that state. However, service of process in the forum state will not give rise to personal jurisdiction if the defendant's presence in the forum state is procured by fraud for the purpose of serving process. As a general rule, a court will not take jurisdiction based on service of process on a defendant who was brought within the reach of its process wrongfully or fraudulently, or by deceit or any other improper device.

Service of process on Ms. Dohm, is alleged [to have been] fraudulently induced into coming to Louisiana by the plaintiffs to be served with process, under the ruse of Ms. Dohm delivering the deceased Mr. Phillip Gatte's ashes to the plaintiffs. Because Dohm was personally served with process while voluntarily present in Louisiana, personal jurisdiction was established as to her unless she was fraudulently induced to enter the state for the purpose of serving process. Dohm states that she "was duped by Mr. Gatte's family into flying to Cancun, Mexico to retrieve Gatte's remains and personal effects due to being led to believe that plaintiffs were too distraught to do so themselves."

On the other hand, plaintiffs states that Judy Dohm contacted them and offered to fly to Mexico and retrieve Phillip Gatte's personal items and ashes from Mexico." Plaintiffs' affidavit, if believed, establishes that she did not trick or defraud Dohm into coming to Louisiana. For purposes of the personal jurisdiction inquiry, this is conclusive.

For the reasons explained above, the district court's dismissal of the plaintiffs' claims for lack of personal jurisdiction is reversed.

SECTION 8.8
CHRISTOPHER V. ROBERTS

PARK, BROWN & SMITH, P.C.
ATTORNEYS AT LAW
MEMORANDUM

PROBLEM EIGHT—A

TO: All Students
FROM: Peter Smith, Esquire
RE: Christopher v. Roberts

Mr. Roberts has been served with the lawsuit over the attack of the next-door neighbor by Joe's pet bear. We need to file a response on his behalf. As strange as it may seem, our client really did keep a bear in his backyard and he may have supplied the animal with liquor. I fully appreciate the fact that most people would be outraged if their neighbor maintained this type of animal in the backyard so I anticipate an uphill battle in defending this litigation.

I have interviewed Joe and he swears that the bear is very gentle. His family has raised the animal since it was a cub and the bear follows the family members around like a puppy dog. In fact, Joe claims that the bear will hide if you raise your voice or yell at him.

I need to ascertain the liability of a person who keeps a non-domesticated animal in a residential setting. Does the law treat the owner of such an animal the same as it would a dog or cat who harms someone? What I really need to ascertain is if we have any defenses to the claim by Mr. Christopher? Joe has a five-foot high fence around his backyard, and the neighbor was found about ten feet inside the client's boundary line. Since Harry is about five feet tall, I have difficulty believing Christopher's story that the bear somehow pulled him over the fence. I think it is more plausible that Christopher climbed over the fence and confronted the bear on Joe's property. If that is the case, can we argue that the neighbor assumed the risk of the attack? Does it matter that the bear was tame and had never hurt anyone previously?

Please review the enclosed case and let me know if it helps our defense.

SCOTT IRVINE V. RARE FELINE BREEDING CENTER, INC.
685 N.E. 2D 120 (CT. APP. IND. 1997)

For the past thirty years, Mosella Schaffer has lived on a fifty-acre farm where she has raised exotic animals.

In 1993, Scott Bullington was renting a room in the garage area of Schaffer's house. Aware of his friend Irvine's interest in wild animals, Bullington informed Irvine of Schaffer's farm and the animals she kept there. Over the next two years, Irvine visited Schaffer's farm several dozen times. During these visits, people would occasionally pet the tigers through a fence.

On the afternoon of December 2, 1995, Irvine arrived at Schaffer's home to see Bullington. The two men drank alcohol and watched television. Because Irvine had consumed a substantial amount of alcohol, Bullington told Irvine he could stay overnight on the couch.

Around 8:00 p.m., Irvine decided to visit the tigers before going to sleep. Irvine approached the wire caging, as he and others had done in the past, placed a couple fingers inside the enclosure, and attempted to pet a male tiger. As he was scratching the male tiger, a female tiger made some commotion, which caused

Irvine to look away. At that moment, the male tiger pulled Irvine's arm through the two inch by six inch opening of the wire fence.

Upon hearing Irvine's shouts, Schaffer came out of her house, banged an object against the fence, and freed Irvine. Schaffer immediately drove Irvine to the hospital and he underwent six surgeries during a thirteen-day hospital stay.

We first address whether strict liability is the common law rule for wild animal cases. We have not found a case specifically applying strict liability to a wild animal case. However, we have little difficulty concluding that Indiana's common law recognizes the strict liability rule for wild animal cases.

We have previously set out the rationale for imposing strict liability against owners for injuries caused by an attack by a naturally ferocious or dangerous animal. Strict liability is appropriately placed upon those who, even with proper care, expose the community to the risk of a very dangerous thing. The kind of "dangerous animal" that will subject the keeper to strict liability must pose some kind of an abnormal risk to the particular community where the animal is kept; hence, the keeper is engaged in an activity that subjects those in the vicinity, including those who come onto his property, to an abnormal risk. The possessor of a wild animal is strictly liable for physical harm done to the person of another if that harm results from a dangerous propensity that is characteristic of wild animals of that class.

With the rationale for the rule in mind, we analyze whether any exceptions or defenses to the strict liability wild animal rule are appropriate. The *Restatement (Second) of Torts* provides: (1) A possessor of a wild animal is subject to liability to another for harm done by the animal to the other, his person, land or chattels, although the possessor has exercised the utmost care to confine the animal, or otherwise prevent it from doing harm. (2) This liability is limited to harm that results from a dangerous propensity that is characteristic of wild animals of the particular class, or of which the possessor knows or has reason to know.

The plaintiff's contributory negligence in knowingly and unreasonably subjecting himself to the risk that a wild animal will do harm to his person is a defense to the strict liability. Although one harmed by a wild animal that has escaped from control of its possessor is not barred from recovery because he has not exercised ordinary care to observe the presence of the animal or to escape from its attack, he is barred if he intentionally and unreasonably subjects himself to the risk of harm by the animal. Thus one who without any necessity for so doing that is commensurate with the risk involved knowingly puts himself in reach of an animal that is effectively chained or otherwise confined cannot recover against the possessor of the animal.

In the same manner, one who voluntarily teases and provokes a chained animal, or goes within reach of a vicious dog, is barred from recovery if he does so with knowledge of the danger. Thus, a plaintiff who voluntarily and unreasonably comes within reach of an animal, which he knows to be dangerous, has no cause of action when it attacks him.

Name   **Please Print Clearly**

1. Is a bear a domesticated or non-domesticated animal? Please explain.

_____

_____

_____

_____

_____

_____

_____

_____

_____

2. From a liability point of view, does the law treat the owner of a bear as the same it would a dog or cat?

_____

_____

_____

_____

_____

_____

_____

_____

3. What defense can Joe Roberts assert to the lawsuit by Peter Christopher?

_____

_____

_____

_____

_____

_____

_____

_____

_____

4. Does it matter that the black bear had never hurt anyone before this incident?

_____

_____

_____

_____

_____

_____

_____

_____

_____

SECTION 8.9
THE PLEADINGS

The purpose of the **pleadings** is to set forth the theories of liability and defenses, and to establish the boundaries of the litigation. In other words, if the plaintiff asserts that the defendant was negligent in the operation of a car, he cannot allege that the defendant intentionally ran him off the road at trial. Likewise, if the defendant has a defense to the lawsuit, such as assumption of the risk or comparative negligence, it must be asserted at this time or it will be waived.

The plaintiff initiates a lawsuit by filing a **Complaint** with the Clerk of the Court or **Prothonotary**. This pleading is like a short story and sets forth the plaintiff's theory of liability against the defendant, as well the damages the claimant maintains that he or she is entitled to receive.

The Complaint will generally follow the following outline:

1. It will identify the parties to the lawsuit and set forth their addresses;

2. It will set forth the facts in a light most favorable to the plaintiff;

3. It will identify the theory of liability such as negligence, invasion of privacy or breach of contract;

4. It will list the plaintiff's damages and/or injuries; and

5. It will conclude by asking for a dollar amount.

Regardless of the merits of the Complaint, the defendant must file a response to the lawsuit within a specified number of days. Generally, the response is called the **Answer** and the defendant must admit or deny each paragraph of the Complaint. The defendant is also required to assert his or her defenses at this time, such as the statute of limitations or assumption of the risk. This is done in a pleading called **New Matter or Affirmative Defenses**.

If the defendant has a cause of action against the plaintiff, it may be raised as a **Counterclaim**. In the alternative, the defendant can simply file a separate lawsuit against the plaintiff.

If a pleading is defective, a party may file **Preliminary Objections**, and the matter will be referred to a judge for a ruling.

THE LITIGATION PROCESS

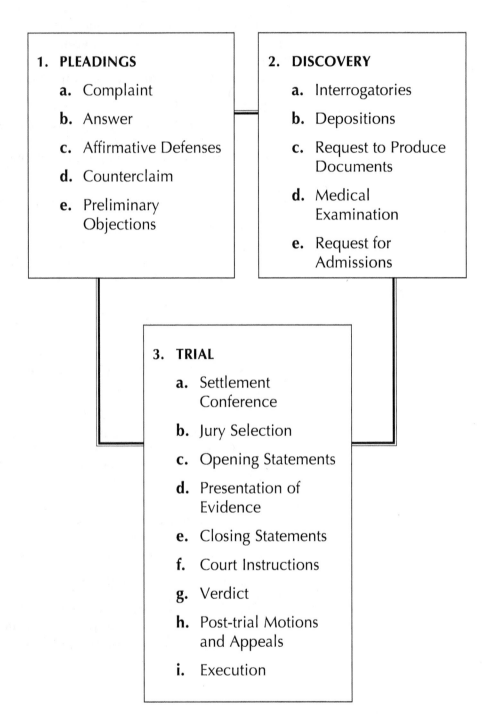

1. PLEADINGS

    a. Complaint

    b. Answer

    c. Affirmative Defenses

    d. Counterclaim

    e. Preliminary Objections

2. DISCOVERY

    a. Interrogatories

    b. Depositions

    c. Request to Produce Documents

    d. Medical Examination

    e. Request for Admissions

3. TRIAL

    a. Settlement Conference

    b. Jury Selection

    c. Opening Statements

    d. Presentation of Evidence

    e. Closing Statements

    f. Court Instructions

    g. Verdict

    h. Post-trial Motions and Appeals

    i. Execution

The following documents are the pleadings in the lawsuit of **Christopher v. Roberts**.

PETER CHRISTOPHER	: COURT OF COMMON PLEAS
v.	:
JOSEPH ROBERTS	: No. 2016-00653

COMPLAINT IN CIVIL ACTION

1. The plaintiff, Peter Christopher, resides at 38 Royal Court in Rydal, PA

2. The defendant, Joseph Roberts, resides at 37 Royal Court in Rydal, PA

3. On or about September 3 of Labor Day weekend, the defendant owned and kept a large and wild bear on his property which was left unchained.

4. A bear is a non-domesticated and wild animal that is dangerous to people.

5. As a result of the defendant's keeping this non-domesticated animal in his backyard, the bear attacked, mauled, and bit the plaintiff causing severe injuries to his body.

6. The defendant is both strictly liable and negligent for keeping such wild animal on his property.

7. The carelessness and negligence of the defendant includes, but is not limited to:

    a. keeping a non-domesticated animal that possessed a dangerous propensity at a residential property;

    b. failing to keep the animal properly chained and secured; and

    c. in otherwise being negligent.

8. Solely by reason of the aforesaid occurrence, the plaintiff was made to sustain great pain and suffering, lacerations and abrasions about the body, along with lost wages, and medical expenses.

WHEREFORE, Peter Christopher demands damages from the defendant in excess of $50,000.

PETER CHRISTOPHER	: COURT OF COMMON PLEAS
v.	:
JOSEPH ROBERTS	: No. 2016-00653

ANSWER WITH NEW MATTER AND A COUNTERCLAIM

1-2.   Admitted.

3.   Admitted. However, the backyard was enclosed by a five-foot high fence which the plaintiff climbed over.

4-8.   Denied. Said paragraphs call for conclusions of law to which no responsive pleading is needed. Furthermore, after reasonable investigation, the defendant lacks knowledge or information to form a belief as to the truth of these averments.

NEW MATTER

9.   Plaintiff's claim is barred by the Comparative Negligence Act.

10.   Plaintiff's claim is barred by the doctrine of assumption of the risk.

COUNTERCLAIM

11.   Joseph Roberts is the owner of a North American brown bear that he kept secured on his fenced-in property.

12.   On the date in question, Peter Christopher trespassed on the property of Mr. Roberts and willfully attacked the bear with a metal pole thereby causing the bear to sustain injuries requiring veterinarian expenses to cure.

13.   Joseph Roberts received $8,750 in expenses to treat the bear as the result of the plaintiff's conduct.

WHEREFORE, the defendant demands that judgment be entered in his favor to the amount of $8,750.

SECTION 8.10
ANTHONY ROBERTS
v. JIM JOHNSON

PROBLEM EIGHT—B

PARK, BROWN & SMITH, P.C.
ATTORNEYS AT LAW
MEMORANDUM

To: All Students

FROM: Peter Smith, Esquire

RE: Roberts v. Johnson

Tony Roberts decided to visit some of his college friends in the Philadelphia area. While stopped in a southbound direction on Broad Street near its intersection with Walnut Street, his car was hit in the rear by another motor vehicle being driven by Jim Johnson.

Apparently, Johnson was so intent on changing the radio station on his stereo that he did not see Tony's car stopped in front of him. While Tony was not hurt, his Corvette sustained $10,000 in property damage. It took two weeks to fix the Corvette and Tony had to rent a substitute vehicle during this time at a cost of $420.

The firm has been hired to file a lawsuit against Mr. Johnson for the damage to Tony's car and the cost of the rental vehicle. Please prepare the pleading so that we can file it with the court. As you know, Tony lives at 37 Royal Court, Rydal, Pennsylvania. Mr. Johnson resides at 805 Broadway in Philadelphia. You are to follow the form of the Complaint involving Peter Christopher, which is described in *Section 8.9*. The cause of action should be based on allegations of negligence. Your document should set forth in detail what Mr. Johnson did wrong in causing the accident. As for the date of the accident, please assume that the collision occurred one year ago on this date.

PROBLEM EIGHT—B

Name   **Please Print Clearly**

Anthony Roberts   :   COURT OF COMMON PLEAS
37 Royal Court   :
Rydal, PA   :
                            :
       v.   :
                            :
Jim Johnson   :
805 Broadway   :
Philadelphia, PA   :   No. 2016-4399

COMPLAINT

SECTION 8.11
DISCOVERY

Lawyers do not like surprises, so between the time that a lawsuit is filed and the case proceeds to trial, the litigants engage in **discovery**. This process allows an attorney to learn more about an opponent's case by the orderly exchange of information between counsel.

The tools of discovery may be classified as follows:

1. Interrogatories

2. Request for Production of Documents

3. Depositions

4. Submission to a Medical Examination

5. Request for Admissions

Interrogatories are written questions submitted to an opponent that must be answered in writing under oath. This discovery tool is used so frequently by attorneys that standard questions have been created for specific kinds of cases. For example, pre-set Interrogatories exist for personal injury cases involving medical malpractice, car accidents, trips and falls, and products liability. Since the issues are generally the same, standard questions may be utilized in various cases. When the circumstances warrant, additional questions can be crafted to cover any situation.

A **Deposition** is the oral questioning of a person under oath in which everything that is said is recorded by a stenographer. Depositions are informal in nature and can take place in a courthouse or an attorney's office. Anyone with knowledge about a case can be deposed.

A **Request for Production of Documents** requires an attorney to turn over to opposing counsel a copy of the file. While an attorney's work product and mental impressions are exempt, statements of witnesses, photographs, employment records, and medical reports must be exchanged.

A party may be required to submit to a **physical or mental examination** if relevant. For example, if a plaintiff institutes suit for personal injury, a defendant has the right to have the claimant examined by a doctor of the defendant's own choice.

Request for Admissions are used to narrow the issues for trial. A litigant can ask an opponent to admit certain facts about the case. If the information is admitted, then it does not have to be proven at the time of trial. For example, a defendant may ask a plaintiff to admit that the claimant had a previous back injury. If the fact is admitted, the defendant will not have to produce the medical records about the previous back injury at trial.

SECTION 8.12
SUBPOENA

A **subpoena** is a court order directing a person to appear in court or at another designated location to provide testimony in a court proceeding. Failure to obey the subpoena can result in a recalcitrant witness being held in **contempt of court**. It is through this process that parties are able to compel witnesses to testify in judicial proceedings so that the facts may best be presented to the finder of fact. Subpoenas are used both at the time of trial and through the pre-trial process of discovery.

There is nothing magical about the subpoena. The forms are generally purchased from the Clerk of the Court and kept in the attorney's office until needed. Subpoenas are pre-signed by the court, and the attorney merely fills in the appropriate biographical information on the document to identify the witness. A representative of the attorney's office, such as a private investigator, must serve the subpoena upon the witness. A witness is entitled to a modest fee for his or her appearance and compensation should be tendered at the time that the subpoena is served. That individual should never ignore a subpoena, since it carries with it the contempt powers of the court. If a problem exists with the date for the witness' testimony, the witness should contact the attorney whose name is listed on the document to see if the date can be changed.

While the court has great discretion in being able to hold a party in **contempt**, the imposition of sanctions must be fair. A finding of criminal contempt will be sustained when the Court finds: **(1)** misconduct in the presence of the court **(2)** committed with the intent to obstruct the proceeding, and **(3)** obstructs the administration of justice. An example of inappropriate behavior includes a case where the defendant removed his clothing down to his underwear, persisted in arguing with the judge, told the judge to go to hell, and failed to return to the courtroom in the afternoon. **Commonwealth v. Odom, 764 A.2d 53 (Pa.Super. 2000).**

REYNALDA MOLINA V. CITY OF VISALIA
2016 WL 373450 (E.D. CAL. 2016)

Plaintiffs filed the complaint in this action [and the] defendants filed a motion to show cause why sanctions should not issue due to Jaime Magana's failure to appear for deposition after being served with a subpoena requiring him to do so.

Mr. Magana explains that he had a court appearance in his own legal matter the same day as his deposition in this action was scheduled for and represents that he has the court paper work to prove that he appeared in his own matter that day. He also repeats his not entirely persuasive explanation that he had lost his deposition subpoena and had no way to contact defense counsel to notify them in advance of the conflict. Finally, he represents that he has a family with small children, works for the minimum wage and cannot afford to pay to defendants the amount recommended by the findings and recommendations.

The record reflects that defense counsel has experienced considerable difficulty in securing the attendance of this witness at deposition. It also establishes that Jaime Magana failed to contact defense counsel directly to notify them that his own court date conflicted with the deposition to which he was subpoenaed and that his explanation for failing to do so was a weak one. Nonetheless, defense counsel's motion established that six days prior to Mr. Magana's scheduled deposition, plaintiff's counsel notified defense counsel that it was his understanding that "Jaimie Managua (sic) will not be at his scheduled deposition because he has a court appearance in another matter." It was also undisputed that the day before the scheduled deposition of Magana plaintiff's counsel advised defense counsel that he had been informed by someone other than the witness, presumably plaintiff herself, that Mr. Magana would not be able to appear for his scheduled deposition. Despite this knowledge, defense counsel chose to commence the deposition and to place on the record Mr. Magana's failure to appear. While the court can understand defense counsel's frustration, apparently in part caused by difficulties encountered in obtaining the appearance of other witnesses,

under these circumstances that frustration does not justify the finding of contempt.

A party moving for civil contempt must prove that the non-moving party violated a court order by clear and convincing evidence. The burden then shifts to the [witness] to demonstrate she took every reasonable step to comply with the subpoena and explain why compliance was not possible. In making its contempt determination, a court considers the witness' history of non-compliance and the extent to which the witness failed to comply during the pendency of the motion for contempt.

Here, witness Magana has represented that he had a court appearance in his own action scheduled for the same day as his noticed deposition and has offered to present evidence that he did in fact appear in that court on the day in question. Defendants have not presented any evidence to the contrary. While Mr. Magana's explanation for not notifying defense counsel directly of the scheduling conflict is undeniably a weak one, the record establishes that defense counsel were aware of the alleged conflict several days before the scheduled deposition. The undersigned has also considered that Mr. Magana has no history of noncompliance with court orders and in fact appears to have complied with the magistrate judge's order issued at the order to show cause hearing. While his manner of communication was flawed, the witness appears to have had an adequate explanation for why he was unable to appear on the scheduled date and thereafter has cooperated in the taking of his deposition. Under these circumstances, he should not be held in contempt.

SECTION 8.13
RULES OF EVIDENCE[1]

Cases are tried by the presentation of evidence. Witnesses are called during trial and questioned by the attorneys. The finder of fact will listen to this testimony and decide who is telling the truth.

Rules of Evidence have been established to govern the way an attorney may examine a witness or ask a question. These Rules cover a wide range of possible situations arising in all types of trials.

The following is an overview of some of the Rules of Evidence. It has been prepared by the staff of the Law Education and Participation (LEAP) Program at Temple University School of Law for use in high school mock trial competitions. LEAP organizes the program in conjunction with the National Institute for Citizen Education in the Law of Washington, D.C.

EXAMINATION OF WITNESSES

A witness is questioned on **direct examination** when he or she is called by an attorney to prove the client's side of the case. The attorney who calls that witness may not ask leading questions on direct examination. A **leading question** is one that suggests to the witness the answer desired. For example, the question "Isn't it true that you last saw Mrs. Jones on January 1?" is leading. The correct way to phrase the inquiry is: "When did you last see Mrs. Jones?" In other words, a question on direct examination should be designed to obtain a short narrative answer.

An exception to the leading question rule exists if an attorney calls the opponent as a witness, or a witness is shown to be "hostile." The Court may allow the attorney to ask leading questions under these circumstances. The purpose of this exception is to prevent a hostile witness from avoiding direct, non-leading questions.

Hearsay testimony is generally prohibited in court. Hearsay is an out-of-court statement made by someone other than the witness to prove the truth of the facts contained in the statement. An example of hearsay is when Mr. Smith testifies: "Joe told me that Harry was wearing a light blue coat." The opposing attorney can object when Smith says: "Joe told me...," indicating that the witness is relying upon what someone else said. To be objectionable, the answer would also have to be relevant to the case that Harry was wearing a blue coat. The Court, however, may allow the hearsay statement if Joe is the opposing party and the out-of-court statement made by Joe was against his interest.

There are a number of exceptions to the hearsay rule. One of the more unusual exceptions deals with a **dying declaration.** If the decedent has been the victim of a crime, is critically wounded, and identifies the culprit on his deathbed, the identification will be allowed in the criminal trial even though the statement is hearsay. The idea behind the rule is that a person is not going to lie just before death. A dying declaration will be admissible even though the statement is hearsay, if **(1)** the victim identifies his attacker; **(2)** the victim believes he is going to die; **(3)** death is imminent; and **(4)** death actually occurs.

Opinion testimony is an expression of non-factual conclusions. Generally, a "lay witness" can only testify as to observed facts and those areas of "opinion" that the Court would consider to be within the general knowledge of the witness. For example, a person may testify as to the speed of a car if the witness has had some experience in driving or observing cars travelling at the speed in question. Opinion testimony, however, may be given by an expert witness. An expert is a person who can be "qualified" as having specialized knowledge in a given field because of professional credentials and/or experience acceptable to the Court. In the alternative, the attorneys for each side can agree, or **stipulate**, that a witness is an expert.

While experts must possess specialized knowledge, their testimony is entitled to no more weight than any other witness. The jury may also disregard the expert testimony if it is not found to be credible.

Relevant evidence is testimony or an exhibit that helps establish a fact which is controverted or necessary to prove one's side of the case. The Court usually allows an attorney to obtain background information from an important witness. For example, an attorney may ask the witness about his age, family, or work experience, even though it is not relevant to the central issue of the case. The opposing attorney is granted leeway in questioning the witness to explore the truthfulness of the person's direct testimony, including omitted facts, bias, or prejudice.

Not all evidence that may shed light on an issue, however, will be allowed into evidence. In federal court, the trial judge is also required to examine the prejudicial effect of the proffered evidence. If the probability of the evidence in establishing a fact is substantially outweighed by negative factors—such as confusion of the issue, unfair prejudice, or misleading the jury—the admissibility of the evidence will be denied.

Would it be relevant in a personal injury case whether the defendant received or did not receive a ticket on the issue of negligence? Do the police use the same standard in issuing a ticket that a jury would use in determining negligence? That is the issue in the next case.

CHRISTIE SOTO V. MCCULLEY MARINE SERVICES, INC.
2015 WL 8921897 (D. CT. 2015)

In 2009, Manatee County had a program to establish artificial reefs offshore from the beaches at the Bradenton Beach. The program required large quantities of concrete debris and other materials to be transported by barge to the desired locations. To facilitate this activity, Manatee County had established a staging area with a dock at the southeast end of Anna Maria Island. This staging area was adjacent to Coquina Beach and Bayside Park. Especially on weekends and holidays, that park is used by many people who are seeking to enjoy the water.

The Defendants were engaged by Manatee County to help build the artificial reefs, and the Defendants were legally responsible for any negligence of the captain who was in command of the tugboat and the barge involved in this project. In 2009, the Fourth of July fell on a Saturday. The Defendants did not wish to work over the long holiday weekend. As a result, the captain moored the tugboat and barge adjacent to the dock in the staging area. The sixty-five-foot tugboat and equally long barge were tied together and moored in a manner that caused them to jut outward into the pass.

Longboat Pass is known to have tidal currents that can be quite strong. On July 4, when the tidal currents were allegedly strong, Mr. Medina was operating a jet ski near the tugboat and barge. The jet ski stalled and he could not restart it. His friends came to help, but Mr. Medina became separated from the jet ski. Apparently, no one witnessed him drown, but he was found under the barge with his life jacket still on. The Estate claims that the current, enhanced by the configuration of the tugboat and barge, caused Mr. Medina to be swept under the vessels despite his use of the life jacket.

The accident was investigated by the Florida Fish and Wildlife Conservation Commission. The investigating officer did not cite the Defendants with any violation of law. During the Estate's case, one of the jurors submitted several questions. One question asked: "Did the FWC officer write a ticket to the captain or owner of the vessel citing the law that was broken?"

Given the large number of negligence cases that have arisen from automobile accidents, it is now very well established that evidence of a citation or lack thereof is inadmissible at trial. The negligence standard employed by juries is not the same as the standard used by individual law enforcement officers when deciding whether to write a ticket. Florida courts have repeatedly emphasized that the admission of such evidence constitutes prejudicial error, even in cases in which the trial court has given a curative instruction. Where fault is an issue, evidence of the presence or absence of a traffic citation will almost always constitute prejudicial error and warrant a mistrial," because "[c]ommon sense ... tells us that to the average juror the decision of the investigating police officer ... is very material to, if not wholly dispositive of, that juror's determination of fault on the part of the respective drivers."

Cross examination is the questioning of the other side's witnesses. An attorney on cross-examination may ask leading questions. For example, an attorney may ask: "Isn't it true, Mr. Jones, that you were wearing a light blue jacket on the night of January 1?" Questions that permit a witness on cross examination to explain the answer are usually avoided.

The Court should restrict the subject areas on cross examination to those matters raised by direct testimony. However, the Court does allow some leeway. Attacking the truthfulness of a witness may be attempted on cross examination if the witness has been convicted of crimes of dishonesty.

Questioning by the Court may occur at any point. These questions, however, should only clarify points that are unclear. The judge should not attempt to prove any part of either side's case.

INTRODUCING EXHIBITS

Physical evidence, if relevant, can be introduced by either attorney when presenting one's case, or during cross examination.

An attorney must follow a specified procedure when introducing exhibits into court. The attorney will ask the judge: "Your Honor, I request that this document be marked as P-1 (if it is a Plaintiff's exhibit) or "D-1" (if it is a Defendant's exhibit). The Exhibit will then be marked by the clerk of the court and will be shown to opposing counsel so that he or she knows what is being discussed. The document is then **authenticated.** This is done by showing the exhibit to the witness and asking, "Mr. Jones can you identify this exhibit for the Court?" The witness will then briefly explain the exhibit and attest to its accuracy.

After the document is shown to the judge and the witness is questioned about the exhibit, the attorney formally offers the exhibit into the record. This is done by the attorney saying: "Your Honor, I offer this exhibit into evidence."

One should note that if an exhibit is authenticated, questions can be asked about its contents even if the document is never offered into the record. Also, the exhibit can be offered into evidence at the conclusion of the attorney's case but before the attorney "rests."

Opposing counsel can always object to the exhibit being offered into evidence if it is not relevant or if it has not been properly authenticated.

OBJECTIONS

Objections are made by counsel when it is felt that the opposing attorney is violating the Rules of Evidence. Objections may be made for a number of reasons. The manner in which these objections are made are outlined below.

Leading Questions: "Your Honor, I object to counsel's leading the witness." A leading question is only objectionable if asked by the counsel on direct examination, not on cross.

Irrelevant Evidence: "I object your Honor—the question is not relevant to the facts in this case." This objection is used sparingly because opposing counsel usually does not care if the opponent is not getting to the important facts.

Non-responsive: "Your Honor, the witness is not answering the question asked." This objection may be used when the witness is not answering the questions presented.

Hearsay: "Objection, Your Honor. Counsel is asking for hearsay testimony." If the witness provides an answer that is based on hearsay, the attorney can ask the court to strike the answer from the record.

Beyond the scope of direct: "Your Honor, I object. Counsel is asking about matters that were not raised on direct examination." This objection is used to limit overly broad cross examination.

An attorney may object to testimony that violates a **confidential communication.** In striving to protect the confidentiality of certain communications, the court allows for privileged communication in four situations:

1. attorney-client privilege,

2. doctor-patient privilege,

3. priest-penitent privilege, and

4. husband-wife privilege.

In these situations, a party to the conversation cannot be forced to testify in court against the other party to the communication.

Throughout a trial, both sides have the opportunity of calling witnesses and presenting evidence. Since the plaintiff has the burden of proof, that party will go first in the presentation of the evidence. In a civil case, the burden of proof is by the **preponderance of the evidence.** In other words, the plaintiff must tip the scale in his or her favor in order to win.

In **Se-Ling Hosiery, Inc. v. Margulies, 70 A.2d 854 (Pa. 1950),** the court explained the meaning of a preponderance of the evidence with the following illustration:

> If we visualize evidence as something weighed in an ordinary balance scale, and if the evidence plaintiff offers in support of his claim is so much more weighed in probative value then the

evidence offered in opposition to it that it tips the scales on the side of the plaintiff, the latter has proved his claim by a fair weight of the evidence.

To put this burden of proof in perspective, it should be compared to the burden of proof in a criminal case, which requires the government to prove each element of the crime **beyond a reasonable doubt**. This higher burden of proof has been defined as follows:

> The defendant is presumed to be innocent and the burden is upon the Commonwealth to prove his guilt beyond a reasonable doubt. A reasonable doubt cannot be a doubt fancied or conjured up in the minds of the jury to escape an unpleasant verdict; it must be an honest doubt arising out of the evidence itself, the kind of a doubt that would restrain a reasonable person from acting in a matter of importance to himself. **Commonwealth v. Donough, 103 A.2d 694 (Pa. 1954).**

The purpose of discovery is to assist the litigants by making them aware of the various witnesses who will testify and the evidence that each side will present at trial. These pre-trial disclosures allow the attorneys to plan their strategies and to prevent surprise. What happens, however, if an attorney learns the identity of a new witness during trial? The court will not automatically allow the presentation of this new evidence because of the prejudice that may be imposed on the other side. The trial judge has several ways of handling this surprise situation: the witness may be prevented from testifying; a mistrial may be declared; or the judge may allow a brief intermission so that the other side may conduct an investigation of the new information, including taking the person's deposition.

SECTION 8.14
EXECUTION

Following the verdict and the court's disposition of post-trial motions, the plaintiff will move to have the verdict reduced to a **judgment**. If no appeal is taken, the aggrieved party is entitled to enforce the judgment in an attempt to collect the money owed. If the defendant will not voluntarily satisfy the award, the plaintiff may seek the help of the Sheriff in seizing the assets of the defendant and selling them at **Sheriff's sale**. For instance, a home owned by the defendant may be sold at Sheriff's sale and money in a bank account can be attached in order to satisfy the judgment. Even property that is transferred to a third person in order to make the defendant judgment-proof may be seized as a transfer to defraud a creditor.

The mere fact that a plaintiff secures a judgment, however, does not mean that the aggrieved will recover the amount owed. If the defendant is judgment-proof, or has no assets, the victorious litigant will collect no money. Certain types of property may also be exempt from execution depending upon the jurisdiction. For instance, some states will not disturb property that is owned by a husband and wife if the judgment is against only one of the marital partners. A debtor's interest in a pension fund or life insurance policy are also safe from seizure. In Pennsylvania, for example, the Judicial Code provides that wages, and commissions shall be exempt while in the hands of the employer from an attachment except for support, divorce matters, board for four weeks or less and for repayment of loans under the Pennsylvania Higher Education Assistance Agency Act. A judgment, however, is valid for a number of years so a plaintiff may be able to seize assets that a debtor accumulates several years after the entry of the judgment.

A number of states allow a driver's operator's privileges to be revoked if they don't pay a judgment arising out of a motor vehicle accident. For instance, Pennsylvania provides that the Department of Motor Vehicles, "upon receipt of a certified copy of a judgment, shall suspend the operating privilege of each person against whom the judgment was rendered." The following case talks about the ability to suspend a driver's license for an unpaid judgment and that law's limitations.

DeEdra Raper Franklin v. Department of Transportation
39 A.3d 453 (Pa. Comm. Ct. 2012)

The Department of Transportation, Bureau of Driver Licensing (Bureau), appeals from an order of the Court of Common Pleas which sustained the appeal of DeEdra Raper Franklin (Licensee) from the Bureau's suspension of her operating privilege. We affirm.

In October 2009, Licensee's minor son, Charles Franklin (Franklin), took an automobile belonging to Thomas and Deborah Kresch without their permission. While operating the vehicle, Franklin was involved in an accident and damaged the vehicle. The Kresches filed a suit against Franklin and Licensee, asserting causes of action for conversion and negligence against Franklin and for parental liability against Licensee under section 5502 of the Parental Liability Act (PLA).

Subsequently, a $2,500.00 default judgment was entered against Licensee under the PLA. To date, Licensee has not paid the judgment. Upon receiving notice of the unsatisfied judgment against Licensee, the Bureau issued a notice of suspension of Licensee's operating privilege pursuant to the Motor Vehicle Financial Responsibility Law (MVFRL).

The issue on appeal is whether the MVFRL mandates the suspension of a person's operating privilege for an unsatisfied judgment entered against that person under the PLA. The Bureau claims that the language "any judgment arising from a motor vehicle accident" of the MVFRL includes a judgment entered under the PLA, where such judgment arises from a parent's vicarious liability for a child's tortious act while operating a motor vehicle. We disagree.

This issue appears to be one of first impression in Pennsylvania, However, we find **Department of Transportation, Bureau of Driver Licensing v. Benner, 151 Pa. Cmwlth. 131, 616 A.2d 181 (1992),** instructive. Nolan Benner threw an eighteen-pound rock from an overpass through the windshield of a truck. The trial court refused to suspend Benner's license under the MVFRL for his failure to pay the judgment that arose from the accident. On appeal, this court stated that "motor vehicle accident" is a term "of common parlance ... and the coverage of the MVFRL is limited to motor vehicle accidents while *maintaining or using the same.*" We further noted that Benner's conduct "did not involve the use of an automobile *owned or operated by Benner.*" Thus, we concluded that Benner's license could not be suspended because the judgment did not arise from a motor vehicle accident.

Here, Licensee's involvement in a motor vehicle accident was even further removed than that of Benner. Benner's act of throwing a rock through a truck driver's windshield was a cause of the motor vehicle accident. Licensee had no involvement in her son's motor vehicle accident. Moreover, Franklin's accident did not involve the use of an automobile owned or operated by Licensee. Licensee's liability under the PLA arose exclusively from her parental relationship to her son, not from the accident itself.

We cannot accept the Bureau's broad interpretation of the MVFRL. Our court has recognized that "the purpose behind the enactment of the MVFRL was to both promote the financial responsibility of drivers and aid in the collection of debts against negligent owners and drivers." We do not believe that the MVFRL's purpose is served by suspending the operating privilege of a parent whose only liability resulted from her relationship to her child and not from her operation or ownership of a motor vehicle.

In sum, we hold that the judgment imposed on Licensee under the PLA is not a judgment arising from a motor vehicle accident under the MVFRL, thereby subjecting her to a license suspension for nonpayment. Therefore, we conclude that the trial court correctly sustained Licensee's appeal.

SECTION 8.15
TRIAL MEMO

PROBLEM EIGHT—C

PARK, BROWN & SMITH, P.C.
ATTORNEYS AT LAW
MEMORANDUM

To: All Law Clerks

FROM: Peter Smith, Esquire

RE: Christopher v. Roberts

I have returned from the trial involving Joe Roberts and the attack of his next-door neighbor by the family's pet bear. The jury is in its third day of deliberation and the judge has declared a recess for the weekend. I have received an expedited copy of the trial transcript since I plan on appealing if we lose.

To prepare you for this assignment, I have dictated the following summary of the key points from the trial transcript. Please read the material so we can talk about the case. I need your honest assessment of what happened. Please be prepared to discuss the following issues:

1. Who should win the case?

2. Were the court's evidentiary rulings correct?

3. Was the court correct in refusing to allow me to produce the bear to show the jury the animal's docile and friendly nature?

OPENING STATEMENT BY MR. LONDON

Members of the jury, my name is David London, and I represent the plaintiff, Peter Christopher. What comes to mind when I hear the words "man's best friend," are images of a dog walking side by side with his owner. In this case, a bear named "Harry" was kept by Joseph Roberts in his backyard as the family pet. You will learn that over the Labor Day weekend, two years ago, my client was viciously attacked by this wild animal. Now members of the jury, this attack did not occur in the woods but in a residential neighborhood. If keeping a bear in the backyard is not bad enough, we will also prove that Mr. Roberts gave this animal alcohol. The bear eventually fell asleep against the fence abutting my client's yard.

Mr. Christopher was cleaning his yard at the time in preparation for a barbecue. Because the bear was nestled up against the fence, Peter gently nudged the animal with a pole so the bear would move to the other side of the yard. The bear, however, awakened in a fury and pulled my helpless client over the fence mauling his leg in the process. Mr. Christopher sustained a number of large lacerations to his left leg and his femur was broken in two places. These injuries have altered my client's life. His leg hurts every day and affects his ability to work. At the conclusion of this case, we will ask you to return with a very large verdict in favor of Mr. Christopher to compensate him for this tragic incident. Thank you.

OPENING STATEMENT BY MR. SMITH

My name is Peter Smith and I represent Joseph Roberts. Members of the jury, there are two sides to every story. I admit that what happened to Mr. Christopher is a tragedy. However, the accident was not caused by Joe Roberts' conduct. Rather, Peter Christopher's injuries were the result of his own actions. While intoxicated, he climbed over a five-foot high fence into the Roberts' backyard and attacked a sleeping bear with a metal pole. I admit that the defendant's choice of a pet is eccentric and not a choice that I would make, but Mr. Christopher took his life into his own hands by confronting the animal. In other words, he assumed the risk of his injuries which the judge will tell you is a complete defense to this claim.

During the course of the trial, you will hear from Mr. Roberts, who will describe his unique pet which he saved from a bankrupt circus and raised from a small cub. The evidence will also show that Harry never hurt anyone before this incident and was a very gentle animal.

At the close of the evidence, I believe you will find for the defendant, and it is in your fair judgment that Joe Roberts places his confidence. Thank you.

THE COURT: *Mr. London, present your first witness.*

MR. LONDON: Your Honor, I call Peter Christopher.

DIRECT TESTIMONY OF
PETER CHRISTOPHER

Q. **Please state your name for the record.**

A. *My name is Peter Christopher.*

Q. **And what did you do for a living?**

A. *I was a private investigator and undercover surveillance specialist. Presently, I am out of work because of my injuries.*

Q. **Turning your attention to September 3, two years ago, can you tell the jury what happened?**

A. *Sure. It was Sunday of the Labor Day weekend and Joe Roberts let his bear out to roam in the backyard. The animal eventually fell asleep against the fence that abutted my property. Because I was about to have a party, I tried getting the bear to move to the other side of the yard. I even tried bribing him with a piece of meat but the bear kept sleeping. So, I gently tapped him with a pole and he was wild from the moment he opened his eyes. The animal pulled me over the fence and before I could get away, the bear had my leg in his mouth. I don't remember anything after that. It was a nightmare.*

Q. **What do you remember next?**

A. *I woke up in the hospital, and the lower part of my left leg was in a cast and the pain was unbearable.*

Q. **Are you receiving any medical treatment at the present time?**

A. *Yes. I go for physical therapy twice a week.*

Q. **Mr. Christopher, are there any activities that you can no longer perform?**

A. *I can't run or squat. This prevents me from doing surveillance.*

Q. **No further questions.**

CROSS-EXAMINATION OF
PETER CHRISTOPHER
BY MR. SMITH

Q. **Where were you when you "tapped" Harry?**

A. *I was in my backyard.*

Q. **Mr. Christopher, you did more than just tap the bear, didn't you?**

MR. LONDON: Objection – leading.

THE COURT: *Overruled.*

A. *I told you, I just wanted to move the animal away from my property.*

Q. **You repeatedly hit the bear with a pole, didn't you, Mr. Christopher?**

A. *I just tapped the animal to wake him.*

Q. **Mr. Christopher, you were intoxicated at the time?**

A. *I had a few beers.*

Q. **You had more than just a few beers, isn't that right?**

MR. LONDON: Objection. The witness has answered the question.

THE COURT: *Sustained.*

Q. **How did you end up in your neighbor's backyard?**

A. *The bear pulled me over the fence.*

Q. **How high is the fence?**

A. *I guess about five-feet high.*

Q. **How big is the bear?**

A. *I don't know. He is much bigger than a person and has huge teeth.*

Q. **Is the bear taller than the fence?**

A. *No.*

Q. **You climbed over the fence, didn't you?**

A. *No. The bear pulled me over.*

Q. **The bear just happened to pull you over the fence even though Harry is not taller than the fence?**

A. *Yeah. That is right.*

Q. **How was that possible?**

A. *I don't know. The bear is powerful I guess.*

Q. **No further questions of this witness.**

REDIRECT EXAMINATION OF PETER CHRISTOPHER BY MR. ROBERTS

Q. Mr. Christopher, tell the jury what you did with the pole.

A. *I merely nudged the bear so he would move to the other side of the property.*

Q. How did you get into Mr. Roberts' backyard?

A. *The bear pulled me over the fence with its claws.*

MR. LONDON: Thank you.

THE COURT: *Mr. London, please call your next witness.*

DIRECT EXAMINATION OF DR. JONES BY MR. LONDON

Q. Please state your name.

A. *My name is Dr. Donald Jones.*

Q. Where do you practice?

A. *I am a surgeon at Temple University Hospital in Philadelphia.*

MR. SMITH: We will stipulate that the doctor is qualified to perform surgery.

THE COURT: *Very well. Mr. London, proceed.*

Q. Turning your attention to September 3, did you treat Peter Christopher?

A. *Yes, I had to perform emergency surgery on the wounds to his leg.*

Q. Can you tell us the nature of that surgery?

A. *Mr. Christopher had rather large and deep lacerations on his left side and his leg had to be reset because of fractures to the distal femur. The size of the wound reminded me of a shark bite.*

MR. SMITH: Objection. The doctor is speculating.

THE COURT: *Sustained.*

Q. Doctor, were these injuries the result of a bear attack?

MR. SMITH: Objection. Leading and asking for an opinion.

THE COURT: *Sustained. You'll have to rephrase that, counselor.*

Q. Dr. Jones, were you able to discover the cause of these injuries?

A. *Yes. They appeared to have been caused by the teeth of a very large and powerful animal.*

Q. Have you treated the patient since the surgery?

A. *Yes. I continue to monitor the wounds.*

Q. Dr. Jones, did the ambulance driver say anything to you when they brought the plaintiff to the hospital?

MR. SMITH: Objection – hearsay.

THE COURT: *Sustained.*

MR. LONDON: Thank you, doctor. That is all I have.

CROSS EXAMINATION OF DR. JONES BY MR. SMITH

Q. Dr. Jones, isn't it true that the plaintiff's wounds healed nicely?

A. *Yes.*

Q. Is the plaintiff able to ambulate successfully following your excellent medical care?

A. *Yes. I believe so.*

Q. Was Mr. Christopher's surgery complicated by the fact that he had been drinking?

MR. LONDON: Objection. There is no proper foundation for the question.

THE COURT: *You'll have to rephrase that, counselor.*

Q. Did you test Mr. Christopher's blood before the operation?

A. *Standard procedure.*

Q. What did you learn from the blood analysis?

A. *There was a clear indication of alcohol in his system so we had to alter the anesthesia.*

Q. Wasn't the plaintiff's blood/alcohol level content .25?

A. *Yes.*

Q. Legally intoxicated?

A. *Yes, this is more than three times the legal standard.*

Q. Did you find any types of drugs in his system?

MR. LONDON: Objection. And, I move to strike the question as prejudicial.

THE COURT: *Sustained*

THE COURT: *Members of the jury, please disregard these last questions.*

Q. **Doctor, do you live near the plaintiff?**

 A. *I live on the same street.*

Q. **Have you heard anything about Mr. Christopher's reputation in the community?**

Mr. London: Objection. This is irrelevant and hearsay.

The Court: *Overruled. Doctor, you may answer.*

 A. *I know of his reputation first-hand. Mr. Christopher is always getting into trouble with the law and he has been in jail several times for intoxication and trespassing.*

Q. **Isn't it true that you treated the plaintiff three months before this incident for a torn cartilage in the left knee?**

Mr. London: Objection. The question is irrelevant to this case.

Mr. Smith: It is relevant. This man had a pre-existing left knee injury.

The Court: *Overruled.*

 A. *He had hurt his knee about a month before the attack and needed surgery which had not yet taken place.*

Q. **Dr. Jones, are you currently being sued by Mr. Roberts for malpractice?**

Mr. London: Objection. That is irrelevant.

Mr. Smith: It is relevant. It shows that the doctor could be biased against my client.

The Court: *Overruled.*

 A. *I don't see what relevance that claim has to this case.*

Q. **I don't care what you think, doctor, I ask the questions.**

Mr. London: Objection. Counsel is badgering the witness.

The Court: *Overruled.*

Q. **Doctor, are you being sued for medical malpractice by Joe Roberts?**

 A. *Yes.*

Q. **No further questions.**

Mr. London: That is the plaintiff's case and we rest.

DIRECT EXAMINATION OF JOSEPH ROBERTS BY MR. SMITH

Q. **Please state your name for the record.**

A. *Joseph Roberts.*

Q. **Joe, what do you do for a living?**

A. *Well, times were tough for the Roberts family for a long while, and…*

THE COURT: *Mr. Roberts, just answer the questions asked.*

Q. **Joe, you may answer.**

A. *I own my own construction company. It is called Joro Construction.*

Q. **Did you own a bear?**

A. *I had a wonderful pet bear named Harry.*

Q. **Mr. Roberts, will you please tell the court why you bought such an exotic pet?**

A. *My children saw Harry at a bankrupt circus and fell in love with him. He seemed so sad so I bought him. We raised him from a cub.*

Q. **Has Harry ever been violent before the incident on September 3?**

A. *No. He wouldn't hurt a fly.*

Q. **Turning your attention to September 3, did anything unusual happen that day?**

A. *It was the Labor Day weekend and we went inside for lunch. Harry was restless because of the heat, but he finally fell asleep by the fence that surrounds my property.*

Q. **Then what happened?**

A. *I heard shouts coming from our yard. I ran outside, and saw Christopher in my backyard, passed out. I told my wife to call an ambulance.*

Q. **Was Harry injured, Mr. Roberts?**

A. *Yes. He had several wounds which had to be treated at the Large Animal Clinic at the University of Pennsylvania.*

Q. **Do you know how Mr. Christopher got in your backyard?**

A. *He must have climbed over the fence.*

MR. LONDON: Objection. This is pure speculation.

THE COURT: *Sustained.*

Q. How high is the fence?

A. *It is a five-foot high fence.*

Q. How tall is Harry?

A. *He is a little shorter than the fence is high.*

Q. Could the bear pull someone over the fence?

A. *No. Harry could not reach over the top of the fence with his paws.*

Mr. London: Objection. This is pure speculation and I move to strike.

The Court: *Overruled.*

Q. How long have you had Harry?

A. *Two years.*

Q. Has Harry ever hurt anyone before?

A. *No. He really is very gentle.*

Q. How long have you and Mr. Christopher been neighbors?

A. *A little more than six months.*

Q. Had Mr. Christopher ever complained to you about Harry before the day in question?

A. *Never. In fact, I occasionally heard him talking to the bear.*

Q. Was Harry treated for his injuries?

A. *Yes. I had to pay $5,000 for his care.*

CROSS EXAMINATION OF JOSEPH ROBERTS BY MR. LONDON

Q. Did you have a license to keep the bear at your home?

A. *No. I didn't know that I needed one.*

Q. Isn't it true, Mr. Roberts, you enjoyed getting Harry drunk?

A. *No. I did not enjoy getting the bear drunk.*

Q. Did you give that bear liquor on the day in question?

A. *He was restless so I gave him some beer. He likes it and it relaxes him.*

Q. Didn't Harry maul your son previously or have physical contact with him?

MR. SMITH: Objection. What does counsel mean by physical contact?

THE COURT: *Rephrase your question.*

Q. Didn't the bear hurt your son previously?

A. *Yes and no., Tony was wrestling with Harry and my son was scratched by the bear's claws. It was an accident. Tony yelled at Harry and the poor animal hid the rest of the day, even though he did nothing wrong.*

Q. Isn't it true that my client was bleeding profusely when you found him in the backyard?

A. *Well, he was bleeding but so was Harry. I am not sure whose blood I was looking at.*

Q. Mr. Roberts, didn't the bear have Mr. Christopher's leg in his mouth when you saw him?

MR. SMITH: Objection, your Honor.

THE COURT: *Overruled. Answer the question.*

A. *Yes. Harry had Christopher's leg in his mouth but Christopher had that metal pole in his hand.*

Q. No further questions.

REDIRECT OF JOSEPH ROBERTS BY MR. SMITH

Q. What did you do when you went outside?

A. *I immediately wrapped Peter Christopher's leg in a towel to stop the bleeding.*

Q. Have you ever let Harry out of the confines of your backyard?

A. *Never. Harry was afraid of strangers and I know better than to let a bear roam the neighborhood.*

Q. Had Harry ever hurt anyone before the day in question?

A. *No.*

Q. No further questions.

MR. SMITH: Your Honor, we have one more witness.

MR. LONDON: Your Honor, the plaintiff is unaware of any other witness and demands an offer of proof.

MR. SMITH: The witness played a very important part in the incident. Actually, he was there.

THE COURT:	*Really. In the interest of justice, I will allow the testimony.*
MR. LONDON:	Oh my God! Your Honor, Mr. Roberts is leading a bear into the courtroom.
THE COURT:	*Mr. Roberts, remove that animal from this courtroom immediately. Mr. Smith, what is the meaning of this stunt?*
MR. SMITH:	Your Honor, we merely wish to show that Harry is a very gentle animal.
THE COURT:	*Counselors, approach the bench immediately, and I mean now!*
MR. SMITH:	The jury is entitled to meet Harry and judge for themselves whether he is a vicious animal. If the jury could merely see Harry, they would have a better understanding of this case.
MR. LONDON:	This request is outrageous.
MR. SMITH:	Your Honor, I believe there is precedent for what I am trying to do. Dogs are routinely used by the police to establish probable cause that drugs are present and their findings are allowed into evidence as long as the dog has a history of providing reputable information.
THE COURT:	*Enough! A bear has no place in the courtroom, and the prejudicial affect of this stunt far outweighs the probative value of the evidence. You will both return to your seats and make closing arguments. Mr. Smith, you are lucky I don't hold you in contempt of court and declare a mistrial. Counsel, I suggest you make your closing arguments.*

CLOSING ARGUMENT BY MR. LONDON

Ladies and gentlemen of the jury, this case is quite simple. Is it reasonable to keep a bear in one's backyard? To make matters worse, the owner of that animal then decides to provide the thing with liquor in order to quiet it down. Are these actions normal and rational? The law is clear. One who keeps a non-domesticated animal, like a bear, on his property is liable to anyone injured by that animal. The only defense is if the injured party assumed the risk of injury. Do you really believe that Mr. Christopher thought he would be harmed by gently nudging the bear with a pole to move the animal away from the fence? I think not! The only real issue in this case is how much money my client should be awarded for his injuries and loss of business. In making this calculation, please remember the massive teeth of a bear as they crushed my client's leg. Consider also that Peter must go through the rest of his life with a permanent injury to his leg. He can't run, or do the things with his leg that we each take for granted.

Peter carries both physical and emotional scars with him everyday. Everyone can see the massive scars on his left leg. No one will hire him at the moment since he can no longer perform his job. Members of the jury, I ask that you please award my client a sum of money that will reimburse him for his past and future losses and that which will send a clear signal that we will no longer tolerate the selfish conduct of people who display a disregard for their neighbors. Thank you.

CLOSING ARGUMENT BY MR. SMITH

Members of the jury, we are truly sorry that Peter Christopher injured his leg. However, this is a legal proceeding and your duty is to assess liability based upon the law and not pity. I must admit that keeping a bear as a pet is a bit eccentric. But, do you really believe that Joe would do anything to jeopardize his family's safety? Harry is a tame pet who was kept enclosed in the backyard. The plaintiff got hurt through his own fault.

The plaintiff incited the incident by attacking the sleeping bear with a metal pole. Wouldn't it have been easier if Christopher had telephoned Joe and asked his neighbor to move Harry? The plaintiff has taken great care during the trial to tell you how he was in his own yard when the bear attacked him. How then did Peter end up in Joe's backyard? Did the bear jump the fence, attack the plaintiff and throw the plaintiff into Joe's yard? I suggest that Mr. Christopher, with pole in hand, climbed over the fence to teach Harry a lesson. After all, the bear is shorter than the fence is tall. There is only one logical answer as to how Mr. Christopher ended up in the backyard. He climbed the fence to attack the bear. By engaging in such reckless conduct, the plaintiff assumed the risk of the attack and he alone must take full responsibility for the consequences.

In fact, not only should you find against Mr. Christopher, but you should award Joe money for the injuries sustained by Harry. The animal was asleep minding his own business when he was violently struck with a metal pole. It is about time that we recognize that animals have rights too and a money judgment in favor of Harry will make more people aware of this fact. Thank you.

CHARGE BY THE COURT

This is the most unusual case I have heard during my tenure as a judge. Issues of credibility have arisen during the trial especially as to how Mr. Christopher ended up in Mr. Roberts' backyard. You are to be guided in deciding whom to believe by your own common sense and life experiences.

As for the law, one who keeps a non-domesticated animal on his property is liable to another who is injured by that animal. A bear is a non-domesticated animal no matter how cute or playful that animal appears to be, and the owner is liable for any harm inflicted by that creature. On the other hand, one who knows of a danger, but yet still exposes himself to that risk is barred from recovery.

You must decide where Peter Christopher was located when the incident happened. Was he in his own backyard and stuck the pole through the fence, or did he assume the risk of the attack by climbing over the fence into his neighbor's backyard in order to confront the bear? In the latter event, the plaintiff is barred from recovery.

If, and only if, you find in favor of the plaintiff, then you must award a sum of money to fully compensate Mr. Christopher for his injuries and losses. In other words, you must award a sum of money that will return the plaintiff to the condition he was in before the incident occurred. Your award will include compensation for medical expenses, past and future lost wages, and pain and suffering.

The plaintiff has the burden of proving his case by the preponderance of the evidence. This means that for the plaintiff to win, you must place all of the credible evidence on a scale, and the scale must tip no matter how slight, in favor of the plaintiff. If the scales are even or tip in favor of the defendant, then you must find in favor of Mr. Roberts. In addition, it is only after the scales tip in favor of the plaintiff that you can consider the issue of damages.

If you find that Joe Roberts is not responsible for the injuries suffered by Peter Christopher, then you will return with a verdict for the defense. In that event, you may consider an award of damages to Joe Roberts for the injuries to the bear.

Please return to the jury room and decide upon a verdict.

ANSWER SHEET
PROBLEM EIGHT—C

Name

Please Print Clearly

1. Who should win the case? Please explain your answer.

_____

_____

_____

_____

_____

_____

_____

_____

_____

_____

_____

_____

_____

_____

_____

_____

_____

_____

_____

_____

_____

2. Were the court's evidentiary rulings correct? Please explain.

_____

_____

_____

_____

_____

_____

_____

_____

_____

_____

3. Was the judge correct in refusing to allow Harry to be brought into court?

_____

_____

_____

_____

_____

_____

_____

_____

_____

Most people have insurance but not everyone know the terms and conditions of their policy pr how to negotiate with the insurance carrier. Many people will obtain the services of an attorney or adjuster to help them deal with the insurance carrier. Others will try and adjust the matter on their own.

It is basic rule that an insurance company must carry out its obligations ethically and in good faith by not taking advantage of a customer in its dealings. How far does this obligation extend when the carrier is dealing with its insured? That is the subject of the following case.

LINDA WILLIS V. ALLSTATE INSURANCE COMPANY
334 GA. APP. 540 (CT. APP. GA. 2015)

This case involves an action on a homeowner's insurance policy issued by Allstate Insurance Company to Linda Willis. While in the process of remodeling her home, Willis rented a portable storage unit to hold some of her possessions. Because the unit was placed in her front yard, some of Willis's neighbors complained, and, without notice to Willis, the owner of the storage unit removed it from her yard and put it in the company's storage yard. Willis reported this to Allstate as a theft. Then, the next day Willis's home burned, and Allstate boarded up the house because it determined the house was unsafe. Willis contends other property of hers was stolen from the boarded-up house. Although Willis filed claims, Allstate never paid any of the claims.

The Allstate policy issued to Willis provided: "No suit or action may be brought against us unless there has been full compliance with all policy terms. Any suit or action must be brought within *one year* after inception of loss or damage." The three losses at Willis' house occurred on February 27, 2006, February 28, 2006, and September 3, 2006. Willis did not file her lawsuit against Allstate until December 16, 2008, well over two years after the date of loss.

Willis argues that Allstate waived the suit limitation in the policy by misleading her during negotiations to "lull her into the false sense of security of believing that liability was clearly accepted ... so as to delay her past the Statute of Limitation, and/or the time within which the policy required her to file her action in the Courts."

An insurance company may waive the contractual limitation provision where the company leads the insured by its actions to rely on its promise to pay, express or implied. If the insurer never denied liability, but continually discussed the loss with it's insured with a view toward negotiation and settlement without the intervention of a suit, whether or not this lulled the insured into a belief that the 12–month clause in the contract was waived by the insurer can become a disputed question of fact for the jury.

In the present case, Allstate never agreed that the losses were covered under the policy, never made any payments for the losses, and continuously warned Willis that it was not waiving any policy provisions. From the time Willis placed Allstate on notice of her claims and throughout the course of the proceedings, "the communications between Ms. Willis and Allstate were prefaced on the part of Allstate by the specific statement that, 'We are not waiving any defenses. We expect our insured to comply with all terms and conditions.' That was repeated on various occasions" until Allstate ultimately denied Willis' claims. The record contains numerous letters and emails from Allstate to Willis, and nearly all of them include similar language. For example, one of the letters included the following:

> Please understand that no action of Allstate or its representatives should be considered by you to be a waiver of any of the terms, conditions, or provisions contained in the Allstate policy of insurance. On the contrary, Allstate will continue to insist upon strict compliance with the terms, conditions, and provisions contained in the Allstate policy of insurance. We are reserving our right to deny coverage obligation under the policy and assert a defense of no coverage under the policy.

On November 29, 2007 and December 4, 2007, Allstate sent letters in which it responded to a request to set forth its position relative to the three claims. Allstate wrote: Please be advised that Allstate will not further consider the above referenced claims. Allstate on numerous occasions requested that you provide further information substantiating your claims. That information was not provided in violation of the terms of the policy of insurance which obligated you to cooperate with Allstate. In addition, during the course of its investigation,

Allstate learned that you had misrepresented material facts related to the claim and your claimed loss and damage in violation of the policy. Finally, please be aware that the time period for you to bring a legal action seeking recovery under the above referenced policy of insurance has expired.

Mere negotiation for settlement, unsuccessfully accomplished, is not that type of conduct designed to lull the claimant into a false sense of security so as to constitute a waiver of the limitation defense. And, where inconclusive settlement negotiations were explicitly conditioned on the policy terms, the policyholder cannot create an issue by claiming a belief that the insurer would waive the contractual limitation provision.

Although Willis argues that Allstate fraudulently induced her to believe that it intended to accept her claims and did not intend to enforce the suit limitation provision, she points to no evidence—slight or otherwise—of any fraudulent inducement. It is undisputed that "Allstate undertook several actions to protect the premises and engaged in discussions with Ms. Willis," but it is equally "clear that any negotiations and any activities that took place were subject to ... repeated representations" that Allstate was not waiving any policy defenses, and Willis has not presented "an affirmative promise or other act waiving the limitation."

There is "no showing in this record of any affirmative statement or other act by Allstate that would lead Willis to believe that the insurer would waive the contractual limitation."

SECTION 8.17 REVIEW CASES

1. Miller was found lying face down in the street and bleeding profusely. A police officer asked Miller who shot him, and Miller identified Griffin as his assailant. At the time of trial, the District Attorney calls the police officer to introduce into evidence the

statement made by Miller before he died in order to prove that Griffin committed the crime. Is this hearsay statement admissible? **Commonwealth of Pennsylvania v. Aaron Griffin, 453 Pa. Super. 657 (1996).**

2. Mathis was arrested in a stolen van. He testified that while hitch-hiking from Georgia to Tennessee to attend a Rod Stewart concert, he was given a ride by an unknown person who fled when the van was stopped by the police. In rebuttal to this testimony, a state witness testified that his firm represented Rod Stewart in obtaining theatrical bookings; he had checked the company's records and they revealed that Rod Stewart was in New Mexico on the day in question. The testimony was objected to as an alleged violation of the best evidence rule. Should this testimony have been excluded on that basis? **Mathis v. The State of Georgia, 228 S.E. 2d 228 (Ga. App. 1976).**

3. During a trial concerning an automobile accident, a witness for the plaintiff was asked to estimate how fast the defendant's car was going before the accident. The defense objected on the basis that the answer would constitute opinion evidence which can only be expressed by an expert witness. Can a witness, who has no specialized technical or scientific knowledge, testify as to the speed of a motor vehicle? **Dugan v. Arthurs, 79 A.2d 626 (Pa. 1911).**

4. Haight was accused of committing burglary by moving electrical equipment from a property. At the time of trial, the prosecution was allowed to introduce into evidence the fact that Haight was unemployed and on welfare at the time of the crime. The Commonwealth argued that this evidence was relevant to show a motive for the burglary, namely a desire for money. Was this line of questioning relevant to establishing a motive for burglary? **Commonwealth of Pennsylvania v. Haight, 31 A.2d 357 (Pa. Super. 1984).**

5. Following the imposition of the sentence on robbery charges, Williams decided to express his dissatisfaction with the court's punishment. He did so by (1) raising his middle finger, and (2) stating: "F - - k you." The judge ordered Williams to return to the court room, at which time the judge found Williams guilty of two counts of contempt and imposed two consecutive sentences of six months for each of the offensive acts. Was it proper to find Williams in contempt of court because he voiced displeasure over the sentence? Was it proper for the court to find him responsible for two separate acts of contempt over the one incident? **Commonwealth of Pennsylvania v. Walter Williams, 753 A.2d 856 (Pa. Super. 2000).**

Footnote:

1. Reprinted with permission from **Simplified Rules of Evidence,** by Temple University School of Law and the Law Education and Participation (LEAP) program.

KEY TERMS

Affirmative Defense

Answer

Authenticated

Beyond a Reasonable Doubt

Civil Procedure

Closing Statements

Complaint

Confidential Communication

Contempt of Court

Contingent Fee

Counterclaim

Court Instructions

Cross Examination

Deposition

Direct Examination

Discovery

Dying Declaration

Examination

Execution

Fee Arrangement

Fixed Price

Hearsay

Interrogatory

Irrelevant Evidence

Judgment

Leading Question

Medical Examination

New Matter

Non-Responsive

Objection

Opening Statement

Opinion Testimony

Overruled

Physical Evidence

Pleading

Post-Trial Motions

Preliminary Objections

Preponderance of the Evidence

Production of Documents

Prothonotary

Quantum Meruit

Redirect Examination

Relevant Evidence

Request for Admission

Retainer

Rules of Evidence

Service of Process

Sheriff's Sale

Submission to a Medical

Subpoena

Sustained

Trial

Verdict

CHAPTER 9

LIMITATIONS TO LAWSUITS

SECTION 9.1
RES JUDICATA

In a bizarre twist of fate, a convicted murderer who had bludgeoned his aunt to death and spent 10 years in a mental institution for sexually assaulting an 11-year-old girl was hired as a special police officer by the city of Scranton, Pennsylvania. Clothed with the official authority of a badge and gun, he sexually assaulted and killed two boys. Suit was filed against a variety of governmental entities for the deaths of the teenagers. This claim was dismissed on the basis that the government could not be sued for its actions. **Freach v. Commonwealth, 370 A.2d 1163 (Pa. 1997).**

Regardless of the merits of a claim, a limited number of defenses exist that will either bar or restrict lawsuits without considering the merits of the dispute. Certain entities such as the government, diplomats, and parents, are often clothed with immunity and are not responsible for their actions. Claims must also be filed with the court within a finite period of time or be forever barred. This chapter will explore these technical defenses starting with **res judicata**.

Res judicata, an historical doctrine, is Latin for "the thing has been decided" and prevents a litigant from bringing the same lawsuit a second time. This principle forces the parties to use their best efforts at trial, insures that the controversy will be concluded at some point in time, and prevents inconsistent results. Res judicata saves time and expense for both the defendant and the court by avoiding redundant litigation even if new evidence is discovered after the first trial or the second claim is being advanced under a different theory of law.

Res judicata will bar a subsequent claim when: (1) the parties are the same as those who litigated the first case; (2) the issue is the same in both suits; (3) the first court had jurisdiction; and (4) the first action concluded with a final judgment on the merits.

This concept does not prohibit an appellate review of a court's decision, which is the normal process for an aggrieved party to challenge an unfavorable ruling.

This principle also applies in a criminal case to bar a subsequent prosecution involving the same crime. However, in criminal matters, this concept is called **double jeopardy.** This protection is contained in the Fifth Amendment to the United States Constitution and guarantees that no person may be tried twice for the same crime. More specifically, the Fifth Amendment provides "nor shall any person be subject for the same offense to be twice put in jeopardy of life or limb." While some may consider this rule harsh or a legal technicality, it serves a very legitimate purpose. Not only does it emotionally and financially safeguard a defendant from multiple trials but it is society's protection against an overzealous or harassing prosecutor who is dissatisfied with the original verdict and wishes to refile the criminal charges until a conviction is obtained. The Double Jeopardy Clause also protects against two other distinct abuses: a second prosecution for the same offense after conviction; and multiple punishments for the same offense. **United States v. Irwin Harper, 109 S. Ct. 1992 (1989).**

Suppose Joe Roberts is involved in an intersectional collision with Lori Brown on his way home from work. Both drivers claim that the other was responsible for the accident. Roberts sues Brown to recover the cost of repairs to his automobile and the court finds in Joe's favor since Ms. Brown was the cause of the accident. Subsequently, Ms. Brown sues Joe for personal injury. That suit will be barred by the doctrine of res judicata since the parties and the issue in both cases are the same.

JOHN QUIRKE V. THE PRIVATE RESIDENCES AT ONTARIO
2015 IL APP 142385-U (ILL. 2105)

John Quirke was evicted by court order in 2011 from a Chicago residential condominium unit and deeded private parking space for not paying monthly assessments and late fees on the property. He filed the current action in 2013 challenging the reasonableness of the late fees. The trial court, however, granted the defendants' motion to dismiss the suit on grounds that Quirke's eviction suit was *res judicata* as to the validity of the late fees.

Both the 2011 eviction suit and the current suit filed in 2013 stem from Quirke's late payment of monthly assessments for his condo unit and parking space. He owned residential unit # 1010 and parking space P–S905. He received monthly invoices which itemized the assessment for his unit, which was approximately $335, and the assessment for his deeded parking spot, which was approximately $55. The two items were presented in a single invoice each month, but a late fee would be assessed for each item that was paid untimely; thus, when Quirke was late to pay his monthly assessments for September 2010, he was charged a late fee of $75 for his residential unit and a late fee of $75 for his parking spot. The payment he tendered in October 2010 was first applied to the September late fees and was insufficient to also cover his October assessment, so he was charged an additional $150 in late fees. Quirke did not make a payment in February 2011 or any month after that. The condominium association filed suit seeking $2,659.50 in past-due charges any subsequently accruing unpaid charges, and possession of Quirke's condo. Judgment was granted for the requested amounts. Quirke's debt was finally satisfied in June 2013 and he sold the property in August

2013. During the 52 months that he owned the unit and parking spot, he incurred late fees 34 times, and ultimately paid a total of $20,239.44.

In November 2013, he filed this suit. Count II [of the complaint] characterized the late fees as being "excessive" and "unreasonable" In the motion for dismissal, the defendants contended that because of the 2011 forcible entry and lawsuit, Quirke's current suit was barred by res judicata.

Res judicata is a legal doctrine that requires parties to litigate, in one case, all the rights that arise out of the same set of operative facts. The doctrine protects a party from being forced to relitigate what is essentially the same case and it minimizes the waste of judicial resources. Res judicata bars not only what was actually decided in the first action but also all issues that could have been decided in the first action. The doctrine bars suits based on facts that would constitute a defense or counterclaim in the earlier suit and where a "successful" outcome in the later suit would either nullify the earlier judgment or bar the rights established in the earlier suit. The defendants argued that the eviction suit, which was based on Quirke's failure to pay monthly assessments and late fees, was where he could have challenged the reasonableness of those amounts and presented his position that the fees were inappropriate.

Quirke could have challenged the validity of the late fees in the 2011 action that was based on his nonpayment of those fees, and thus, res judicata barred his separate suit in 2013 challenging the validity of the fees.

[Plaintiff's] res judicata arguments are unpersuasive. Res judicata bars not only what was actually decided in the first action but also all issues that could have been decided there. Res judicata bars suits based on facts that would constitute a defense or counterclaim in the earlier suit and where a "successful" outcome in the later suit would either nullify the earlier judgment or bar the rights established in the earlier suit.

Res judicata applies where three requirements are met: (1) an identity (sameness) of the parties or their privies, (2) an identity of the causes of action, and (3) a final judgment on the merits. Quirke takes issue with only the second element. He does not dispute that there is an identity or sameness of the parties in the two suits. The condominium association was a party in both the forcible. Eviction on behalf of the condominium association also involved the amount of the bill and apply to this dispute.

For these reasons, we find that, despite Quirke's arguments, all the elements of res judicta have been met.

SECTION 9.2
STATUTE OF LIMITATIONS

If the debtor fails to repay a loan or damages your car, how much time do you have to file a lawsuit? The **statute of limitations** refers to the time period within which an aggrieved party must institute suit or the claim will be barred. This rule is designed to force a claimant to act within a specified period of time so that the party being sued can take the necessary measures to properly defend the action. With the passage of time, people lose track of witnesses, misplace important evidence, and memories fade. By knowing that a lawsuit must be filed by a certain date, a party can safely assume that the matter is no longer of legal significance if the statute of limitations has expired and no suit has been instituted.

The statute of limitations has equal application in both criminal and civil cases. Even the Internal Revenue Service is mandated to act within a specified time. The IRS is generally required to reassess a tax within three years after the filing of a tax return. The Statute of Limitations, however, does not apply to a false or fraudulent return that has been filed with the intent to evade taxes.

Statute of limitations are established by the legislature and will vary from jurisdiction to jurisdiction and type of action. These time periods merely reflect an attempt by the legislature to establish a reasonable time frame within which a party must file suit. For instance, California requires a lawsuit for personal injury to be filed within two years of the date of the injury, or when a person discovers that an injury has occurred. Another state may require that the lawsuit be filed within one year. Is justice served, however, by the dismissal of a lawsuit because a claim for personal injury is filed one day after the two-year period? The statute of limitations provides ample time for the institution of suit so an aggrieved party should not wait until the last minute before seeking judicial relief. Therefore, a specific cutoff date will be enforced even if a party is late in filing the suit by one day.

When does the clock start to tick on the statute of limitations? A party is usually aware when an actionable wrong has occurred. Loans are to be repaid by a certain date and people know when they are involved in car accidents. The statute of limitations starts to run or "accrues," on the first day the loan is past due or when the collision occurs. If the statute of limitations for a car accident is two years and the incident occurred on August 1, 2006, the lawsuit must be filed no later than July 31, 2008.

There are a few exceptions to the statute of limitations. There is no bar to bringing criminal charges against a party for murder regardless of the time period that has elapsed. People with a legal disability, such as a child, also have extra time to bring a lawsuit since the statute of limitations is tolled or stopped during that period of disability. This is particularly true with minor children. For instance, the statute of limitations on a personal injury claim involving a child does not start to run until the minor has reached majority, since the child was previously under a legal disability.

The question in the following case is whether biological parents who executed a surrender of their child to an agency for purposes of adoption may revoke that surrender after the statute of limitations where they have alleged both fraud and a conflict of interest by the attorney representing the prospective adopting parents.

In Re Adoption of J.W., A Minor Child v. Family Choices
2016 IL App 150203 (Ill. 2016)

Jennifer J. and Adam H. are the biological parents of J.W. Petitioners Janet and Gregory W. are Jennifer's aunt and uncle. J.W. was born on August 4, 2012. On October 9, 2012, Jennifer and Adam executed surrenders for adoption papers. Their intent was for J.W. to be adopted by the W.s. However, they executed surrenders to an agency for adoption rather than consents to adoption by the W.s. The surrenders were prepared by the W.s' attorney, Deborah Cobb. The adoption agency involved, Family Choices is owned by Cobb's mother, and the caseworker assigned to the case is Cobb's sister, Susan Wolk.

The W.s filed a petition to adopt J.W. in January 2013. The matter came for a hearing on November 22, 2013. Cobb told the court that she treated the adoption as an agency adoption for two reasons. First, due to issues involving Jennifer, the Department of Children and Family Services (DCFS) was likely to become involved. Second, Gregory W. was involved in proceedings in which a child was removed from his home 15 or 20 years prior to the proceedings involved here. Family Choices refused to consent to the adoption based on the findings in a psychological evaluation of the W.s. The court denied their petition to adopt J.W. and ordered that J.W. be surrendered to Family Choices for placement in another home.

On December 11, 2013, Jennifer and Adam filed a motion to revoke their surrender for adoption. They alleged that (1) Cobb, acting in concert with Wolk, fraudulently induced them to sign irrevocable surrenders to the agency even though she was aware of their intent that their child was to be adopted by the W.s; and (2) Cobb had an actual conflict of interest because Family Choices was owned by her mother.

Family Choices filed a motion to dismiss noting that the motion was filed more than 12 months after the surrenders were executed and as such, the statute of limitations barred revocation.

The Adoption Act provides that "no action to void or revoke a consent to or surrender for adoption, *including an action based on fraud or duress,* may be commenced after 12 months from the date the consent or surrender was executed." Thus, the statute of limitations, by its express terms, is applicable to cases involving allegations of fraud.

The petitioners argue that we should find that their allegations of conflict of interest fall within an exception to the statute of limitations. They point out that neither the statute nor any Illinois decisions directly address allegations of conflict of interest.

The statute of limitations applies to both agency surrenders and consents. In addition, it applies regardless of whether an adoption has been finalized. The fact that the statute does not explicitly state that its limitations period is applicable to cases involving allegations of conflict of interest does not create an exception to this absolute time limit.

For these reasons, we conclude that allegations of fraud and/or conflict of interest do not create an exception to the 12-month statute of limitations.

PARK, BROWN & SMITH, P.C.
ATTORNEYS AT LAW
MEMORANDUM

TO: All Students

FROM: Peter Smith, Esquire

RE: The Medical Malpractice Claim

Joe Roberts is the clear victim of medical malpractice. However, Joe's claim may be barred by the statute of limitations because there is a two-year time limitation for bringing this type of lawsuit. While Joe did not discover the malpractice until a few months ago, the surgeon's act of negligence actually occurred more than two years ago. Thus, we must ascertain when the statute of limitations begins to run. The following facts are provided to help you assess the situation.

Joe's problems stem back to the evening of December 31, 2003. Joe and Estelle were celebrating New Year's Eve with some friends. While eating dinner, a piece of food became lodged in Joe's throat. Luckily, Dr. Jones was at the gathering and quickly dislodged the food. The surgeon, however, was not convinced that Joe was out of danger since Joe's breathing was still labored. The doctor told Joe to go to the hospital. After some tests, Dr. Jones suggested exploratory surgery to determine the nature of the problem. As it turned out, a chicken bone was lodged in Joe's esophagus.

Joe's initial post-surgical recovery was uneventful. At his six-month check-up, Mr. Roberts appeared to be in perfect health. But in December of 2005, Joe began experiencing mild discomfort in his abdomen. At first, Dr. Jones wasn't concerned. This type of problem was common and represented the formation of scar tissue at the incision site. Joe's symptoms continued on a sporadic basis over the next six months. In June of 2006, Joe made another appointment with the surgeon who ordered x-rays that revealed a surgical sponge in the patient's stomach. Joe had to undergo additional surgery to remove the foreign object, which procedure was performed in July of 2006.

Our client wants to sue Dr. Jones for medical malpractice. Assume the current date is January of 2008. Please review **Bayless v. Philadelphia National League Club** in order to ascertain when the statute of limitations begins to run. Please let me know if we should take Joe's case, or does the two-year statute bar recovery?

Patrick Bayless v. Philadelphia National League Club a/k/a The Phillies
579 F.2d 37 (3rd Cir. 1978)

This diversity action presents the question whether the Pennsylvania two-year statute of limitations bars an action by one who did not discover the cause of his injury within the two-year period. Because there exist genuine issues of material fact as to when the limitations period began to run, we reverse the summary judgment granted the defendant.

The facts, considered in the light most favorable to the plaintiff, are as follows. Upon his graduation from high school in 1966, Patrick Bayless was hired as a baseball pitcher by the defendant Philadelphia National League Club, popularly known as the Philadelphia Phillies. In May of 1971, while playing on a Phillies' minor league team, Bayless began to experience severe pain in the lumbar-sacral area of his back and in his right leg. He complained to the team trainer and physician who treated him by administering massive doses of the pain-killing drugs, Decadron, Xylocaine, and Butazolidin. He claims to have been compelled to pitch while in a drug-induced stuporous condition. Bayless' pitching performance deteriorated. On August 12, 1971, the Phillies gave him his unconditional release.

Within thirty days, Bayless collapsed; an emergency laminectomy was performed. Nonetheless, he continued to suffer pain in his back. In September of 1971, Bayless began to exhibit erratic behavior and to suffer from severe depression. He was thereafter confined in state mental institutions on numerous occasions and has been diagnosed as a paranoid schizophrenic. He alleges that this condition was triggered by the drugs he was administered. He seeks damages from the Phillies for injuries associated with his back condition and for the mental illness he has suffered.

On October 15, 1976, more than five years after ingesting the drugs but, or so he claims, less than two years from the time that he discovered that it was the drugs that caused his mental illness, he filed this action. The defendant moved for summary judgment on the grounds that the action was barred by the Pennsylvania statute of limitations.

The district court ruled that Bayless's claims arising out of his back condition and those involving his mental illness were both governed by Pennsylvania's two-year limitations period for personal injuries, but it treated the two claims separately. It held that the cause of action based upon the back injuries arose no later than September 12, 1971, the date on which Bayless underwent the emergency laminectomy. It was then that Bayless knew of his back injury, and the district court held this was more than two years prior to filing the present suit. Thus, the court held that this claim was timebarred. Bayless does not challenge this aspect of the trial court's ruling on appeal.

With respect to the claim for mental illness, the trial court ruled that the limitations period began to run "when plaintiff knew or reasonably should have discovered the extent of his mental illness." The court ruled that this occurred no later than January 23, 1973, the date on which Bayless was discharged from Napa State Hospital diagnosed, according to hospital records, as a paranoid schizophrenic. In other words, the court held that the limitations period began to run when Bayless learned that he suffered from a mental illness. Accordingly, the court held that this claim was barred as well.

The Pennsylvania statute of limitations for personal injuries reads, in relevant part:

> Every suit hereafter brought to recover damages for injury wrongfully done to the person, in case where the injury does not result in death, must be brought within two years from the time when the injury was done and not afterwards;

Our task is to decide when the limitations period commences to run. The court below held that it runs from the moment that the injury is known to the plaintiff, in this case, from the moment he knew of his mental illness. We hold that the rule in Pennsylvania is that the limitations period begins to run from the time that the plaintiff knows or reasonably should know the cause of his injury.

Analysis begins with the case of **Ayers v. Morgan, 397 Pa. 282, 154 A.2d 788 (1959).** Plaintiff Ayers underwent surgery for an ulcer in 1948. He was discharged within two weeks but he continued to suffer pains in his abdomen. In January of 1957, he returned to the hospital for tests. At that point it was determined that the surgeon who had performed surgery nine years earlier had left a sponge in his body. Defendant raised the statute of limitations as a bar; the trial court granted summary judgment in its favor. The Pennsylvania Supreme Court reversed, holding that the statue of limitations did not begin to run until Ayers knew, or by the exercise of reasonable diligence, could have learned of the presence of the foreign substance within his body. Because Ayers had averred that he did not become aware of the sponge until January 1957, and he had filed suit within two years of that date, the Court held that he was entitled to go to trial on his claims.

In **Irrera v. Southeastern Pennsylvania Transportation Authority, 231 Pa. Super. 508, 331 A.2d 705 (1974),** plaintiff suffered a fall due to a hole in a street surface. Pennsylvania law required that a notice of claim be filed within six months. Plaintiff gave notice more than six months after the accident, but within six months after ascertaining that the defendant was responsible for road maintenance. The court equated the notice statute with a statute of limitations. After discussing **Ayers** and **Daniels v. Beryllium Corp., 227 F. Supp. 591 (E.D. Pa. 1964),** it stated:

> From these cases it appears that the rule that best manifests the legislature's intent… is that time begins to run on the date of injury unless, because of fraud or concealment by the authority, or *in spite reasonable diligence by the claimant, knowledge of the negligence or its causes cannot be discovered until after the six month period.*

Because there was no evidence in the record to suggest that plaintiff could not have learned of the defendant's responsibility had she exercised reasonable diligence, summary judgment in defendant's favor was affirmed.

The *Daniels* case, which was cited with approval in *Irrera*, stands directly for the proposition that the statute of limitations does not begin to run until the plaintiff, in the exercise of reasonable diligence, could have discovered that his injury was caused by the defendant. In *Daniels*, plaintiff brought suit for beryllium poisoning caused by contamination of the atmosphere by defendant's manufacturing plant. Plaintiff first became ill in 1943, but her illness was not diagnosed as beryllium poisoning until 1953, and she did not bring suit until 1958. The court held that the statute began to run not when her symptoms first appeared, and not when the diagnosis was made, but rather when plaintiff should have known the causal connection between her illness and defendant's activities. This was deemed to be a jury question. Judge Higginbotham, now a member of this Court, had earlier interpreted Pennsylvania law in this matter in a wrongful death action. In **Gemignani v. Philadelphia Phillies National League Baseball Club, Inc., 287 F. Supp. 465 (E.D. Pa. 1967),** the deceased, like Bayless, played for the Phillies. In 1959, an examination by one of the Phillies' team physicians revealed a symptomatic blood condition.

Nevertheless, the deceased was not treated, nor was he informed of his malady. In August 1960, he was hospitalized because of a serious kidney problem. He died as a result of uremic kidneys on September 3, 1960. On August 31, 1962, plaintiff instituted suit on the theory that the Phillies' failure to treat or to advise the deceased more than two years earlier permitted his condition to develop into one which was terminal.

Notwithstanding that the defendant's allegedly wrongful acts or omissions occurred in 1959, more than two years before suit was filed, the court ruled that the action was not time-barred. It framed the dispositive issue as follows; whether the statute of limitations begins to run from the date on which the plaintiff knows facts from which, through the exercise of reasonable diligence, he could learn the cause of the injury; or whether the statute begins to run from the time the plaintiff, through the exercise of reasonable diligence, should have learned both the facts in question and that those facts bore some causative relationship to the injury. The court opted for the later view:

> It is true that in **Byers v. Bacon, 250 Pa. 564, 95 A. 711 (1915); Smith v. Bell Telephone Co., 397 Pa. 134, 153 A.2d 477 (1959); Ayers v. Morgan, 397 Pa. 282, 154 A.2d 788 (1959),** the courts spoke in terms of discovery of facts. However, it is also clear from reading those cases that discovery of the causative facts necessarily gave us, simultaneously to discovery of the causative relationship. Moreover, it would require the most narrow reading of the language of those cases and the ignoring of the policy basis thereof to fail to recognize that "discovery of the cause of harm" must comprehend discovery of both the facts or occurrences and also discovery of reason to believe that those facts might bear a causative relationship to the harm.

Because the record was devoid of any evidence that prior to August 31, 1960, plaintiff reasonably suspected or should have reasonably suspected that the examination, the facts which it revealed, and the failure of the Phillies to either treat the condition or to inform the deceased's family about it were causally connected to the deceased's terminal illness, the suit was deemed timely.

We think that *Gemignani* accurately states the law of Pennsylvania. If common sense and reason dictate that the limitation period is not to run at least until a plaintiff knows that he has been hurt, then it should not run until he can reasonably determine what or who hurt him. Ordinarily, the two events will occur simultaneously, but this need not always be so. There are cases where one knows of an injury, but not its cause. This may be such a case.

The record here shows that Bayless began to develop symptoms of mental illness in September of 1971. His condition became so serious that he was institutionalized as early as 1972. According to the record, however, the first suggestion that Bayless's mental condition might have been caused by his ingestion of pain-killing drugs is a Neurology Clinic Consultation Report, dated January 15, 1973, prepared by a physician one week prior to Bayless's release from the Napa State Hospital in California. This report states in part, "One thought to keep in mind could be a toxic reaction to some of the drugs such as Butazolidin which does at times cause rather severe mental disturbances." The report, on its face, is titled, "Confidential Patient Information." There is nothing in the record to suggest that its contents were disclosed to the plaintiff or that the report was made available to him. In any event, under the circumstances of this case, the question when Bayless knew or should have known that his mental illness resulted from the Phillies' treatment of his back complaint is for the jury.

The order of the district court granting summary judgment to the defendant will therefore be reversed and the case will be remanded for further proceedings.

**ANSWER SHEET
PROBLEM NINE**

Name   **Please Print Clearly**

1. According to **Bayless,** when does the statute of limitations begin to run?

_____

_____

_____

_____

_____

_____

_____

_____

_____

_____

_____

_____

_____

_____

_____

_____

_____

_____

_____

_____

_____

2. Should we take Joe's case, or does the two-year statute bar it?

_____

_____

_____

_____

_____

_____

_____

_____

_____

_____

_____

_____

_____

_____

_____

_____

_____

_____

_____

_____

_____

_____

Section 9.4
Immunity from Suit

Part of the fabric of our common law is the recognition that certain entities are immune from suit. Those who traditionally enjoyed protection may be classified as follows:

1. sovereign or governmental authorities;

2. judges;

3. charities;

4. claims between certain family members;

5. parties who create immunity by contract; and

6. diplomats.

Charitable immunity and intra-family immunity are outdated concepts, and the majority of jurisdictions have abolished these types of immunity or have severely limited their application. Sovereign immunity and immunity by contract are complex topics which are still recognized by the courts and warrant further discussion.

Section 9.5
Sovereign Immunity

Sovereign immunity essentially means "the king can do no wrong." In application, this ancient English concept prohibits suits against any governmental unit unless the sovereign gives its expressed consent to the litigation. As Justice Holmes stated: "A sovereign is exempt from suit... on the logical and practical ground that there can be no legal right as against the authority that makes the law on which the right depends." **Kawananakoa v. Polyblank, 205 U.S. 349 (1907).**

The justification for sovereign immunity is that:

1. such liability would open a floodgate of litigation;

2. governmental bodies have no available funds to pay damage awards; and

3. public policy favors the idea that it is better that one individual bear the burden of the loss rather than inconveniencing the public.

It is not hard to imagine the injustices suffered over the years by unsuspecting plaintiffs who are denied "a day in court" simply because the government happens to be the wrongdoer. While the courts are reluctant to bar an aggrieved party from pursuing a claim, sovereign immunity is constitutional and recognized by the courts.

Has the government ever given its expressed consent to be sued? In 1946, Congress enacted the **Federal Tort Claims Act**, which requires that the federal government agree to be responsible for the wrongful conduct of its employees committed within the scope of their employment. Actions by federal employees that constitute intentional torts or discretionary acts are still exempt. As a United States Court of Appeals noted, the *Federal Tort Claims Act* is a general waiver of the immunity for the federal government. The legislation is designed to afford easy and simple access to the courts for persons injured by the activities of the federal government without having to ask the legislature for a special appropriation of funds for the sole purposes of providing compensation to an aggrieved party. The Act has also been expanded to allow claims when the wrongful conduct arises out of an assault, battery, false arrest, abuse of process, or malicious prosecution.

In those sectors of the government that have not passed legislation on the issue of immunity, the courts make a distinction between functions that are "governmental" and those which are "proprietary." **Governmental functions** are those tasks which can only be performed adequately by the governmental unit. In carrying out a governmental function, the political unit will retain its immunity from suit. Examples include the police department, fire department, and public schools. **Proprietary functions** are those activities which are performed by the government but can be delivered just as well by the private sector. These functions include rubbish collection or providing utilities. Suit against the governmental unit for these types of activities are allowed.

In those states or municipalities that have passed legislation on the topic, one must examine the terms of the law to see when suit has been authorized.

The following is a sample listing of areas in which governmental units will consider waiving their immunity for the torts of their officers and employees:

1. the negligent operation of a motor vehicle

2. improper custody or control of personal property;

3. dangerous conditions relating to government owned real estate, highways, and sidewalks;

4. dangerous conditions relating to utility services; and

5. the care, custody and control of animals.

Even though the government may waive its immunity defense, it will still impose a cap on the amount of recovery. For instance, the City of Philadelphia has imposed a $500,000 cap in the aggregate on any personal injury recovery against the municipality.

An exception to the immunity rule exists when the conduct of the state or local government employee is willful. In that situation, the immunity defense will not protect the governmental unit from tort liability.

For instance, Pennsylvania has waived its immunity defense if an employee engages in willful misconduct in carrying out the duties and functions of the job. In **Ramona Africa v. City of Philadelphia, 938**

F. Supp. 1278 (E.D. Pa. 1996), the court discussed this concept in an action filed by MOVE members to recover damages for the bombing of their home by city officials in 1985. The court noted that the liability of a governmental unit for personal injury is limited to those situations involving injuries arising out of the operation or management of motor vehicles, streets, sidewalks, traffic control systems, reality, utilities, personality or animals, which are possessed or controlled by the municipality. However, in the case of egregious conduct, the city will remain responsible for the actions of its employees. This statutory waiver of immunity provides:

> In any action against a local agency or employee for damages on account of an injury caused by the act of an employee in which it is judicially determined that the employee caused the injury, and that such act constitutes a crime, actual fraud, actual malice, or willful misconduct, the defense of immunity shall not apply.

In those jurisdictions where the legislature has not clearly established the circumstances under which they will waive their immunity, courts frequently have to decide if a particular act constitutes a governmental function or a proprietary function. During the winter and spring many motorists hit potholes and ruin their car's tires or rims and some are even involved in accidents because of the road condition. It is estimated that potholes costs motorists about $3 billion a year and 16 million drivers around the nation have sustained pothole damage.[1] A pothole falls within the category of a dangerous road condition in the immunity statute that allows suit against the government but the law requires the municipality to have notice of the pothole before the event in question in order to bring suit. **Nicole Walthour v. Commonwealth of Pennsylvania** examines the question of what constitutes notice.

NICOLE WALTHOUR V. COMMONWEALTH OF PENNSYLVANIA
31 A.3D 762 (PA. 2011)

Appellant alleges that she suffered serious personal injuries on March 30, 2005, when the motorcycle on which she was a passenger hit a pothole on State Route 837 in the City of Duquesne, and she was thrown approximately 120 feet. Appellant further alleges that the Department had received written notice of the dangerous condition. The Department asserted the defense of sovereign immunity.

The Political Torts Subdivision Claims Act, "governing recovery of damages caused by potholes and other dangerous conditions," requires that the Department have actual notice of the pothole or dangerous condition.

Generally, the Commonwealth enjoys sovereign immunity and is immune from lawsuits unless this immunity has been waived by the

Legislature. Section 8522 provides for waiver of sovereign immunity in certain circumstances, stating in relevant part:

> The following acts by a Commonwealth party may result in the imposition of liability on the Commonwealth and the defense of sovereign immunity shall not be raised to claims for damages caused by:
>
> (5) Potholes and other dangerous conditions.—A dangerous condition of highways under the jurisdiction of a Commonwealth agency created by potholes or other similar conditions created by natural elements, except that the claimant to recover must establish that the dangerous condition created a reasonably foreseeable risk of the kind of injury which was incurred *and that the Commonwealth agency had actual written notice of the dangerous condition of the highway* a sufficient time prior to the event to have taken measures to protect against the dangerous condition. Property damages shall not be recoverable under this paragraph.

Hence, the Act requires a plaintiff to prove two elements of notice: "(1) that the Commonwealth had actual written notice of the dangerous condition; and (2) that the actual written notice had been given sufficiently prior to the incident giving rise to plaintiffs claim so that the Commonwealth had a reasonable opportunity to remedy the dangerous condition."

In the case before us, the question is whether a letter written by Senator Logan before the accident constituted actual, written notice sufficient to inform the Department of the dangerous condition on State Route 837.

[In response to the Senator's letter about the general poor condition of the highway], the Department's acknowledgment sent to the Senator stated that "[t]he Department would like to make major improvements to this section of roadway but has been unable to secure the necessary funding. We will certainly keep this project at the top of our priority list.

There is no question that Senator Logan's Letter constituted actual, written notice about a particular road. Senator Logan's letter, was sufficient to give notice to the Department of the dangerous condition Appellant alleges has caused or contributed to her injuries.

The Department argues that the notice was not sufficient because it did not identify *the specific pothole* so that the Department could have "fixed it." The Department maintains that Senator Logan's Letter focused upon gravel and loose chips, and did not alert it to a pothole. However, there is no dispute that Senator Logan's Letter named State Route 837, stated that it had "fallen into disrepair," called attention to patchwork repairs "that seemingly has caused more problems than solved," and specifically requested that "this road be evaluated and subsequent repairs be undertaken as soon as possible." We note that the Department's Letter acknowledged these conditions and stated that it intended to make major improvements to this section of roadway, and that its "Maintenance Crews have been patching."

A defendant's awareness of dangerous conditions has often been considered sufficient to provide the requisite notice. [T]he dangerous condition created a reasonably foreseeable risk of the kind of injury which was incurred and that the local agency had actual notice or could reasonably be charged with notice under the circumstances of the dangerous condition at a sufficient time prior to the event to have taken measures to protect against the dangerous condition.

Here, we cannot conclude that Senator Logan's Letter is insufficient notice as a matter of law. The sufficiency of the notice, is a material fact that is disputed, and will be determined after a trier of fact considers whether the Department would have been on notice of the dangerous condition alleged to have caused or contributed to Appellant's injuries upon a reasonable inspection of the section of State Route 837 to which Senator Logan's Letter refers. Because this material fact is disputed, it is a question for the jury and the trial court's grant of summary judgment was in error.

In accordance with the foregoing opinion, the Order of the trial court granting the Motion is vacated.

SECTION 9.6
JUDICIAL IMMUNITY

A judge has immunity from suit when he or she acts within the scope of judicial authority and in the discharge of official duties. The purpose of **judicial immunity** is to insure that a judge will be free to render a decision on the merits of a dispute without fear or influence of being sued by an aggrieved party. The concept, however, does have its limits. A judge remains liable for actions that are of a non-judicial nature, such as a charge of sexual harassment by a law clerk or improper disciplinary actions involving an employee.

CATHERINE LANGELLA. DOMINIC CERCONE, JR.
34 A.3D 835 (PA SUPER. 2011)

Dominic Cercone, Jr. is a Magisterial District Judge located in McKean County, Pennsylvania. On October 22, 2007, Catherine Langella was charged with assault and harassment for striking her husband, then the McKean County Chief Public Defender. Langella was arraigned before Judge Cercone, a colleague and friend of Langella's husband, who set bail at $5,000.00. Langella posted bail and was released.

On November 2, 2007, Langella's husband reported that Langella violated the terms of her bail and Langella was arrested. That afternoon, Langella appeared for a hearing before Judge Cercone, who revoked her bail. Langella alleges that during the hearing, she attempted to testify that she had not intentionally violated the terms of her bail, but Judge Cercone told her to "shut up." When Langella pleaded with Judge Cercone to allow her to go home to care for her more than forty rescue animals, Judge Cercone told her she had "more important things to worry about than her cats" and remanded her to jail. Langella was then transported to Prison where she served forty-two days.

During Langella's time in prison, Judge Cercone denied Langella's requests for reinstatement of bail, and, according to Langella's complaint, falsified an official court document that kept her in prison without conviction or legal representation. Langella was finally granted a preliminary hearing. During the hearing, Judge Cercone threatened Langella with involuntary commitment to a psychiatric facility. Langella subsequently saw a psychiatrist who determined that no psychiatric commitment was necessary. Following the evaluation,

Langella was allowed to return home, at which time she found her home destroyed and many of her rescue animals dead.

Langella subsequently filed a suit naming Judge Cercone as a defendant. Judges are absolutely immune from liability for damages when performing judicial acts, even if their actions are in error or performed with malice. Thus, judicial immunity requires a two-part analysis: first, whether the judge has performed a judicial act; and second, whether the judge has some jurisdiction over the subject matter before him. The rationale in support of such protection is that for magistrates to exercise their discretion freely and apply their understanding of the law to the facts before them, they must be granted such a measure of independence that they are not compelled to respond in damages for mistakes honestly made provided they have not acted beyond the pale of their authority."

In determining the limits of judicial immunity, courts have attempted to draw a line between truly judicial acts, for which immunity is appropriate, and acts that simply happen to have been done by judges. "[T]he factors determining whether an act by a judge is a 'judicial' one relate to the nature of the act itself, i.e., whether it is a function normally performed by a judge, and to the expectations of the parties, i.e., whether they dealt with the judge in his judicial capacity." For actions taken by judges outside of the regular legal proceedings, the courts have looked to four factors that support a finding that a judicial act is involved:

(1) The precise act complained of ... is a normal judicial function; (2) the events involved occurred in the judge's chambers; (3) the controversy centered around a case then pending before the judge; and (4) the confrontation arose directly and immediately out of a visit to the judge in his official capacity.

Judge Cercone's presiding over the criminal proceedings is a judicial function that falls squarely within the category of protected judicial acts. Further, all of Judge Cercone's statements during the proceeding, including the alleged falsification of a court document, were made within his jurisdiction to preside over criminal proceedings. That Judge Cercone allegedly acted with prejudice and malice in performing these judicial acts does not eliminate the protection of judicial immunity. Langella's claim against Judge Cercone for his actions are barred by judicial immunity.

SECTION 9.7
CHARITABLE IMMUNITY

Historically, charitable organizations, such as churches, hospitals and community organizations enjoyed immunity from claims for personal injury. This protection was based on the idea that charities should not be concerned about financial liability for their mistakes. Rather, they should focus their efforts on serving the public good. The law also wanted to guarantee that funds raised by the charities would not be depleted by civil judgments rendered against them. Most jurisdictions, however, have abolished **charitable immunity** as an obsolete doctrine or have curtailed its application since non-profit organizations may protect themselves through insurance.

In Green v. Pennsylvania Hospital, 123 A.3d 310 (Pa. 2015), the Pennsylvania Supreme Court provided a good discussion of the status of charitable immunity when it said:

> At one time, hospitals enjoyed absolute immunity from tort liability. The basis of that immunity was the perception that hospitals functioned as charitable organizations. Hospitals have evolved into highly sophisticated corporations operating primarily on a fee-for-service basis. The corporate hospital of today has assumed the role of a comprehensive health center with responsibility for arranging and coordinating the total health care of its patients.

> Thus, in 1965, this Court abolished the doctrine of charitable immunity for hospitals. Thereafter, the concept of hospital liability in Pennsylvania further evolved in 1974 when we held that the hospital was not as a matter of law immunized from any liability for negligence of its personnel during an operation, thereby recognizing respondeat superior as a basis for hospital liability. We also went on to recognize that a hospital could be held liable under the doctrine of corporate negligence, if the hospital fails to uphold the proper standard of care owed to a patient.

SECTION 9.8
INTRA-FAMILY IMMUNITY

Traditionally, spouses could not sue one another. **Spousal immunity** stemmed from the idea that a husband and wife became one legal entity upon marriage. Before states began passing Married Women's Property Acts, a wife had no standing to initiate legal action against her husband. These acts established a woman's right to property and the capacity to sue and be sued. However, spousal immunity continued to exist because courts feared that suits between spouses would be disruptive to the peace and harmony of the family unit. There was also concern that husbands and wives would fabricate fraudulent claims. Most recent decisions, however, have abolished spousal immunity and allow suits between married couples.

Immunity between children and parents did not exist at common law but was first recognized in 1891 in **Hewlett v. George**. This Mississippi decision established that minor children could not sue a parent because it would disrupt the peace and harmony of the family unit and deny parents the right to exercise discipline and parental control over their children. As the court noted, "So long as the parent is under an obligation to care for, guide and control, and the child is under a reciprocal obligation to aid, comfort and obey, no such action can be maintained."

Many jurisdictions now limit the application of parental immunity. The availability of insurance relieves parents of direct responsibility to their children in tort actions so these states allow suits between parents and children. To be more precise, eleven states have abrogated the concept, but at least thirty-two jurisdictions have limited its application to the negligent acts of a parent, which involve a reasonable exercise of parental authority or the exercise of ordinary parental discretion concerning the care and necessity of a child. Most of these jurisdictions, however, have determined that the granting of immunity does not protect a parent against intentional acts such as an assault of a child. As an example, Texas recognizes three exceptions to the parental immunity defense: (1) intentional or malicious acts; (2) acts committed by parents in an employer-employee relationship with their child; and (3) the negligent operation of a motor vehicle.

Immunity between family members has always been confined to spouses, or parents and their children. It has never extended to siblings suing each other.

STEPHANIE NEEDHAM v. ROY PRICE
780 S.E.2d 549 (N.C. 2015)

Stephanie Needham and defendant had been involved in a long-term domestic relationship but they separated before November 2009 when the events described below occurred. The couple had three children during the course of the relationship, all of whom were minors at the time of the incident that led to the present action.

On September 26, 2012, plaintiff filed a complaint alleging claims against defendant on behalf of the three unemancipated minors seeking compensatory damages. Plaintiff alleges that on November 20, 2009, when she and the minors still occupied defendant's home, defendant surreptitiously entered the home through the garage and attic. As defendant attempted to penetrate into the interior of the home, via the attic stairs, he caused the attic ladder to unfold, striking plaintiff Needham on the back of her head, neck, and, shoulders. Needham sustained serious injuries. The unemancipated minors awoke because of the noise, observed plaintiff being struck by the ladder, and "recoiled in terror screaming and watched in shock as defendant descended the ladder shouting obscenities at their fallen mother. Needham alleged that the children suffered emotional distress and psychological injuries.

Defendant argues that no issue of material fact exists regarding the unemancipated minors' claims because plaintiff's claims are barred under the parent-child immunity doctrine.

The parent-child immunity doctrine bars actions between unemancipated children and their parents based on *ordinary* negligence. Injuries sustained by unemancipated minors arising from a parent's willful and malicious acts may be actionable. The terms "willful and wanton conduct" and "gross negligence" are used interchangeably in describing conduct falling between ordinary negligence and intentional conduct.

This Court recognized that the purpose of the parent-child immunity doctrine is "maintenance of family harmony" so that "suits by children against their parents for negligent injury" do not "destroy parental authority and undermine the security of the home." Therefore, this Court concludes that except where statutorily abrogated, the parent-child immunity doctrine "bars actions between unemancipated children and their parents based on *ordinary* negligence. This Court also concludes that the parent-child immunity doctrine in North Carolina has never applied to, and may not be applied to, actions by unemancipated minors to recover for injuries resulting from their parent's willful and malicious acts.

This Court took great care to emphasize the importance of allowing unemancipated minors to seek damages for injuries suffered as a result of a parent's willful and malicious. An act is willful when it is done purposely and deliberately in violation of law or when it is done knowingly and for a particular purpose. An act is malicious when committed deliberately without just cause, excuse, or justification, and is reasonably calculated to injure another. Therefore, the term willful and malicious acts refer to intentional acts. Anything short of willful and malicious conduct does not support a valid claim against a parent.

Notably, the unemancipated minors here were bystanders to plaintiff Needham's injuries. There was no evidence to show that defendant's conduct was directed towards the unemancipated minors. There was also no evidence to show that defendant's conduct rose to the level of malicious conduct reasonably calculated to injure another.

SECTION 9.9
IMMUNITY BY CONTRACT

People are often cavalier in their conduct and take many risks unaware of the full consequences of their actions. We think nothing of leaving cars and other valuable possessions in the hands of strangers. Think about the last time that you parked your car in a garage. In exchange for your automobile, the attendant provided a ticket which probably contained phrases such as; "We assume no liability for loss or damage;" "Park at your own risk" or "We are not responsible..." These phrases provide immunity by contract and are known as **exculpatory clauses**.

The courts allow parties to allocate their risks by contract but will invalidate an exculpatory clause which results in unfair surprise to one party. The courts examine the subject matter of the contract, the relationship between the parties, the equality of bargaining power, and whether the agreement is against public policy. For instance, exculpatory clauses relieving a party from liability for intentional misconduct or for personal injury due to negligence are not favored. On the other hand, immunity from suit for property damage claims is not so easily challenged.

The following case involves a skiing accident and focuses on the criteria the court will use in deciding whether to enforce the exculpatory clause.

Karl Kotovsky v. Ski Liberty Operating Corporation
603 A.2d 663 (Pa. Super. 1992)

WIEAND, Judge:

While participating in the second heat of a downhill ski race, Karl Kotovsky failed to negotiate a turn and collided with a wooden fence post. As a result of this accident, he received serious injuries. Alleging negligence in failing to pad the post, Kotovsky commenced an action for damages against Ski Liberty Operating Corporation (Ski Liberty), the owner of the slope. In its answer to the complaint, Ski Liberty pleaded two exculpatory agreements and releases which Kotovsky had executed prior to participating in the downhill ski race. By the terms of these agreements and releases, Kotovsky expressly assumed the "risks, conditions and hazards which may occur whether they now be known or unknown." He also released the ski area, as well as the promoters, sponsors, organizers and others, "from any and all liability, whether known or unknown, even though the liability may arise out of negligence or carelessness on the part of persons or entities mentioned above."

Downhill skiing is a dangerous activity. Downhill racing is even more dangerous. In recognition of the hazardous nature of such activity, the legislature has expressly provided that assumption of the risk shall be a complete defense to actions for downhill skiing injuries. **42 Pa. C.S. Section 7102(c).**

In **Zimmer v. Mitchell and Ness, 385 A.2d 437 (1978),** the Superior Court laid down the following standards for a valid exculpatory agreement.

> The contract must not contravene any policy of the law. It must be a contract between individuals relating to their private affairs. Each party must be a free bargaining agent, not simply one drawn into an adhesion contract, with no recourse but to reject the entire transaction.

The agreement in the instant case was not one of adhesion. Appellant was not required to enter the contract, but did so voluntarily in order to participate in a downhill ski race. This activity was not essential to appellant's personal or economic well-being.

The releases also did not contravene public policy. They were contracts between private parties and pertained only to the parties' private rights.

The exculpatory agreement and release in this case demonstrated clearly and unequivocally the intent of the parties. Its purpose, as stated expressly therein, was to release the "ski area" from all liability for injury to appellant caused by natural or man made obstacles on the slope, including hazards resulting form negligence by the owner.

There was no compulsion for appellant to participate in the downhill ski race which caused his injuries. In order to participate in this hazardous event, he agreed to assume the risk of injury and released the owner of the slope, as well as others, from all liability for injuries resulting therefrom, including injuries caused by another's negligence. Appellant's exculpatory agreement and release bars the present action. Therefore, the trial court properly entered judgment on the pleadings for appellee.

Judgment affirmed.

SECTION **9.10**
WORKERS
COMPENSATION

Employees are frequently hurt on the job so remedial measures have been enacted to provide workers with a humanitarian, fast, and easy way to obtain compensation for those injuries. Dubbed **workers compensation,** employers are required to maintain a form of accident insurance that will provide employees with the prompt payment of medical bills and wages in the event a work-related injury. These benefits will be paid regardless of fault on the part of the employer or employee, and without the need to engage in time consuming litigation against the employer. In other words, even if the employee assumed the risk of the injury or if the employer is fault free, the benefits will be paid to the worker.

In exchange for these automatic benefits, the worker has surrendered his or her right to sue the employer for pain and suffering damages. As noted in **Kramer v. W.C.A.B., 883 A. 2d 518 (Pa. 2005)**, this statutory scheme balances competing interests: while offering the prospect of specific recovery to employees regardless of fault on the part of their employers, the laws also provide employers relative cost-certainty in the form of limited exposure in the event of a work related injury.

The key to this compensation scheme, however, is that the aggrieved party must be an employee at the time of the injury and the injury must occur within the scope of the employment. An employee is one who performs services for another and whose employment is not casual or occasional. In determining whether a person is an employee as opposed to an independent contractor who would not be entitled to collect benefits from the employer, the critical factors are: (1) who controls the manner in which the work is performed, (2) which party supplies the equipment, (3) whether compensation is by the job or by time, and (4) whether the task is part of the regular work of the employer. For instance, a horse jockey who rides horses for a variety of owners, supplies the saddle, and controls the manner in which the horses are ridden during races, is an independent contractor and not an employee. On the other hand, a professor or instructor at a University is an employee of that institution.

The following case illustrates the difficulty in determining whether the employee's injury occurred within the scope of the employment.

MORRIS v. W.C.A.B
879 A.2D 869 (PA. CMWLTH. 2005)

Claimant was employed at Walmart Stores, Inc. On the date of her injury, Morris' shift was to begin between 5:00 p.m. and 6:00 p.m. In the early afternoon, Claimant and her two daughters walked from their apartment to Employer's store to purchase school supplies, using Claimant's employee discount to do so. It was Claimant's intention that, after the shopping was completed, her daughters would return home and she would stay at the Employer's premises to begin her shift. While walking in the "big aisle" of the store, Morris slipped and fell, injuring her right knee.

Claimant asserts that she was within the course and scope of her employment at the time of the injury and, thus, it is compensable. An injury falls within the scope of employment under two possible situations. The first is where the employee, while injured, is actually engaged in furtherance of the employer's business or affairs. Alternatively, an employee who is not actually engaged in the furtherance of her employer's business or affairs is eligible for workers' compensation benefits if: (1) she is on premises occupied or under the control of the employer, or upon which the employer's business or affairs are being carried on; (2) she is required by the nature of her employment to be on the premises; and (3) she sustains injuries caused by the condition of the premises or by operation of the employer's business or affairs thereon.

Claimant argues that she was actually engaged in the furtherance of the employer's affairs when she was injured. She relies on **Hoffman v. Workers' Comp. Appeal Bd., 741 A.2d 1286 (Pa. 1999)**. There, an employee was injured when she stopped at her employer's premises on her day off to pick up her paycheck. This method of collecting pay was one of three alternatives specifically approved by the employer. The Supreme Court, in concluding that the employee was acting within the course and scope of her employment, explained that receipt of wages is a "fundamental aspect of the employment relationship" and a "necessary affair" of the employer.

Claimant asserts that her employee discount was also a fundamental aspect of her employment. We disagree. Payment of salary is a legal obligation on the part of an employer. Providing an employee discount is not; rather, a discount is only a perquisite of employment. Therefore, an injury sustained by an employee collecting wages under an employer-designated method is distinguishable from an injury incurred by an employee who is using an employee discount while shopping during her non-work hours. We conclude that Claimant, while shopping, was not functioning as an employee who was furthering Employer's business; rather, she was only a member of the general public.

Employees still retain the right to sue any third party who causes the work related injury. For instance, an employee who is injured by a defective forklift will collect wages and medical expenses from his employer but will still be able to sue the defective product's manufacturer for such things as pain and suffering damages. Also, an injury sustained while the worker is traveling to and from work is generally not considered within the course of employment for purposes of workers compensation benefits nor is an injury incurred as the result of intoxication.

SECTION 9.11 DIPLOMATIC IMMUNITIES

Diplomats and their immediate families enjoy special privileges and immunities under the law because of the need to develop and maintain friendly relations between countries. This protection is firmly embedded in history and is known as **diplomatic immunity**. Simply put, a foreign dignitary is afforded immunity from suit or criminal prosecution while in the host country.

This principle was given uniform recognition around the world in 1961 through the **Vienna Convention on Diplomatic Relations** which noted that a diplomat shall not be subject to any form of arrest or detention. Also, the diplomat shall not be subject to service of process and shall be immune from suit in civil cases. These principles ensure the efficient performance of the functions of diplomatic missions and serve the needs of the foreign sovereign.

There are, however, three exceptions to this grant of immunity. The diplomat can be sued over a private real estate holding in the host country unless that property is being used as the diplomatic mission. Immunity is also waived when the diplomat acts as the personal representative of a decedent's estate or in an action relating to any commercial activity outside of his or her official functions.

The United States codified the requirements of the Vienna Convention in 1978 when Congress enacted the **Diplomatic Relations Act**. That legislation provides:

> Any action or proceeding brought against an individual who is entitled to immunity with respect to an action or proceeding under the Vienna Convention on Diplomatic Relations... or under any other law extending diplomatic privileges and immunities, shall be dismissed.

This grant of immunity can become controversial such as when a diplomat kills someone while driving under the influence of alcohol and is set free, when a diplomat's son, who was suspected of committing multiple rapes, is allowed to leave the county, or when millions of dollars in parking tickets go unpaid because the cars' operators are attached to a foreign embassy.

JAMES CRUM V. KINGDOM OF SAUDI ARABIA
2005 WL 3752271 E. D. VA. (2005)

This matter is before the court on Defendant's Motion for Judgment on the Pleadings.

James Crum began working as a limousine driver in the spring of 1986 for Defendants Royal Embassy of Saudi Arabia and the Kingdom of Saudi Arabia. During the time that Plaintiff worked for Defendants, he was well-qualified to do his job and fulfilled his employer's requirements for the position; he never had an accident or called in sick during sixteen years of service to the defendants.

According to Plaintiff's Complaint, after the attack on the World Trade Center Towers in New York City on September 11, 2001, Plaintiff alleges that his supervisor and other employees of the Embassy began making anti-American comments to Mr. Crum, including cursing at the plaintiff, calling him a "stupid American" and a "dumb-ass American." Drivers who were not American were not called these names.

Plaintiff's Complaint also alleges that in October 2001, Mr. Crum placed decals of the American flag on his personal automobile. Prince Bandar Bin Sultan's wife asked Mr. Crum questions about his patriotic feelings, including whether he knew anything about the individuals being held as prisoners in Guantanomo Bay, Cuba. Shortly thereafter, two other employees of the defendants told Mr. Crum that if he did not remove the American flag decals from his car, he would be fired. Mr. Crum did not remove the decals from his car and was fired on August 1, 2002. Other limousine drivers who were not American who placed American flag decals on their personal cars were not terminated by Defendants.

On November 12, 2003, Crum filed suit alleging national origin discrimination under **42 U.S.C. § 2000e**. Defendants filed a motion for judgment on the pleadings. In essence, Defendants argue that this Court has no jurisdiction to hear this claim of employment discrimination based on national origin because hiring a limousine driver does not constitute "commercial activity" within the meaning of the Immunity Act.

The Court holds that it does not have jurisdiction to decide this case under the Foreign Sovereign Immunities Act because the hiring of an individual to drive a limousine does not constitute a "commercial activity". The FSIA states that a foreign state shall be immune from the jurisdiction of the Courts of the United States and of States. However, one of the exceptions to the rule granting immunity is when a defendant engages in actions based on a "commercial activity." A "commercial activity" means either a regular course of commercial conduct or a particular commercial transaction or act. A foreign state engages in commercial activity where it exercises only those powers that can also be exercised by private citizens, as distinct from those powers peculiar to sovereigns.

Mr. Crum's case does not constitute an exception to the FSIA's grant of immunity because it does not pass the test for "commercial activity." Being employed as a chauffeur for the Saudi Arabian Embassy does not constitute a "commercial activity." The Fourth Circuit rejected a claim similar to Mr. Crum's in **Butters v. Vance International, Inc., 225 F.3d 462 (4th Cir.2000)**. In **Butters**, the plaintiff, a female security agent, argued that by hiring and firing employees, the Kingdom of Saudi Arabia engaged in the type of conduct ordinarily undertaken by any private company in commerce. The Fourth Circuit however determined "the relevant act" as the "foreign sovereign's decision as to how best to secure the safety of its leaders"-an "act peculiar to sovereigns." The Fourth Circuit concluded in **Butters** that the employment decision was "not a commercial act in which the state was acting in the manner of a private player within the market," and therefore could not trigger the FSIA's commercial activity exception.

Accordingly, the Court holds that it does not have jurisdiction to decide this case under the Foreign Sovereign Immunities Act because a foreign embassy hiring an individual to drive a limousine does not constitute "commercial activity" within the meaning of the Foreign Sovereign Immunities Act.

Section 9.12
Other Immunities

There are a number of other limited immunities afforded by the law as the result of special interest groups who have succeeded in having legislation enacted to protect a specific group from lawsuits. Other immunities have been granted as the result of society's desire to achieve a certain result such as the development of a vaccine when the drug manufacturer is afraid to become involved because of potential litigation if the product does not work or to encourage health care professionals to help people in an emergency situation without the fear of being sued.

The fast food industry received a jolt a few years ago when a class action lawsuit was filed against McDonald's because its food products allegedly caused obesity in children. That suit was largely unsuccessful but it prompted the enactment of legislation in a number of states to prohibit these types of claims. Known as the "Cheeseburger Bill," legislation has been introduced to limit the liability of food manufacturers, retailers and marketers for claims stemming from weight gain or other health problems as the result of fast food consumption. According to the National Restaurant Association, at least 25 states have enacted statutes limiting civil liability for obesity claims including Arizona, Colorado, Georgia, Florida, Idaho, Illinois, Louisiana, Michigan, Missouri, South Dakota, Tennessee, Utah and Washington.

The following is an example of the Cheeseburger Bill. This one was passed in Illinois, the national headquarters for McDonald's. The legislation is called the **Illinois Common Sense Consumption Act:**

> No person shall bring a civil liability action in state court against any seller of a qualified product which is defined as food under the Federal Food, Drug and Cosmetic Act.
>
> This immunity shall not extend to:
>
> (a) an action in which a seller of a qualified product knowingly and willfully violated a federal or State statute applicable to the marketing, distribution, advertisement, labeling, or sale of the product, and the violation was a proximate cause of the claim of injury resulting from a person's weight gain, obesity, or health condition related to weight gain or obesity; or (b) an action for breach of contract or express warranty in connection with the purchase of a qualified product.

Spectators at sporting events are routinely exposed to the risk of being hit by a foul ball or hockey puck that goes into the stands. The reader may even remember the child who was killed at a Columbus Yellow Jackets' hockey game when an errant puck struck her in the forehead. Most suits by injured spectators for damages, however, fail because of the doctrine of assumption of the risk. It is commonly assumed that people are aware of these types of dangers when attending a sporting event, and are barred from recovery if he or she is injured at the game. Stadium personnel also make periodic announcements that balls and pucks leave the playing field and people should be vigilant for these dangers.

This established defense was restricted in the following New Jersey case.

Louis Maisonave v. The Newark Bears Professional Baseball Club, Inc.
185 N. J. 70 (2005)

Plaintiff suffered a facial injury when a foul ball struck him in the eye as he stood on the mezzanine at Riverfront Stadium, home field of minor league baseball team, the Newark Bears. The mezzanine is an open walking area exposed on one side to the baseball field. Vendors sell food and beverages on that level, and restrooms are located there. At the time of the incident, the stadium used movable vending carts for the sale of beverages because the built-in concession stands were not operational. The carts dotted the mezzanine along both the first and third base lines on the field-side of the mezzanine. The vendors stood with their backs to the diamond while the patrons faced it.

In **Hopkins v. Fox & Lazo Realtors**, we held that a landowner "owes a duty of reasonable care to guard against any dangerous conditions on his or her property that the owner either knows about or should have discovered." 132 N. J. 426 (1993). The operator of a commercial recreational facility, like the operator of any other business, has a general duty to exercise reasonable care for the safety of its patrons.

The (assumption of the risk rule) is a specialized negligence standard that has protected stadium owners and operators since the early days of modern baseball. Since the early twentieth century, courts have held that one of the natural risks assumed by spectators attending professional games is that of being struck by batted or thrown balls.

We now must decide whether the (assumption of the risk rule) should apply to areas other than the stands. We recognize that a different standard of care may be appropriate for areas of the stadium outside of the stands. Transformations in tort law and the game of baseball suggest boundaries to the (assumption of the risk rule).

Fans foreseeably and understandably let down their guard when they are in other areas of the stadium. Once the fan has disengaged him—or herself from the activity on the field and has left the stands, that individual is no longer trying to catch foul balls or even necessarily watching the game. It is all harmless fun—until that one foul ball comes screaming at the wrong time and in the wrong place.

Nothing about the game of baseball distinguishes it from other businesses in a way that justifies preferential treatment for stadium owners and operators for injuries that occur outside of the stands. Indeed, in areas outside of the stands, including concourses and mezzanines such as the one in this appeal, a commercial sports facility is no different than any other commercial establishment, and we do not hesitate to apply general negligence principles in virtually all other tort situations.

We conclude that the proper standard of care for all other areas of the stadium (outside of the stands) is the business invitee rule, which provides that a landowner owes a duty of reasonable care to guard against any dangerous conditions on his or her property that the owner either knows about or should have discovered.

The New Jersey legislature quickly responded to this change in the law by enacted legislation that provides baseball owners with immunity when a patron is struck by a ball anywhere in the stadium. Known as the **New Jersey Baseball and Spectator Safety Act of 2005**, the legislature noted that assumption of the risk is a complete bar to suit against a baseball team owner by a spectator who suffers an injury resulting from an inherent risk of attending a professional baseball game. The owner shall remain liable, however, if warning signs are not posted that contain the following notice:

> ### WARNING
>
> Under New Jersey law, a spectator of professional baseball assumes the risk of any injury to person or property resulting from any of the inherent dangers and risks of such activity and may not recover from an owner of a baseball team or an owner of a stadium where professional baseball is played for injury resulting from the inherent dangers and risks of observing professional baseball, including, but not limited to, being struck by a baseball or a baseball bat.

Does the law impose a duty upon a person to go to the aid of another in a position of danger? Examples have been well documented of those who turn their backs on victims of crimes, the injured and the sick. This conduct is ethically reprehensible but there is no legal duty to help another. The law, however, does require a person who harms a third person to go to that individual's assistance. Also, a legal duty is imposed to help in those situations where a special relationship exists between the parties such as in the case of a parent and child or an employer and employee.

Must a physician, however, stop and render emergency aid to the victim of a car accident? Despite the doctor's specialized training, the answer is no. Physicians are reluctant to become involved because of their fear of being sued for malpractice. To encourage healthcare professionals to render emergency help, many states have passed **Good Samaritan statutes,** which impose liability only in the event of gross misconduct.

The following is an example of one such law:

> Any physician or other practitioner of the healing arts or any registered nurse, who happens by chance upon the scene of an emergency or who is present when an emergency occurs and who, in good faith, renders emergency care at the scene of the emergency, shall not be liable for any civil damages as a result of any acts or omissions by such physician or practitioner or registered nurse in rendering emergency care, except any acts or omissions intentionally designed to harm or any grossly negligent acts or omissions which result in harm to the person receiving emergency care.

This limited immunity also extends to a lay person offering emergency aid if that individual possesses a current certificate evidencing the successful completion of a course in first aid or basic life support sponsored by the American National Red Cross or a similar organization. A lay person will not enjoy the protections of the Good Samaritan statutes if the emergency aid extends beyond one's specialized training. For instance, a person trained in CPR cannot perform open-heart surgery or administer intravenous drugs to regulate the rhythm of the heart.

SECTION 9.13 PROBLEM CASES

1. Witte sold his beer distributorship in 1987. His accountant prepared Witte's tax returns. However, he did not include payments on Witte's individual income tax return for which the buyer of the business was making payment to an escrow account on Witte's behalf. Nevertheless, the bank reported the payments to the Internal Revenue Services; which audited the seller in 1994. As the result of the accountant's negligent actions in 1987, Witte had to pay approximately $325,000 in taxes, penalties, and interest. At the end of 1995, Witte sued the accountant for malpractice. The accountant argued the statute of limitations as a defense to his 1987 act of negligence. That statute of limitations in South Dakota provides that an action against an accountant for malpractice must be commenced within four years after the alleged occurrence in the absence of fraudulent concealment of the negligence advice. Is this claim for the account's malpractice barred by the statute of limitations? **Witte v. Goldey, 590 N.W. 2d 266 (S.D. 1999).**

2. A family court judge ordered Jamerson to provide child support and health insurance for his minor children. The father defaulted

on this obligation, so the judge ordered Jamerson's wages attached. The father's employer sent a letter to the judge indicating that the employee had no health coverage available at work. The employer also told the judge to "get a real job" and to leave the employee "alone." The judge issued a contempt citation against the employer, which charges were subsequently dismissed. The employer then sued the judge for abuse of process. The employer claimed that the judge acted outside the scope of his jurisdiction in issuing a rule to hold the employer in contempt of court since he was not a party to the underlying litigation. Will the judge be protected by the doctrine of judicial immunity? **McEacheran v. Block, 496 S.E. 2d 659 (S.C. 1998).**

3. Mrs. Hack was injured in an automobile accident while she was a passenger in a car driven by her husband. She sued her husband to collect for personal injury. The negligent spouse claimed interspousal tort immunity. Will Mr. Hack be responsible to his wife for her injuries since Pennsylvania no longer recognized the doctrine of interspousal immunity? **Hack v. Hack, 433 A.2d 859 (Pa. 1981).**

4. A father opened a window in a second-story bedroom two inches in order to increase the air circulation in the room. He then left for work with the baby sitter asleep on the couch. The child awoke, opened the window, and fell out. The parents instituted suit against the owner of the building for negligent removal of the storm window and in failing to provide a guardrail to prevent the child's fall. In turn, the owner of the building sued the parents for contribution or indemnification in the action brought on behalf of the child. In New York, a parent cannot be liable for contribution or indemnification unless the act of the parent violates a duty owed to the "world at large," or unless a dangerous instrumentality was entrusted to the child, the use of which caused injury or harm. Will the parents be held liable for the injuries sustained by the child in the New York lawsuit? **McNamara v. Banney, 672 N.Y.S. 2d 569 (N.Y. App. 1998).**

Footnote:

1. George Matar, "Potholes Can Cost Drivers Big Bucks, Bucks County Courier Times, February 15, 2016.

KEY TERMS

Assumption of the Risk
Charitable Immunity
Diplomatic Immunity
Diplomatic Relations Act
Double Jeopardy
Exculpatory Clause
Federal Torts Claim Act
Good Samaritan Statute
Governmental Function
Immunity by Contract

Intra-Family Immunity
Judicial Immunity
Proprietary Functions
Res Judicata
Sovereign Immunity
Spousal Immunity
Statute of Limitations
Workers Compensation
Vienna Convention on
Diplomatic Relations

GLOSSARY OF TERMS

Administrative Agency–a governmental body charged with administering and implementing particular legislation; administrative agencies have legislative, executive, and judicial powers.

Affirm–when a decision is affirmed, the appellate court determines that the lower court reached the correct decision.

Appellee–party against whom the appeal is filed.

Appellant–person who appeals the lower court's decision.

Arbitration–a form of alternate disputed resolution often used in a commercial setting where both parties agree to have a third party or arbitrator resolve a controversy.

Assault–the intentional tort consisting of an act intended to put another in fear of an immediate battery.

Assumption of the Risk–a defense to a negligence action asserting that when the plaintiff knows of the danger but voluntarily exposes himself to the harm, the plaintiff will be barred from recovery.

Battery–the intentional tort consisting of an intentional touching of the body of another or an object closely associated with the body in an offensive or harmful manner.

Bench Trial–a trial with no jury where the judge decides both factual and legal questions.

Bill–the form used for the introduction of proposed legislation.

Business Visitor–one who enters the premises for a business purpose.

Caption–part of a case that identifies the parties to the lawsuit.

Charging the Jury–the situation where the judge explains what law the jury must consider in reaching a verdict.

Closing Speech–a speech given by each side after the evidence has been heard arguing to the jury how and why the evidence supports their view or theory of the case.

Comity–the principle that allows the recognition of the rules and laws of a foreign jurisdiction in this country.

Comparative Negligence–a defense to a negligence action that as long as the plaintiff's negligence is not greater than the defendant's, the plaintiff may recover damages, but the verdict will be reduced by the percentage of the plaintiff's negligence.

Compensatory Damages–a sum of money that will return an aggrieved party to the status quo as though nothing ever happened.

Compurgation–one of the three English prejury methods of trial that was necessary when a person's oath was questioned; compurgation required the accused person to bring forward 11 supporters, called compurgators, making 12 people in all who would be willing to take an oath on behalf of the accused.

Compurgators–the 11 persons who would swear on behalf of the accused in a compurgation; they did not swear that what the accused said was true but served more as character witnesses.

Concurring Opinion–an opinion written by a judge who agrees with the outcome of the case but wants to note a difference in logic for reaching the decision.

Constitutional Relativity–the concept that the constitution was intentionally written in broad vague terms to ensure that the constitution could adapt to changing times.

Continuance–a situation in which a case is postponed until a later date.

Contract–the exchange of promises voluntarily made by those whose agreement is enforceable in court; the five essential elements of a contract are offer, acceptance, consideration, capacity, and legality.

Contributory Negligence–a defense to a negligence action asserting the failure of the plaintiff to act as a reasonable person under the circumstances.

Crime–a violation of those duties which an individual owes to the community and for breach of which the law requires that the offender make satisfaction to the public; an offense against society or the state that violates a penal law and carries a possible punishment of imprisonment.

Criminal Complaint–a statement of facts about a crime which later becomes the basis for formal charges against the accused.

Criminal Homicide–a unlawful killing of another; includes murder and manslaughter.

Defamation–a statement that is false and tends to harm the reputation of another or to lower him in the estimation of the community.

Defendant–party who is being sued.

Derivative Suit–litigation brought by a minority shareholder on behalf of the corporation to contest the illegal or improper acts of the majority.

Dissenting Opinion–a judge writes a dissent when he or she disagrees with the result reached by the majority; the dissent has no value as precedent.

Double Jeopardy–the right guaranteed by the Fifth Amendment of the United States Constitution that no person shall be tried twice for the same offense.

Duty of Care–establishes the type of behavior a person must exhibit in a given situation; the basic rule is that a person must conform to the standard of care of a "reasonable person under the circumstances."

Excusable Homicide–a killing by accident or mistake where the wrongdoer does not have criminal culpability.

Fair Use–an exception to the Copyright Act which permits the utilization of copyrighted work for the restricted purpose of criticism, comment, news reporting, teaching, scholarship or research.

False Imprisonment–the unlawful detention of a person against his or her will.

Felony Murder–an unintentional killing of another committed during the commission of a felony; also called "second degree murder."

First Degree Murder–an unlawful killing of another with malice aforethought and the specific intent to kill.

Forum non-conveniens–means that the place of the trial is inconvenient for the parties and the witnesses involved in the trial.

Gift–a transfer of title to property without payment or compensation.

Good–personal property that is both tangible and movable.

Homicide–the killing of another human.

Hostile Environment–a type of sexual harassment that does not involve specific consequences like economic loss, but under which a victim suffers a down-graded work atmosphere, pervaded with unpleasantness.

Imputed Negligence–the concept that because of a special relationship that exists between the parties, one person can be held liable for the negligence of the other; also called vicarious liability.

Insanity–a defense to a crime based on the criminal's failure to appreciate what he or she did is wrong or the person did not know the difference between right and wrong because of some mental disease or defect.

Intangible Property–property that is not a physical object, e.g. a patent or trademark.

Intentional Tort–when a wrongdoer purposely sets out to harm another.

Intoxication–not a defense to a criminal act unless it negates a specific mental state.

Invasion of Privacy–the intentional tort consisting of an unwarranted intrusion upon a person's right to be left alone.

Involuntary Manslaughter–an unintentional killing of another which is the result of outrageous conduct or gross negligence.

Joint Ownership–a term used when ownership to property is shared and title is held by two or more people (see also "concurrent ownership").

Joint Tenancy with the Right of Survivorship–a form of concurrent or joint ownership in which the co-owners have essentially equal rights to the property; if one co-owner dies, her share will pass to the surviving co-owner.

Judge–the person who presides over the trial and decides questions of law.

Judgment on the Verdict–the final pronouncement by the court of a defendant's guilt or innocence after the verdict has been announced.

Judicial Immunity–a judge has immunity from suit when he or she acts within the scope of judicial authority and in the discharge of official duties.

Jurisdiction–refers to the power of a court to determine the merits of a dispute and to grant an aggrieved party relief.

Jury–the individuals who decide questions of fact.

Justifiable Homicide–a killing in self-defense or an execution carried out by court order.

Larceny–the taking and carrying away of property of another without consent and with the intention of depriving the other of the goods permanently.

Lease–an encumbrance upon property where a landlord holds property as a fee simple absolute but has given a tenant the rights to possess and use the property exclusively.

Legal Capacity–the capacity of the organization to sue and be sued in its own name.

Lessee–a tenant who is given the rights to possess and use the property exclusively by a landlord who holds property as a fee simple absolute.

Lessor–a landlord who holds property as a fee simple absolute but has given a tenant the rights to possess and use the property exclusively.

Libel–the publication of defamatory matter by written or printed words.

Majority Opinion–a decision reached by more than half of the judges of an appellate court panel; a decision rendered by the majority of the court which is the law.

Malice Aforethought–describes the conduct that exhibits a wanton disregard for the safety of others.

Mediation–a form of alternate dispute resolution used primarily in disputes between labor and management; mediation is advisory in nature.

Mens Rea–the necessary state of mind that a perpetrator must have to be found guilty of committing a particular crime; criminal intent.

Mini-trial–a form or alternate dispute resolution where the parties submit their case to a panel of experts or neutral advisor who suggest the likely outcome if the case were to go to court.

Negligence–the failure to do what a reasonable person would do under the circumstances; the three elements of negligence are 1) a duty, 2) breach of duty, and 3) the negligence must be the proximate cause of the harm.

No Duty to Rescue Rule–the rule under which the law does not force a person to help a stranger in an emergency unless that person has somehow caused the problem or has a special relationship to the party.

Nominal Damages–provide a remedy where a technical wrong has been committed but no actual harm has resulted.

Opening Statement–a speech given by each side at the beginning of the case describing what the evidence will prove.

Personal Property–consists of all property that is not land or attached to land; the two kinds of personal property are tangible and intangible; includes such things as a car, book, clothes, and furniture as well as bank accounts, stocks, bonds, patents and copyrights.

Plaintiff–party who initiates the case.

Precedent–the process whereby judges apply the decision and rules or prior cases to the present case over which they are presiding; see also *"stare decisis."*

Private Judging–a form of alternate dispute resolution used when parties are constrained by time and can afford to hire a private judge; private judging proceeds as a normal trial would be conducted.

Private Law–involves matters between individuals; most common forms are contract, tort, and property law.

Procedural Law–the way that substantive law is made, enforced, and administered.

Products Liability–the concept of holding sellers of defective products liable for harm caused to the user, consumer, or his property even though the seller has exercised all possible care in the preparation and sale of the product; also called strict liability.

Property–everything that may be owned, either as real property or personal property.

Property Law–deals with the rights and duties that arise out of the ownership or possession of real or personal property; defines and enforces the rights and responsibilities that accompany ownership.

Proximate Cause–requires that there be a reasonable connection between the negligence of the defendant and the harm suffered by the plaintiff.

Public Law–involves the rights of society as a whole, and those interests are usually handle by a government agency; most common forms are criminal, constitutional, and administrative law.

Punitive Damages–a sum of money awarded to punish the tort-feasor for his or her misconduct so that the type of incident in question will never occur again.

Rape–the unlawful carnal knowledge of a person another through force or the threat of force and without consent.

Real Property–land and everything attached to the land.

Receiving Stolen Property–intentionally obtaining property of another that has been stolen, or believed to be stolen.

Remand–the appellate court remands—or sends back—a case to the trial court when the appellate court finds that the trial judge committed an error in deciding the case or additional evidence must be obtained.

Res Judicata–"the thing has been decided."

Reverse–the appellate court reverses a decision when it finds that the lower court's decision was incorrect.

Rights Theory–the ethical theory that focuses on the reasons for actions.

Robbery–larceny with the additional requirement that the taking be accomplished by force or threat of force.

Second Degree Murder–an unintentional killing of another committed during the commission of a felony; also called felony murder.

Self-defense–the right of a person unlawfully attacked to use reasonable force to protect himself.

Slander–a defamatory statement that is verbal or oral in nature.

Sovereign Immunity–the concept that prohibits suits against any level of the government unless the sovereign gives its expressed consent to the litigation.

Standing–the concept that a plaintiff in a lawsuit must have a direct and substantial interest in the outcome of the case that he or she intends to bring.

Stare Decisis–the process whereby judges apply the decision and rules or prior cases to the present case over which they are presiding; (see also "precedent").

Statute of Frauds–requirement that certain agreements be in writing in order to enforceable by the court.

Statute of Limitations–the time period within which an aggrieved party must institute suit or the claim will be forever barred.

Statutory Rape–generally occurs when a man over the age of 16 has sexual relations with the consent of a girl under sixteen; her consent is presumed meaningless because of her young age.

Strict Liability–see "products liability."

Substantive Due Process–the requirement that the law be fundamentally fair; legislation must be capable of serving a legitimate public interest, and the law cannot be vague.

Substantive Law–the "actual law" which defines the duties and rights of members of society.

Tangible Property–a physical object.

Tenancy by the Entirety–a special form of coownership for married couples which carries the right of survivorship; however, neither spouse can convey his or her interest in the property since each spouse owns a 100 percent interest in the property.

Tenancy in Common–a form of concurrent or joint ownership in which the co-owners have essentially equal rights to the property; if one co-owner dies, his share will pass to his heirs.

Third Degree Murder–a killing of another with malice aforethought but with no specific intent to kill and not occurring during the commission of a felony.

Trespasser–one who comes upon the premises of another without consent and with no legal right to be on the property.

Tort–a private or civil wrong against an individual for which the court will award money damages; torts are classified into the categories of negligence or intentional torts.

Tort Damages–a sum of money that should place the injured party in as substantially a good position as she occupied before the injury.

Trial by Cold Water–a form of trial by ordeal where the accused was bound and placed in a body of water that had been purified by prayer. If he sank, he was considered innocent because the water would "accept" one who was pure; floating indicated that the accused's body was polluted by sin by rejecting it.

Trial by Fire–a form of trial by ordeal where the accused was tested with some type of fire, for example holding a hot iron or walking across hot coals. The accused was guilty if burned or innocent if not burned; sometimes the test was not whether the person was burned but how well the burn healed.

Trial by Hot Water–a form of trial by ordeal where the accused would remove a ring from a cauldron of boiling water after being cleansed by prayer; if he was burned he was considered guilty, and if he was unharmed he was considered innocent.

Trial by Ordeal–an old fashioned method of determining justice where the accused was subject to some sort of physical test, the results of which were supposed to indicate guilt or innocence; e.g. trial by hot water, trial by cold water, trial by fire.

United States Constitution–the legal document which establishes the fundamental rights of United States citizens and protects them from unlawful governmental interference.

Venue–the place where a case should be heard.

Verdict–the decision regarding a defendant's guilt or innocence made by either a judge or jury.

Vicarious Liability–see "imputed negligence."

Voir Dire–process for selecting a jury by which members of the jury are questioned by the judge or attorneys to ascertain whether they are suitable to serve at trial; issue of prejudice, conflicts of interest, and philosophies of life are explored.

Wager of Law–one of the three English pre-jury methods of trial that simply required the accused person to take an oath, swearing to a fact.

STUDENT NOTES